Where on Earth are We Going?

Where on Earth are We Going?

Maurice Strong

Alfred A. Knopf Canada

PUBLISHED BY ALFRED A. KNOPF CANADA

Copyright © 2000 by Maurice Strong

All rights reserved under International and Pan-American Copyright
Conventions. Published in 2000 by Alfred A. Knopf Canada,
a division of Random House of Canada Limited, Toronto.
Distributed by Random House of Canada Limited, Toronto.

Knopf Canada and colophon are trademarks.

Canadian Cataloguing in Publication Data

Strong, Maurice, 1929–
    Where on earth are we going?

ISBN 0-676-97247-0

I. Title.

PS8576.A42L23 2000   C813'.54   C99-932756-9
PR9199.3M344L23 2000

First Edition

Printed and bound in the United States of America

10 9 8 7 6 5 4 3 2 1

To my parents who, despite the difficulties under which they laboured, gave me a loving home and the values and principles that set the direction for my life; my brother Frank and sisters Shirley and Joyce, who never wavered in their love and support through many of the ups and downs of the life we have shared; Pauline and Hanne, my wonderfully supportive wives at different phases of my life; to my children, Fred, Maureen, Mary Anne, Ken and Alice; my grandchildren, Curtis, Sarah, Colin, Samantha, Laura, Ben, Katie, Heather, Joe, Jenna and Zachary, who are such great sources of pride and pleasure at this stage of my life; and to their entire generation, whose future will be largely shaped by the issues I have been working on for so long.

CONTENTS

Foreword

I F THE WORLD SUCCEEDS in making a transition to truly
sustainable development, all of us will owe no small debt of
gratitude to Maurice Strong, whose prescience and dynamic
presence on the international stage have played a key role in con-
vincing governments and grassroots alike to embrace the principle
—if not yet the practice—of adopting a new, long-term, custodial
approach to the global environment.

But if the world fails to transform its relationship with the
planet and its bounty of natural resources—if, alas, the oft-
predicted environmental catastrophe does come to pass—no one
will be able to say that Maurice Strong was part of the problem, or
that he was ever less than fully committed to the goal of reconciling environment and development, ecology and economy, and the
needs of the present with the needs of future generations.

It would be a mistake to think of Maurice solely as one of the
world's leading environmentalists. His main cause has been people. Whether he was helping to put the environment on the international agenda in the 1970s, orchestrating the landmark "Earth
Summit" in Rio de Janeiro in 1992 or assisting me to reform the
United Nations to face the challenges of a new era in world affairs,
his wish has been to see men and women in all countries leading
peaceful lives of dignity, security, freedom and opportunity, in
harmony with nature and themselves.

In his long career he has struggled against powerful and entrenched interests, from businesses to bureaucracies. He has made allies out of former antagonists. And he has compiled a solid record of achievement in both the public service and the private sector. I have worked with him for many years and have always valued his advice, enjoyed his friendship and admired his commitment to international co-operation and to multilateralism's main instrument, the United Nations. I have no doubt that readers will find in this book the same qualities that have made Maurice Strong a unique and important force in our lives; they may also, not least, derive some hope for our shared future.

Kofi A. Annan
Secretary-General of the United Nations

Acknowledgements

IOWE A VERY SPECIAL debt of gratitude to Marq de Villiers, himself a distinguished author whose work I have long admired. I was delighted when he agreed to help me with the book, and I would never have been able to do it without him. It was a great learning experience for me. He gave me wise advice and helpful criticism, and edited my original texts. This, together with the guidance of Louise Dennys and Michael Mouland at Knopf and the skilful work of their own editors, made the book far more coherent and readable than it might otherwise have been. My own style tends to be on the pedantic side as most of my experience has been in writing policy memoranda and public service papers. Marq de Villiers is in a real sense the co-author, though he declined my offer of naming him as such. I'm not quite sure whether this is from the generosity of spirit that I came to appreciate so much in him or an understandable desire to distance himself from some of the book's shortcomings, for which I am solely responsible.

I would also like to acknowledge Marilyn Voss and Kim Peters, who were my right arms in helping to produce the book, and the others who gave such helpful advice and support: Alex Crutchfield, Nitin Desai, Stephanie Foster, George Greene, Larry Onisto, Phyllis Pandovski, Lesly Puyol, John Ralston Saul, Fred Strong, Sondra Sullivan, and Peter S. Thacher.

Introduction

I WATCHED them filing into the room—heads of state, presidents and kings and prime ministers, tyrants and democrats and dictators and builders of consensus, men (and a few women) who represented all the teeming billions on the planet. They milled around a little uncertainly because they were there without aides or minders. Heads of government are used to having attendants escorting them and giving them directions; but now they were all together, here in a private room at the Rio convention centre, Rio-Centro, and they had to find their own seats.

That was my doing. I had insisted they come in by themselves, just the leaders of the world around a single big table. I wanted them to be able to sit down informally. Maybe for an hour or so they could look past their political problems, their national agendas, their opportunism, their mutual suspicions and paranoias, look past the alliances and trading blocs and leftover Cold War animosities to see what was really at stake here, in this summer of 1992, at the Earth Summit in Rio.

Maybe, I thought, maybe they'll see how small the problems that preoccupy them really are compared with what they must now confront.

But I doubted it, even then, as I watched them move through the doors. Heads of nations, like the rest of us, are locked into the boxes of their experience, their pressing preconceptions and—unlike the rest of us—their own sense that what they do is important.

They came in slowly, nodding and smiling. There were 116 of them, more heads of government in one place than on any other occasion in history, at what had been billed in the press, with only minor hyperbole and little contradiction, as "the most important political meeting in world history." Many had come to Rio eagerly. Many had had to be persuaded. I had spent years cajoling and persuading and shaming others to come to this ecological summit; often my efforts had nearly been derailed, sometimes by substantive issues—the developing countries still suspected that "the environment" was another stick the rich had chosen to beat them with—and sometimes by irrelevancies (George Bush didn't want Al Gore to be in the room when he spoke, and it was one of my most piquant private moments when then Canadian prime minister Brian Mulroney, unaware of their antipathy, cheerfully brought the two together in the conference hall). Many of the people in the room were together for the first and only time—Fidel Castro with Bush, Israelis with Iranians and Jordanians, Iraqis with Syrians and Turks, enemy with enemy and rival with rival, rich with poor, developing countries with industrialized ones. National delegations and non-governmental organizations had been meeting for days, hammering out agreements. Now it was the leaders' turn.

Slowly they took their seats at the huge oval table we had constructed specially for them. Oval because . . . well, bringing 116 leaders together in a room poses delicate problems of protocol, as you can imagine. That table was one of the logistical challenges for the conference—you couldn't have anyone appearing to take precedence.

Just the leaders of the world, the UN secretary-general . . . and me.

I had preceded them and sat down, going in even before Secretary-General Boutros Boutros-Ghali, and watched them come in, one by one, deferring to each other (but not really), scrambling not to be left out or be beaten to a seat, in some global version of musical chairs.

Eventually they all found places and sat down, and silence fell in the room. They turned in my direction, waiting for me to speak. For a few seconds—it may have been longer—I said nothing.

I looked at the expectant faces, and then it hit me all at once. What am I doing here? Is this really happening? What am I going to say?

I had a sudden flutter of nervousness. I could not help reflecting on the long series of events in my life that had culminated in my presence here and wondering where it would lead—for the world community and also for me personally. For a few fleeting seconds I felt myself what I had once been, a poor boy from rural Manitoba, son of a railway worker devastated by the Depression, his fortunes redeemed only by the war, and here was the world, waiting for me to say something, to lecture to the leaders of the planet. It was of course a defining moment for me, but it was also an important, a crucial, moment historically. After all, we were meeting to consider the very future of our planet.

I spotted the Swedish prime minister—I had a special affinity for the Swedes. I saw Castro, and he smiled—we had joked earlier about the length of his speeches, and I had playfully threatened to call time on him if he went on too long.

"Each of you," I said after the Secretary-General had made his opening remarks, "is preoccupied with issues at home—important issues, sometimes urgent issues. But let me submit to you that none of those will be nearly as important to the future of your people as the issues here. Long after your national concerns are forgotten or have become footnotes in the history books, these issues will be central to humanity. So what you do—or fail to do—here, and when you leave here, is of absolutely central importance to your people—and to the world . . ." I was trying to give them context, trying to make them see that there were issues alive in the world that transcended national frontiers, that couldn't be solved in the context of the old nation-states—the very states that they represented and in some cases incarnated. I went on in this vein for a few moments, but not too long; if there is anything that I think is in character with me, it's that I always quickly move to the practical side of things. Okay, we've had our epiphany, our global togetherness. Now, what do we do about it?

Well, I thought, will they go home to indulge in high-minded rhetoric rather than press for action?

I looked around again. I couldn't tell. The faces were attentive, but bland, giving nothing away.

"We have to continue," I said. "We must. We have no other legitimate choice. The future of the earth as a secure and hospitable home for those who follow us is in our hands."

When the conference was over, they all flew home to confront their own peoples and their own problems, and I went back to my own business. The Halifax G-7 conference came and went, the fiftieth anniversary of the United Nations, Rio+5, more G-7 meetings, as the years passed. The Kyoto meeting on global warming and climate change ended with an agreement, but a feeble one. I watched and waited. On the substantive issues, the determination that Rio had helped express seemed to slip away, the momentum dissipating. On the really tough issues there was very little progress at all.

We had changed some minds at Rio, got some people, states and even alliances to shift ground, but we had, it appeared, failed to effect the fundamental change in political motivation that I know is called for—that I know the planet most critically demands.

The doomsday clock is ticking toward a day of reckoning if we fail to change our ways.

The political will to stop it seems lacking.

Late at night in the witching hours, or when I am weary, the questions intrude: Have we the collective political, moral and ethical will to do it? Do we have a chance?

Someone asked me again recently, "Don't you ever get frustrated with this saving-the-world business?"

Well, I said, the patient's still alive. In bad shape, yes, but still alive.

I was moved to write this book on the initiative of Michael Levine, who since I first met him as an idealistic young aid worker in Tanzania has become a highly successful lawyer and literary agent. I didn't really want to do an autobiography and had shied away from earlier proposals that I had to do one. But I had to agree with Michael that if I were ever going to do it, I should not put it off any longer. And he agreed with me that the main theme and purpose of the book would be to recount the pathway through which I developed and pursued my deep interests in international affairs, development and the environment, and the lessons I have drawn from my own experiences.

Particulars of my life are admittedly complex to anyone who looks casually at it. So it is perhaps not surprising that media coverage of my views and activities, whether excessively positive or excessively negative, has often been ill-informed and in some instances ill-intentioned. But it is understandable that the many career moves I have made raise questions about my real interests and motivations. As I hope this book will make clear, the causes and the values that have motivated me in all the career decisions I have made are rooted in my earliest and deepest motivations and values—a desire to work for a more fair and equitable society, at home and internationally, a deep affinity for nature and the environment, and a strong belief that our economic system should serve and support our social goals and human values rather than become an end in itself. While I have made many changes in my jobs and roles, I have not changed my values or causes, and these have provided the basis for my decisions along the way.

I am often asked whether I am a pessimist or an optimist. Simply put, I guess I am both. I am an optimist in the sense that I believe it is feasible—indeed more so than ever before—to shape a peaceful, secure and equitable future for all humankind; pessimistic in the sense that I believe we have not yet made the fundamental shift in priorities and behaviour that will enable us to achieve this.

I believe that change is still possible, and this book seeks to make the case for change, based on years of work and observation in the environmental field, in business and in government. The maxim "Think globally, act locally" is only partly valid. The time has come when we need to act both globally and locally, and that requires the co-operation of all of us, from individuals to grassroots groups to business, governments and supranational organizations.

It may seem that I have spent an inordinate amount of my time on the phone, in boardrooms, at dinners and conferences. Perhaps that is true, but the fact is that these places are where many of the most important battles have been won—or lost.

This book is not a memoir, but it draws on my personal experiences where they may help elucidate issues or inspire others as I have been inspired. The result, I hope, is both an interim report card on how far we have come and some guidelines for getting where we need to go.

Maurice Strong
Lost Lake
September 1999

CHAPTER 1

Report to the Shareholders

This is how it might go, unless we're very, very lucky, or very, very wise:

1 January 2031

Report to the Shareholders, Earth Inc.

THE BEST THAT CAN BE SAID of the past year—and the past tumultuous decade, the most devastating in human experience—is that it's behind us. If this were a business, the board of directors would have recommended shutting the doors and padlocking the gates, turning the workforce loose to pick up scraps where they might. But of course this is not a business; it is the Prison of Life, and there is nothing beyond the gates of Planet Earth but the formless void. Since we cannot escape, we must endure, and since we cannot give up, we must continue the struggle. We must also grasp at what straws there are. Perhaps the past decade has been so awful that it must get better. Perhaps in the chaos and degradation we have experienced, the seeds of a new order have finally been planted, and deep in the muck strong new wood is growing.

Perhaps not. But life without hope is a living death.

The Year in Politics

The year began with another grotesque failure, that of world leaders at the Global Summit held in The Hague to agree on how to reverse the accelerating breakdown in relations between states, to agree even on co-operating to discuss the lack of international co-operation. The summit was supposed to bring nations together on key issues affecting the security and future of the world community. It was also supposed to revive the United Nations as the only available forum for doing this, to attempt to bring that once august body back to a semblance of the prestige and authority it had briefly enjoyed at the end of the Cold War between the former Communist empires and the former American one—a prestige dealt a fatal blow by its contemptuous dismissal by an America confident still of its own manifest destiny.

On both these issues the summit failed dismally, with the predictable consequences we have all seen: the chaos that has engulfed the world in the past decade shows no signs of abating. Central authority has now broken down in thirty-two more nations, from which sixty-nine (or is it seventy? seventy-one?) new nations emerged, declaring themselves sovereign and independent. The greatest of these was of course China, whose central government finally had to succumb to the centrifugal forces that had already resulted in the breakup of Indonesia and smaller states like Sri Lanka. A severely weakened government in Beijing has had to acquiesce in conceding virtually full autonomy to Guangdong, Tibet, Manchuria, Hunan and the former commercial enclaves of Shanghai and Hong Kong, which insisted on fully independent status and resisted inclusion in what Beijing is forlornly describing as a "new Chinese Federal Union."

India has long since disintegrated. It's hard to remember what really set the process off—the Sikh separatists in the northwest, or the squabble between Tamil Nadu and Karnataka over the water of the Cauvery River. In a way it no longer matters: frontier posts have gone up all over the formerly united subcontinent, and minor conflicts flare every few months.

The other formerly great power in Asia, Japan, has thus far been able to contain these tendencies. But it has, nevertheless, had to concede a much greater degree of autonomy to its principal regions, while at the same time resorting to an increasingly authoritarian style of government.

Korea split apart again at the beginning of the decade and this year continued to fragment.

Attempts to revive the moribund European Union collapsed— again. The European Parliament, which hadn't met for five years, was called into special session, but it failed even to achieve a quorum— no one could agree on how to assess the credentials of many of the delegates who bothered to show up. Was Scotland an independent country, as its delegates declared? Was Alsace? Brittany? The new Basque state carved from parts of Spain and France at least seemed viable. The big news from Eastern Europe was the further breakdown of what had been called Russia. The small "states," governed mostly by warlords, that had sprung up along the banks of the Volga met briefly in the Tatar city of Kazan, but failed to agree not only on a constitution but even on a style of government, and after the convenor was assassinated, the delegates fled. A whole series of new "countries" sprang up around the Black and Caspian seas, and some of the Siberian tribes declared that their allegiance to Moscow had ended, following the lead of the Asian republics, some of whom had joined with Iran earlier in the decade, only to split again in a disastrous civil war as the mullahs came into conflict with the oil oligarchy.

Almost everywhere in the region law and order have disintegrated, and local governments are run by strong autocratic leaders who ignore or are no longer bound by normal principles of accountability. Some are closely allied with and others strongly influenced by criminal elements, which wield much of the economic power. In other cases there is no distinction at all between the local "mafias" and government, and governance has become a protection racket. Gang warfare, too, is common: the region is rife with local conflicts that claimed the lives and property of many thousands of citizens while terrorizing and exploiting the remainder.

In other places there is precarious order. The tiny nation of Chechnya has exploited the breakdown of government and order in its neighbours and has assumed de facto control of the region. Although it has imposed its rule and the constitutional measures purported to legitimize it, it has nevertheless received the passive support of the people concerned for the discipline, order and stability that the regime has restored. Much of the economy of the region has been paralyzed by shortages and disruption of energy supplies.

Of the seventy-three nuclear power plants in Russia, only three are now functioning, and attempts to refurbish others have foundered for lack of capital and components. As we have learned to our cost, there is a flourishing criminal trade in the deadly components of nuclear weapons, many looted from power stations or the former Russian arsenals. The sabotage of transmission lines and relay stations has deprived large segments of the population and industry of power supplies. Gas pipelines also have been sabotaged, which has severely disrupted supplies to domestic markets and to Ukraine and Western Europe, where it has exacerbated already serious energy shortages. Massive forest fires in Siberia have effectively destroyed a number of key towns, cities and industries there, while the continuing drought in the Trans-Ural regions and torrential rains in the Ukrainian lands mockingly called the "breadbasket" area have devastated crops and produced severe shortages of food.

Nine more countries in Latin America reverted to military dictatorships, but the reversion to authoritarianism has been even more extensive, as the democratic process in many countries that retain a formal commitment to democracy has been effectively subverted by or come under the control of the military, often in collaboration with criminal elements.

In the United States, where the office of the president has been severely weakened since the assassination of President Brady in 2023, President Reynolds has become even more politically impotent with effective power increasingly concentrated among the extremists who now control Congress in concert with the military and the FBI. Their action in pushing through Congress a motion calling for a new constitutional conference constituting a powerful Preparatory

Committee under the chairmanship of Senator Torrence McKelvie, ostensibly to deal with the decisions taken by the state governments of Texas and Florida to secede from the union, has effectively consolidated the shift of power to this group and left the president with the formal trappings of power but devoid of its substance. Speculation about why they did not use their majority in power to impeach the president centres on their need to resolve rivalries within their own group before acting to claim the presidency.

At the same time there is effectively a state of guerrilla warfare in several mountain states, as "citizen militias" become increasingly assertive.

Canada has been luckier. Two decades ago, prodded by Quebec and British Columbia separatist movements, the Canadians opted for an innovative system that divided the country into four separate sovereign states united in the Canadian Union, which helped to keep a functioning democracy. The members of the Canadian Union have suffered the same economic devastation experienced worldwide, and many parts of the union have reverted to locally managed subsistence-level economies. Overall, Canadians have thus far done a better job of managing their crisis than most. They have been able, with the help of volunteer brigades, to maintain security, so violent conflicts have been avoided or contained. A notable exception was the outbreak of violent clashes in Vancouver's Chinatown in July, when it was invaded by a large mob bent on seizing the hoards of food and medicine they believed had been stockpiled there. The rioting was eventually brought under control, but not before much of the area had been looted and destroyed.

The State of the Environment

The short period of benign weather experienced in many parts of the world as the year began inspired hopes that there would be a return to more stable and reliable weather. Unfortunately, it was not to be: 2030 gave us hitherto unprecedented extremes of weather. Hurricanes, tornadoes and record rainfall took more lives and caused more damage than both world wars of the twentieth century. Much of Florida is now under water, and the lowlands of the Carolinas are lagoons. The devastation of much of the California coast has accelerated the exodus of people from what was once one of the most attractive places in the world to live. Its economy has been shattered by the almost complete devastation of its infrastructure, particularly the road system, much of which was earlier destroyed or weakened by the Great Earthquake of 2026. Many other coastal areas around the world were similarly devastated. An estimated 6 million people died as a result of the flooding of the low-lying plains of Bangladesh, and many more are now dying of starvation and disease. Widespread flooding has also occurred in the Netherlands, despite reinforcements of its unique system of dikes, and much of its productive farmland has been lost. The rise of several centimetres in the sea level has exacerbated the effects of storms and required the evacuation of many coastal areas and several South Pacific Islands as well as the Maldives in the Indian Ocean.

Another consequence of the turbulence and destructiveness of the weather in the past year has been the disruption of water supplies. Shortages and the progressive contamination of existing supplies have deprived many cities and towns of potable and even non-potable water. In Central Asia, cities like Bukhara and Tashkent have faced the forced evacuation of most of their residents and the closing-down of industries. Twenty years ago more than a billion people were without safe water. The number has more than doubled and is still increasing.

Oil supplies are increasingly erratic. Seizure by remnants of the military of some of the principal oil and gas fields and related facilities has been tolerated because they have restored production, despite the fact that they control the output in order to sell it to the highest bidders in a world market starved for energy.

The heavy blanket of grey smoke that hung over Siberia during the summer afflicted the people of this once pristine region with air pollution, while, paradoxically, their compatriots in most of the cities of the region who had long suffered from air pollution experienced some relief because of the closing of the industrial plants that had caused it. Unemployment became so bad that people were actually clamouring for pollution—at least that would have meant the re-opening of the factories and plants that provided their jobs. Later in the year the pollution indeed resumed. But it was useless, unproductive pollution, the result of the coal and wood fires that warmed houses when gas and oil supplies dried up.

In the Middle East the precarious peace persisted. Iran and Iraq consolidated their control of the oil-producing states of the region, which now produce some 70 percent of the world's oil. Their reconciliation in 2021, for the purpose of freeing the region of foreign control, led to a joint guardianship of Gulf States that has proven remarkably effective, particularly now that both Kuwait and Saudi Arabia are ruled by regimes installed with the support and agreement of both Iran and Iraq.

During the year there were renewed but increasingly futile calls in the United States in particular for military action to assert Western control of the region on which its economic lifeblood depends. Cooler heads knew it was too late. It might have been feasible immediately following the rapprochement of Iran and Iraq, but was then judged unnecessary. No one expected the alliance to survive, and there were fears even then that an invasion would seriously disrupt oil supplies. A year or two afterwards was already too late. By then Iran and Iraq (the United Islamic Republic) had demonstrated their power and their joint control of OPEC by raising oil prices again to $50 a barrel. All the West could do was bluster futilely: the UIR had by then made elaborate and sophisticated arrangements for the demolition of all oil fields and facilities in the region in the case of an attack. America made noises but took no action. The price would have been too high—much higher than just paying up.

In point of fact most sober observers now admit that the new Middle Eastern power has conducted itself responsibly vis-à-vis the rest of the world and has ensured security and a certain stability of supply in an otherwise uncertain international political climate.

Although the stability of the oil situation in the region was reinforced during the year, there has been no end to the conflicts over water—which is now, barrel for barrel, more expensive than oil in many arid regions of the world. Concerted attacks by Arab guerrillas supported by Iraq have failed to dislodge Israel's control of the Jordan River, but they have demonstrated Israeli vulnerability to future attacks, particularly as the weakened economy makes it extremely difficult for the Israelis to maintain, let alone strengthen, their occupation of the basin. After an incursion of Iraqi troops deep into Turkey the two countries have reached a truce of sorts in their conflict over the Tigris, but the fundamental problems of sharing the depleted water flows of the river have not been resolved. Even more complicated is the struggle over the Euphrates. Iraq's control of Syria has strengthened its hand in the conflict with Turkey, but its preemption of a major portion of Syria's historical share of Euphrates water is creating immense human and economic problems for Syria and strong resentment against its new overlord.

Elsewhere, the Great Plains area of the midwest United States and Canada suffered the seventh consecutive year of drought, and the dried-out soil of what was once the world's most productive farming region has been swirling away on great clouds of dust, which have darkened the Prairie skies and buried whole farms and towns. Grain and animal production now barely meet local needs, and no one foresees the time when surpluses will again be available for export to those who had long relied on this source of supply. Elsewhere, too, the granaries of the world have been ravaged by either continuing drought or debilitating floods—Ukraine, Australia, the grain belt of Argentina, all have suffered. And even where grain has been produced in export quantities, the deteriorating infrastructure has meant it can't get to markets. As a consequence the price of wheat rose above $50 a bushel, but with the disruption of commodity markets, much of what was traded was sold in the black market at even higher prices.

The Ogallala aquifer, which had been the main source of groundwater for eight of the states of the Great Plains, has been sucked dry and is not being replenished. Which means the whole area—comprising farms and cities—is entirely dependent on rainfall. Consequently, the plains are among the areas hardest hit by the drought.

The Colorado River was long since stolen from the Mexicans by California, but now only a trickle is reaching California itself, and farmers in the Imperial Valley have either reverted to subsistence farming or have fled. For the first time water vendors with armed guards roam the streets of Los Angeles, providing the only source of water for the few people left in those parts of the city where the water system is no longer functioning.

Last summer's record heat wave added to the toll of deaths and suffering in many parts of the world. Washington, D.C., came to a standstill as the failure of electric power left the city without air conditioning. The deaths from heat-related causes exceeded a hundred thousand, many of whom could undoubtedly have been saved if the district's remaining hospitals and medical services had not been overwhelmed.

The year has been catastrophic for humans, but insects and rodents have thrived, and the explosion in their populations has contributed immensely to the death and suffering. The outbreak of plague, which took so many lives in Russia and Central Asia, is attributed to the proliferation of the rat population; a new strain of killer bee played havoc in the southern and western United States; great swarms of locusts devoured what little there was of crops in North Africa; and mosquitoes and flies have multiplied to the point that they have made many places in the tropics as well as in northern regions virtually uninhabitable for humans. For example, a new and virulent strain of mosquito-borne malaria has emptied the bayous of Louisiana and turned New Orleans into a shrinking fortress held only with poisonous amounts of increasingly lethal pesticides.

The fires that continue to rage in the Amazon region and the forests of West Africa have reduced these to some 20 percent of their original size, and unusually dry weather, in some cases bordering on drought, combined with the relentless cutting of trees, seems to ensure that these regions will be stripped of their original growth within the next five years.

Reliable figures are not available at this point, but one of the world's leading experts at the Smithsonian in Washington has estimated that in this year alone some 25 percent of the world's prime concentrations of biological diversity have been lost, and something like the same proportion of species of animal and bird life have become extinct. There is no sign that this process is being arrested. Not only is it robbing many people who are immediately dependent on these resources for their livelihoods, but it is depriving all people of the resources that will be required to create a sustainable future for those who survive the current tumult.

The human tragedy is on a scale hitherto unimagined. In earlier periods there would have been an outpouring of sympathy and convoys of relief to the stricken areas, but no longer. People preoccupied with their own survival have little alternative but to turn their back on the more distant tragedies of others.

It's not possible to more than hazard a guess at the total number of those who have died as a result of these calamities. But for the decade it certainly must be on the order of 200 million if the victims of disease are included, a large proportion people weakened by hunger and malnutrition. The outbreak of cholera in Brazil in June has claimed at least 1.5 million victims and has still not been brought under control. A combination of famine and pervasive outbreaks of malaria, cholera and other water-borne diseases, as well as a particularly virulent virus for which there is no known cure, has further devastated the populations of much of sub-Saharan Africa, deepening the region's slide into economic chaos and anarchy. The populations of China, India, Pakistan, Bangladesh, Indonesia and other Asian countries have suffered deaths that surely exceed 100 million. Europe, America, Australia, New Zealand and Japan have not escaped, as some 2 million people in these countries have fallen victim to the virulent nerve-destroying "virus X," originating in Africa, and to resurgent communicable diseases.

One consequence of these multiple disasters is that the troubled peoples of the world are on the move, in numbers previously beyond imagining. In great urban centres such as Cairo, Bangkok, Lagos and São Paulo, the lack of potable water and food and the breakdown of services have forced the exodus of the majority of the population. In the countryside they are almost always met with hostility by the rural population. There is frequent violent conflict. Some people resort to every possible means of entering America, Europe and other countries thought to offer refuge, waves of desperate refugees crashing against every border. Even the brutal measures that these countries have adopted to keep them out have not been sufficient, and the number of illegal immigrants to the United States, Canada and Western Europe has increased by at least 50 percent in the past year. Armoured vehicles patrolling the full length of the border between the United States and Mexico with "shoot on sight" instructions have failed to stem the flow. It has proven impossible to monitor the thousands of kilometres of coastline, and tens of thousands more come by boat. Refugees are even entering North America from the north, stumbling over the polar icecaps, perishing in their hundreds.

The Europeans have set up huge "confinement camps" to contain the flow, but they have proven unmanageable. Even basic services are lacking, and in the past few months alone, rioting inmates have broken out of at least a third of the camps in Europe and are to be seen everywhere along the roads and in the streets and cities and towns. Feelings against immigrants run high, and they are often shot on sight. The authorities are helpless to intervene.

Some take comfort from the fact that no new official war was declared last year, but it is scant comfort indeed. By year's end there was scarcely a region in the world free of conflict and few places where life and property were secure. If there are no new wars in the formal sense, it is because the limited capacity of most governments to mobilize and deploy conventional military forces is needed to try to keep order at home. Most conflicts involved armed gangs, criminal syndicates or local warlords. In many places police and former military forces have become the main predators, and those who do still provide security do so at a steep price. The wealthy retreated into gated and armed enclaves long ago, but even their guards are now turning on them, and the number of incidents of the wealthy becoming the hostages of their hired security are increasing.

Some of the most dramatic conflicts of the past year have taken place at sea. The shrinking of land-based food supplies drove many more to turn to the sea for sustenance. A number of the main species have been depleted to the point of extinction, and the lesser species are following as the oceans are sucked clean of life. There has been a resurgence of piracy on the seas. Much of the conflict is between individual boats or groups of boats, or between those who resort to piracy when their fishing is unsuccessful. A hysterical mob recently hacked to pieces a whale that had been beached on the coast of Maine, and when they had finished with the whale they turned on each other. One of the most dramatic fights at sea occurred in August, when private gunboats sank a fleet of twenty-seven Spanish fishing boats in international waters on the Grand Banks.

What about the good news, if any?

There is, of course, good news—much of it from people who have faced up to their difficulties—but even some of the good news is in fact bad. For example, the best estimates of emissions of carbon dioxide and other greenhouse gases from human sources indicate that they have now stabilized and should be in the process of receding somewhat. But this is not because we have become more prudent or disciplined. Our use of fossil fuels has been drastically reduced because of the breakdown of the world economy. Scientists can only speculate about the degree to which this may be offset by the large-scale desecration of the forests and grasslands, which provide sinks for the absorption of carbon dioxide.

And there is still one island of relative calm. The strongest and most resourceful political leader of the year is undoubtedly Germany's new chancellor, Rolf Schmidt. Elected in a landslide on a platform of restoring stability and discipline in Germany, he has set out to make it an island of strength, security and survival in a troubled world. He's no Adolf Hitler, but he nevertheless borrowed from Hitler the tactic of winning his office democratically and then granting himself emergency powers, giving him virtually total authority. Unlike Hitler, however, he has in his few months in office demonstrated a remarkable combination of benevolence, fairness and toughness. In instituting reform and marshalling the resources of German society he has sought to ensure that all Germans work together for the common good and share equitably in both the sacrifices and the benefits achieved through a total mobilization of citizens to deal with their problems. Schmidt's initiatives have ignited a new spirit of determination and optimism among his people, and at this point he enjoys their virtually unanimous support. Already the tough new regimen of national mobilization he has imposed is producing results in establishing personal security throughout the country, increasing food production and ensuring that food and other essential supplies are made available to all on an equal basis.

But benevolent dictators are increasingly rare. The majority of other authoritarian regimes that have emerged around the world are neither so benevolent nor so effective.

Still, other scattered islands of sanity and order are to be found in many regions, beacons of civility and hope, playing the same role in our modern chaos as the medieval monasteries did in the European Dark Ages, keeping alive the flickering embers of learning and wisdom. In Crestone, Colorado, for example, a community created as a spiritual retreat in recent materialistic times has proven to be a haven for the virtues of sustainability, harmony and "ethical husbandry."

Similar havens have appeared in the Altai in Russia and in the remote fastnesses of Tibet, a traditional refuge for asceticism and spirituality. A farmer in Manitoba has synthesized the best attributes of the Hutterite self-help communities and the Amish farmers and has set up a refuge around a large groundwater reservoir. Its ready success has prompted him to expand it to include others, as the capacity to absorb them permits, giving priority to displaced children and young families. Everywhere, indigenous peoples are rediscovering their traditional way of life. The Inuit in the Chesterfield Inlet of northern Canada have once again established a community like that of their ancestors; tribes in the Brazilian Amazon have abandoned their new-found reliance on chainsaws and tobacco and are once again dwelling in harmony with the forest—albeit with an "educational facility" set up for foreigners who wish to learn how it is done. In the war-ravaged cities of Mozambique, a demobilized soldier named João has helped to restore order and basic amenities through an innovative system of volunteer cadres supported and paid for by the grateful community. A similar system was set up in Texas by an enterprising former colonel of the u.s. Army, Mike Ryan, who put together a volunteer security service for schools, hospitals and other institutions serving the needs of people, particularly young people. This "volunteer security corps" has spread rapidly to other parts of America and Canada, and counterparts are now springing up throughout the world.

The State of the Soul

In the face of these multiple disasters, massive numbers of people turned away from science, which was blamed for the chaos, and toward religion. There was a resurgence of religions and spiritual movements of all sorts. Some have been promulgating messages of hope and calling on their followers to help relieve the distress and suffering of others, while an increasing number have been pointing to the current travails as a sign that the end of the world is near. The prudent habits and communal practices of the Mormons have enabled them to maintain a reasonable degree of security, order and subsistence in the communities they dominate. But their commitment has been challenged by the growing migration of others to these communities, and their hostility toward these newcomers has in some cases turned violent.

Old ethnic and religious conflicts, such as the continuing open warfare between Catholics and Protestants in Ireland, have flared up again. The return to "the church militant" has also given rise to new conflicts as religious groups band together to stake competing claims to living space and livelihoods.

One of the more dramatic events of the past year was the emergence of a new movement for spiritual unity under the charismatic leadership of the man who calls himself Tadi.

As almost everyone by now knows, his message is deceptively simple, little more than an exhortation to people to return to the roots of their own religions, while tolerating and respecting all others as differing expressions of a universal spirituality that unites all people. Simple, perhaps, but exceptionally sophisticated: Tadi has persuasively isolated the basic spiritual, ethical and moral values underpinning all the world's religions, from the imperial legions of Christianity and Islam to Judaism, the many variants of the Tao, Buddhism and even the smaller, more isolated philosophies like those of Nummo, the great god of the Dogon in North Africa. Ecumenism or unitarianism is not, of course, a new notion. What is new and remarkable is that people of all faiths have embraced Tadi's formulations. This is due as much to the timeliness of the message as it is to the exceptional qualities of the messenger.

Tadi is of mixed Welsh, Armenian and Moroccan origin. After being educated in the United States and spending some ten years as a Christian missionary in Guyana, he came to reject his own narrow fundamentalist vision of the world, concluding that in this Time of Troubles God must call all to a new and transcendent unity. By now he has come under intense media and security service scrutiny, but nothing has been found that would cast doubt on his integrity. His modest style of living sets an example for all to whom it has become a necessity as well as a virtue, and he works tirelessly not only to promulgate his message but to give effect to it in practical ways. Tadi disclaims formal leadership of the movement, yet he is clearly the inspiration for the proliferation of Spiritual Unity groups and communities throughout the world.

The movement has also evoked vigorous and often hostile responses from fundamentalists of various religions. Tadi has been condemned by the Christian Alliance in the United States as the voice of the devil who seeks to undermine the commitment to Christ as the only saviour and the exclusive route to heaven. In the Sudan fundamentalist Muslims have rallied to the call of a new Mahdi, personally leading attacks on Christian churches and communities and threatening death to anyone who joins the Spiritual Unity movement. A few of the more militant Orthodox rabbis in Jerusalem have labelled Tadi a blasphemer.

Prognosis

Most people can't afford the luxury of looking to the long term. But at year-end we must have faith that there will be a future for the human family. Those who survive and the generations that will follow them will eventually benefit from the traumatic chastisement that nature has visited on our generation. Soothsaying is always risky, but surely it is revealing (as well as ironic) that some of the concerns commonly expressed at the beginning of this century have proven unfounded, and that certain worrying trends have even reversed—as a result not of good sense but of cataclysm.

Population growth, for instance. At the end of the twentieth century the exponentially expanding human population was perceived as the greatest problem facing humankind, the "ur-problem" underpinning all others. Yet now population growth has ceased; population levels are declining precipitously almost everywhere, and some areas of our planet have been almost entirely depopulated. More people are dying, and dying younger—birth rates have dropped sharply while infant mortality increases. At the end of the decade, the best guesstimates of total world population is some 4.5 billion, fewer than at the beginning of this century. And experts have predicted that the reduction of the human population may well continue to the point that those who survive may not number more than the 1.61 billion people who inhabited the Earth at the beginning of the twentieth century. A consequence, yes, of death and destruction—but in the end a glimmer of hope for the future of our species and its potential for regeneration.

Tadi teaches us what we should already know: that we must inculcate in those of our children who survive the bitterest lesson of all, which is that the human suffering and cataclysms we are now experiencing need never have happened, that they occurred not through chance or the will of malevolent gods, and that the revenge of nature and the devastation of our civilization are direct results of the uncaring arrogance of our forebears and of our own self-indulgence, greed and neglect. What we have suffered is our own fault, and only through our own efforts can it be reversed and a hopeful and sustainable future secured.

CHAPTER 2

The State of the Non-Union

I S EVERYTHING I HAVE WRITTEN in the previous chapter just sour fantasy, the dismal fiction of a doomsayer?

Many readers will think so, will decry it as totally implausible, as scaremongering, the ravings of an activist with a hidden agenda, or write it off as the thoughts of a credulous fool.

I don't pretend, in fact, that it's in any way a prediction (sooth-saying really is for lounge magicians, not to be taken seriously). But I would contend—out of a lifetime of study and of deep involvement in the environmental movement—that the conditions it depicts are entirely plausible, and outcomes like them even probable if we do nothing but what we're doing now, if we merely carry on carrying on, doing "business as usual," putting off the future until the future is the past, in the way we have long become accustomed to doing.

People say to me, "You haven't proven your case beyond all doubt." And I reply, "On the fundamental question of the future of life on Earth, can we seriously insist on the kind of proof that only a post-mortem could provide?"

Ecological problems creep up on the unsuspecting. At first no one notices. Or at least some people notice, but scientists—most of the good ones—seem incapable of polemics, and the ecologists are simply

dismissed as so many Jeremiahs crying in the wilderness. "The cra-
zies," as a professor at MIT described them contemptuously.

The little things first. Signs go up on the beaches—water unfit for
swimming. Fish disappear from the oceans; poisonous algae bloom.
People's skin burns more readily in the sun. Viruses mutate and
cause mysterious new diseases. The wilderness shrinks to national
parks, their own condition damaged, and outside those parks the
streams are poisoned with industrial runoff, pesticides from farms,
acid rain, debris from urban dwellers. The soil, leached of nutrients,
turns saline. There are occasional waves of panic. Mad cow disease
or something else hitherto unknown is the malady of the month.
Trout are unfit to eat. Fishermen trip over submerged rubber boots,
broken televisions and rusty iron bedsteads. Tampon applicators
and other detritus wash up on beaches.

Denial of the obvious is everywhere. Those active in business and
politics are fixated on free-marketism (the new orthodoxy), unable
to see past the next quarter's results, the next election. Media commentators are their fellow travellers, dispatching the same message.
Scientists argue about global warming, about whether the case has
been proven, but the insurance industry doubles, triples, quadruples
its payouts to victims of hurricanes. News of typhoons and tornadoes is heard from unfamiliar places. Towns are flooded or flattened
by gales. Water tables shrink and aquifers dry up. Careless irrigation
turns the soil saline. The deserts spread. On the oceans, red tides
bloom, and the fish retreat to the deep seas. Politicians dispute
whether the hole in the ozone layer means anything, but melanomas
increase and the cancer wards in hospitals across the planet are increasingly crowded with those facing premature deaths that could
have been avoided. Out of the paranoid secrecy of the former Soviet
Union the reports finally trickle out—of ecological tragedies, nuclear
accidents, the poisoning of rivers, the runoff of radioactive wastes
into the Bering Sea . . .

The political and economic establishments become ever more
fixated on growth. If growth falters, the markets panic. Growth is
the prevailing orthodoxy. Entrepreneurs become ever more inventive in turning out consumables. A failure to consume begins to be

equated with sabotage. The refuse dumps of industrial civilizations fill with unwanted and unneeded artifacts.

An enormous factory turning out consumer electronics is accused of poisoning a nearby river. At a weepy press conference, the chief executive protests. He has children who love camping, cherish the forests—why would he destroy the world of his inheritors? He had to protect the company's quarterly earnings, his employees' jobs. He was just doing his job.

The same thing happens in politics. The political equivalent to the quarterly earnings report is the next election. The first imperative is to be re-elected, and that requires distortion, exaggeration, even prevarication dressed up in "spin." After a while, politicians hardly even bother to disguise their lies or the fact that the promises they make will never be kept. They can't risk the wells of money drying up. And the money comes from the same corporations whose focus is the short term.

Geopolitically, the developed countries may just pull themselves together, though the signs are lacking. But China and India, the world's two largest countries, and potentially the planet's largest economies, are still dependent on fossil fuels, especially low-grade coal, to drive their industries. What if half a billion Chinese buy cars? And why, in justice, should they be denied the right to do so?

The "environment" isn't just an issue, something to be fixed while everything else remains the same. Ecological destruction is a sign of the imbalance in the way our industrial civilization sets its priorities and governs itself. There is an increasing dichotomy between industrial capitalism's victors and victims. The rich become richer, more elusive, more mobile, less constrained by national laws. They withdraw, moving out of reach of national taxation systems. Their money, however, is in ever greater demand. It is necessary to lure that money in order to make society work. Competition is increasing for their resources, which means less and less control over them. The gated communities growing in Western countries will develop globally. The rich will live in enclaves of luxury while the rest of the world festers. The result? The so-called market economies risk spiralling into class war.

Do we really want this? Do we want Marx to be proven right, after all?

Nation-states will become less and less dominant. City-states will reappear on the one hand and transnational authorities on the other. The criminal syndicates were the first to lead the way. Multinational corporations followed. Politics will surely emulate such exemplars.

The doomsday scenario will be reality if we do nothing. What will produce it is simply this: our doing business as usual. If we don't change, radically, thoroughly, systematically, we ensure our own downfall.

Do we have the collective wisdom and political will to prevent that?

Why is a doomsday outcome probable if we do nothing? Because our global, interdependent civilization is itself a complex system, and we have all come to rely on the functioning of that system for the standards of living and security we take for granted. When complex systems break down, the process of disintegration becomes self-reinforcing, and a downward spiral becomes almost impossible to arrest. I contend that we can prevent this apparently inevitable downward spiral by taking a number of steps to ensure the sustainability of the main elements that the functioning of our civilization depends on. (I will outline those steps in my program of action, later in this book.)

We don't even need to concede that doomsday is inevitable if we fail to take these measures, but we must accept that it is possible. And though most of the measures we must take will call for major changes in our attitudes, policies and behaviour—and, yes, some will be very costly—many of the changes will be good for us in any event, and I believe that the costs can be met largely through the shifting of expenses within our current economy—which will improve economic efficiency as well as environmental security.

So yes, the remedies are known, are available, will be good for us and can be absorbed. Do we have the will to bring them about, or will inertia and apathy continue to propel us along the pathway to doomsday? Do we really have the "lemming instinct"?

In telling the story of my own participation in the evolution of the international environmental movement, I will necessarily be recounting the past. But the lessons I have learned and the insights I have derived from these experiences have given me a profound concern for the future of our Earth as a secure and hospitable home for those who follow us. I am convinced that the human future will be determined largely, and probably decisively, by the course we set within the next two decades. All the evidence I have seen reinforces this conviction. I want to outline my thoughts about where we are headed and what we can do to shape our common future.

For many of the media commentators and politicians in the West who speak for the privileged minority (a minority enjoying the best of times among these worst of times), there is little immediate incentive to change. Why listen to the doomsayers who warn that we are heading for disaster? The doomsayers have usually been wrong, haven't they? Look at Thomas Malthus and his predictions of famine and pestilence. Look, to take a modern example, at the dire warnings of the Club of Rome, and how the apocalyptic dangers that that body forecast have receded ever since. In any event, if we are doing so well, why not continue as long as we can?

Although those who are profiting are in the minority, their ranks have been expanded during the recent period of strong economic growth and surging financial markets, and the occasional faltering of those same markets has hardly dented their confidence. These are also the people who monopolize the levers of economic and political power. Today the dominant ethos is individual self-interest, its mechanism the unfettered market. Since the collapse of Marxism, it has become axiomatic that market capitalism is synonymous with maximizing freedom and opportunity, and equally axiomatic that untrammelled freedom is synonymous with future security.

What's missing in this sunny picture? There can be no question that individual rights and freedoms constitute the foundations of our society. But in order to be able to exercise these rights and freedoms, we must accept the constraint and discipline required to enable us to enjoy them, as well as a high sense of responsibility to others and to future generations.

And where, in this obsession with efficiency of markets and the maximizing of returns, is responsibility to be found?

Many of the privileged minority do take their responsibilities to society seriously. They manifest this by their support of charitable and voluntary organizations. Particularly noteworthy are George Soros, who donates hundreds of millions of dollars a year through his Open Society Foundation, largely in the countries of the former Soviet Union, and the billionaire media genius Ted Turner, who made the largest single charitable contribution in u.s. history by committing $1 billion to support United Nations programs and activities. His generosity has since been topped by the computer software king Bill Gates, the first person ever to have his personal net worth reach $100 billion. They follow in the tradition of the great philanthropists of the past—notably the Rockefeller family, which continues in its current generation to set a remarkable example of enlightened and innovative philanthropic leadership.

Overall, the level of charitable giving reached us$135 billion in the United States and $4.53 billion in Canada in 1997. But because much of it is targeted for causes of particular interest to donors, gifts do not make up for the cuts in social and welfare support for many of society's poorest and neediest people and thus contribute little to the empowerment of the disadvantaged and underprivileged or to offering them permanent relief from dependency and a sustained improvement in their living conditions.

Fundamental change almost always occurs in response to crisis or the perception of crisis. The inequities in Western societies are not yet perceived as a crisis. Many do deplore the worsening disparity, but realistically most people have become accustomed to studiously avoiding street people and insulating themselves against appeals for help, rationalizing that "the poor will always be with us" and that their plight is a necessary and tolerable evil in a free and open society. A sustained level of unemployment is therefore regarded as a proper lever for the functioning of an economy, a view that manages to put out of sight the sufferings of people reduced to an economic statistic.

The tendency to ignore a gathering storm is especially apparent in the response to the threat to the global environment, climate change perhaps being the prime example. Evidence that we are permanently damaging our environment is dismissed as a non-issue, the latest scare tactic of "extreme environmentalists," in spite of the considered view of a majority of scientists that early action is imperative to limit the controllable buildup of greenhouse gases in the atmosphere that permanently affect climate. People in government and business in both their work and personal lives routinely make decisions on matters of much less importance on the basis of evidence far less persuasive, but on this issue, which could affect our very survival, many argue that we should wait for scientific certainty. Business, in short, as usual—until business is no longer possible.

Where do we go from here?

Well, we are gods now, gods in charge of our own destiny, and gods can't be capricious.

The environmental crisis is a new kind of crisis altogether, something our leaders don't seem to have grasped.

There have been crises before, some of them grave. Even a cursory reading of history shows that human excesses and failings have contributed to the demise of past civilizations. But however devastating were the effects on the people concerned, in broad historical terms they were limited in both space and time. Some civilizations disappeared, but others endured.

Now, everything has changed. As we move into the new millennium, we are confronted with a situation unprecedented in human experience—the civilization that has emerged as a result of rapid advances in science and technology is global in scope, so what happens in any part of it affects the whole. We face the grave responsibility for the preservation of life on Earth. We are only beginning to comprehend the magnitude of this responsibility, and we're far from ready to accept it.

Let me quickly sketch some of the elements that I believe make my "business as usual" scenario depressingly plausible, as outlined in my report on 2030. Although we have learned not to trust projections extrapolated from current trends, we also know that well-established trends are not shifted quickly or easily. Inertia affects human affairs, as it does the physical world, making the decisive alteration of events difficult without major changes in their underlying components. We have been accustomed to acknowledging that the rate of change experienced in our lifetime is unique, without precedent. But we have failed to translate this perception into a real awareness of its implications for our future prospects and have generally avoided the need to make real change in current policies and patterns of behaviour that will determine these prospects.

Obviously, the changes that have produced our global, interdependent civilization are rooted in the advances in knowledge, technology and production capacity that have taken place over the past several millennia, particularly during the twentieth century. Even in my own lifetime the changes have been unusually rapid— my birth in 1929 coincided with the beginning of the Great Depression, resulting from the breakdown of the economic order. The level of global economic activity has greatly increased, and the number and structure of nation-states have changed dramatically. In 1929, most of Africa, much of Asia and the Caribbean region of America were still under colonial rule. Even in the developed countries, automobile ownership was still the exception, and railroads were the principal mode of long-distance transport. Although radios were widely available in the more industrialized countries, telephone use was on a limited scale, and telecommunications were confined to sending signals in Morse code by telegraph and wireless. Computers, television and atomic energy, all major forces driving globalization, had not yet entered our lives. Airplanes were a novelty, with limited commercial application. Tuberculosis, smallpox and diphtheria were widespread threats to health.

The real effects of scientific inquiry and research cannot be predetermined even by those who produce them. All we can say for sure is that the knowledge generated by science and the capacity to translate it into technologies that alter our ways of living and working are transforming our civilization and determining its future. A greater proportion of the results of scientific research is finding applications as "intellectual property," and its commercialization is now the dominant source of new business opportunities. The largest and most rapidly growing corporations in the world are those that have been most adept at identifying new technologies and moving them into the marketplace.

This change is a mixed blessing. On the one hand it has provided support and impetus for research and development, particularly helpful in redeploying R&D capabilities following reduction in defence budgets, notably in the United States, formerly the main source of R&D support in the post–Second World War period. On the other hand commercialization also imposes new constraints on the free flow and exchange of ideas among researchers, which has been one of the most important guiding principles in the scientific community. Any strictures will almost inevitably constrain the R&D process itself and the universal dissemination of the benefits—and problems—it produces.

That benefits are often offset by negative consequences has not always been accepted and indeed still isn't. The benefits, at least, are easy to see, and are most evident. An example is mass immunization against such killer diseases as smallpox, typhoid fever, yellow fever, diphtheria and malaria, as well as the development of antibiotics as a cure for a wide variety of infectious illnesses. These spectacular advances in medical science have reduced individual human suffering and increased lifespans. Life expectancy in Canada at the time of my birth was sixty years for men; it is now seventy-seven years. In many developing countries life expectancy has increased even more dramatically to sixty-four years. For individuals, a longer life, but for society? The consequences are more ambivalent. Increased lifespans have added to the population explosion in developing countries, which are growing faster than their capacity to provide the basic infrastructure, services and livelihoods required to sustain the greater number of people. This in turn is contributing to the persistence of poverty, as the benefits of economic growth are absorbed, and in some cases negated, by the increase in population. What is the measure of gain here?

The use of pesticides and chemical fertilizers, which made possible vast increases in food production, has also contaminated soils, water and the food chain, with considerable impacts on human health. Mother's milk in Central Africa contains levels of DDT beyond the levels set by the U.S. Food and Drug Administration and beyond what local usages would have predicted; similarly, the fragile ecosystems of the Arctic are being affected by pollutants that originate thousands of kilometres away. Trace contaminants are now being found in breast milk in even the most developed of countries.

The car is perhaps the best known and most extensively studied example of positive and negative effects. Widespread automobile ownership has meant freedom and mobility for individuals, but cars are also the source of air pollution and growing traffic congestion worldwide, and a leading contributor to global climate change. On a recent visit to Beijing I was interviewed for a local television show. They asked me, "Mr. Strong, you have come to Beijing many times over the years. What are the main changes you have seen?" I replied, "When I first came here the streets were crowded with bicycles, and there were very few cars. Now the streets are crowded with cars, and there are fewer bicycles, but the bicycles go faster than the cars."

Atomic energy is another example. Although it has provided a new and potentially unlimited energy source that does not contribute to climate change, it is not benign: the environmental and health risks are still unresolved.

And what about genetics? Recent advances in genetic sciences give us the capacity to manipulate the life processes of plants, animals and human beings. One of the potential consequences is a truly industrial agriculture—the movement away from land-based farming to a capital- and technology-intensive food production system, which would have devastating consequences in dozens of developing countries. And this even without the profound ethical dilemmas posed by our capability to clone complex organisms (including humans) and to "manufacture" entirely new species.

Clearly, the manifest benefits of science and technology are accompanied by a series of imbalances that compel our response. Impact on the environment is not just an inconsequential side effect of the processes that have driven industrialization and urbanization, processes that have benefited modern society. Rather, science and technology have created fundamental imbalances. Fundamental imbalances require fundamental rebalancing—an apparently tautological formulation that is the absolute nub of the matter.

"Globalization" is just a shorthand way of saying that everything affects everything, that what we do affects others and what they do affects us—all on a global scale. Sophisticated telecommunications have made possible a worldwide financial market that now functions on a round-the-clock basis. Massive movements of money and transactions in securities and commodities are initiated on the basis of impersonal decisions taken by institutions and corporations, often deploying assets larger than those of many nations. Funds derived from criminal and illicit activities can also be moved swiftly and anonymously into safe havens. It is estimated that money generated from the illegal trade in drugs and endangered species of wildlife, as well as other criminal activities, has reached a level rivalling legitimate trade. This has put immense financial power in the hands of an uncivil society of organized crime and terrorist groups, which are becoming more and more sophisticated. In some cases, this underground financial activity is linked with corrupt elements in the political and corporate worlds to the point that political parties and even national governments risk becoming the allies and even the agents of uncivil society.

Changes in the weather that affect crops of major commodities such as coffee, wheat, fruit and vegetables have an almost immediate impact on prices we pay in the marketplace. Disease that originates in any part of the world can be transmitted through the movement of people and products to any other part. In centuries past such scourges as AIDS would almost certainly have been confined to the regions where they began—devastating to the local populace, to be sure, but not a global catastrophe.

Despite the end of the Cold War, the capacity for nuclear annihilation still exists. The number of countries possessing nuclear weapons is growing, and they are, or soon will be, within the reach of terrorist organizations as well, so the potential use of nuclear weapons has become an even more complex, continuing challenge to the international community. At the same time the capacities for more insidious forms of bacterial and chemical warfare have increased significantly, and access to such means of mass destruction by rogue nations and terrorists is not subject to effective control.

Globalization has meant that the culture of the wealthy and influential West has become internationally pervasive—a culture of materialism and self-gratification. Its symbols and agents are the heavily marketed brands and the lifestyle they promote, as well as pop music, television and movies. For the majority of people of other cultures, this international culture is both seductive and alien. They experience it primarily as consumers, or aspiring consumers, and underpaid labour. It tends to undermine and detach them from their roots. The result is too often frustration and alienation and a reversion to the more familiar and supportive cocoon of tradition. Thus the movement toward religious and cultural fundamentalism must be seen as a reaction to the universalizing pressures that accompany globalization.

Globalization has also reinforced the parochialism deeply entrenched in all societies. Even in the United States, globalization's vanguard, there is a backlash, showing itself in a resurgence of isolationism, a growing resistance to free trade and a reluctance to respond to humanitarian crises in "remote" parts of the world.

Post–Cold War change has left the United States the sole superpower and weakened its support for multilateral organizations—notably the United Nations. American ascendancy enables the U.S. to work with other nations bilaterally (so they can be easily influenced and even bullied) rather than multilaterally (which might permit the others to unite against, or "gang up on," American leadership). Public opinion polls in the U.S. show continued support for the UN by ordinary Americans, but there are powerful forces in the U.S. who see international organizations as a threat to U.S. sovereignty and supremacy. The demise of the United Nations wouldn't trouble them at all; short of that, they prefer to see it weak and dependent on the United States. Indeed, the right-wing media in the United States have recently been targeting me as a dangerous leader of a conspiracy to establish a world government that would subvert the sovereignty of the United States.

The end of the Cold War seemed to signal the final triumph of market capitalism, which is now being embraced by virtually all governments, even those, like China, that continue to maintain an ideological commitment to communism. The sense of triumph is premature. Russia and the other countries of the former Soviet Union are discovering that embracing a capitalist, market-driven economy does not produce immediate benefits for all. Market economies are intricate and complex systems. It takes a great deal of time to develop the culture, attitudes, behaviour patterns and institutional structures required for the market system to function effectively and benefit the majority. And there is growing concern even in the most developed economies and democracies that market capitalism will give rise to its own negative consequences. The short-term effect, as we are seeing in Russia and to varying degrees in other countries of the region, is a breakdown in the structures and disciplines that existed under the ponderous command and control system of communism. The opportunistic few are able to take advantage, all too often on an illicit basis, while the rest of the people are frustrated and adrift, deprived of the basic security and services that they had become accustomed to under communism. No doubt if they can stay the course, these societies will accommodate in their own ways the opening-up of their economies and the realities of globalization. But the growing disparities of wealth and power in the most advanced economies, particularly the United States, inevitably raise concerns about the effects of unregulated capitalism.

If social upheaval follows before stability and relative prosperity can be created, the conflicts thus generated could deepen into societal breakdown and anarchy. History is replete with examples of how people embrace, and radical leaders exploit, such conditions—look at the takeover of Russia in 1917 by the Bolsheviks and the rise to power of Adolf Hitler in Germany in the 1930s. It is important to remind ourselves that Hitler's rise to power came about through the democratic, constitutional processes of the Weimar Republic, and it was only after he became chancellor that he subverted the constitution and concentrated all power in Party and Führer. As Erich Fromm has pointed out in *Escape from Freedom*, people for whom freedom means insecurity, vulnerability, frustration and wounded pride will be prone to yield it to strong leaders and radical political movements promising to solve their problems. Signs of this are already evident in the revival of support for the Communist party in Russia and the willingness of many to support extreme nationalist parties like that led by Vladimir Zhirinovsky.

Democracy in countries that have little experience with it is at best a fragile concept. Some countries of the former Soviet Union, notably the Czech Republic and Poland, have made the transition to functioning democracy quite well. In Russia the process has at best produced a shaky and tenuous compromise among the principal political parties, which has permitted the government to function on a crisis-to-crisis basis but has not enabled it to deal effectively with some of the country's fundamental problems. While democracy and market capitalism do not necessarily go hand in hand, as China demonstrates, they are closely linked and in many ways mutually reinforcing. The more open an economy, the more difficult it is to maintain a closed political system, as China is finding.

Even in the more mature democracies, the dichotomies of unfettered market capitalism are becoming evident. A growing backlash against globalization is directed at the multinational corporations, seen as its main drivers and beneficiaries. This was manifested at the recent annual meeting of the World Economic Forum in Davos, Switzerland, where a group of demonstrators protested the evils of globalization. It may well be a portent of things to come.

As governments have removed many of the controls they have exercised over their economies and privatized government-owned enterprises, there has been a widening gap between those who are able to benefit from concomitant new opportunities and those who lose out. Figures for 1994 indicate that the top 10 percent of the U.S. population enjoys 28.5 percent of its wealth, while the bottom 10 percent of the people share 1.5 percent of the wealth. The situation is much the same in Canada, where the top 10 percent earned 23.8 percent of the wealth, the bottom 10 percent only 2.8 percent.

In Europe, where governments have been slower to relinquish control or to reduce social benefits, the gap is less, though unemployment remains high.

It's true that since 1980 a dramatic surge in economic growth in some fifteen countries has brought rising incomes to many of their 1.5 billion people, more than a quarter of the world's population, says the UN Development Program's 1996 report. But in the same period, economic decline or stagnation has affected one hundred countries—again, more than a quarter of the world's population. Globally, the gap between rich and poor has continued to widen. The difference in average per capita incomes between the more developed and the developing countries increased by a factor of three between 1960 and 1993, and the richest 20 percent of the world's population increased their share of global income from 70 to 85 percent.

Among developing countries may be seen different economic responses to the global stimulus. Asia and Latin America have been leading and, despite recent setbacks, seem likely over time to be the primary drivers of world economic growth. In stark contrast to this is the stagnation prevailing in some of the least developed countries, notably the low-income ones of sub-Saharan Africa, whose economies are based primarily on agriculture and, in some cases, mineral development. They depend heavily on foreign aid and are least able to attract private investment capital. All this exacerbates their vulnerability to changing external conditions—commodity prices, reductions in development aid and shifts in trading patterns and financial markets.

Overall, we are witnessing the first stages of a major shift of economic power from North to South, which will be slowed down but not arrested by the severe economic setbacks and financial shocks experienced by some of the most rapidly developing countries of Asia.

A recent World Bank report points out that in the two decades from 1974 to 1993, developing countries as a whole grew at a rate slightly higher (3 percent) than the rich industrial countries (2.9 percent) and are expected to grow by almost 5 percent a year in the next decade, compared with 2.7 percent in the traditional industrial countries.

On this basis, as *The Economist* noted in a survey of the global economy, China will replace the United States as the world's largest economy by 2020, and nine of the top fifteen economies of the world will be today's developing countries. India will replace Germany as the fourth largest economy. And the same survey projects that developing countries' share of world output will increase to 62 percent by 2020, while that of the rich industrial countries will decline to 37 percent. It's always dangerous to give too much weight to surveys based largely on extrapolation from current trends, particularly those limited to narrow economic indicators; nevertheless, there seems little doubt about the direction in which the world economy is headed.

The basic character of the economies of some developing countries is also undergoing a major transformation. Although most of the poorest and least developed have been largely bypassed, many others have moved beyond their traditional role as exporters of raw materials and commodities. Manufactured goods now constitute some 60 percent of developing countries' exports, compared with only 5 percent in 1955. And their share of world manufacturing exports rose from 5 percent in 1970 to 22 percent in 1993.

In light of these forecasts, the G-8, which today does not include a single developing country, has become an anachronism. The current world order continues to be rooted in the past, particularly our notions of North-South relationships. We in the West have not yet really begun to appreciate, let alone come to terms with, the immense geopolitical implications of this growth of economic power in the South. Despite the movement toward a global economy and a more open trading system, I see signs of a "fortress North" mentality developing in the wealthy industrial countries, which would not bode well for future relationships with the developing world.

Export industries in the Organization for Economic Cooperation and Development (OECD) countries have welcomed—and been quick to exploit—the opportunities that have opened up in the rapidly growing economies of the developing world. They've seized on a recent OECD report that suggests that if China, India and Indonesia continue to grow at recent rates, some 700 million people in these three countries alone—more than the combined populations of America, the European Union and Japan—will, by 2010, have an average annual income roughly equivalent to that of Spaniards—US$14,000. This compares with only 100 million today. Indonesia's economic free fall and the slowing growth elsewhere in Asia have modified the OECD's optimism somewhat, but the numbers are still indicative of basic trends.

On the other hand OECD countries increasingly look on developing countries as competitors. Low labour costs and rising productivity —which really means the exploitation of workers and sweatshop production conditions—are making their manufactured products highly competitive in Northern markets—helping to keep consumer prices down but evoking strong and growing resistance from those in the industrial countries who see their investments and jobs at risk.

The late British financier and European Parliamentarian Sir James Goldsmith predicted that freer trade with developing countries would lead to massive movement of industry to the Third World and large-scale unemployment in OECD countries as well as in developing countries. When you look at people and not capital, however, the flow is all the other way. Political turbulence and economic hardship in the developing world, as well as in parts of Eastern Europe and the former Soviet Union, are creating increased pressures for emigration. Now, new "Berlin Walls" are being erected against those who are uprooted, dispossessed and persecuted; these barriers are creating a new iron curtain separating rich and poor. The same countries that are tightening their borders against the poor and dispossessed welcome and even woo those with capital and marketable skills.

Rapidly as developing countries are growing, much of the world's poverty is still to be found there. Changes are deepening the difference between countries that are growing and those that continue in the grip of economic stagnation and poverty. These changes have immense implications for all of us. In environmental terms alone, they could be decisive for the human future.

None of the specific events of the twentieth century could compare in their impact on our global society with the astounding growth in the world population. In 1999, the world population reached 6 billion.

The latest UN statistics indicate that population will level off as economic growth provides more people with access to education, health care and birth control measures. But this will not for some time result in a stabilization of world population at 11.6 billion, which will likely occur sometime toward the twenty-third century. However, as early as 2050, the world population could be as low as 7.3 billion or as high as 10.7 billion, with 8.9 billion considered most likely. Population pressures will continue to exacerbate the problems of developing countries and drive both internal and external migrations, with their potential for serious conflict. By far the majority of this growth is in developing countries, where there are already many people struggling to lift themselves out of poverty on a diminishing base of natural resources. It is not so much that the world as a whole could not accommodate this level of population but that its distribution and rate of growth overwhelm the capacity of governments to provide even the most basic necessities. Some of the most densely populated areas on our planet are among those experiencing the highest standards of living—the Netherlands, Japan and, within the developing world, Singapore and Hong Kong. But a common denominator is the high degree of political and social discipline and stability in these societies—something extremely difficult to achieve in cultures with a greater degree of ethnic and regional diversity.

The more mature industrialized countries face a different, but just as difficult, demographic dilemma. Low birthrates and extended life expectancy is producing aging populations and pointing to a decline in numbers. This will increase the pressures for migration from outside—and the resistance to it.

As I saw at the Stockholm Conference on the Environment in 1972 and later at Rio in 1992, many people in the developing world were initially wary of the environmental issue. But they have become increasingly sensitized as they experience, often in acute form, some of the environmental problems that first emerged in the more industrialized countries. The cities of the developing world have been growing at rates beyond anything experienced in the countries that were first to industrialize—outstripping their capacity to provide even the most basic housing, infrastructure, health, education and social services to their exploding populations. Cities like Cairo, Manila, Bangkok, Calcutta and Mexico City are among the most polluted and congested in the world; and in rural areas depletion of the forests and the degradation of the soil are robbing developing countries of the natural capital on which the future livelihoods of their people depend.

This is unquestionably the political challenge for the twenty-first century. If developing countries follow the same growth pattern as the more mature industrialized countries, the impact will move us beyond the thresholds of safety and sustainability. Some of the most environmentally devastated areas of the world are in the former Soviet Union and Eastern Europe. We have a compelling interest in helping to ensure that they rebuild their economies on an environmentally sound and sustainable basis. While in some respects the environment has benefited from the slowdown of industry, there is little evidence that new industrial initiatives reflect a significant improvement in environmental responsibility.

Developing countries are contributing more and more to the larger global risks, such as climate change, ozone depletion, degradation of biological resources and loss or deterioration of arable lands. China has already become the second largest source of CO_2 emissions and will almost certainly succeed the United States in the dubious honour of being number one. Meanwhile, in Western countries, as these issues have receded somewhat from our own immediate experience, it has become more difficult to maintain the levels of public interest and commitment required to support the actions needed to deal with them. It is sobering to remind ourselves that all the environmental deterioration and risks that have arisen to date have occurred at levels of population and economic activity much less than they will be in the period ahead.

In other words the planetary environmental future will be largely determined by what happens in the developing world. Yet how can we, who created the risks in the first place, and who benefited most, deny the right of developing countries to grow? How can we possibly be surprised that, in doing so, they emulate our model? It would not be fair or reasonable or practical for us to unilaterally impose constraints on them in the name of the environment. But if we collectively don't accept just those restraints, we all face the doomsday scenario I have already outlined.

Unfair but safe, fair but unsafe? Are those the only options? What is the right policy?

The reluctance of developing countries to put up with measures that would impose constraints and higher costs on their development was brought into sharp focus by the negotiations on the Climate Change Convention in Kyoto in 1997. The South contended—once again—that the principal responsibility rests with the industrialized countries, which had caused the problem in the first place and had already enjoyed its associated benefits. Let the "rich" countries act first. Let them bring down their own emissions first. Let them leave "space" for developing countries to grow. And let the advanced world help out with new money and access to the best technologies to help bring emissions down.

Somewhat reluctantly the industrialized countries acknowledged a special responsibility to take the lead, but insisted that their efforts alone would not reduce emissions close to tolerable levels. Most of the current increases in emissions come, after all, from developing countries, and it will only get worse—the more they develop, the more they emit. In the end, an agreement, sort of, was patched together. The industrialized countries agreed, with a number of caveats, to targets and timetables for their own emission reductions. But the victory may yet prove hollow, because the u.s. administration, bowing to the pressure of the Republican majority in Congress, said it wouldn't even submit the Kyoto Protocol to Congress for ratification until developing countries have agreed to participate. At the subsequent meeting of the Parties to the Climate Change Convention in Buenos Aires in November 1998, continuing controversy limited progress to a modest step forward.

Climate change is shaping up as the mother of all environmental battles, and it will not be resolved quickly or easily. The controversies surrounding the Kyoto negotiations have reignited public and political interest in the issues and moved them back into the centre of the agenda. This has demonstrated clearly the deep differences and strong feelings that the issue evokes, both within and among nations.

In my view the rhetoric and controversy swirling about the issue sound like the clamour surrounding earlier fundamental changes in the way business was done—that is, the movements to abolish the slave trade and later child labour. Then as well, the dominant economic ethos of the times clashed with a new moral and ethical sensibility. Then as well, the business doomsayers of the day resisted the abolition of slavery or ending child labour. The rhetoric then, too, was typically extravagant and typically wrong-headed. The economy would collapse. Mass unemployment would ensue, the towns starve, the countryside go untended, the factories idle, it was all much too expensive and radical and unnecessary, and besides, the present system was the natural order of things, the best way to do things, and undermining it was a threat to an established way of life . . .

All the arguments are familiar in the present debate. The only difference is in tone: the existence of our mass media (and the added incentive that the current controversy concerns not just an economic way of life but the very survival of the human species) has added a shrillness to the rhetoric and a fundamentalism to the political posturing that is new. Still, every day you can hear the same arguments that business deployed to keep children in the mines: it would be economically ruinous to change, would impose unacceptable costs and constraints on business and on individual freedom.

This line of argument was wrong-headed then and it is wrong-headed now. If its proponents take the trouble to look, there is already persuasive evidence that, at least initially, many of the measures required to bring CO_2 and other greenhouse gas emissions under control can actually be advantageous in economic as well as environmental terms.

And that's the point. We should take these steps because they are intrinsically good steps to take. If they also head off catastrophe . . . well, who loses from that?

CHAPTER 3

Beginnings

W HO AM I, and why should anyone listen to me?
If you attend to the peculiar legends of the paranoid
right, there's a conspiracy. According to that view, a shadowy group of men, unelected, unrepresentative of anyone and
accountable to no one, set out to remake the world. They exercise
their secretive power in committees, in international and in non-
governmental organizations, in regulatory agencies. They gain influence by manufacturing artificial crises, by creating doomsday
scenarios of planetary degradation and by subverting and diminishing the sovereignty of nations. Cautiously, carefully and cunningly,
over many years, they have placed their people in key posts. They
are using the UN for their own designs, working surreptitiously to
turn it into an undemocratic proto—world government. They are
creating institutions that bypass nation-states. They are undermining the Western way of life. The unfettered workings of free markets
disturb their bureaucratic minds. They are a fundamental threat to
free men everywhere.

There's more, but that's the essence of it. I am sometimes said to
be at the centre of this sinister cabal. I've been collecting the quotes
over the years. Maurice Strong, "anti-charismatic to a fault," the
"Michelangelo of networking," a "very dangerous ideologue," a
"would-be king of the world." The American right-wing *National
Review* put it this way in a cover story in 1998: "... the actual peril is
subtle. A small cadre of international bureaucrats are hard at work

devising a system of 'global governance' that is slowly gaining control over ordinary Americans' lives. Maurice Strong, a 68-year-old Canadian, is at the center of this creeping UN power grab." The article went on in this alarming vein for three thousand words or so.

Of course there are also men who believe that the black helicopters of the UN armed forces are poised to swoop down on remote American hamlets and farmsteads and take over the world by force. Here's a not untypical excerpt, from a book called *Toward a New World Order*, by Donald McAlvany:

> Maurice Strong is a man to watch! The billionaire Canadian businessman is an employee of the United Nations; an employee of the Rockefeller and Rothschilds trusts and projects; a director of the Aspen Institute for Humanistic Studies; the organiser of the first World Conference on the Environment in 1992 [sic]; the founder and first head of the UN Environment Program; the secretary general (and chief organiser) of the UNCED Earth Summit in Rio in June 1992, and a leading socialist, environmentalist, New World Order manipulator, occultist, and New Ager. In the mid-1980s, Strong joined the World Commission on the Environment [sic] where he helped produce the 1987 Brundtland Report widely believed to be the "incendiary" which ignited the present "Green movement." Strong, who spearheaded the Earth Summit, has complained that "the United States is clearly the greatest risk to the world's ecological health . . ."

And so on and so on; there's much more of this stuff, both in print and bouncing around from Web site to Web site on the Internet, with a perverse life of its own.

Sure, these are but the deluded and paranoid ravings of the Western far right, and I wouldn't normally trouble to mention them at all except that my reaction when I hear a few of these charges is that I wish I had a smidgen of the power (and money!) they say I have. I wish I could accomplish a few of the things they already attribute to me. Not all of them, of course—most I wouldn't like to see happen. I do wish I could assist my many friends and colleagues in all the

organizations I belong to to remake the political and economic landscape. To make the world understand that the environment is not
just an issue but a symbol of the way industrial civilization has gone
terribly wrong. To help bring about a change in global thinking—
a change that might seem sentimental to hard-headed professionals
but that I believe necessary to the human future—to recognize that
the motivating force of political will, and human and social will,
really is based on the deepest moral, spiritual and ethical principles
that human beings of various persuasions respond to.

I would like to help change the world, yes, because I believe the
world really is in peril, but not change the world in my own image or
according to what I think right. I want to help change the world to
enable it to be itself, in all its glorious diversity.

My critics—and some of my friends—have occasionally expressed
puzzlement at the course of my life. They see it as a quixotic series of
zigzags, impromptu changes of course. I've been in business—I seem
to have some aptitude for it despite some notable failures. I've given
it all up several times and gone into public service. I've run oil companies. I've been—and am still—an environmentalist. I was once a
partner in a company with plans to develop the aquifers of Colorado
and was vilified in the local press (portrayed, among other things,
as a water-sucking Canadian plutocrat). I've been secretary-general
of the Earth Summit in Rio, yet a few years afterwards was chairman
of Ontario Hydro, one of the biggest producers of nuclear energy in
the world. Over the years I've worked with religious leaders, rock
stars, presidents, kings, diplomats, academics and entrepreneurs.
I've been at the UN many times, once as a lowly clerk in the pass
office, seven times as undersecretary-general.

Do I know, therefore, what I'm talking about? Not necessarily,
but these experiences have given me some very strong and deep con-
victions. I have received a good many criticisms and brickbats, not
all of them from the loony right or the loony left. At the same time, I
have had more than my share of honours and awards. In addition to
forty-two honorary doctorates, I've lost track of all the environmental awards I've been given, but I know they include the Tyler Ecology

Prize, Japan's Asahi Prize and the Onassis Award. From my own government I have received the Order of Canada, from the King of Sweden the Order of the Polar Star and a number of others. And on the recommendation of Brian Mulroney when he was prime minister of Canada, I was invested as a privy councillor to the Queen, an honour that carries with it no powers or duties but confers status equivalent to cabinet rank. I point out these things only to indicate that when I speak on the environment it is from a lifetime of study and involvement, sometimes deep within the councils of the great, sometimes on the fringes where so much of the creative thinking is done.

My business friends are often suspicious of my environmentalism, which marks me as a little flaky, and my colleagues in the environmental movement often regard my business life as somehow irreconcilable with the ideologies that drive them. Yet to me there are no contradictions here. To me the economy and business are not separate from the environment. You cannot affect one without changing the other. In the current state of human affairs, business is, in some senses, the environment. And so to me my life, while it has in some ways been a series of responses to expected and unexpected challenges, has always been consistent in its purposes and direction. If I look back down the long tunnel of memory I can clearly see the two impressions that dominated my childhood and shaped my attitudes and my actions: a revulsion at the notion of poverty and how it saps the human spirit, and a fascination with the intricate interconnectedness of nature. To me, I've always been headed in the same direction. I know what it is that governs my life: an urgent, overwhelming anxiety for the future of our planet and our species and a desire to do whatever I can to improve its prospects and dreams of a better future.

I was born in Oak Lake, a small town in rural Manitoba, in April 1929, just before the onset of the Great Depression.

The Depression was one of the great shaping forces in my life, a calamity visited not just on my family but on my community and my country and on many millions of people around the globe. The results of that calamity were everywhere to be seen. Its cruelty stripped my father of his livelihood and his sense of self-worth. It ruined my mother's health, and in the end it killed her. Human life, politics, the way society was ordered, had gone dreadfully wrong, that was clear enough even to me as a child. But no one seemed to know what to do, or indeed if there was anything that could be done. I used to watch the trainloads of the homeless and the desperate passing by my house, crossing the prairies, torn from their families by need and hunger, and their worn, pinched, anxious faces haunted me for years afterwards.

I was a quick learner as a child, I think—schoolwork, at any rate, seemed effortless to me—but I don't know whether I was any more sensitive than other children. Perhaps they felt the same way I did, that life was a series of threats and uncertainties. Perhaps they hid their doubts, as I did. And perhaps they needed as much as I did the sense of orderliness and purpose that seemed so lacking in adult life. If so, I don't know how they dealt with their anxieties. It would never have occurred to me to discuss these things with anyone. I was a private child and kept to myself. Thus it was that I found refuge in nature; it was there, in the richness and intricacy of the natural world, that I found the serenity that I longed for, a serenity so absent in human affairs. And so, a rather solitary boy, I immersed myself in both the tiny and the grand patterns of the non-human world.

Our part of Manitoba largely escaped the ravages of the droughts and plagues of grasshoppers that accompanied the Depression and turned parts of the prairies into a vast dustbowl. Despite the poverty of our human society, Oak Lake was full of trees, plants and flowers and a variety of nesting and visiting birds. I sought refuge in this fragile but stable world, in the transformations of spring, when the waters began to run, the trees to bud, the fresh green of grass and plants emerged from the receding snow, and the robins and orioles returned. All through my boyhood I spent many hours alone in the low hills on the edge of town, which remained untamed, with tall poplar and oak trees towering over dense, low brush, a refuge for small animals and birds. I learned to track and observe them for hours at a time, wondering at the grand patterns—how had they become what they were, how had I become what I was, what were the links between us? I was especially fascinated by insects and the busy communal lives of ants and bees. I became more and more aware of the great varieties of life that existed in the soil, much of which, as I learned from my nature studies, was not visible to the human eye. I grew to love the Manitoba fall, when the leaves turned golden and red, and the rabbits and weasels exchanged their summer browns for winter whites.

I often walked the three kilometres to the Assiniboine River outside town, where I put a fishing line in the water and lost myself in watching the flow of the river. Visits to the lake from which the town gets its name were a special treat, though less frequent as it took a long bicycle ride or the good fortune of a lift in our neighbour's Model T. I used to sit there and dream of building a boat to sail around the world.

When I was ten I created a secret "dungeon," a small cave in the side of a hill, hidden from intruders. I began to spend several days at a time there, playing truant from school, watching the landscape and the passing animals, wondering about God and the why and the how of His creation. I never minded being alone. I'd sit quietly for hours, listening to the busy silence. I'd watch the ants at work. I'd study the small scurryings of the mice and voles, and the innocent ferocity of their predators. At night I'd lie in my little bunker and stare upward, looking at the stars, wondering about the nature of time and space—I already knew I was "seeing" a universe that no longer existed, so great were the distances between and within the galaxies. I'd watch how nature's cycles worked, how the sap rose in the spring, the ebbs and flows and how everything fitted together, how harmoniously it all worked. Those hours alone gave me an emotional connection with the natural environment that never left me.

If nature could be so right, how could human society be so wrong? I asked my mother this once, but she just looked wistful and talked of better times when she was a girl, and the better times that would surely come for me and my brother and sisters.

Everything I've done as an adult has in some way been a response to that question.

My parents, Frederick Milton and Mary Strong, had four children: I was followed at two-year intervals by my brother, Frank, and sisters, Shirley and Joyce. My father's parents, Frederick and Ida, from Loyalist stock, had moved as a young couple from the Grafton/Cobourg area of Ontario to a farm near Brandon, Manitoba, before Oak Lake. Frederick Sr. kept the family going by working as a carpenter on odd jobs. He died before I was born.

My mother's background was very different. She was a Fyfe, also from Ontario stock, but her grandfather had been mayor of Sarnia and a founder of Imperial Oil, which was a Canadian company from 1880 until 1898 and is now Exxon's Canadian subsidiary. Her father had been a medical doctor and her mother a journalist with a column in the *Regina Leader Post*, in Saskatchewan.

I was just an infant when my father lost his job as an assistant station agent at the Canadian Pacific Railway Oak Lake station—he operated the telegraph machine, among other chores—and for the next decade he found nothing but occasional work for the Manitoba Hydro company, which was bringing electricity to our area, and odd jobs, for which he was often paid in kind—butter, milk, meat and wood. When he could get work, he worked very hard, and he had a deep sense of responsibility toward his family, but our existence was at the subsistence level. These were tough times for everyone, and we lived mostly on the produce my father got from local farmers in exchange for unremitting toil and on berries and wild things my mother managed to pluck from her garden and the woods. There were days when we were reduced to eating dandelions and pigweed. The strain on my parents was immense. With little money at the best of times, and none at all much of the time, my mother had to improvise day to day. The few essentials she needed were "bought" through the generosity of a local grocer, a Mr. Wallace, who extended her credit, though he knew the chances of being paid were meagre. Despite his own financial problems he never cut us off during the bad years, but kept us going with the small fiction that he was giving us "credit" and not a gift—one of many virtuous acts of kindness that filled the Depression years.

The long and extreme prairie winters were especially difficult. At times my father had to go out into the bush to cut wood without proper shoes; he'd wrap his feet in rags to keep them warm. We moved from one rented house to another, but none had central heating or indoor plumbing, and because we couldn't afford the luxury of coal to keep the stove burning all night, the temperature inside on winter mornings was much the same as outside; our clothes would freeze stiff during the night, and just getting the household up and started was a major chore. When my father was away, this became my job.

The Depression was hard on my father, but hardest of all on my mother. She did her best, coping as well as she could with the relentless worry of feeding and clothing her family, but the grind slowly wore her down. She had a brilliant mind and took care to introduce her children to issues beyond the immediate and the mundane. We had only a small library, but it contained some of the best of the classics, and my mother used to read Tennyson, Longfellow and Shakespeare to me—which served as a relief from her own anxiety as well as a benefit to me.

I remember her as a caring, gentle soul totally devoted to her family and subordinating her own interests and aspirations to the drudgery of domestic life, which her own privileged upbringing had not prepared her for. Her love of ideas gave me a permanent interest in the wider world that I might not have gained any other way. And she left me with a single overriding message: never hold yourself back from trying to achieve what you want. Always press to the limit.

After the birth of her third child she had what was to be the first of a long series of breakdowns and was admitted to the mental hospital in the nearby city of Brandon. When she came home, she was again the exemplary wife and mother, throwing herself into caring for her husband and children. Very likely this only compounded her distress. She invariably sacrificed for her family, but despite her heroic efforts she could never give them the lives she felt they needed, the lives she felt she owed them. The Depression defeated her, and she broke down again. The periods of treatment became progressively longer and longer, until at last she went back to the hospital and never came out again. She died when she was fifty-six.

Poor as we were, there were many times when life was good. The daily grind was punctuated by special occasions, like trips in a borrowed car to see our cousins in Saskatchewan. Christmas was always a time of great excitement, when Uncle Alex, who owned the local hardware store, made sure that Santa Claus was generous to us, and we always found under the Christmas tree some of the favourite toys that he had seen us looking at longingly in his store.

Thus, despite our poverty, we had the sense that we were better off than many others. Oak Lake was built around the main line of the Canadian Pacific Railway, and the freight trains travelling in both directions carried swelling numbers of people who had cut themselves adrift in search of food, a job, a little hope. When the train stopped, many of these destitute and desperate people would come to our house, seeking a drink of water or something to eat, and they'd tell us their sad stories and their dreams of a better future. We always shared what little we had, and none were ever turned away from our door.

At first I treated this pathetic stream of homeless strangers as a natural part of life—I had, after all, never known any other existence. But as I grew old enough to ponder these things, what I saw made less and less sense. How could there be so many impoverished people, eager to work yet unable to do so? Why were the factory doors closing when there was a willing workforce, and when so many people so clearly needed so many of the goods the factories had been producing? What was wrong with a system that permitted this to happen?

Later I put the questions to the man who was my principal all through my school years, Clarence "Curly" Heapy. He was an exceptional person by any standard, a largely self-educated man with a great capacity to foster in his pupils a love of learning. He was a man who took a deep interest in each of his pupils, identifying and fostering the best in them, giving each one a sense of direction that had an enduring influence on their lives.

I told him of the men who came to our door, their longings and their fears. Why, I asked him, could this happen? Why were so many people out of work?

He responded to my queries in the best way possible, by taking them seriously. He would launch into a passionate and forceful discourse on the injustices of the country's political and economic system and the need he saw for radical change. He told me many sad stories of people who had fallen victim to the system. He made it clear, too, that his political sympathies lay with the new prairie socialist party, the CCF (Co-operative Commonwealth Federation), headed by the populist J. S. Woodsworth. I think he found in me fertile ground for his ideas about social justice.

Heapy helped me in other ways. He saw that schoolwork was easy for me, though he never approved of my solitary days in my "dungeon" in the woods—particularly since I cut classes to get there—or accepted my excuse that I learned more out in the hills than I did in the classroom (something he later was good enough to acknowledge). But he did allow me to follow his own version of an accelerated program at school, and I ended up skipping three grades. Science and nature studies were my principal interests, and with his guidance and the encouragement of my mother I eagerly devoured books on the subjects to help me to understand the mysterious processes of nature that so excited and challenged me. At the same time Heapy fostered in me an interest in history and political science. The regimen he designed for me enabled me to pass my junior matriculation just after I turned fourteen, fulfilling requirements for entry to first-year university.

In what proved to be my final year of school, I won a cash prize intended to contribute to the cost of university. Instead I took the cheque down to our grocer, the generous Mr. Wallace. This was not a heroic or virtuous act—it was simply giving something back to a man with a great heart, paying a moral as well as a financial debt.

Many lessons can be learned from a terrible Depression, not all of them grim.

When Hitler's war began in 1939, it signalled a great change in our world, even in our small corner. The economy began to improve and jobs became more plentiful. Young men from Oak Lake and district rallied to the call of patriotism and adventure to join the armed forces. My father enlisted in the Royal Canadian Air Force and was about to realize his fondest aspiration—to be trained as a wireless operator—when my mother had to go back to the hospital. In an act of real sacrifice he accepted demotion to the lowest rank in order to be posted at an air base in Brandon, where he could be close to our mother and able to get home on weekends to care for his family.

The terrible Depression was followed by a terrible war, and yet spirits immediately lifted. Heapy believed passionately that the war was a product of the bankruptcy of our system.

"Why," he asked, "does it take a war to produce jobs and the resources required to get the economy moving?"

It was a question, of course, that many others asked, and answered in a variety of ways. In me it struck a responsive chord that haunted me for many years.

In 1943 the war was at its height, and the armed forces made a strong drive to enlist new recruits. I was only fourteen, too young to join up, but I was indignant that age alone should prevent me from serving my country when my classmates, with whom I had been able to keep up in school, were going off to war. It seemed to me to present both a patriotic obligation and a convenient opportunity to see the world—like most young people at the time, I didn't consider that war could kill or maim me; the war seemed to me almost wholly a good thing. In an act for which I have always felt embarrassment and remorse, I got out my birth certificate and carefully doctored it to add four years to my age, rather cunningly inking 1925 where 1929 had been. I knew my parents weren't likely to give me permission to enlist, so I left without telling them, reasoning optimistically that I'd let them know once I'd joined up and seek their understanding and forgiveness at that time. Off I went with a friend to the recruiting office in nearby Brandon. When they wouldn't take us—for some reason we were unable to meet the requirements, though my newly altered document was not the problem—my friend went back to Oak Lake, but I doggedly moved on to the Lakehead, as the twin cities of Port Arthur and Fort William were referred to (they're now known as Thunder Bay).

First I hitchhiked to Kenora, then took a freight train for a slow and lonely ride through the rugged Canadian Shield wilderness of rock, trees and pristine lakes. Here, nature was still largely untouched and unspoiled; the sparse population was concentrated in small villages along the railway and a few mining and paper mill communities. I remember it made an impression on me, even though my preoccupation was hunger—I'd taken nothing with me, and had nothing to eat along the way except a bunch of carrots I had pulled from someone's garden. When I arrived in the Lake Superior port city of Fort William, I was exhausted and half starved. I found a small restaurant near the railway yard and ordered a big meal, only partly inhibited from enjoying it by the knowledge that I had absolutely no money. When the bill came, I asked the waitress if I could see the manager. He turned out to be a very friendly man.

"I have something to talk to you about," I said solemnly. He sat down.

"I've been without food for a couple of days," I said. "I can't pay for my meal. But I am prepared to work for it."

I watched his face. To my great relief he was sympathetic. He'd been in my position himself, he said, and I should come into his restaurant any time I was hungry. "The best repayment you can make is to do the same for someone else," he said. This is another lesson from the Great Depression that I've never forgotten.

I spent that night huddled shivering in the covered entrance of a school, taking refuge from the rain. But the morning dawned bright and clear, and as the summer warmth dispelled the chill of the night, my spirits soared. I knew what to do. I headed for the port area and was delighted to see moored there a ship much larger than anything I had imagined. It proved, indeed, to be the largest passenger ship of the Canada Steamship Lines, the *Noronic*. I asked one of the seamen how one applied for a job on the vessel and was told to see the second steward. I went in search of that worthy, but he was much too busy to talk to me and waved me away. The ship was leaving shortly, he said, but would be back next Wednesday, and there might just be an opening for me then. At that, the ship's gong sounded, and an announcement came over the PA system that the ship would be leaving in ten minutes. "All visitors must now go ashore," the announcer brayed. I wasn't going to wait until next Wednesday—it seemed like an eon to me. Instead, I hid in a closet and waited until the sound of the engines and the swaying of the ship told me it was under way. I came out and went looking for the second steward again. He gave me a dressing-down, but he also gave me a job in the ship's galley, peeling potatoes and cleaning pans. I couldn't have been happier.

The experience on the *Noronic* confirmed my interest in seeking war service and adventure by going to sea. I met a young man on board who shared my ambition, and later we set out together by freight train, bound for Vancouver and the Pacific. Our comradeship was not to last. One stormy night in Kenora we were chased by railway police and were separated. The next morning I went in search of him but was warned off by a policeman. I must have looked even more like a tramp than usual, having spent the night in a freight car that had been used to haul coal, and the coal dust had clung to my damp clothes and body. The cop said he'd arrest me for vagrancy if I didn't leave town immediately. So I went on alone, hopping the next freight west out of Kenora.

In the early hours of the morning the train stopped briefly at Oak Lake, and I had to fight back the temptation to terminate my journey and return to the warm welcome I knew I'd find at home. But I felt that to come back under these circumstances would be to accept defeat of the mission for which I had left home only a few weeks earlier, so I resisted and held on until the train began to move off on its long journey to the Pacific.

It was on that trip from the known to the unknown, rumbling along the track through the endless prairie, in the optimistic flush of fourteen summers, that I had the first of the two epiphanies that were to shape my life. I was sitting in the railway yard at Broadview, Saskatchewan, waiting for the next freight train, basking in the sun, my spirits rising after the near-capitulation at Oak Lake, when a light breeze rustled the pages of a discarded newspaper nearby. I wandered over to pick it up and settled in the sun to read. It was, I recall, the *Regina Leader Post*. I read that Churchill and Roosevelt

had met on a warship in the Atlantic and had issued a pronounce-
ment that after the war a global organization would be created to
ensure that the world would never again have to experience the
horrors of war. I was transfixed. I remember the story so clearly. I can
still see in my mind the tattered broadsheet, the smudgy ink, the
words that resonated so strongly in my mind. I was still a boy, but
great international affairs had long impinged on my consciousness—
not just the Great Depression, but the war itself. All around me
people were going off to the front. People I knew were being killed
or injured, and tales of human devastation were daily fare. So when
Churchill and Roosevelt met and said that the world was going to be
a different place afterwards, I knew at once that I wanted to be part
of that endeavour.

Does that seem too neat, too pat—a fourteen-year-old with in-
flated political notions? But it was true. What a grand vision it was!
It was all there: everything that had been churning in my mind, all
my unfocused ideals, all my puzzlement at the way the world had
gone wrong, all my aspirations to do something, anything, to engage
in the struggle for change—I could hardly contain my excitement.
That short news report gave me a new purpose. In the years that
followed I read everything I could about the old League of Nations
and its dismal fate and watched carefully for any sign that the vision
of the two leaders would be fulfilled. I was thrilled when I read after
the war of the San Francisco Conference, at which the UN was
constituted, and I continued to read all I could of it and talked to
everyone who might be even slightly informed on the subject. It
remained an obsession with me.

I headed west, taking a freight train to Calgary. I was in good
spirits—riding those trains always gave me a feeling of freedom,
even exhilaration.

Coming into Calgary was another wonderful moment. It was a
clear crisp morning, and I was thrilled to see on the distant horizon
the shapes of the "shining mountains," as La Vérendrye had called
the Rockies. I didn't stay long in this city, which figured so prominently in my later life, but instead hitchhiked up to Edmonton.
Along the way I was picked up by a contractor from Leduc, who

hired me to work on one of his building projects in Edmonton. That lasted for about a month before I decided to move on to my main destination, the Pacific, working my way in the kitchen of a train carrying troops to Vancouver. The first thing I did when I got there was go down to Stanley Park to see the ocean.

There was a man sitting on a park bench, staring out to sea.

"Is this really the Pacific Ocean?" I asked.

He politely assured me that it was indeed, and I filled a bottle with water to send back to my brother and sisters.

I needed the cheapest possible place to stay and found a dosshouse in Chinatown that offered beds for $1.25 a night. The proprietor was an elderly Chinese man who kindly offered to let me sleep in his own room without payment. With a mixture of apprehension and appreciation, I accepted. His offer wasn't as kindly as I'd thought, because later that night I was startled awake as the old fellow climbed into my bed and began to snuggle up to me. I was both frightened and repelled, and hurriedly started dressing to leave. Chagrined, he assured me that he meant no harm and that I could stay in the room by myself and lock the door. With some trepidation I did this, and he didn't bother me again.

With my doctored birth certificate I enlisted without difficulty in the merchant marine, and signed on a CPR ship, the *Princess Norah*, under contract to the U.S. Army to transport troops to Alaska. I loved the life and took every chance I could to marvel at the marine life, at the mountains and the rugged forested islands as we made our way up the Inner Passage to Alaska.

On this voyage I made my first foray into entrepreneurship. I had been assigned a small cabin, which I shared with another fellow. The cabin had once been the ship's barbershop and proved a good place for the American officers to play poker. So I paid my roommate to find a bunk elsewhere and made a deal with the poker players to take a small amount (I think it was 50 cents) out of each pot for the privilege of using the room. It made me quite a bit of money.

Earlier I'd written to my parents, telling them I hoped to get another ship to take me into the South Pacific area. There I would surely see some real action. Writing that letter served to frustrate my plans. When the ship docked in Vancouver on the return voyage, I was met by two police officers who politely but quite firmly escorted me to a detention home to await the arrival of my father. This was my first and only experience on the "inside," and I vowed never to repeat it. When my father arrived, he was greatly annoyed to find that I'd been locked up, but the officers patiently explained that they'd seen no other way of ensuring that I'd stay put until he got there.

My father made me an offer. If I'd return home for a year, he said, I'd then be able to leave with his full blessing. I agreed.

What could I do with my life? I was restless. I wanted something to do with nature, somehow and somewhere. I wanted adventure. I wanted far-flung travel, international places, a long way from the prairies of Oak Lake. I remember sending letters all over the world, including one to a company that hunted whales in the Antarctic; even at that time I was not attracted by what they did, but I loved the prospect of high adventure it offered. Then, in the spring of 1945, after I'd spent the year in Oak Lake that I'd promised my dad, I saw in the Winnipeg paper a small ad: "Wanted. Young lads for far northern trading posts. Apply Hudson's Bay House." I wrote them a note, and they told me to come in for an interview. Off I went. I had my interview. And I was hired by the Hudson's Bay Company as an apprentice fur trader.

I didn't hesitate. How could I? The Arctic appealed to my sense of adventure. I'd be out in nature at its most dramatic, and I'd have the chance to be with the Inuit people, whose lives fascinated me. I'd always been interested in Canada's aboriginals. There was an Indian reserve near Oak Lake, and their culture and way of life had appealed to both my curiosity and my romantic instincts. The Eskimos, more properly referred to as Inuit, surely would be more exotic still. I'd not given any thought to the fur trade and its cruelty—at the time it just seemed part of life. It was only when I witnessed it firsthand that my uneasiness developed.

I was to go to Chesterfield Inlet, which is on the east coast of Hudson Bay. I had to go by boat, for at that stage there were no scheduled flights. The supply ship *Nascopie* brought the year's provisions on its annual trip to each of the main Arctic settlements, its arrival always the highlight of the year. A small schooner, the *Fort Severn*, from Churchill filled in the gaps and made occasional visits. I was booked on this schooner.

I got to Churchill by train, a trip that lasted five days, because not only did we stop at night, sleeping in small hotels in the villages along the way, but we also stopped for any tracker or trader or trapper who flagged us down. The railmen would often do the trappers' shopping for them, in The Pas or Winnipeg, and the trappers would wait patiently by the track until their supplies arrived. From Churchill I took the schooner to Eskimo Point, where I spent two or three weeks, and then went up on the same schooner to Chesterfield Inlet.

It wasn't much, a small settlement with a Roman Catholic mission, a Department of Transport radio weather station and of course the Hudson's Bay post. There was only a handful of people, but it was still quite a little centre—why, it actually had a medical doctor! I was an apprentice fur trader. My boss was the post manager, Alan Scott. I was assigned an upstairs room in the house in which he lived with his wife, Eileen, and their two small children.

I was put to work the moment I arrived, supervising the Inuit who were helping to unload the schooner, something that had to be done rapidly because of the constant pressure of the short shipping season and the risk that bad weather or the movement into shore of the ice floes would trap the vessel. If the ship wasn't unloaded quickly, the post could lose vital supplies, and they could not be replenished until next year, or the ship might get trapped and not reach its next destination in time.

Chesterfield Inlet had no wharf or quay; unloading was entirely dependent on catching the tide, so every able-bodied person had to work every hour the tide was right and then again at next tide. But how to keep the Inuit, who lived in tents scattered all over the region, from simply going home between tides? If they went home, they'd never be rounded up again in time for the next tide.

My job was to keep them close by until the turn of the tide. I had to find some way of interesting them so that they wouldn't just disappear.

Alan Scott was a tough Scot with a brusque manner. I had to find a way, he told me, whatever it was, or else . . . Well, I couldn't speak the language, and I was just fresh off the boat. What to do?

I sat with the Inuit for a while, trying to think of something. How could I keep them amused without speaking a word of their language? Then it came to me. There were ducks everywhere in the Arctic and especially around the post. One of them, an eider duck, makes a peculiar *aaarh aaarh aaarh* sound and waggles its wings as it moves in an odd waddling walk. I saw a few of them and started to imitate them. I got to my feet, flapping my elbows and making, as best I could, their harsh, croaking *aaarh aaarh aaarh*, strutting up and down the inlet like the purest fool—and I was a hit! The Inuit had never seen a white person acting undignified in quite such a spectacular fashion, and they began to roar with laughter. They responded as though it was the funniest thing they'd seen in years. They laughed, called more people over, laughed again, and the new people called more people, until they were all laughing. This was exhausting work! Never have tides seemed so far apart. Whenever I stopped to rest, they would urge me on. They couldn't speak any more English than I could their language, but their gestures were admirably clear: do it again! Make like a duck again! I tried a few other creatures, but they liked the eider duck best.

In this way, I passed my first test—I managed to keep them there until the next tide. Scott was surprised when more of the Inuit than ever turned up to help unload, and the job got done.

It stuck with me, too—for the rest of my time in the Arctic the Inuit called me Metik, which means Boy-that-makes-like-a-duck. Whenever they saw me after that, whenever they came back after their weeks or months away, they'd come by the post and call for Metik, and ask me to make like a duck again.

When I got to know them, the Inuit fascinated me more than ever. It's hard to think of a people closer to nature. They had lived for centuries in a brutal climate without the benefit of either wood or metal. But they were patient, persistent and innovative and, before the white man's civilization intruded into their world, had evolved a way of life and a value system that enabled them to live in harmony with their Arctic surroundings. What struck me was how they could be so happy living in one of the harshest climates in the world.

I got to like them enormously. I learned their language and developed a real rapport with them. Jacqueline, a young Eskimo girl who worked in the factor's house, was cheerful and friendly and enjoyed flirting with me. And her little brother, Anikiloo, attached himself to me wherever I went. Their father was a wise and reliable man called Apik, who did the chores around the post and had earlier worked for the Danish explorer Peter Freuchen. I also understood pretty quickly that the factor, Scott, was much too tough on the Inuit; he treated them like unruly children, with a harshness that I thought was uncalled for. I spoke to him about this; I was never one to hold my tongue when I felt strongly about something. He dismissed my protest summarily.

"You just don't understand these people," he said. "They're good people, but you don't want to let them get on top of you."

So dismayed was I by his treatment that not long after I arrived, I went over to the radio station and reported him to the Hudson's Bay headquarters in Winnipeg. When they found out, the Scotts were understandably angry. For about six months they treated me with frosty disdain, though I continued to live and work with them. I didn't care—I suppose I was sustained by the fact that I had done what I thought was right. The time I had spent in solitary contemplation of nature in Oak Lake had taught me to value privacy, and I enjoyed being alone. In any case, when the spring came, I moved out of the trading post and pitched my own tent. I still did my work at the post and had to get my food there, and we later repaired our relationship, though for six months I lived apart.

I got along fine with the native people, who soon found out what I'd done. Once I'd become quite fluent in their language, they'd invited me into their own circle. I'd go out with dog teams—there were no snowmobiles then—and I learned a good deal about how the Inuit stalked the seals, how they only killed for food for themselves and their dogs, how patient they were, how they knew where to wait for the seals, how to call caribou, how to build an igloo, how to survive and how to make the most of life.

The whole experience profoundly influenced my regard for other cultures. I learned for the first time to respect people who spoke a different language, who reacted differently to circumstances. I developed a tremendous curiosity about other cultures that never left me.

The Inuit took me into their tents and their igloos. I was the only white person there, and though I didn't understand all I heard, I knew enough to get the sense of it. They would sit in a circle and sing the long and melancholy songs of their people, not really singing but a slow chanting, recounting the exploits of their history, telling the tales of their survival, of their heroes and villains, of the beneficent spirits and the malignant ones, of their survival in the face of the overwhelming power of nature, which they felt so personally and viscerally. They told stories about their ancestors, about the land, about animals, about animal spirits. They would also tell stories about the idiotic things the *kabloona*, the white man, had done. They looked with amusement at the *kabloona*, who had all the power in the world but was so ignorant of so many things. They enjoyed stories that showed how naive and inexperienced the white people were, stories told without malice, only with amusement. The word *Inuit*, they pointed out to me, means "the real people." White people were interesting, but not real in the same way, and definitely peculiar.

Often after a particularly powerful tale, or a deeply conjured image, the conclave would fall silent, contemplating what they had heard, savouring the image, admiring its flavour. They would be still sometimes for an hour, two hours or more; the silence was an integral part of their communication. It took me a long time to understand this and to feel comfortable with it, coming as I did from a culture where blather is constant and silence is either rude or embarrassing. Later in life I used this understanding to good effect, when I spent some time with the Indian prime minister Indira Gandhi, who was wont to lapse into long silences in conversations, whether from calculation or habit I never knew. In any case she saw that I was not troubled by her silences, and it made her comfortable with me.

The Inuit had other customs that seemed peculiar to me, until I understood the cultural matrix that they sprang from.

There was an old woman I was fond of. One day she was not there. I asked about her.

"She has gone," I was told.

"Gone? What do you mean, gone? Is she dead?"

"Well . . . she's gone."

It meant that she had said goodbye to everybody she knew, to her family, and had walked out into a storm, never to return. I only understood this later. The Inuit were a nomadic people living in a savage environment, surviving on meagre resources, and it was an individual's duty to help the people survive. It was unthinkable to become a burden. And so they knew when it was time to go, when it was time to say goodbye.

Not all customs were so bleak. I was very surprised one night when a young fellow I liked very much brought his wife along to my tent and offered her to me. I was very young, very taken aback and therefore awkward and embarrassed. Even had I been tempted I wouldn't have known the proper protocol, the manners. So, probably gracelessly, I demurred. He was surprised in his turn and a little hurt. He proceeded to make quite a good case for her, that she was a nice woman, a good woman, an attractive woman. He made an effort to sell me on her manifold virtues; it was a gesture of friendship.

The Inuit had learned to depend on goods procured at the Hudson's Bay Company trading post in exchange for their furs—rifles, ammunition, tea, biscuits, primus stoves, cloth and other basic merchandise. But most still lived nomadic lives in search of the best hunting and trapping grounds, inhabiting igloos in winter and tents in summer. Dogsleds were their principal mode of transport, supplemented by canoes in summer. Most still favoured their traditional clothing—caribou-skin parkas, sealskin pants, mitts and boots. And Apik's wife, Daisy, made me a complete outfit, which I soon found the most comfortable and sensible thing to wear, particularly in the winter.

The Inuit didn't have money, not then. It was still a cashless society. But of course I was a junior representative of a global trading company, which very definitely used money. We used sticks to make the translation.

It worked this way: when a trapper came in with his furs, the trader counted them and evaluated them, if only in a rudimentary way. Then for each fur you'd put so many sticks on the counter and say, "Well, this one is worth twelve sticks, this one fifteen," and so on. By the end of the session the counter was covered with sticks. Then the trapper would start to buy. He'd say, "I want two cases of tea. How many sticks?" You'd pull the right number away from the pile. "A case of ammunition?" Another selection of sticks. All the while they would look carefully and studiously at the diminishing pile of sticks. A few of the more sophisticated would want to store some of their sticks as a kind of deposit account. They insisted on watching while the trader took the sticks, counted them and transferred the number into a ledger. When they returned, in weeks or months, you would take out the books, count out the actual sticks and put them on the counter. Some even wanted credit: they wanted us to advance them some sticks. We didn't do that often.

During the winter, when there were few Inuit people around, I frequently visited the other residents and formed a particular attachment to Bishop Marc Lacroix, the Roman Catholic bishop of the Arctic who was resident there and said to be the youngest bishop in the Church. He patiently instructed me in the basic tenets of his faith and dealt with my doubts in a friendly, understanding way. I admired him greatly and had a high regard for the other priests and brothers at the mission, but I could not in the final analysis accept some of the fundamental beliefs of the Church, though this experience gave me an enduring respect for it.

There were others who helped me understand the Inuit in the larger, ethnological sense. One was a French anthropologist who later became a senior scientist in the Musée de l'Homme in Paris, Jean Philippe Michea. He arrived by ship in the spring. The Inuit called him Tablookie, Man-without-a-chin. He was looked on as an eccentric by the other whites because he seemed to have no other business but to study the Inuit.

I also learned a great deal from the writings of the Danish explorer and author Peter Freuchen, who had spent some time in the same region. In the trading post storeroom I found a bundle of old files, including a collection of letters from Freuchen. Apik told me many stories about his experiences with the man, including how he'd had to help him amputate his own leg after severe frostbite. Freuchen wrote a number of interesting books about the Inuit, which I devoured. Later, when I went to the UN, to my astonishment I found Freuchen one day in the delegates' lounge, a great big magnificent man with a peg leg. He had been sent to New York by the Danish government just after the war; the U.S. wanted to buy Greenland, and the Danes had sent Freuchen over to negotiate. I introduced myself and he was delighted to reminisce about his days in the Arctic.

I was in the Arctic at the end of an era. The local people were just becoming exposed to modernization. There was no regular air service then—most travel is by air now. There were no snowmobiles then— it's all snowmobiles now. The people were nomads and their culture was more or less intact then—they live in permanent houses now and their culture is fractured. In some ways they're better off—they have access to medical treatment, for instance. When I was there, there was no market for Eskimo art, not as a source of income. Now, though it may have been overdone, some with artistic talent can actually make a living from their art. But in certain ways it is not so good—the culture is deteriorating and nothing much has replaced it. The people have lost their nomadic ways and have become less self-reliant. The "gods" of government, believing that the Inuit needed access to the benefits of modernization, and responding to the hardships they had experienced during the famine that afflicted the North in the late 1940s, gave them homes in permanent communities, which separated them from their traditional way of life. Governmental intervention has had a debilitating effect on Inuit culture and sense of self-worth. Observing this, I began to realize what a mixed blessing modernization is for traditional peoples.

I was at Chesterfield Inlet a little over a year. In the end I came to resent the fur trade and the way the Inuit had become servants of its commercial purposes. I didn't want to work there any more and applied for a transfer. I was refused, so I quit, and when the supply ship came in the summer of 1946, I went back to Oak Lake.

A short while after my return there was a polio epidemic in the

North. Many people were flown to hospitals in Winnipeg, and the call went out for interpreters. I volunteered my services. When the patients started to recover, I was recruited by *Time* magazine to take these Inuit around Winnipeg and get their reaction to the city— they had never seen a city before. Indeed, most of them had never seen a tree before. I remember that they asked me about telephone poles, why these odd trees didn't have branches. And they couldn't get over the fact that we'd drive down the street, apparently going somewhere purposefully, and then suddenly stop. Then we'd start up again, go fast again, then stop. Stoplights were one of the most puzzling things to them.

My interest in native affairs continued long after I left the Arctic. Some years later I helped to set up the Native Business Council of Canada, and I was appointed to a three-man commission set up by the government of Canada to study the future governance of the Arctic, though I never actually got to serve on it.

Those early experiences of living and working among the Inuit helped me later in life in working with the people of developing countries. Not, of course, that developing countries are alike—people of other cultures think differently and approach life differently. But while I'm not very good at languages, I've always had a high degree of cultural sensitivity—which I certainly didn't get from my home-town, where the Catholics and Protestants were always at odds, and people would whisper nastily about "foreigners." I, on the contrary, was always fascinated by the otherness of different cultures. I wanted to make my life among them. I was determined I would do so.

My experience with the Inuit in the Arctic thus added a third thread to the fabric of my life. To my revulsion at the way people are at the mercy of politics and my fascination with nature, I now added an engagement with the cultures of others. These three have run through everything I've ever done. Sometimes one of them would be uppermost, sometimes another. But they were all present in some form, always. They have shaped my life and informed everything I have tried to accomplish.

Through the Back Door

I PASSED MANY LONG HOURS with the Inuit, but the Arctic nights were long and I also spent a good deal of time studying. I'd got hold of a copy of a correspondence course in prospecting designed by the University of Toronto and the Ontario Prospectors' Association, and I pored over it through the winter. I had one advantage other students didn't—I asked my Inuit friends to collect rock samples for me wherever they could, and by the time I finally left Chesterfield Inlet in mid-summer I'd built up quite a collection. I was even able—at least to my own satisfaction—to identify a number of commercial prospects in the eastern Arctic.

By a happy coincidence, a man who was to play a significant role in my life came up on the boat I was to take home. He was W. A. (Bill) Richardson, a flamboyant, somewhat eccentric genius of a fellow from Tennessee whose handsome looks and silver tongue charmed and intrigued most everyone he met—particularly women. Known to his often bemused colleagues as Wild Bill, he'd come to Canada during the war, joined the air force and married a wealthy Torontonian, a socialite named Mary McColl. After the war ended he decided to go into prospecting, an activity that suited his restless energy and hunger for the dramatic. I managed to spend quite a bit of time with him as I waited for the boat to return to take me south.

Having studied prospecting myself, here I was, meeting the real thing. He had all the latest equipment, too, every gadget and piece of gear you could imagine. I was fascinated by him.

He was impressed in his turn with my own rock collection—my samples came from a broad swath of the eastern Arctic but mainly from around Baker Lake and Rankin Inlet. Richardson gave me his address in Toronto and said, in his lofty but well-meant way, "When you're in Toronto come and work for me."

Well, I took him up on it. After spending a few months back at my home in Oak Lake, I went down to Toronto by bus. Of course, I had no money, but I was buoyed by Richardson's promise of work. I found a rooming house through a small ad in the paper and went to see it. I looked at the room and told my landlady-to-be that I'd take it.

"I'll need a down payment," she said.

"I'm sorry," I said, "but I just can't."

She asked me whether I had a job.

"Well," I answered, "I think I have a promise of a job."

She took a chance on me and let me have the room.

The next day I went down to see Bill, only to find that while he had meant the invitation seriously at the time—he always meant everything at the time—there really wasn't anything for me to do. He was friendly and helpful, but he had no work for me.

I got a job eventually on my own, delivering stationery on a little wagon to the back doors of the city's great office buildings.

In time, though, Bill Richardson came through and arranged for me to be hired by a company that had grubstaked him, Vincent Mining Corporation, as an accounting clerk. I studied bookkeeping and accounting at night and practised it by day, acquiring by default much more responsibility than my youth and inexperience warranted because of the frequent absences of the chief accountant, a brilliant person who was trying desperately to hide an addiction to alcohol. I helped cover for him by doing much of his work. It proved to be an intense learning experience for me.

Bill Richardson must have been satisfied. He was putting together a new company he called New Horizons Explorations to prospect over the vast Keewatin District, and at the age of seventeen I found myself featured in its prospectus, a nice piece of fiction, as one of the company's prime assets, its so-called five men of the North. I even found myself nominated a director and secretary-treasurer. The brochure staked out an ambitious program of exploration in the North, including some of the prospects I had helped to identify in the eastern Arctic. New Horizons wasn't one of Bill's great successes—it was wound up only a year later, its investors paid off with shares in other mining companies.

All this time my obsession with the United Nations remained undiminished. I devoured every bit of news about it and was always looking for ways to pursue my interest in international affairs.

Mary McColl Richardson, Bill's wife, was the daughter of John McColl, a major player in Toronto, who had controlled the McColl-Frontenac Oil Company until it was taken over by Texaco. Mary was a lovely woman but somewhat spoiled by her upbringing among Toronto's establishment. Still, she was John's only daughter, and he was very protective of her. Being a conservative fellow, he had always been dubious about the merits of his flamboyant son-in-law, but he took a shine to me, for even then I had a bit of a flair for numbers and for business, though I didn't know very much about either. He found me a reassuring contrast to his wayward son-in-law, I think, and took a special interest in me.

Mary invited me to live in the Richardson home. This was not the first time such an offer was made to me, and it was to be far from the last. I'm rather at a loss to explain why. I was a polite and soft-spoken young man, and I suppose bright enough, but what possessed her to make the overture? In these more cynical days it would be supposed there was something dark about it, some suppressed eroticism, but I rather think I aroused her sisterly instincts—she certainly treated me like a younger brother. Somehow, without doing anything but trying to be polite and forthright, I ingratiated myself with people. Perhaps it was because I was so obviously eager to learn. In any case the Richardson household was my introduction to the world of big oil, big business and geopolitics. At the Richardson home I met many members of Toronto's business elite and other prominent people. Among them was Paul Martin, MP for Windsor, Minister of Health and Welfare, and—more important to me—leader of the Canadian delegation to the UN.

Before her marriage Mary had had a boyfriend, a French aviator, who had been killed in the early part of the war, and he in turn had a very good friend, Noel Monod, who had become treasurer of the United Nations, an important and influential position. He visited Toronto in the summer of 1947 while I was there—his mother was a delegate to a world conference of women, and she stayed with the McColls.

Mary, supportive of my youthful aspirations, said to him at dinner one night, "Well, Noel, Maurice is just consumed with the United Nations. Would you mind spending a little time just talking to him?"

If he resented the invitation to spend time with a seventeen-year-old, he was far too diplomatic to show it. Dutifully he went down into a basement family room with me after dinner, and we began to chat. Soon he became interested. He could see I really did know an extraordinary amount about the UN. "It just so happens," he said at one point, "that I'm on the personnel selection board of the UN. Let me look into this for you and see what I can do."

And he did. He went back to New York and set up an appointment for me with the personnel department. As soon as he called I took a bus to New York and showed up at UN headquarters the next day, as instructed.

The UN was new and very popular then, a desirable place to work, and the personnel department anteroom was jammed with people. I thought I didn't have a chance. I found myself sitting next to a fellow who told me he had a Ph.D.; he had been waiting eight months or so for his opportunity.

"How long did it take you?" he asked.

"I just got to town yesterday," I said.

Looking around the room at all those probable Ph.D.'s, I was convinced I'd never make it. But to my surprise a woman came out into the room and called out, "Mr. Strong?" So I was in, on a very temporary General Assembly appointment. (Temporary appointments are much easier to secure, not requiring all the rigmarole of the permanent ones.)

Monod, too, had taken something of a shine to me, perhaps because of my youthful enthusiasm, though I later had occasion to wonder if there were not some other dimension to his interest. I stayed briefly at his apartment, where I was first introduced to young David Rockefeller, grandson of J. D. Rockefeller. David had been assigned by the Chase Bank to handle the UN account. This had brought him into contact with Monod, and indeed I found out later that he had been largely responsible for Monod's appointment as treasurer of the UN. I had a long and cordial relationship with David in later years.

Monod's notion was to attach me to the senior administrative office of the Palestine Commission, which was then being set up under Count Folke Bernadotte. Palestine was the burning issue of the time, and I was going to have a very junior clerical role in the commission. I was thrilled. But the complicated politics of the UN delayed the mission, and then delayed it again—in fact, Bernadotte was assassinated later—and my appointment was up in the air; the job for which I had been hired didn't yet exist. So in the meantime I got a job in the pass office, as a junior clerk issuing building passes. There were press passes and several levels of delegate passes; it was part of the security of the place, and thus important enough.

Because I was young (I was still adding four years to my real age, and even then I was written up as the youngest person around) and also eager, I came to the notice of the head of security, who liked me and made me his unofficial assistant. I'd run around to the conference rooms and lounges on his behalf, a minor part of the organization's security apparatus. The great benefit for me was that I had access to any place; I could go into any conference room. I was there when Israel was created, for instance. I heard Vyacheslav Molotov speak and even Andrei Gromyko, who was then a young man with the Russian delegation. He was very dour, but as I was just a young fellow and no threat to anybody, I got to know him slightly—he'd say hello to me in the men's toilet and that sort of thing. It was Gromyko who delivered the Soviet Union's blessing for the creation of Israel, not vetoing the division of Palestine into Israel, Gaza and Jordan. In my later life, when Gromyko briefly became president of the Soviet Union, I spent a memorable hour with him in his office in the Kremlin, and we reminisced about those early days in the UN. I was surprised that he remembered me. The open and animated way that he discussed both current and past issues with me was in stark contrast to the dour reticence that had been his hallmark through most of his career.

I got to know many people—not very well, of course, because I wasn't on their level—but I remember, for example, Warren Austin and Lester B. Pearson of the Canadian delegation. John Green, a journalist who was dating my first cousin, was the son of Howard Green, who later became Canada's minister of external affairs. He went to New York, and because he'd heard I was working at the UN came to see me. He thought I was a guard of some kind. Actually, guards were probably better paid and more senior than I, but when he asked for me, one of the guards said, "Oh, yes, Mr. Strong!" They thought I was a bigger shot than I was because I was helping the boss. Green was surprised that I seemed to be so well known. But of course the only reason was that I got around, I was curious, I asked questions, I was always keen to talk to anyone—I always found them willing to talk to a young fellow who was both polite and interested.

I used the UN's procedures to my advantage. There is always a lot of time spent waiting at the UN, as delegates wait for meetings to begin, wait for other meetings to finish, hang around in the halls. There was a small office outside the main conference room that I used when I could, and I talked to all kinds of people while they were waiting. I made myself useful when I could. I watched and listened and learned. The General Assembly period is when all the senior ministers come to the UN, so for me it was a great experience, a traumatic, revealing, exhilarating, enlightening, enriching experience.

Working there, I became even more obsessed with the place. I used to read copies of the debates. Andrei Vyshinsky was the president of the General Assembly for a while, and I clearly remember some of his memorable and thunderous interventions. "I am an atheist!" he famously declared at one point. The Cold War had already set in, and there was much fractiousness and division within the UN. It shocked me to think that the organization, set up to preserve peace, so noble a purpose, was being torn apart by Cold War politics.

Exhilarating as the experience was, and though it entrenched in me my resolve to seek a career in international service, I knew my job wasn't leading me anywhere. I noted in my diary that it was simply not realistic for me, a person without academic qualifications or political connections, to rise in the ranks of the UN—I'd only be able to work at the administrative or "general services" level. I'd have to return to Canada and find some way of accumulating the necessary credentials and experience.

My first such effort was through the armed services. Months before, I'd applied to the Royal Canadian Air Force for an officers' training course, which came with the equivalent of a university degree. Just about the time I was mulling over my UN future, I heard that my application had been accepted. This, I decided, could open the door to the kind of career I was seeking. I went back to Toronto and did well in the course. But I was not really cut out to be an active-service military man. I went from the officers' course to pilot training, and though I enjoyed it and proved pretty good at aero batics, I lacked the depth perception required to land safely. Since it wasn't much use to the air force if a pilot performed well in the air but was a hazard to himself and his colleagues getting back to the ground, I was washed up as a pilot. They gave me a chance to become a navigator, but this didn't interest me at all, and I took the other option—discharge.

I returned to Oak Lake to ponder the possibilities. What else could I do that would give me the credentials and experience I needed? I didn't have the money to go to university, so I knew I'd have to work. But what kind of work?

In the spring of 1948, just turned nineteen, I got a promising job as a trainee statistician (what would now be called a securities analyst) for the firm of James Richardson and Sons, one of Canada's leading stock brokerage firms, headquartered in Winnipeg. My specialty was to be mining and oil securities, but after a few months on the job I came to focus primarily on oil. This was when the Alberta oil boom, triggered by the discovery at Leduc, was moving into high gear.

Richardson's had already developed considerable expertise in the oil business, which had given them a clear lead among investment dealers in the field. I worked and studied hard to make myself an oil and gas expert. I used my spare time to set up a system of well cards to track every well then drilling in Alberta, among other stratagems. When the firm decided to move one of its experts from Winnipeg to Calgary to be even closer to the action, I was quick to volunteer. That didn't go anywhere. The statistical department was headed by a slight, dapper and fastidious Englishman, Noel Fowler, who sported a well-groomed handlebar moustache and conducted himself as though he were still in the military. He derided my proposal. I was still too new and inexperienced, he said.

But I wasn't to be diverted. A few days later an envelope had to be delivered to the general manager, R. D. Baker, a stocky, gruff, red-faced man who ran the Richardson investment business with an iron hand. No messenger was immediately available, so I offered to take it myself.

He ignored me when I entered his office.

Timidly and tentatively I said, "I'm sorry to bother you, sir, but I know that the firm is sending an oil specialist to Calgary. Mr. Fowler thinks I'm too young for the job, but I know I can do it, and if I were given a chance would expect to be fired in six months if I did not perform."

He finally looked up. He stared at me. After a few very long seconds he said gruffly, "We'll see."

I scurried out of his office, not knowing whether my venture would lead me to Calgary or to the streets.

I heard nothing for two weeks. Then Fowler called me in and said simply, "Well, you're going to Calgary, after all. I have to tell you it was not my choice. Mr. Baker has decided it for his own reasons, and I only hope you can handle it."

I never did explain the overture I had made to the general manager.

This was a time of great activity and excitement in Calgary, and

I found myself very much in the centre of it. I began to make money and to acquire a reputation. At the same time there were happy developments in my personal life. In Winnipeg I'd met a girl named Pauline Williams, who was at the Winnipeg normal school studying to become a teacher. She was very attractive and engaging, and when I learned how she had overcome the obstacles of growing up in a poor and somewhat divided family, putting herself through high school by working as a night operator in the local telephone exchange, my respect for and interest in her deepened. After I became established in Calgary, I asked her to marry me, and to my great delight she accepted.

But there was a problem—my "age." I was still not quite twenty, but my "official" age had me almost twenty-four. Before marrying, I had to resolve this self-inflicted problem. Accordingly, and with great trepidation, I went to see Swift Hodgson, who was then the regional supervisor for Richardson's in Calgary, and confessed. I hadn't meant to deceive them, I said—I explained that I'd needed to be "older" to get into the services. I offered my resignation. I was greatly relieved and taken aback when Hodgson laughed. "We'll just treat it as a change of records," he said reassuringly. Pauline and I were married in Calgary on July 29, 1950.

Shortly afterwards Jack Gallagher, who had just been recruited by Dome Mines from Standard Oil of New Jersey (now Exxon) to head the newly formed Dome Exploration (Western), invited me to come in as his assistant. I accepted this as a great opportunity to learn the operating side of the oil business. Gallagher was highly intelligent, a shrewd and visionary person with a perpetual smile and a congenial, persuasive personality, for whom I developed great affection and admiration. At the time the team consisted only of Jack, his secretary, Ethel Cairns, and me, but Jack had already arranged for a senior engineer, Charlie Dunkley, to come in as a vice-president. It was a good choice. Dunkley was a competent petroleum engineer, had a wry sense of humour and a sceptical attitude toward anything that had not been proven to his satisfaction. A slide rule was always in his hands or within reach, and he consulted it at some point in virtually every conversation.

Under Gallagher's tutelage I performed a variety of tasks and took on increasingly larger responsibilities as the company developed to become one of the largest independents in the Canadian oil business. Initially I did many of the office chores, including keeping track of production reports, land and legal records and our then-rudimentary accounts. As the staff expanded, others took over more of these responsibilities, and I concentrated largely on the land, legal and financial sides of the business, including liaison with our principal investors. Dome Mines was controlled from New York. Among the investors were a syndicate led by John Loeb of Lehman Brothers, who later became Edgar Bronfman's father-in-law; Harvard University's endowment fund; and Empire Trust, managed by Henrie Brunie, a friend of John McCloy, legal adviser to the Rockefellers, who had helped set up the CIA.

Like a number of people in the Calgary oil community, Jack Gallagher had had a great deal of international experience. He was very sympathetic to my own international aspirations. But the person with whom I was able to share them most fully was Gus van Wielengen, a Dutch petroleum engineer who had come to Canada after the war, during which he and his wife, Betsy, had been confined to a Japanese prison camp in Indonesia. During long evenings stretched out on the rug in front of the fireplace of their home, we discussed their wartime experiences and speculated about our future activities. Gus went on to become one of the most enlightened and respected figures in Canada's oil industry and one of the most loyal and staunchest friends from my Calgary days. We have since continued to share our international interests and experiences.

After my first two years with Dome, the company was developing rapidly, I was enjoying my job and doing well. Pauline and I were able to move out of our small basement suite and buy our first home.

Doing well, indeed. But for what purpose? Where was it taking me? Business was all very well—but business for what?

In the summer of 1951 I went back to the family home in Oak Lake for a visit. For one long evening I sat on the steps of my old school and mulled over my life. I was twenty-two. I had a good job with a growing oil company and was well positioned for promotion. I had made a small fortune. Yes, I was doing well, but . . . here I was back in Oak Lake, and the memories crowded in. This was the place where Principal Heapy and my mother had helped me open my mind. This was the place where I had observed the ravages of the Depression and its effects on the human spirit—it had destroyed my own mother, after all. From here I had heard the siren song and seen the terrible trap of war. My solitary walks in the woods around town and my contemplation of the natural world had given me a longing for something greater, more useful to society than I had known. All evening the ghosts of my past crowded and jostled in my mind. I so vividly remembered my excitement at first reading about the notion of a United Nations, and its chance to become a body that was greater and wiser than any nation. I remembered my months in New York, the UN's huge promise and deep troubles. I yearned for something meaningful to do, some service I could perform. I remembered I had come back to Canada not to be an oilman or to succeed in business but to make myself ready for international service. It was a complicated time internationally. The Korean War was raging. The Cold War was at its frostiest, and in the United States Senator Joseph McCarthy was doing his evil work.

No, I decided, things were going well for me, but it wasn't enough. By the end of the evening, I had determined what to do.

I returned to Calgary the next day and announced to an astonished Pauline that we were going to pull up our roots and take a trip around the world. Naturally enough, her first reaction was trepidation, but she soon became fully supportive and even enthusiastic. Jack Gallagher, for his part, was disappointed but understanding.

"I'll keep a job open for you at Dome, for when you return," he said. I was grateful, I told him, but I'd prefer not to have any commitments. This wasn't supposed to be a sabbatical I was taking. I wanted a change. I hoped the trip would lead to opportunities in the international world.

We sold our house, I left my job and we set out just after Christmas, taking a ship from New York to Genoa. For six months we travelled through Europe, by bus, train and thumb, staying mostly at youth hostels. We were in Paris when Stalin died. Then we took a Union Castle–line passenger/cargo ship on a slow route through the Suez Canal to South Africa. Pauline was a wonderful companion, and this shared experience solidified our relationship and gave me some of the best times of my life. Our plan, hazy as it was, was to travel north through South Africa to what was then Rhodesia. But we never got that far. The ship stopped for several days at the Kenyan port of Mombasa, and there I learned from a fellow Canadian of the Mau Mau uprising in upcountry Kenya. Because of the conflict, he said, there were many job opportunities in Nairobi. The combination of a job and adventure in an exotic country was irresistible, and it wasn't difficult to decide to terminate our voyage in Mombasa and take the train to Nairobi.

The train ride itself was an adventure. As we wound our way up to Nairobi, the lush tropical landscapes of the coast gave way to arid plains, where in the early light of dawn we caught our first sight of the magical African wildlife—herds of zebras, gazelles, giraffes and in the distance several elephants. At every stop along the way lively people swarmed around the train.

On arrival in Nairobi we checked into the venerable New Stanley Hotel, knowing that we couldn't afford to stay there very long. The Stanley was the watering hole of choice for Nairobi's affluent white settlers, and it was expensive. That same evening we had our first taste of the dangers that we learned we had to be constantly on guard against. The Mau Mau movement, under the canny and charismatic Kikuyu leader, Jomo Kenyatta, had mounted a campaign against the government and made white settlers, police and native collaborators targets of violent and often deadly attacks.

After dinner at the New Stanley we walked about two blocks and paused to look in the windows of a large sporting goods and safari supplies store. Another couple from the hotel followed us about half a block behind. Just as we got back to the hotel we heard what we thought were a couple of shots, but—not yet used to the notion of urban terrorism—we concluded it must have been something else, perhaps a car backfiring. Later we learned that one of the other two, a Ford executive from Canada, had been shot dead while he and his companion stood in front of the same window we had looked into just minutes before. Apparently the store had been broken into, presumably by Mau Mau seeking arms, and he had the misfortune of being in their way when they left.

As we soon discovered, Nairobi was a lively city, well laid out, with many impressive buildings and broad tree-lined avenues. It had no particular reason for being there—it had been established at the whim of a railway engineer pushing his way from the coast to Uganda—but it had plenty of merits. At an altitude of over 1500 metres, it had an ideal climate—warm but never sticky, temperate all year. The social divisions, however, were stark, sharply drawn and, for the most part, rigorously maintained. The racial divide had been worsened by the rise of the Mau Mau movement. Kenyatta was revered by the Africans but regarded as the devil incarnate by the white community and by the colonial government, which imprisoned him. The British colonial regime was winding down, but the white minority remained obviously dominant; there was also a large and visible Asian population, the country's principal retail merchants, tradesmen and service providers, and they were relatively affluent. These Asians far outnumbered the whites and were disliked and resented by both Europeans and Africans, all the more so, no doubt, because the effective functioning of the society depended on them.

The African majority was largely confined to menial occupations, and the seemingly affluent city was surrounded by teeming black shantytowns. Their traditional tribal society and value system had been undermined and exploited by both immigrant populations, and they found themselves a subject people in their own homeland. Except for a few who, largely through the mission schools, were able to get an education, some of them going abroad for studies in medicine or law, there were few opportunities for Africans to obtain the education and skills they would need to play a larger role running society. In the colonial society, of course, the Africans were generally written off as childishly impossible; whites thought of them not so much as fellow inhabitants but rather as a temperamental resource to be managed somehow. As an outsider, I was struck by the perversity. I was already familiar with cultures other than my own and knew how easily differences can be misinterpreted. As I got to know the black Kenyans I appreciated more and more that my instincts were right: their difficulties in adapting to the modern world that had been imposed on them were not due to deficiencies in their intelligence, diligence or initiative, as the white Kenyans supposed, but rather to the denial of opportunity. I resolved to do everything possible to help them.

It was in Nairobi that I received my introduction to the YMCA, an organization I would do much work with in later years. I found that it was the only place during that period of inter-racial tension and conflict where Europeans, Africans and Asians came together to share interests. It seemed to be an oasis of sanity and promise and an incubator of the kind of future that was possible for Kenya.

As I'd been told, there were many job opportunities—most of the colony's able-bodied men had been conscripted into either the police or the armed services. I soon found interesting work for the oil company Caltex, helping locate and develop service station sites throughout East Africa. I was thus able to travel extensively throughout my "territory," which included Kenya, Tanganyika (now Tanzania), Uganda, Zanzibar (where I helped to establish the first service station), Madagascar, Mauritius, Eritrea and Somaliland (now Somalia). We rented a large house in the pleasant suburb of Muthaiga, and for a while lived the privileged colonial life and made many friends within the expatriate community. The primary topics of conversation at the "sundowners," the end-of-the-day gatherings, were the latest atrocities committed by the Mau Mau, lurid tales confirming the evil nature of Jomo Kenyatta and stories about the growing insolence of the Africans. I particularly remember the spluttering indignation of one matron who had encountered a couple of Africans who had refused to step aside, off the sidewalk, or to take off their hats as she passed.

We couldn't tolerate this kind of thing for long. The gross inequities of the colonial regime revolted us both. We grew to identify with the Africans and their aspirations, and I took advantage of my role at Caltex to train African candidates in the operation and management of service stations, in defiance of traditional colonial logic and custom. I learned Swahili and got to know the Africans well; it was obvious to me that, despite our cultural differences, we shared basic human qualities and aspirations. I was particularly impressed with the importance they attached to family and community, the core of their traditional social and security system.

So well did I get on with them that I was warned by the police that if I continued my "subversive" activities I'd be expelled from the country. The police superintendent who conveyed this warning made it clear that he considered me a naive and meddlesome outsider who didn't understand the situation.

"If you give these people an inch," he said, "they'll take a mile and before long will want to be running the place."

"Isn't that the idea?" I asked. "Aren't you supposed to be preparing them to run their own country?" To this I got no answer.

East Africa was then, as indeed it still is, a paradise for the nature lover. The Nairobi National Park on the edge of the city was home to an incredible profusion of wildlife, including lions and the occasional rhino. Beyond Nairobi was the African savannah, the golden plains spotted with thorn bushes and acacias, home to the largest herds of antelope and deer on Earth and all the great African predators. There were also in the country pockets of dense tropical foliage, home to monkeys and colourful birds and larger animals.

It soon occurred to me that the unique wildlife of Africa was an invaluable and precious resource for the world community. My assignment with Caltex helping to develop new service station sites gave me the opportunity to travel extensively and see a good deal of East Africa's rich wildlife resources and its fascinating diversity of people. The wildlife was not an unmitigated blessing for its farmers and villagers, who had often to suffer the ravages of elephants and attacks from lions and leopards. Clearly a balance needed to be struck between the needs of the people and the importance of conserving Kenya's wildlife. I had much to ponder as I tried to understand the complex cause-and-effect system through which the human populations interacted with and affected the natural environment. Clearly the processes of modernization and development were much more complex and challenging than the simplistic notions I had brought with me to Africa.

Pauline entered fully into my life there, and we made many close friends. Except for a period when she was seriously ill, she travelled with me much of the time, and shared experiences that were very good for our relationship.

We left Kenya in July 1953 for reasons other than our conflicts with the system. True, as a foreigner I could do little to change the regime from within, but it wasn't just that. I had promising career prospects with Caltex, but it wasn't what I wanted—I hadn't left the Canadian oil patch just to get a job with another oil company, and in any case the oil business wasn't what I'd contemplated as a career in international service. I didn't really know how to find what I wanted, but I knew this wasn't it. I needed a broader canvas. I was becoming more and more interested in the problems faced by developing nations in managing the transition to modernity. It was best, I thought, to return to Canada and seek a career in development assistance.

We went home the long way, on a slow boat to Calcutta. For a couple of months we travelled extensively in India, including two weeks in the Himalayas, the beginning of my strong affinity for this exotic region of such stark and awesome beauty and richness of human life.

India impressed me greatly. As the home of some of the world's most advanced ancient civilizations, the country was then experiencing a new awakening as an independent nation. It was asserting itself on the world scene and pressing for the independence of other developing countries. Despite the trauma that accompanied independence, there was everywhere a great sense of pride in having achieved it, and a confidence in the future. India faced huge challenges, that was clear, but its people had the talents, the skills and the qualities needed to run a great nation. The primary need was financial and technical support.

While I was in India I visited a number of YMCAs, mostly because I'd become involved with the organization in Nairobi. I greatly appreciated their ability to build bridges of co-operation among diverse ethnic and religious communities and to create a broad range of practical activities in the fields of education, training, sport and community development in both urban and rural areas. As a non-denominational Christian organization, the YMCA was satisfied to manifest its Christian commitment in its programs rather than by proselytizing. And while most of the programs had been developed by expatriate YMCA professionals, leadership and most management were invariably local.

From India we took another slow cargo ship that visited a variety of Asian ports, including Singapore, Saigon and Hong Kong. I made my first excursion into mainland China. The next stop was Japan, where we stayed for several weeks, travelling in the countryside, staying at small Japanese inns. We were immensely impressed with the diligence and discipline of the Japanese in rebuilding their war-shattered nation and with the distinctive cultural and spiritual traditions that underlay their remarkable economic progress. The final lap of our round-the-world journey was on a Danish cargo ship that landed us in Vancouver.

We got back to Calgary in December 1954, and I checked in with my old friends. I was flattered that both my two past employers, Richardson's and Dome, offered me positions. But it wasn't enough. I hadn't returned just to go back to the life I had left—I'd come back with a purpose. Having seen so many developing countries first-hand, I was more determined than ever to pursue my ambition to seek a career in international development and co-operation.

There were several ways to do it. I could join one of the many international volunteer organizations, so many of which were doing good work in Africa and Asia. But I decided that my first priority was to work on a governmental level. I wanted to join the external aid office of the Canadian government. Accordingly, I went to Ottawa to make an application and seek an interview, hoping that my experience in Africa might compensate for my lack of formal education.

There I was summarily and curtly dismissed. They couldn't so much as accept an application from me, I was told peremptorily, for I didn't have even the minimum qualifications. It was one of my life's greatest disappointments, and I returned to Calgary frustrated and dispirited.

But out of frustration came decision. In the depths of my disappointment I had the second of the two epiphanies that shaped the course of my life.

I knew what I wanted. But as long as I lacked the minimum educational qualifications, a direct route to my aspirations was closed—I'd never get in by banging on the front door. I had no more money—my travels had used it up. There was only one thing to do—find a back door in. That would have to be a successful business career. After all, I reasoned, business is an important power in society, and I seemed to have some talent for it. Why not use it to get to where I wanted to go? I could get a job easily enough, so I could probably make some money. Perhaps as a businessman I could earn the credentials I needed to catch the attention of those who could help me achieve my real aspirations. I already understood that power is augmented by influence derived from extensive and diverse networks. Business would be my platform for the realization of my ambitions—for me, a means rather than an end in itself.

CHAPTER 5

The Levers of Business and the Corridors of Politics

S O I REJOINED DOME.
I re-entered business life with a new enthusiasm and sense of purpose and soon concluded it had been a good decision. A business career did indeed open up pathways to the kind of international service opportunities I was seeking.

This is not to say I neglected my "other track." While I was establishing myself in business, I did volunteer work. Remembering what the YMCAs had accomplished in Kenya and India, I walked into their Calgary office, introduced myself to the general secretary, Bill Kingersley, told him how impressed I'd been with the work of the YMCA in my international travels and volunteered to help.

Kingersley immediately put me on the local World Service Committee. Rapidly, through the guidance and inspiration of a remarkable cadre of YMCA friends—Les Vipond, Bob Torrance, Don Brundage and John Magwood in particular—I moved through a number of positions to the presidency first of the Calgary YMCA and then of the National Council and chairmanship of the Committee on Extension and Intermovement Aid of the World Alliance of the YMCA, headquartered in Geneva. This gave me my first experience of participating in, and then chairing, international meetings and introduced me to some of the finest people I have ever met, among the professional staff as well as the lay leadership. There I first met Léonard Hentsch, one of Geneva's most prominent and respected private bankers, who was treasurer of the World Alliance. He became a valued friend and later a business partner. During this period I also served on the Vatican's Society for Development, Justice and Peace (SODEPAX) and became active with the World Council of Churches. I was an early member of the Overseas Institute of Canada, founded by the great Canadian educator and internationalist J. Roby Kidd, and was invited to speak in various places across the country.

I spoke first at YMCAs, where I focused on the strong impression made on me by the work of the YMCA I had seen during my travels in Africa and Asia. I told how these experiences had convinced me that the principal challenge of our times was to ensure that the developing countries, constituting some 75 percent of the world's population, could meet their aspirations for a better life for their people. I made the case that this was a mission that should provide a special opportunity for Canada. It was one for which both our history and our national character had prepared us well. We had ourselves made the transition from a colony to an independent nation. We had never sought to conquer or exercise control over others. Even Canada itself was made up of an increasingly representative cross-section of the world's peoples. Our economy was based largely on the development of our natural resources, and we were very dependent on international trade, so our skills and experience would be of use to the developing world. I argued that Canada should take the lead in the movement to support the aspirations of developing countries and that this indeed should be our primary role in the world. I developed this theme as I received invitations to speak to Canadian clubs, service clubs, church groups and others right across the country.

Jack Gallagher was very sympathetic to my international interests, as he'd had an international career himself. Nevertheless, as the invitations I had to speak and participate in various meetings and seminars increased, I had to keep them down to a level that enabled me to discharge my principal job responsibilities at Dome.

During this period I had some encounters with politicians, particularly Arthur Smith of the Conservative Party in Calgary and Carl Nickle, who became a local Conservative candidate. Indeed I joined with Art Smith in managing his campaign. I also began to meet representatives of the department of foreign affairs and others who travelled through Calgary and to stop over in Ottawa to meet international officials from time to time.

At Dome, I was quickly given expanding responsibilities and soon became vice-president and treasurer. Jack Gallagher gave me a good deal of running room. The company was growing rapidly, and he held out the prospect of my succeeding him as president. Clearly I had a promising career there if I chose to pursue it. But that wasn't what I wanted. I really wanted to launch out on my own so I could have more control over my life and spend more time pursuing my public service interest.

I left Dome in 1956 on a friendly basis, Jack's understanding and goodwill having stood the test of my disappointing him a second time, and set up my own company, M. F. Strong Management. I became the Calgary connection in identifying and helping to negotiate investment opportunities for a number of national and international financial institutions interested in Alberta oil. One of them was Henri Brunie's Empire Trust, a company that had been an investor in Dome. The senior vice-president who looked after Canada was Robert Heim, a wise, thoughtful man who became a mentor and lifetime friend. Robert also introduced me to a person he described as an exceptionally promising young Australian, Jim Wolfensohn. Bob Heim asked me to take over a small, troubled company, Ajax Petroleums, which supplied natural gas to a major chemical plant in Edmonton, offering me equity if I could solve its problems. This wasn't exactly what I'd intended by getting out on my own, but it was a good opportunity and I took it on. I assumed the chief executive's role in the company and began a rebuilding process that ultimately transformed it into what is now one of Canada's leading oil and gas companies, Norcen. That first summer at Ajax, Paul Martin Jr., later Canada's finance minister in Jean Chrétien's government, came to work for us during the university vacation. He once wrecked one of the company's trucks and was briefly fired, a story he has often told with some relish.

On a personal level Pauline and I were blessed with four children. Fred was born in 1956, followed at two-year intervals by Maureen, Mary Anne and Ken. In 1961 we added a foster child, Alice, whom I'd located through my YMCA work helping to resettle Hungarian refugees. She soon became a full and permanent member of our family. I had always had an affinity for children, but until we had our own I never really understood what a joy it is to be a parent. Despite my busy business and public service life my greatest pleasure was being with Pauline and the children. If I have any regrets at this point in my life it is that I did not spend enough time with them.

During this period we made some of the friendships that have been our most important and durable. The Calgary oil community was very dynamic, and one of the oilmen I respected most was Ed Galvin, who was putting together a number of smaller companies and later became a close colleague and friend when they merged into the company that developed out of Ajax, Canadian Industrial Gas and Oil. He became its president and chief executive officer.

I also became an elder of Central United Church, one of Canada's largest congregations thanks to its congenial and persusive minister, Jack Lowery. I recall being very disappointed that the elders seemed to spend a lot of time talking about business and financial matters— almost more than they talked about matters of the spirit. But I came to realize that religious and charitable organizations also need good management and, of course, money.

I still didn't have the business platform I needed to combine my business career with an expanding commitment to public service. I could continue to build my own company, of course—the contacts and experience I had gained made this a plausible option. But I lacked any significant amount of personal capital. And there are other ways of doing things. I was willing to take risks and was confident that I was ready to take on larger responsibilities, so why not consider taking over a major national company? If I found the right target I felt sure I could find the financial backing.

I spent many hours poring over the profiles of Canadian companies that might be suitable. One on my short list was Power Corporation of Canada Limited, a holding company headquartered in Montreal with extensive interests in power generation, especially in Quebec, Manitoba and British Columbia, and in the resources and financial fields. I wasn't so concerned with its size—size is just a matter of money—as with its asset mix. Its portfolio included control blocks of many oil and gas companies. One of them was Canadian Oil, Canada's leading independent refining and marketing company. W. Harold Rae, head of Canadian Oil, was on Power's board.

I'd already met Rae through the YMCA, where he'd been the national president. I had come to admire him as a person who combined superior qualities of leadership in the business field with exemplary values and devotion to the public good.

One evening at an industry dinner in Calgary I found myself seated next to him and used the opportunity to ask him some very detailed questions about Power Corporation. He invited me up to his room after the dinner to continue the discussion and said pointedly, "Maurice, you seem to know a good deal about Power. Why are you so interested?"

I had utmost confidence in his integrity, so I told him. "I'm looking into the possibility of trying to get the funds together to make a bid for the second preferred stock of the company," I said. I knew, as of course he did, that with ten votes a share, the second preferreds represented control.

"You'll never succeed," he said. He pointed out that voting control was now in the hands of Peter Thomson, son of the founder of one of Canada's leading investment firms, Nesbitt Thomson. He then suggested what he thought would be a better way of coming into the company. He explained that the board had agreed that young Peter should become chairman, but as he had a number of other interests and did not really want to be a full-time chief executive, they'd

decided to recruit an outside person for that role. Rae was chairing
the committee set up by the board to recruit a new president. "Are
you interested?" he asked.

I demurred. I wasn't looking just to run a company, I said, no
matter how important. I wanted ownership. I wanted enough independence to pursue my public service interests, including the
YMCA.

Rae didn't see any inconsistency. Power had an important position in Canadian business, he pointed out. Since the company had
been put together in 1925, many past and future politicians and
other influential people had worked on its staff or served on its
board. Working there would open up many new opportunities for
me, provide new contacts. These would surely help further my long-
term goals. He urged me to become a candidate.

The notion of those contacts was persuasive, so I agreed to go for
an interview, though I was not at all persuaded that this was the
course I should follow.

I duly went to Montreal and spent some time with the interviewing committee. I could easily see the board's dilemma. Many of its
members were also heads of the corporations that Power had a major
interest in; they made it clear to me that they wanted someone as
president who could get along with the controlling shareholder
without being his creature. Accordingly, they said, my meeting with
Peter Thomson was a crucial one. Before I went back to Calgary,
they set up a meeting with him. I immediately liked him, and we
seemed to hit it off, but I could also see that he was sensitive to the
fact that the board wanted to dilute his influence. Whoever took the
job, it would be a delicate balancing act.

I mulled it over and made my position clear to the committee.

Then I returned to Calgary.

"How did it go?" Pauline asked.

"It won't be happening," I said, somewhat to her relief. I explained that I'd laid out a set of conditions that a great corporation like Power would never accept from a young, little-known
executive from the West.

"What were they?" she asked.

Well, I said, in the course of the discussions the interviewing committee had offered me options on a significant block of company stock at a discount from the market price, but I had declined this.

"I'd rather have five times as much stock under option," I said, "but at double the market price. That way I'll only profit after the shareholders double their values."

I thought they could have lived with that. It was confident to the point of arrogance, perhaps, but there are worse faults in a CEO.

But I also demanded a clause in my contract acknowledging that I could spend up to a quarter of my time on my public interests, providing they didn't conflict with my primary obligation to the corporation. I also felt that I couldn't desert Canadian Industrial Gas and Oil. I'd have to maintain my ties with the company for enough time to see it through what was an important phase in its development.

All in all, a demanding set of requests from a young man with limited credentials. I was surprised, therefore, when Harold Rae called me to say that the board had largely accepted my conditions and that I should come down to work out the details of my contract.

In the meantime I'd been mulling over my obligations to Canadian Industrial Gas and Oil, and when I went back to Montreal to meet Rae, I suggested a new tack.

"I need to maintain a link with my company for, say, a two-year period. If there are any conflicts, of course they'll be resolved in Power's favour. So why don't I become not president but executive vice-president and managing director for those two years?" I knew that Peter Thomson would be pleased to have the additional titular role of president and chief executive officer during this period, though he'd need to understand that I'd have the principal day-to-day executive responsibilities and would succeed him as president and CEO in two years.

When they accepted this arrangement, we had a deal. Its great virtue was that it helped me establish my relationship with Peter. We had our differences, particularly when I had to fend off friends of his who were always bringing their deals to Power Corporation. A small cadre of them would gather at the end of each business day in Peter's office. Peter would urge me to join them but finally accepted in good grace that I preferred to keep my distance. Despite this, and perhaps even because of it, we developed a good working and personal relationship.

It was on this unusual basis, then, that Pauline and I, with our children, moved to Montreal. Thus, at the age of twenty-nine, I found myself as a rank outsider invited into the Canadian business establishment.

My new colleagues at Power Corporation had earmarked a large house in the affluent Mount Royal district for me and were surprised when I chose instead a much smaller, middle-class one in the suburb of Beaconsfield. This was neither modest nor parsimonious on my part, but in keeping with a long-standing agreement between Pauline and me: we'd not adopt the affluent lifestyle of a senior executive, or accustom our family to it, but rather live in a style that could be easily supported by a public service salary. This would simplify my eventual transition to public service and wouldn't require the family to somehow feel they were backtracking in their standard of living.

The beginning of the 1960s was an interesting time to be in Montreal and Quebec. I was a product of the Anglo-Saxon culture of Western Canada and spoke only rudimentary high school French. Now I found myself in a society stirring with potential change. Power Corporation was not exactly enthusiastic about the Quiet Revolution then occurring in Quebec—as one of the principal centres of English-speaking power in the province, Power was a bastion of the status quo. I was appalled to find that in a city where most people were French-speaking, our switchboard operator spoke no French at all. The only French Canadians in the company's employ were in menial support and service positions—and they had even been told not to speak French in the office. The parallel with my experience under the colonial regime in Kenya was striking. Except of course that this regime was far more subtle and discreet in the exercise of its dominant role.

One of my first acts was to replace the operator with one who could speak French; then I invited francophones to use their language freely in the office. After that, I hired two very capable French-Canadian vice-presidents. At this point, enough seemed to be enough for the old guard—I was called in by the former chairman, J. B. Woodyatt, who continued to have an office with the company. He was a competent executive and a highly principled man, but he was nevertheless—to put it as delicately as possible—a product of the old order in Quebec.

He hesitated to interfere, he said, going ahead anyway. Then, in no uncertain terms, he told me I was on the wrong track.

"I have a high regard and respect for French-speaking Canadians," he said with great sincerity and no understanding of the new political realities. "But we're a minority here, and if we don't protect ourselves against the majority, they'll take us over." What an echo that was of the Kenyan police officer who'd warned me about giving an inch lest "they" take a mile.

I replied, as respectfully as I could under the circumstances, that this would surely be in accord with the principles of democracy. "As one of the major players in the Quebec economy, Power should reflect the character of the society and strongly identify with its interests," I said.

Woodyatt was clearly disappointed in my response. After that, we had only the most cursory relations.

We were soon caught up in politics, in any case. One of the central objectives when Jean Lesage assumed the premier's office in 1962 was provincial takeover of the electric power industry, in which Power Corporation was dominant. Spearheading the move as the energy minister in Lesage's cabinet was René Lévesque, an intelligent and hyperactive man with a strong commitment to Quebec nationalism. I found Lévesque engaging and a man of principle and integrity.

With some reluctance the Power Corporation board accepted the inevitability of nationalization and decided to co-operate while negotiating for the highest possible price. The fact that the corporation had close ties to the Lesage government enabled the negotiations to be conducted on a civil basis, despite a good deal of public huffing and puffing. The result was the creation of Hydro-Québec, which has become one of the largest electric power utilities in the world and a cornerstone of the Quebec economy.

I was soon involved in another expropriation, this time by British Columbia's Social Credit government under W. A. C. "Wacky" Bennett, which was, paradoxically, strongly committed to private enterprise. The principal target in this case was the British Columbia Electric Company, which served most of the province's market. I'd just become a member of its board, representing Power Corporation as the major shareholder. The move by the B.C. government was highly controversial, and my colleagues on the Power board reacted with outrage and hostility. As the new boy on the scene I took the view that it would be counterproductive for us to try to fight the battle on the political level, where the government clearly held most of the cards. We should concentrate on trying to win the economic battle for a higher price.

At the same time the other two power companies we controlled, East Kootenay Power and Light Company, in the southwest corner of the province, and Northern B.C. Power, serving the Prince Rupert area, would be orphaned by the takeover. I convinced the board that it would be in our best interests to have them included in the deal on a friendly, negotiated basis. Fortunately, I had a good relationship of trust and communication with Dr. Hugh Keenleyside, then co-chairman of the B.C. Hydro and Power Authority. He was an eminent former Canadian diplomat whom I'd met through our common interest in the YMCA. This was not the first or the last time that the Y acted as a catalyst in my life, though I had never looked at it from that point of view. Over time I found that with the many links between the corporate, political and non-governmental communities, the contacts and friendships I built in one world spilled over to the others, until there were very few areas where I didn't have at least the beginning of a network of trusted associates.

In this case Keenleyside and I were able to quietly work out the modalities of a deal that I then negotiated one-on-one with Premier Bennett.

Bennett was an ebullient personality with a keen political sense. He was comfortable giving us a higher price for B.C. Electric and the other two utilities because the takeover enabled him to validate his political stance and claim victory. When the deal was done, I joined him for a radio broadcast. We exchanged more or less sincere compliments, and I reiterated Power Corporation's continuing commitment to investment in B.C.

The result of these two takeovers, followed by Shell Oil's acquisition of our Canadian Oil, was to leave Power Corporation with over $100 million in cash, a great deal of money at that time. I then set about rebuilding the company's investments, reducing their number and concentrating our interests in a few areas—primarily finance, pulp and paper and a move back into the oil and gas industry through acquisition of control of my earlier property, Canadian Industrial Gas and Oil, and the merger into it of other Power Corporation interests —Quebec National Gas, Greater Winnipeg Gas and Abasand Oils, which had built the first Athabascan tar sands extraction plant and had one of the best leases in the area. After a later merger with Northern Ontario Natural Gas, the combined company, Northern and Central Gas, was consolidated into Norcen.

The presidency of Power gave me all the opportunities W. Harold Rae had said it would. I had easy access to the Canadian political and business establishment. Power controlled many companies, and through its creative use of contributions and appointments to its various boards and ready access to political leaders, the company had a significant degree of influence with them.

Politicians got to know me and I them. I recruited many young people who later went on to brilliant careers, among them Jim Wolfensohn, who ran our new Australian-based subsidiary. He later distinguished himself on Wall Street and created his own firm, which was subsequently run by Paul Volcker after Wolfensohn moved to the presidency of the World Bank.

At the Montreal YMCA, I had met a tall, thoughtful young man from Toronto, William Turner, who impressed me with his sound approach to business and to life. An engineer, he had moved into a senior management position at equipment manufacturer Ingersoll-Rand. As I got to know him, I saw that we shared values and objectives but had very different personalities and professional backgrounds. This made him an ideal candidate as my senior teammate at Power Corporation, so I invited him to come in as executive vice-president. It was one of the best choices I have ever made. We worked closely and well together in reshaping Power Corporation. Bill Turner went on to head Consolidated-Bathurst, one of the world's largest newsprint companies, which resulted from the merger we engineered of Consolidated Paper with Bathurst Power and Paper, which Power Corporation already controlled. Over the years, as Bill has gone on to be one of Canada's most respected and influential business leaders, he has remained one of my closest friends, as well as a partner in several ventures.

Another of my appointments was Paul Martin Jr. as my executive assistant. I had known him since his student days, and he had told me of his aspirations to become a businessman rather than pursue the legal career that his education was preparing him for. I urged him to qualify as a lawyer by being called to the bar and told him that if he still wanted to go into business at that point, he should come and see me. Which is exactly what he did. I brought him into the company, and after a few bumpy episodes, he soon became a star performer. But he really made his mark as a businessman when he joined in purchasing control of Canada Steamship Lines from Power Corporation. Canada's largest lake shipping company, it also owned one of the country's major trucking firms. He moved out of Power Corporation to run Canada Steamship Lines and did a remarkable job, soon arranging to acquire full control. This set the stage for his inevitable entry into political life, where he is now Canada's highly respected minister of finance. Yet to be determined is whether he will have the opportunity to lead the country as its prime minister, a job for which he is now so eminently qualified.

I found, from my new position at the head of Power, that I had no trouble getting to members of the Canadian establishment and indeed lived very much in their world. But I was never really taken over by it, instead concentrating my attention on identifying and getting to know younger people who were excellent candidates for the next generation of leadership. This was also very much part of my main responsibility at Power Corporation—helping to find promising candidates for our various boards and managements. I also convened a series of informal meetings, usually in the Laurentians, bringing together people with promising leadership potential in the business, political and public policy fields. At one such meeting we had the young Pierre Trudeau and five of the people who later served in his first cabinet when he became prime minister, as well as Bill Davis, later premier of Ontario, Allan Blakeney, who became premier of Saskatchewan, Peter Lougheed, who became premier of Alberta and Quebec's Claude Ryan, to name but a few. It was at one of these meetings that I met Paul Desmarais, whose business moves had attracted my attention but who was still relatively little known in the larger business community.

During this period I was introduced by Jim Coutts, then Prime Minister Pearson's principal secretary, to the minister of finance, Walter Gordon. Gordon had been trying to sell the notion of a Canadian development corporation to help build strong Canadian companies in key sectors and was running into scepticism and resistance from the business community at large. Gordon asked me to advise him, knowing that I was one of the few business people who approved of the idea.

I made several speeches to Chambers of Commerce, Rotary Clubs, other service organizations and church groups focused on Canada's role in international affairs and particularly in assisting developing countries, as well as commenting on current business and economic issues. I brought in Tony Hampson, whom I'd earlier appointed vice-president of Power Corporation in charge of the company's financial investments. Hampson was extremely intelligent, highly competent at his best, but opinionated and difficult. He was really more at home in the field of economic policy than in the hurly-burly of business. He later became the chief executive officer of the Canada Development Corporation and soon made it his own, easing out the very sound and able Marshall Crowe, who had been one of its principal architects and its first chairman. (Tony very much resented my own later re-entry into the situation, when then prime minister Trudeau asked me to become chairman and gave me the government's proxy with instructions to vote the entire board out if they refused to go along. I chose instead to make peace with the board and became vice-chairman, but thereafter my relationship with Tony was somewhat strained.)

In 1964, I was asked by Prime Minister Pearson to help launch the Company of Young Canadians, a Canadian version of the Peace Corps, and was appointed to its board. The organization accomplished some useful things initially, particularly in mobilizing young volunteers to work in a variety of social projects in some of Canada's native and other underprivileged communities. But it never really caught on and had a limited lifespan.

For some years I'd been close to Paul Martin Sr., who had become Canada's minister of external affairs. Among his responsibilities was Canada's External Aid Office. I had taken a special interest in the External Aid Program and had been urging that it be expanded to strengthen Canada's support of the multilateral organizations like the World Bank and the United Nations Development Program (UNDP), as well as to provide closer links with non-governmental organizations. When its director-general, Herb Moran, left his post in 1966, I remember asking Martin on the phone about his possible successor.

"Some of my officials think it should be you," he said. "I told them it would be out of the question, that you'd never leave the presidency of Power for the Ottawa bureaucracy." I later found out that it had been Ed Ritchie, one of the finest and ablest products of the Canadian diplomatic service, then acting as senior adviser to the minister, who had proposed me for the job.

Martin was dumbfounded, I think, when I disagreed. "If it were seriously offered, I'd seriously consider it," I said.

Well, the offer duly came. It was made over a lunch with Prime Minister Pearson at his official residence.

"You know," I said at one point, "some years ago external affairs declined to even consider an application from me for a junior position in the External Aid Office. You were undersecretary of the department then."

"You were lucky," he replied in his disarmingly good-humoured manner. "Lucky you didn't have the qualifications. If we'd taken you, at your age, even if you'd performed well under our system, you could never have been at more than the lower-middle ranks at this point in your career. It would have been impossible for me to offer you the job of heading up External Aid."

My handicap—my lack of education or experience—had turned out to be an advantage. I thought back to what I still regarded as my second epiphany, my realization that a business career could be the back door I needed into public service. How true that had proven, and how much more effective it had made me in the end.

It never entered my mind to decline the offer. After all, it finally opened the door to the career I'd sought for so long. So it was never a question of whether, only of when. By that time I was deeply entrenched in Power Corporation and on some forty boards of directors of associated and other companies. It would require several months for me to unwind my business responsibilities and it was therefore agreed that I would take up my new post as director-general in December 1966.

A minor aspect of this transition was an irritant later in my life. A journalist asked me at the time what I had been earning at Power and what I could expect to earn in government. I refused to say, considering my private income none of the media's business. Of course, they went ahead and stated that $200,000 was my Power salary, as though the information had come from me.

Later someone discovered that my base salary at Power had been some $35,000, thus leading to the claim I had exaggerated my own income.

In fact, base salary in a holding-company structure like Power has little to do with actual overall compensation levels, which consist of salaries and fees from various subsidiaries and affiliates. Ironically, the real number was much higher than even the $200,000 figure mentioned. But as with many media stories, the "facts" once printed seem to take on an independent existence of their own, and the story was being repeated as recently as 1998.

The move from Montreal to Ottawa was not far in terms of distance, but it was a move into a whole new world. It was unusual (though

exceptions had been made during the war) for an amateur to be invited into the top ranks of the civil service. Nevertheless my new
colleagues gave me a warm welcome as a new deputy minister and
treated me well. I was very fortunate to have as my deputy one of
the finest and ablest professionals from the department of external affairs, Peter Towe, who had served as Herb Moran's deputy and
agreed to stay on with me. His congenial, boyish and good-humoured
demeanour concealed an intellectual and professional rigour and
sound judgment that were my principal source of guidance and
support during my first two years.

The same year I took on the job for the federal government, I
became president of the Canadian YMCA. One of the things I did as
president was to sever our "special relationship" with the U.S. on the
YMCA's International Committee. The relationship had worked
quite well over the years, but Canada was clearly very much the
junior partner and was now ready to undertake its own world service
program and forge co-operative links with other national YMCAs,
while retaining a close and friendly relationship with the U.S.

I soon discovered that having some impact and visibility was a mixed
blessing. A frightening incident provided an early example of something I was to experience on a broader canvas as my life progressed—
that my influence was vastly exaggerated, even in some obscure and
unlikely circles. One stormy winter day a young couple, a person-
able young man and woman, appeared at the door of our Ottawa
home. I don't recall why I was still home at mid-morning, but it
seemed like the polite thing to do to invite them in.

"We have to kill you," they said. "We have no option but to kill
you and also the prime minister."

They were very civil about all this. There was nothing personal in
it, they said, but only the prime minister and I could have implemented their ideas about how to fix the world, and we'd both ignored
their letters.

We all sat down in our living room and remained there for several uneasy hours, trying to maintain an outward calm and a civility
of manner, not very easy in the circumstances. Pauline even served

them coffee. Eventually I managed to persuade them that in order to give serious consideration to their proposals I'd need access to my files, and suggested that I rent a room in a hotel across the street from my office. "It would be best to continue our discussions there," I urged.

In the end they agreed. With great relief I left my family at home and the three of us set off for a room at the Beacon Arms Hotel, where we duly continued our "discussions." Still, I said, I needed my files. "I have to go across to the office to pick them up." They finally agreed, and off I went. Of course, I alerted the RCMP, who were expeditious in moving in on them in the hotel and arresting them. I was the principal witness against them at their trial. They were convicted of uttering threats to the prime minister and to me. I always wondered whether they would try to get back at me, but I never heard from them again.

Not all problems turn out to be so manageable.

Real-world problems—including managing the bureaucracy and swinging the ever-cumbersome apparatus of government into action—proved more complex than managing the arrest of a couple of clumsy would-be assassins. I'll give an example, at perhaps more length than the actual transaction requires, but usefully so, I think, because it indicates my learning curve and how I came to understand how to manipulate—no, that's too strong—to deal with bureaucracies.

It was 1967. Canada's international development assistance, which had begun early in the pre-war period through the Colombo Plan, was becoming an ever more important factor in the country's external relationships. I had developed some clear ideas about how I thought this assistance should be managed and had discussed them with a number of knowledgeable people both within and outside government. There were, I thought, too many people and organizations involved, and not enough co-ordination. The External Aid Office ran the country's program of direct bilateral assistance to developing countries, but Canada's relationships with the World Bank and other regional development banks were overseen by the ministry of finance. To complicate things further, many other multilateral programs existed, co-ordinated by the department of external affairs in co-operation with the departments that looked after relations with, for example, the specialized agencies of the United Nations.

I believed that each of these components should be managed within a common framework, which would allow Canada to pursue a set of coherent and consistent objectives in its relationships with developing countries. This management should also include input into the other activities of government that affected developing countries. Dispensing aid was, after all, only one element in these relationships, and the impact of aid could often be negated by policies that, for instance, limited trading opportunities or otherwise had a deleterious effect on countries that received our aid.

When I explained all this to him, Prime Minister Pearson said he liked my ideas and agreed with me. I naively assumed that this informal approval, nodded to over lunch, meant a green light for the change. I soon learned one of my first real lessons about the realities of government—that the verbal approval of the prime minister in a one-to-one meeting at which no minutes were kept and that had not been followed up by the necessary formal processes was—at best—an indication of the prime minister's personal view and far from a decision by his government.

To my disappointment I found that I had to start at the beginning, trying to convince the other key deputy ministers involved that my policy change was a good one. The undersecretary for external affairs, Marcel Cadieux, was a zealous guardian of his department's prerogatives in the domain of international affairs, and he strongly resisted my efforts. He tried, on the contrary, to persuade the minister to let him take over responsibility for External Aid.

I was learning. I didn't want to negotiate directly and bilaterally with external affairs—if there were just two of us at the table, I couldn't hope to muster sufficient weight to prevail. So I set about enlarging the forum where the issue could be worked out. I activated what I called the External Aid Board. As director-general of external aid, I was its chairman, but it also included the deputy ministers of other key departments, including finance, trade and commerce, and the Bank of Canada. With these players at the table, I was able to get a version of my plan adopted. The responsibilities of the External Aid Office were enlarged to include the co-ordination of multilateral as well as bilateral assistance and an input into trade and other important policies that affected relationships with developing countries. At the same time we worked out better ways of involving the other departments in overall decision making, particularly in the areas of their respective special responsibilities.

I did have allies. The enlightened attitude of the deputy minister of finance, Bob Bryce, was especially helpful and supportive. When he agreed to yield to us working responsibility for relationships with the World Bank and the Canadian executive director, Denis Hudon, to transfer to our office, our multilateral role was given real substance.

Did we need legislation to give formal effect to our new mandate? I pondered this and at first thought it would be the best way of formalizing our new structure. I soon realized, however, that this would involve negotiating the details of the arrangements with the officials of the much more powerful departments. In these matters the devil is clearly in the details, but I realized we could well lose in this process. Much of what we had gained in obtaining overall agreement to our new structure and mandate could be lost in working out its particulars, which could end up restricting rather than enhancing our flexibility. It would be best, I thought, to leave our mandate to be more vaguely defined by Orders-in-Council than to set it in concrete legislation, at least for the time being. I assumed, however, that legislation would be needed in due course.

To give effect to the enlarged role of the External Aid Office, its name was changed in 1968 to the Canadian International Development Agency (CIDA)—the word *agency* designed to signal that it had taken on much of the character and flexibility of an operating agency in addition to its role as a de facto department of government. To signal further the distinctive nature of the agency, I had proposed that its head be designated president and was pleased when Mitchell Sharp, who by then had become external affairs minister, agreed. Despite many changes since then, the basic structure we set in place at that time has remained intact.

Finally, I was where I had wanted to be for so long—I was now a participant in international affairs, so long my aspiration. Because of my interest in the UN, I began attending meetings to which a deputy minister would normally have assigned subordinates. I became active in the World Bank and set about making contacts and establishing links with the major players in the development assistance field. They were heady days.

I particularly valued the relationships I made with some of the leaders of the international development community. Notable among these was Paul Hoffman, administrator of the United Nations Development Program, the UN's principal development organization. In many ways he was at the time the grand old man of development assistance, having earlier headed the Marshall Plan for the U.S. I also got to know George Woods, president of the World Bank, and later Robert McNamara. Having had some initial reservations before I had even met him about whether McNamara was the right person to lead the Bank following his controversial role as U.S. Secretary of Defense during the Vietnam War, I rapidly became one of his greatest fans and developed a close personal friendship with him that I enjoy to this day. He led the Bank into a new era: it shifted from being primarily a financial institution to one whose primary objective was to alleviate poverty and improve the conditions and prospects of developing countries. Despite his image as a coldly efficient and numbers-oriented technocrat, I found him to be a person of great compassion with a deep commitment to improving the human condition, a commitment he has continued to pursue vigorously and effectively since leaving the Bank. It is a shame that this great man, who had the courage to acknowledge and learn from mistakes in policies with which he was identified, has been so misunderstood and underappreciated.

CIDA's initiatives found a hospitable international climate. An important one that I was personally involved in was Canada's key role in establishing a network of international agricultural research institutes and in mobilizing financial and technical support for them. The Rockefeller and Ford foundations had pioneered the establishment of agricultural research institutes to develop the new varieties of rice and wheat that were the basis for the "green revolution" that vastly increased the capacity of such important developing countries as India to feed their growing populations. They wanted to expand support for these institutes by mobilizing development assistance agencies, and I agreed to take a lead in helping them to do this. There was some apprehension about this in our ministry of agriculture—they were worried we were financing and fostering competition for Canada's farmers, but in the end they went along, and Canada took the high road as one of the leading supporters of the new organization, called the Consultative Group on International Agricultural Research (CGIAR).

Because Canada was a member of La Francophonie, we had paid considerable attention to French Africa at the time. After discussions with Prime Minister Pearson in 1966, we had decided to send his new parliamentary secretary, Pierre Trudeau, to West Africa to look into ways we could help further. It was Trudeau's first international assignment as an MP.

We found an innovative way of implementing some of our aid projects, combining the policy directions of government and the flexibility of the private sector. At that time Canada did not have embassies in most of the francophone countries, and the way government processes work, it was going to take at best several years before new embassies could be approved, budgeted and set up. But I was eager to get off the ground quickly with our francophone program, so I made an arrangement with a Quebec-based engineering company, SNC, to offer technical facilities and administrative support to our efforts in West Africa. SNC was to act as general contractor to help identify, evaluate and oversee our program, but it could not bid on projects or do the actual work. I made a condition that this arrangement be overseen by one of their vice-presidents, Jacques Gérin, whom I had first met on the board of the Company of Young Canadians. He proved to be a good choice and later was recruited into the federal government itself, first as vice-president of CIDA and then as deputy minister for Indian and northern affairs. We have since worked together in various ways and become close friends.

Another condition I made was that SNC would undertake to hire anyone I recommended for jobs in the field, which short-circuited the normal government recruitment processes and incidentally enabled us to tap some exceptionally capable people, at least two of whom later became ambassadors.

The department of external affairs was totally taken aback by this unusual, and to them irregular, arrangement. But they rose to the challenge and moved expeditiously to establish embassies for Canada in some of the key countries with which we had initiated development co-operation. And overall there were important political implications—domestically, we were giving francophone Canadians a much greater stake in our development aid programs, and internationally, we were establishing much closer relationships with the francophone countries of Africa.

One of our many successful projects was the construction of a series of microwave towers across northern Africa, which permitted African countries for the first time to telephone each other directly instead of routing calls through Europe.

Another Canadian initiative gave rise to the annual, informal meetings of senior development officials organized by the Development Assistance Committee of the OECD, the body set up to co-ordinate the development assistance policies of the OECD countries. Again, it arose out of an informal discussion I had with Bill Gaud, head of USAID, and Andrew Cohen, our counterpart in Great Britain, over dinner at a sidewalk café in Paris following my first participation on the committee. I explained that it was somewhat disappointing to me to find that we all simply made formal statements prepared for us by our own bureaucracies, with virtually no time for real discussion and an exchange of views and experience of the kind that would have been especially helpful to me as a new boy in the field. I asked why we couldn't have an informal session for such frank off-the-record exchanges, which could be extremely helpful to all of us. They agreed in principle and we put the idea to Ed Martin, a very able U.S. ambassador who was just taking over as chairman of the Development Assistance Committee. He agreed to take the initiative in setting up a first meeting, which was held in conjunction with the annual meeting of the International Monetary Fund and the World Bank in 1968 at the Tidewater Motel just outside Washington, D.C. This gave the name to what has become an important annual event on the development calendar. However, it has lost some of its informal character, as it has expanded to include most of the key people in the development community.

I became active in our relationships with the principal multilateral organizations, particularly the World Bank, UNDP and the regional development banks then being established. I was particularly involved in negotiations leading to the establishment of the Asian Development Bank and participated in its inaugural meeting in Tokyo.

I continued to reshape CIDA's structure and programs in ways designed to give effect to our new mandate. We established a policy unit that enabled us to have an active and sometimes influential role in development-related policy processes, particularly in the trade field, focusing on the need to give developing countries access to our markets. And we initiated a new program of support for Canadian NGOs in development co-operation. To head it I recruited an exceptionally talented and committed Canadian of Asian origin, Lewis Perinbam, who had been the World Bank representative at the UN and prior to that an influential and effective leader in the international student movement. He built the program into one of the most effective of its kind, supporting non-governmental organizations and using their skills and more flexible operating capabilities as agents and partners in our development program. This made Perinbam something of an icon in the movement. We also established a business development unit to help bring the Canadian business community into a more active participation in our development programs, principally by offering them incentives to investigate business opportunities in developing countries and other supporting services.

I was coming to understand some of the fundamentals of development in an increasingly technology-driven world. Developing countries simply didn't have the scientific and technological capabilities and institutions that real development now demanded. In fact, developing countries as a whole accounted for only some

2 percent of the global money spent in these areas. In a world where science, technology and knowledge were the principal sources of added value and competitive advantage, it seemed clear that unless this imbalance was redressed, the rich–poor gap could only widen. The most effective response, I decided, had to be an entirely new institution, funded largely by government but with the kind of intellectual capacity and independent character of the major U.S. foundations. We called it the International Development Research Centre (IDRC).

The original idea was for the centre to have a domestic as well as an international role. We thought it might be located at the site of the Montreal world's fair, Expo 67, then winding down but with its facilities still intact. But before it got off the ground it ran into a storm of protest from external affairs. It came about this way: Jim Coutts, who was still principal secretary to Prime Minister Pearson, had heard about my idea for the new centre and had mentioned it to the prime minister, who asked me about it over lunch in his office one day. I gave him a summary of the proposal, and to my great surprise two weeks later in a speech in Montreal he announced it as a proposed initiative by the government.

Marcel Cadieux was furious, accusing me of making an end run around the interdepartmental consultative process. "Don't you understand," he said passionately, "that you do not bring a proposal to ministers, let alone the prime minister, until it has the sanction of senior officials?"

At a later meeting with Pearson, he asked innocently if I'd been pleased with his speech. I was candid. I appreciated his support for the project, I told him, but it had landed me in real trouble with my colleagues, particularly Cadieux.

Pearson was amused. With a twinkle in his eye he said, "You know, Maurice, I was undersecretary of the department myself, and I know the way the bureaucracy works. The reason they're upset with you is that they know the government will now be committed. Once the prime minister has announced the creation of this centre, the government has to make it happen. So you'll get your centre. And to ensure your innocence, I decided not to let you know I was going to mention it in my speech. It may help you a bit with Marcel if I tell him this."

This was just one of the many lessons I learned from this remarkable man, who had moved so easily from the top levels of the public service to the Prime Minister's Office.

But government officials know how to resist and often bury the initiatives of their political masters if they are not adequately prepared. Realizing this, I selected one of the most respected Ottawa mandarins, Wynne Plumptre, to head a task force composed of a galaxy of senior officials. They ultimately resolved the initial objections to the process, gave it their stamp of approval and joined in recommending it to cabinet. The process began when Paul Martin Sr. was my minister and I had his support. By the time it was ready for cabinet consideration, Mitchell Sharp was my minister and his strong and enthusiastic support was decisive.

So the IDRC came into existence through an Act of Parliament in 1970. Its structure was designed for maximum flexibility and independence. Legislation establishing it gave it the character of a corporation, reporting to Parliament through the minister of external affairs. The majority of its board of governors were private citizens, nearly half of whom were foreigners. Decisions on program priorities and funding were entirely the prerogative of the board. It was able to receive charitable donations from individuals and corporations.

In effect, we had created a unique, federally funded organization with much of the character and freedom of action of a private foundation.

Appropriately, Prime Minister Pearson after he left office agreed to be the first chairman and we recruited an exceptionally talented Canadian scientist-cum-economist named David Hopper, who had extensive experience in the field in India with the Rockefeller and Ford foundations, as CEO. This was a superb leadership combination that helped IDRC to become a unique and influential member of the international development fraternity.

The fact that it operated separately from CIDA created occasional tensions and rivalries, but for the most part the roles were complementary, and the result was to give Canada significant additional leverage and impact on the development process. It became an active participant, contributing both intellectually and financially to CGIAR and undertaking many innovative programs designed to support development of indigenous scientific and technological capacity in developing countries. Particularly valuable has been its support of leading developing-country scientists, policy-makers and institutions.

I was fortunate in the two ministers I served during this period, Martin and Sharp, both exceptional people, though very different in their experience and personalities. Martin was the consummate politician, shrewd and canny, especially in his handling of difficult issues with his cabinet colleagues. He taught me a great deal about the politics of building the consensus required for cabinet approval and, in some cases, how to proceed without the necessity of seeking formal approval from cabinet. He was always a congenial and gregarious man who kept in touch with a vast network of friends and supporters. People throughout the country received telephone calls from him, usually in the early morning, on the occasion of their birthdays or other important events. His affable manner and outreach to everyone he met was dismissed by some as the manifestation of his political ambitions. But the man I got to know had a genuine interest in people and their problems. We once travelled together to the Caribbean, and he'd frequently stop to talk to local people who could not possibly have been of any political value to him. Martin was well read, with a broad knowledge of, and interest in, religion and philosophy, a side of him never apparent to the public. He was later Canada's high commissioner in London, where I visited him several times, and I particularly recall a long conversation he had at his official residence there with Barbara Ward, the economist and conservationist. Both were devout Catholics, and I was moved by the evening's conversation, both profound and candid, in which they discussed their commitment to their faith and their very considerable doubts.

Sharp, Trudeau's external affairs minister, was a very different person from Martin—both in his experience and in his personality. As Martin was the consummate politician, Sharp was the consummate civil servant, exemplifying the very best of Canada's career public service. He had a clarity of thought, a soundness of judgment and a soft-spoken way of expressing his views that had earned him a special place in the top ranks of the civil service as a senior deputy minister and the highest esteem of his colleagues, before he decided to leave on a question of principle when John Diefenbaker was prime minister. During a stint in the private sector, as a senior executive of Brascan, he became active in the Liberal Party and eventually a candidate for its leadership. Moving his support to Pierre Trudeau at a crucial point in the leadership convention earned him Trudeau's gratitude. This, together with Trudeau's great regard for his competence and professionalism, led to his appointment as secretary of state for external affairs, deputy prime minister and one of Trudeau's most valued and influential colleagues.

My own situation was somewhat paradoxical, as I was a deputy minister from outside the service serving a minister who was one of its most experienced and accomplished products. Although I didn't know him well at that point, the fact that we both came from Manitoba and had worked for James Richardson and Sons and that he had relatives on his wife's side in my hometown of Oak Lake gave us some common denominators. I soon developed a great admiration for his insightful policy views and expertise. His long period as a civil servant gave him a clear view of which matters should be left for the decision of the senior officials and which required the political authority of the minister. Despite the disparities in our experience, and perhaps in part because of them, we got along well and I learned a great deal from him. Our relations were greatly facilitated by his competent and congenial senior secretary/assistant, Jeanette Dugal, who later became his wife.

CHAPTER 6

Toward Stockholm

OMETIME DURING THE LATE 1960S the term *the environment* began to take on its contemporary meaning, complete
with its undercurrent of urgent concern, and emerged as a real
issue in industrialized countries. Environmentalism as an issue was
rooted in, but different from, the conservation movement. Conservationists had for years been calling on the public to understand the
need to conserve natural resources and to establish parks and nature
reserves. Conservationist concerns were overwhelmingly preservationist and their underpinnings essentially spiritual. Environmentalists, on the other hand, focused on the larger risks to the future of
the resource and life-support systems of the entire earth. Grassroots
organizations, with a wild diversity of tactics and points of view but
an essentially similar philosophy, sprouted everywhere. The International Union for Conservation of Nature and Natural Resources
(IUCN), at the international level, and a revitalized Sierra Club in the
United States, which had broadened its role from the original voluntary conservation organization, became leaders of what began to be
known as the Green Movement.

One of the Green concerns was population, and some elements of
the Zero Population Growth (ZPG) movement were adopted by the
environmentalists and their scientific allies, the ecologists. It was not
hard to see why. Between 1900 and 1960 the number of people on the
planet had doubled, from 1.61 billion to 3.02 billion. During the same
period, scores of nations entered the industrial age. "Development"

was therefore putting enormous strains on the Earth's systems. These were the key facts underlying the movement. And its agenda reflected largely the concerns and values of the industrialized world—the "rich" countries.

I was in no real sense a pioneer in this movement, but I followed the increasingly passionate debate with special interest. I knew there was a role for me to play here—environmentalism represented an authentic synthesis of my increasingly active development role and my early and continuing interest in nature. I also began to sense one of the great underlying truths of environmental politics: the environment is supranational. It transcends the nation-state. At the very least it has to be dealt with multilaterally.

In my business life I'd seen for myself the damage economic development caused nature. I was particularly involved in the petroleum and mining industries, which is precisely where the damage was so obvious. I hadn't recognized it at first—like my colleagues, I'd accepted environmental degradation as a necessary and inevitable part of our way of life. I was much more preoccupied with opportunities than with their environmental consequences.

But the issues impinged on everyone. Air pollution in Montreal had reached the point of being noticeably irritating. The water in the lake near our Beaconsfield home had become so polluted that swimming was prohibited. In Ottawa, the river running past the Parliament Buildings was dark with waste from the paper mill across the river in Hull. My interest and concern deepened as my awareness sharpened. Rachel Carson's book, *Silent Spring*, a cry of alarm for the health of the planet, confirmed and explained much of what I had been observing.

About the same time I read an article by the Italian industrialist Aurelio Peccei, in which he outlined his pessimistic analysis of what he called "the predicament of mankind." He laid out the systemic processes by which we were undermining the very foundations of our industrial civilization. I was so impressed that I went to see him in Rome and found him a charming, persuasive and highly intelligent man. From the moment we met I felt a great affinity for Peccei, and we became friends and collaborators. He was well known in

Europe as a business leader and management theorist but had become so profoundly disturbed about the human future that he devoted the rest of his life to developing and disseminating his solutions. His main vehicle was the Club of Rome, whose members were leading scientists, philosophers, policy experts and others who shared his interests and concerns. He resisted all attempts to give the club any more than the minimum structure and organization—it was always a place for ideas, not politics.

The first report of the Club of Rome, *Limits to Growth*, ignited widespread controversy. The report was in some ways premature— its predictions of impending shortages of key resources didn't take adequate account of rapid advances in materials technology—but its prognosis, that growing environmental impact would constrain growth, was prescient.

In some ways the club's methods were more important than its conclusions. Participants developed a form of systems analysis to produce a model of the complex cause-and-effect process by which human activities produce ultimate consequences. Pioneering this work was Jay Forrester at the Massachusetts Institute of Technology and his brilliant young colleague Dennis Meadows. The techniques they used were still rudimentary, and the results highly dependent on the quality and reliability of the information that could be fed into the models, but I read everything I could on the subject and was convinced that systems analysis provided the best set of tools for understanding the forces shaping our future and guiding our own interventions. For instance, air and water pollution result from industrial processes and practices and from their products. To reduce their environmental impact requires significant change throughout the production and consumption system, which in turn requires change in management practices, in technology and in consumer attitudes. Individual, one-shot solutions are seldom effective.

My work at CIDA gave me new insights into the complexities of development. I could see first-hand our propensity to perpetuate problems—to help developing countries grow in much the same way we had. I was troubled by the environmental and social disruption caused by some of the major infrastructure projects we supported—the Warsak Dam in northwest Pakistan, the nuclear energy plant in India and the giant Tarbela Dam on the Indus River. I still accepted the premise that most of these projects made a net positive contribution to the economies of the countries concerned, but more and more I understood that we needed to pay attention to their environmental and social impacts. But conventional attitudes and practices were deeply entrenched among the professionals who conceived and managed these projects, and it was not easy to effect real change, even from the top.

It wasn't long before I became even more directly immersed in environmental politics.

In 1969, at Sweden's initiative, the UN General Assembly decided to convene the first major global intergovernmental conference on environmental issues, the UN Conference on the Human Environment. The meeting was to be held in Stockholm in 1972, but by early in 1970 hardly anything had been done to prepare for it. The Swedes began to worry. Eventually their ambassador to the UN, Sverker Astrom, who had spearheaded the idea, contacted me through a mutual friend. We met at his residence in New York, hit it off and he recommended to Philippe de Seyne, UN undersecretary-general for economic and social affairs, that they approach me to head the conference secretariat. A young Canadian friend, Wayne Kines, who was a media consultant to the UN at the time, arranged a meeting with de Seyne. I was then invited to spend Saturday afternoon at the Washington home of Christian Herter Jr., U.S. undersecretary of state, who made a persuasive case for my taking it on. This was followed by an offer from UN secretary-general U Thant to become secretary-general of the conference and undersecretary-general of the UN responsible for environmental affairs.

Colleagues in Ottawa warned me against accepting. In their view the preparations were a mess and the conference was already beyond redemption. There was no way it could succeed. If this was intended to warn me off, it had the opposite effect. I regarded their pessimism as a challenge, and their warnings simply gave me another incentive to take the job and try to turn it around. Not that

I really needed the incentive: this was an offer I was incapable of resisting. After all, it was a unique intersection of my three major interests—development, the environment and the United Nations. Besides, to be undersecretary-general of the UN . . .

Some twenty-three years after I was handing out security passes and deciding I had no future in the place unless I left and found some other way in, I was duly appointed undersecretary-general of the UN. Now I was in with a vengeance, a long-standing ambition fulfilled.

In January 1970 I moved my family to Geneva, where the conference secretariat had been set up. We took a house in the small village of Gingins, outside the city, and our children went to local schools. I had the unique experience of simultaneously enjoying bucolic Swiss village life while being buffeted by the political cross-currents that make it so difficult to achieve agreement in international affairs—even on issues that would seem to compel agreement in everyone's interests. The environment issue was no exception. My colleagues' warnings in Ottawa had scarcely been exaggerated—preparations for the conference were marred and almost derailed by East-West and North-South conflicts.

This was the time of the Cold War, and relations between the Western alliance and the U.S.S.R. and its allies were at a very low ebb—fractiousness and antagonism were the normal operating modes for both sides. Even before I got to Geneva, the West was insisting on excluding East Germany—the German Democratic Republic—from the conference on the grounds that it wasn't a "real" country but a creature of the U.S.S.R. The Soviets argued, correctly I thought, despite their cynical political motives, that the environment was a universal issue and that participation in international measures to deal with it should also be universal. The West, led by the U.S., was equally insistent that until the overall issue of the two Germanies had been resolved, the G.D.R. had to remain excluded from the UN, which included any UN conference. Their view was that letting the East Germans talk about anything, even such a non-ideological notion as the environment, was the thin edge of the wedge leading to full UN membership.

I did my best to engineer a compromise, even meeting with the East German foreign minister in Cuba, but to no avail. As a result, the U.S.S.R. and most of its allies withdrew from participation in the conference. This could have had disastrous consequences. No effective environmental action could be taken by the UN without the East Bloc. I therefore kept my own lines open to them, making sure that they were fully briefed on conference preparations and that their views were taken into account by our secretariat.

The Soviets took a hard-nosed and coercive attitude to the UN secretariat, and I ran into their obduracy early. I needed someone from the Soviet Union on my small staff, and their ambassador to the UN came to me with a single candidate who clearly was not the kind of person I needed. I told him so politely but clearly.

"Mr. Strong," he said blandly, "this is the only candidate of my government, and if you do not accept him, there will be no representative of our country on your secretariat and that will be very bad for you."

"I very much want a Soviet person on my staff," I replied, "but to have a person I can't use would not be good either for the United Nations or for the Soviet Union. What I need is one of your distinguished scientists."

When I escorted him out beyond earshot of the others in the room, he politely said to me, "Mr. Strong, I completely understand your position and will communicate it to Moscow." In the end I was able to get a leading Soviet scientist and former head of the Hydrology Institute, Vladimir Kunin, who was also a great character with a wry sense of humour.

That wasn't the end of it. When the Soviet Union decided to boycott the conference, I'd been in the process of recruiting a second Soviet expert to my staff. Naturally, I moved to cut this off. But when I told Kunin, he just laughed and said, "Maurice, you don't understand our system. You know how long it took to get the approval of my government to make him available. Now the Politburo itself would have a hard time stopping our bureaucratic processes from sending him here." Sure enough, he appeared and we took him on.

At the conference itself I met almost every day with the Soviet ambassador in Stockholm to brief him on the proceedings so that he could keep Moscow informed.

But the East-West issues weren't the only obstacles to be overcome. The biggest single threat to the conference was the ambivalence, even antipathy, that developing countries felt toward the whole issue of the environment.

From the beginning, developing countries had regarded the West's concern with "the environment" as just another fad of the industrialized countries; in their view pollution and environmental contamination were diseases of the rich, which could only divert attention and resources from their principal concerns, underdevelopment and poverty. They were understandably sensitive to the possibility that measures designed to protect the environment would impose new constraints on their development. Most of them would gladly exchange a little pollution for the benefits of economic growth. Their case was argued persuasively in the Preparatory Committee by Brazil's Miguel Almeida Ozorio. There was a growing movement to boycott the conference.

I knew the conference would fail if we couldn't persuade the developing countries to take part, and I knew they'd never agree to come unless their concerns were addressed. The draft conference agenda I'd inherited didn't even attempt to do so. On the contrary, it was heavily skewed toward issues affecting the more developed countries—air and water pollution and deterioration of the urban environment. If I was to get anywhere, I'd have to radically remake the agenda—which had already been accepted by the Preparatory Committee.

I went away to do some serious thinking. Then, when I was clear in my own mind what approach we should take, and with the astute guidance of the committee's Jamaican chairman, Keith Johnson, I called its members together for a special meeting.

I laid out for them my revised agenda. The key concept called for a redefinition and expansion of the concept of environment to link it directly to the economic development process and the concerns of developing countries.

Well, it sounds good. Nice linkage. But it means what? I could see their scepticism.

The basic thesis, I said, is simple: environmental and economic priorities are intrinsically two sides of the same coin. Of course, there will be conflicts and trade-offs in particular cases, but I pointed out that it was, after all, the process of economic development that has an impact on the environment, both positively and negatively. Only through better management, therefore, can the basic goals of development be achieved—to improve the lives and prospects of people in environmental and social as well as economic terms. My new agenda recognized that national priorities were dependent on the stage of development currently attained and would therefore vary. The key was to insist that the needs of developing countries would best be served by treating the environment as an integral dimension of development rather than an impediment. By integrating it in this way, richer countries could support a renewed commitment to the development process itself, and the developing countries could see the environment issue as a basis for such additional support for the development. In fact, they insisted on this—that their participation in environmental co-operation be contingent on agreement by the industrialized countries to provide "new and additional" resources to cover the incremental costs of providing for environmental protection in their development programs.

The Preparatory Committee went along with this approach. More important, I received the conditional but encouraging support of the developing countries.

Still, we were far from finished. What I'd presented seemed to me logical and sensible, but it was still only an intuitive notion rooted in reflections on my own experience; it lacked the benefit of rigorous analysis and a well-developed policy thesis. With the help of Barbara Ward, one of the most articulate and influential gurus of the development field, who had the trust of developing countries as well as the ear of leaders of the industrialized world, I assembled in New York a small group of leading development experts, primarily from the developing world, and invited their comments on my thesis.

Comments I got, in spades. Pakistan's Mahbub ul Haq, one of the most brilliant and provocative development economists, made a spirited attack on the whole concept of "the environment." Like a skilled lawyer, he hammered home all the reasons why developing countries should not be drawn into participation in the conference on the terms set by the industrialized countries. He then proceeded to attack point by point the arguments I had made. His position was devastating and simple: industrialization had given developed countries disproportionate benefits and huge reservoirs of wealth and at the same time had caused the very environmental problems we were now asking developing countries to join in resolving. The cost of cleaning up the mess, therefore, should be borne by the countries that had caused it in the first place. If they wanted developing countries to go along, they'd have to provide the financial resources to enable them to do so.

The Sri Lankan Gamani Corea, another noted development economist, supported this argument, as did Enrique Iglesias of Uruguay, the ebullient protégé of the influential Argentine economist Raoul Prebisch. I was impressed with their concerns, which I thought had validity. I knew that the conference could never succeed unless its agenda could incorporate these issues and find sound ways to address them.

I therefore dipped into my evolving fund of experience in dealing with conflict and diplomatic processes. I had learned never to confront but to co-opt, never to bully but to equivocate, and never to yield. When I entered the world of diplomacy as an amateur, a seasoned professional advised me to learn how to say "hmm" in negotiating difficult issues when I didn't agree but didn't want to be offensive. I understood now, as I could never have when I was younger, that the oblique approach can often be the most direct one.

I therefore responded with a challenge. "If you're right, then I've made a mistake in taking on this job. But if there's anything at all to my thesis, it could offer a new and more positive basis for the development relationship between North and South. We can all agree that a basis like that would be invaluable. Why not, then, at least join me in a rigorous, objective process of evaluating the concept? Perhaps you'll be proven right. But let's at least determine whether we can devise from it a new basis for North-South co-operation."

I felt it would be hard to deny my appeal, because I knew that Haq, despite his strongly held views, was intellectually honest and couldn't turn down a challenge like that. I knew that once he was into it, his fertile mind would find a way to formulate the issue in a way he and others like him could live with. Gamani Corea, too, agreed to help with the analysis, with the continued support and guidance of Barbara Ward. It was the beginning of a long, stimulating and satisfying professional partnership and personal friendship with all three.

In the next few months we set out to build the intellectual and policy underpinnings for our—it had become "ours" now—primary thesis, which was the essential relationship between environment and development. In the process, I consulted widely, flying from one country to another. In my role at CIDA I'd already established a network of relationships with politicians and development experts in the developing countries. This helped not only in defining our theme but in persuading developing countries to participate—by taking part, they could protect as well as assert their interests. It also helped that I was already known as a person with a strong commitment to development and had at least a certain credibility with and good access to developing countries' governments. This enabled me to meet with the leaders of a number of them soon after I took up my office. Everywhere I went I conferred with presidents, prime ministers, business leaders and scientists, arguing, explaining, listening, learning, cajoling, co-opting.

The most important single event in the run-up to Stockholm was an informal meeting we convened in June 1971 in a motel in Founex, outside Geneva, with twenty-seven leading experts and policy-makers. The meeting was chaired by Gamani Corea, with Mahbub ul Haq as rapporteur. Others present included David Runnalls and Jim MacNeill, who have each gone on to hold senior positions in both Canadian and international environment and development organizations. The discussions were intense and passionate, characterized by a degree of intellectual integrity and rigour that ultimately enabled the participants to find common ground despite diverging opinions and interests. The meeting is inscribed in my memory as one of the best intellectual exchanges I have ever participated in. It had a profound influence both on the Stockholm Conference and on the evolution of the concept of the environment–development relationship.

By now both Corea and Haq had essentially bought into the thesis, and they had become the architects of elaboration, adding to it the logic that made it credible and persuasive. The two of them co-operated in producing the report of the meeting. I regard this report as a milestone in the history of the environmental movement, an absolutely seminal document.

The report argued that while the degradation of the environment in industrialized countries derived from production and consumption patterns, the environmental problems in the rest of the world were largely a result of underdevelopment and poverty. It called for the integration of development and environmental strategies and urged the rich nations in their own interests to provide more money and help to enable the poorer nations to achieve the goal. "If the concern for the human environment reinforces the commitment to development, it must also reinforce the commitment to international aid."

This was not in any sense charity, the wealthy helping the indigent. Helping the developing nations would be self-help for the rich countries as well—it was their environment too. That's how we'd sell it to the rich countries: do it because it's intrinsically a good thing to do—for you.

About this time I persuaded the scientist René Dubos and Barbara Ward, along with dozens of other experts, to produce a book called *Only One Earth*. In doing so, I once again ran head-on into the UN bureaucracy and rediscovered how it can sometimes act as a barrier to rather than a facilitator of initiatives in its interest.

I went to see the chairman of the Publications Committee, who seemed to take satisfaction in telling me that "we have already considered the possibility of publishing a book for the Stockholm Conference," thereby saying that my idea was a non-starter.

But of course I wasn't ready to give up. I asked a colleague with more experience in the UN if there was any reason why I, as secretary-general of the conference, could not commission a book to be written, as a report *to* the conference rather than an official UN publication. There seemed to be no such explicit prohibition, though apparently it had not been done before. Accordingly, I set up a separate non-profit organization specifically to produce the book, raised money for it outside the UN and gave Barbara Ward and René Dubos the green light. The book subsequently became a best-seller, produced enough revenue for printing in twelve languages, more than double the number of official languages used for UN publications, and made an important contribution to the conference itself. It was an impassioned call to arms, sounding an urgent alarm about the impact of human activity on the ecology of the planet, yet it shared my optimism that humankind could still put aside their differences in the face of an overwhelming common danger.

Only One Earth was to become the theme and the rallying cry of Stockholm.

Two countries in particular were key to whether the conference would work—Brazil and India. Brazil had taken a strong position on the issues, a position derived not from mere political impulse but from a well-reasoned policy analysis of the constraints that international environmental action might impose on their development—they had, after all, "custody" of that extraordinary global resource, the Amazon basin. One of the first things I did, therefore, was initiate a close and constructive dialogue with the Brazilians. India was important because it was especially influential among developing countries; one of my first overseas visits was therefore to New Delhi, where I hoped to see Prime Minister Indira Gandhi.

My friends at the Indian foreign ministry warned me that I almost certainly wouldn't get to see her. She was preoccupied with the war in Pakistan and with difficult domestic issues, they said, and it was not reasonable for me to expect to see her on a marginal issue like the environment. Nevertheless, through my friendship with one of India's most eminent intellectuals and policy leaders, G. P.

Parthasarthy, who was very close to Mrs. Gandhi, I did get to meet with her.

It was immediately clear that she had a deep interest in and knowledge of the environment. I then raised a point I thought would get her attention. "If the developing countries sit out the conference," I suggested delicately, "it would leave the issue in the hands of the industrialized countries." I found, as I had expected, that she was keenly sensitive to the political implications.

"Why not come to the Stockholm Conference yourself, as you are the best possible person to articulate the concerns and interests of the developing world?" I asked. "I can promise you a special place on the program."

She immediately accepted, much to the surprise and, in some quarters, consternation of her officials, and gave me her permission to let it be known that she'd be attending. Thereafter, India became one of the leading participants in preparations for the conference and a strong and effective proponent of the developing countries' position.

This immensely enhanced the prospects of participation by other developing countries. A boycott now seemed unlikely.

It was an auspicious day, beautifully clear and sunny, and there was excitement in the crowd assembled in the streets for the opening-day parade.

True, not everyone was enthusiastic. The Swedish Security Service was worried about threats they had received from radical groups to disrupt the conference, which apparently included threats against me. They tried to dissuade me from taking part in the parade and followed me closely when I insisted on doing so. At our suggestion the Swedes had provided a fleet of bicycles, painted in the UN white and blue, which were freely available for anyone within a defined area around the conference site. I rode one of them in the parade. At one point a young man with long hair broke through the crowd and pushed an old, beat-up bicycle at me, yelling loudly, "If you really believe in what you're saying about the environment, you should get off your new bicycle and take this old recycled one!"

I didn't stop. "So you don't believe in recycling!" he bellowed.

I turned and shouted back, "Young man, not only do I believe in recycling, I am personally made entirely of recycled materials!" This was sufficiently Delphic to give him pause, and I proceeded without further difficulty.

In my opening speech I steered the attention of the delegates to the Action Plan that our Preparatory Committee had managed to get into their hands several months earlier. I reminded them that the plan had two components: a series of recommendations for international action, and a framework to group all such recommendations in their functional categories.

I remember looking down at the attentive faces of the multitude as I outlined the plan's three principal categories: the Global Environmental Assessment or "Earthwatch" Program, which was a co-operative approach to accumulating the necessary data and to providing objective assessments of potential problems or opportunities; the Environmental Management Activities, to provide support at the international level for good management initiatives; and the Supporting Measures, which would be education and training programs but also a way of putting money where our mouths were, a way of backing each agreed-on action with financial and organizational support.

The Action Plan wouldn't solve all our problems, even were it implemented fully, I pointed out. "The Action Plan cannot be a comprehensive approach to all problems of the human environment. It does offer, however, a blueprint for continuing environmental work for the international community, and [it outlines] a first indication of priorities." Then, to some applause, I said, "I hope this conference will lose no time in accepting the framework as the basis for the Action Plan."

Also at the opening session Prime Minister Gandhi made what was one of the most influential speeches of the entire conference, with its theme that "poverty is the greatest polluter of all."

When the conference got down to its real work, the divisions between East and West that had characterized and threatened the preparatory process were soon in evidence as delegates from the 113 nations present began to take to the floor with their opening statements. There was still intense suspicion, especially among newly independent countries, that the "ecology movement" was just another way of curtailing their hard-won freedom, a subtle form of neo-colonialism. The special conference newspaper put out by Friends of the Earth and *The Ecologist* magazine proclaimed in its headlines after the first day, "Only 113 Earths," a sardonic contrast with the "Only One Earth" theme of the conference.

In the absence of most other East Bloc countries, special importance was accorded to the role of the Chinese. This was their first major world conference since they had taken their seat in the United Nations. They maintained a very tough line, generally in support of the developing-country position. I worked closely with their delegation, meeting at their request early every morning to review with them the program for the day and the points that would be of special interest to them. The delegation was headed by Vice-Premier Ku Mu, and while they seemed very much to appreciate my briefings and advice, they never let me know how they intended to respond.

During the second week, negotiations were seriously bogged down not only on the Action Plan but even on the Declaration of Principles, which jointly were to be the main outputs of the conference. It was looking grim—there was a serious prospect that negotiations would break down entirely and the conference would make things worse rather than better, entrenching the conflicts and differences that divided participants. The presence in Stockholm of a colourful and diverse group of representatives of indigenous peoples and NGOs (holding their own unofficial conference on land outside the city lent by the Swedish government and dubbed the Hog Farm) helped somewhat. So did the presence of some influential and well-known personalities, notably Barbara Ward and Margaret Mead, who helped to elevate the spirit of the occasion and strengthen the will of the official delegates to overcome their differences. I had also invited special guests and a number of other interested friends—the noted British scientist Sir Peter Medawar and his equally talented wife, Jean, the Canadian diplomatic veteran and China expert I had so long admired, Chester Ronning, and the then little-known Jim

Wolfensohn. Even at that early stage of his career he evidenced a remarkable prescient knowledge of and interest in the issues being addressed by the conference, and I well remember the lively discussion we had when he joined me for a working lunch in the prime minister's office, from which I managed the conference.

As time became shorter, our working days became longer, with the two main committees meeting into the early hours of the morning. On the Thursday night, the day before the conference was to end, there was no final agreement on the Declaration of Principles. By four in the morning negotiations were still at an impasse.

I had asked a colleague to spell me off in the secretariat's place at the negotiating table while I sat musing on the sidelines, my eyes drooping as the tedious process seemed to be getting nowhere. On an impulse based as much on frustration as inspiration, I quietly got up from my seat, went over to where I had noticed the interpretation facilities had been plugged in to the electricity supply, and surreptitiously pulled the plug. Somehow this seemed to provide just the right jolt to rouse the delegates into getting the process moving again. When even the French, who are normally adamant on the subject, agreed to continue in English, some kind of a breakthrough had been obtained. It was nearly dawn before agreement was reached and the wording settled. The breakthrough owed much to the relentless leadership of the committee chairman, Dr. Mostafa Tolba, minister of science and technology for Egypt and head of his country's delegation. I marked him as a promising candidate for international leadership.

There remained, however, the Chinese. At our early-morning meeting on the last day, the Chinese explained that they couldn't take a final position on the declaration, and more particularly on the population issue, without authorization from Beijing. With the time difference they'd never be able to get authorization by the hour of the final vote later that day. They saw no alternative to walking out of the final session.

Such a walkout would cast a pall over the whole proceedings, and I needed—very quickly—a plan to finesse the problem. Mercifully, an idea flashed into my mind.

"When the final vote is called," I said, "your entire delegation could rise from their seats at the table, but instead of leaving altogether you'd merely move to the seats immediately behind you. You'd not register a vote, but you wouldn't abstain either, or walk out of the meeting. The records of the meeting could then show you as present and implicitly, but not explicitly, participating in the consensus. For your purposes, on the other hand, it could be shown that you hadn't voted in the absence of authorization from your government."

This may seem excessively subtle, even for the UN, but it had its merits. The point was that when the report of the meeting was drafted, it would show the Chinese in the room. It wouldn't say they'd approved, but neither would it say they hadn't—their presence, however, could be taken as an implicit endorsement. But in looking at the actual votes, they could show their government that they hadn't done anything against policy or without permission.

The chief delegate, Vice-Premier Ku Mu, questioned me closely, probing for flaws, and had me explain my idea carefully several times. Then he thanked me without giving any indication what he would actually do about it.

After our meeting I sought out the secretary of the conference, Diego Cordovez, a careful but innovative Ecuadorian who later became an undersecretary-general himself and then foreign minister of his country. He was one of those rare people who combine fastidious attention to detail and proper procedure with a flair for innovation. He'd never heard of such a thing, he remarked, and couldn't think of any precedent for it, but he saw no reason why it wouldn't work.

I still didn't know what the Chinese would actually do. As the chairman called for the vote on the final resolution, my heart raced. My eyes were fixed on Ku Mu. For a few moments after the chairman called the vote, he sat impassively, then rose slowly from his seat. Would he walk out or would he take the seat behind as I had suggested? To my profound relief he turned and moved into the seat behind him. Hearing no objections the chairman pounded his gavel and declared the resolution passed by consensus. The Stockholm Conference had moved into the history books as a major landmark launching a new era of international environmental diplomacy.

One of the issues that had most excited attention in the media and had agitated activists and NGOs was the matter of whaling. Over at the Hog Farm they displayed a large plastic whale, which became transformed by the media into a symbol of the conference itself. So effective were the NGOs on the issue that the main conference ended up proposing, with my strong support, a ten-year moratorium on whaling. After the decision I took time off from my official duties to visit the Hog Farm and was subjected to a raucous display of support for my position on the whaling issue but also sharp admonishment for our lack of progress on other issues.

I knew that the regular meeting of the International Whaling Commission was scheduled to take place in London immediately following the Stockholm Conference, and when the conference wound up I went directly there. I had no official invitation, and though they protested that the matter of a moratorium was not on their agenda, they reluctantly yielded to the clamour of the media and finally let me speak at the meeting. I made as strong a case as I could in favour of a moratorium, and in due course, after some stormy debate, they did agree to a limited moratorium.

Stockholm marked the first real entry of environmentalists into international politics; their ability to arouse public opinion gave them a permanent role in decision making thereafter, and their achievements in Stockholm helped give rise to national environmental movements where none had existed before, including some in developing countries.

Many of the environmentalists had argued for a "steady-state" theory of economics, a no-growth strategy. The industrialized countries, on the other hand, argued for business as usual, and the developing countries for expanded growth. My view, consistently expressed then as now, was to argue that growth was imperative to alleviate poverty and to allow the peoples of the developing world to achieve their aspirations. But, as I argued before the conference, we had to rethink our concepts of the purposes of growth. We had to shift our thinking, see growth as a means of enriching the lives and enlarging the opportunities of all humankind. It followed, then, that the more wealthy societies—the privileged minority—would have to make the most profound—not to say revolutionary—changes, in attitudes, values and behaviour.

It was also the first time that sovereign nations acknowledged a responsibility for domestic actions that affected the environments of other nations and the planet as a whole.

The Action Plan I mentioned in my opening speech was a 109-point document, dealing with an extremely wide range of issues. They included the environmental quality of human habitations; natural resource management; management of pollution; environment and development; and—key—a recommendation that developing nations be given additional assistance to help them meet environmental standards.

No, of course pollution wouldn't instantly disappear or ecological destruction stop. But many nations awoke to the problem, and in the years that followed, hundreds of laws were passed in scores of legislatures. Of the 140 multilateral environmental treaties that have been signed since the 1920s, more than half have been concluded since Stockholm. Stockholm was just a start, but it *was* a start.

Nevertheless, the global environmental crisis continued to unfold.

CHAPTER 7

UNEP,
Petro-Canada
and the
Politics of Water

IT'S ONE THING TO HAVE A CONFERENCE, quite another to ensure proper follow-up. Conferences, when they work, can often be exhausting as well as rewarding. Significant decisions can be made—as indeed they were in Stockholm. But it's what happens afterwards that is important. Otherwise talk is just talk, resolutions just good intentions.

The Stockholm Conference participants recognized this. One of the recommendations was to set up a new UN body that would monitor progress on the environment and ensure that the conference's hard-won conclusions were actually implemented. This notion, as well as the conference itself, was widely debated at the next UN General Assembly, in the fall of 1972. There, to everyone's surprise, Kenya's delegation, led by its able and respected ambassador, Odero Jowi, strongly supported by Foreign Minister Njoroge Mungai, offered Nairobi as the headquarters of the new organization. Other countries, India included, had already indicated a similar interest, but the Group of 77 (the term used to describe the developing-country members of the UN that consult and frequently vote as a group—the "77" because the group originally comprised 77 members, although the numbers have since grown substantially) showed their solidarity, and the Indians joined other developing countries in supporting the Kenyan bid.

Although they couldn't very well say so, the feeling among the Swedes and other industrialized countries was not so much surprise as consternation. They had nothing against Kenya as such, but a new organization like this one (it came to be called the United Nations Environment Program, or UNEP) would have a difficult enough time under the best of conditions, but to be so far from the other international organizations it would have to work with and influence would make its job even more difficult. Under these circumstances distance was seen as a real impediment.

Partly because of this, some of the interested countries sent a delegation to urge me to accept the job of heading the new organization, at least during its formative years.

I could see their point. They wanted to minimize the difficulties of the Nairobi location by at least avoiding a potentially divisive and uncertain search for an acceptable head, and they knew I'd have broad support from all regions. But seeing their point didn't mean having to accept it. This was not at all what I had planned. I had made it clear that I did not aspire to and would not accept an appointment to the organization that might be created as a result of the conference. For one thing, I had an obligation to return to the government in Ottawa. Also, I felt that if I were seen to be a candidate for this post, it could compromise my objectivity and effectiveness in working for General Assembly approval of the new organization. But representatives of a number of other governments joined the Swedes in importuning me to change my mind. So I consulted Prime Minister Trudeau, and he agreed to my taking the new post for an initial start-up period. I accepted. I agreed to take a full five-year term—any hint that I was there only for a short term would have left me a lame duck—but it was privately understood that I'd return to Canada as soon as I felt the new body had been firmly established.

My original appointment to head the Stockholm Conference had been made by U Thant, but by this time Kurt Waldheim was Secretary-General. For reasons unrelated to the subsequent controversies he was involved in, I was unwilling to accept an appointment directly from him. He had let me down in undertakings he had made for me in the past, most recently by sending to the General Assembly a budget and manning table for the new organization very different from what we had agreed on. Accordingly, I insisted that if I were to be a candidate for the job, I must be elected directly, by the General Assembly.

Waldheim didn't like this one bit, but instead of confronting me on the issue, he sent another undersecretary to replace me at the committee where the matter was being discussed. I simply sat back and didn't try to intervene. But I could hardly suppress a smile when his objection was entirely rejected—not a single government supported it. It was a reassuring vote of confidence in me, and I was subsequently elected unanimously to the post. This gave me a certain degree of political independence within the secretariat, while worsening my already difficult relationship with Waldheim.

For me, going back to Kenya was something of a homecoming. Of course, the country had changed utterly since I had last lived there. The Mau Mau were a distant memory. The once-demonized Kenyatta had become a revered Father of the Nation, and an independent Kenya was one of the most dynamic countries in Africa. I had many old friends there and soon made new ones.

UNEP still, however, consisted of nothing more than a General Assembly Resolution and me, and I needed to start from the ground up in translating it into a reality.

For our official headquarters the Kenyan government offered us a new building complex in the heart of Nairobi consisting of a high-rise tower and conference facilities bearing Kenyatta's name. They wanted us to make it our permanent headquarters, but I demurred. An environmental agency needed something different. We had to build distinctive structures symbolic of our environmental purposes. We also needed room for the long-term expansion that seemed inevitable. After looking at a number of potential sites, I located a large coffee farm in an attractive location on the outskirts of Nairobi that I understood could possibly be made available, though it was not the site the government preferred. When I walked over the land, I knew immediately that this would be the right place for us, and eventually the Kenyans agreed. We had our new headquarters completed and occupied by the end of our first year. The buildings were simple but practical and made full use of the beautiful natural setting and the lush tropical foliage that surrounded them.

My first priority was to recruit our top executive team. Nairobi at that time was an attractive place, and though it was difficult to get good people to move there permanently, it proved relatively easy to recruit them for stints of a few years. I already had a deputy. I'd taken the long way around to Nairobi, via Cairo, to meet the Egyptian minister who had impressed me so much at Stockholm, Mostafa Tolba. He yielded to my persuasion and would perform as deputy with great skill and dedication.

UNEP officially opened in a splendid ceremony on October 2, 1973. The UN flag was raised to a fanfare of trumpets, there was a march past of forest rangers and game wardens, and then Jomo Kenyatta appeared in his tribal regalia, to huge shouts of acclaim.

"*Harambee!*" he yelled, his trademark slogan. "*Harambee!* Let's pull together!"

"*Harambee!*" the crowd yelled back.

It was perfect, I thought. Pulling together was the slogan of the new country, but it also expressed our mission with great clarity: it was our job to pull together the nations of the world in the critical fight to protect our planet.

With our new Governing Council in place, I began to spend a great deal of my time travelling the world. A major task was to help developing countries set up environmental ministries or agencies and then to use the recommendations of Stockholm to develop policies and legislation. We also dispensed advice on how to establish links with the principal scientific and policy institutions.

At the same time, we set about exercising our co-ordinating role within the UN system. This was not easy. I was chairman of the UN's Environment Co-ordinating Board, which was made up of the heads of the principal agencies, including the World Bank and the International Monetary Fund. But the reservations Sweden and others had expressed about Nairobi proved correct: our location was a handicap, not because we were in a developing country but because of our distance from those we had to persuade. Thus our co-ordinating function never became as effective as it was intended to be.

UNEP worked well enough, though, particularly when we took the initiative—and a number of our initiatives helped to shape the direction of the environmental movement in the period ahead. We established an "outer limits" program to identify some of the major global risks that needed to be addressed. One of our first targets was the issue of climate change, and I convened a meeting of scientists in 1973 to review the state of the evidence on this emerging issue. This gave UNEP an early leadership role, notably through the efforts of my colleague and successor, Mostafa Tolba, and led to the establishment of the Intergovernmental Panel on Climate Change (IPCC) of leading scientists to provide objective analysis and guidance.

We also took a lead in tackling the issue of ocean pollution, first by convening a meeting of Mediterranean countries, including both Arab nations and Israel, which led to agreement on a convention to protect the marine environment of the Mediterranean. This was followed by the establishment of a Regional Seas Program, through which similar agreements were reached in other regions, including the Caribbean and the Red Sea. We initiated programs on combatting desertification, establishing an International Register of Potentially Toxic Chemicals (IRPTC), initiated processes that produced conventions regulating the international transport of toxic substances, and piloted a process that created the Convention on Trade in Endangered Species. We initiated an ambitious program of monitoring, assessment and early warning of potential environmental risks, and we established offices in each of the main regions of the world. Another important aspect of our activities at that stage was forging links with other organizations with common interests whose

co-operation and capacities we could draw on. Of particular importance was the International Union for the Conservation of Nature
(IUCN), and we contracted with them to use their extensive network
of conservation expertise.

Examination of UNEP's program during these early days is a
reminder of the many areas in which it was the source of initiatives
that have since grown into major international agreements and programs. In many cases other organizations have since become the
principal actors, which is as it should be, for UNEP was designed to
be a catalyst, initiator and co-ordinator in issues not requiring it
to be the prime force.

On a personal level I enjoyed the house I had purchased with
some two and one-half hectares of beautiful grounds, well cared for
by an experienced houseman, Timothy, and his two helpers. Pauline
and I were living apart at that point, though not yet formally separated. Hanne Marstrand, the lovely and charismatic Danish interior
designer I had met in New York, became my partner and spent quite
a bit of time with me in Nairobi.

By the last half of 1975 things were going well in Nairobi, and I was
continuing to find my life there both personally enjoyable and challenging. On the other hand I realized that the time was coming
when I would need to confront my obligations to return to Canada.

While I was mulling this over, I got a call from Jack Austin,
Canada's deputy minister of natural resources. The prime minister
wanted me to come home, he said, to head Petro-Canada, the
national oil company that had just been created as a response to the
OPEC-induced oil crisis. Petro-Canada was a political compromise.
Public opinion polls in Canada at the time indicated strong support
for total nationalization of the industry, but this the government
was not prepared to do. Some of the principal oil exporters were
giving preference to national oil companies. I had earlier proposed the creation of just such a company, so when they had difficulty finding a person to run it who knew the industry and was
also trusted by Ottawa, they thought of me.

I went back to Ottawa to meet with Trudeau and his principal advisers on the matter, his minister of energy, mines and resources, Donald Macdonald, who soon afterwards became finance minister, and Michael Pitfield, the Clerk of the Privy Council, who was a good friend of the prime minister's and his most influential adviser. Both these men were suspicious of my environmental interests and had obviously suggested several other prospects. But Trudeau prevailed, reminded me of my undertaking to return to Canada and suggested that this was the time and Petro-Canada the reason.

I didn't have to mull it over very much. I accepted.

The decision to leave an international UN posting to take up this new challenge requires a little explanation. The move seemed inexplicable to some of the people who were following my career, and it led to the conclusion some of them drew that my career had been a series of odd lurches in peculiar directions: what was a committed environmentalist—after Stockholm and UNEP, one of the globe's more visible environmentalists—doing going back to a small country to head an oil company, of all things? But to me there was nothing incongruous in any of this. I had come from the oil business and understood it intuitively. I knew how important it was—and how devastating its effects on the environment could be. Wouldn't that be an interesting challenge, to set up a new oil company—and to do it right?

Trudeau made my exit from UNEP easier by writing a letter to key governments explaining that in leaving the organization I was responding to an important need that had arisen in the Canadian government.

And it was important—and contentious. To say that the creation of Petro-Canada had been extremely controversial was an understatement—the industry itself always had a strong anti-government bias, and this only made it worse; it was regarded both as intolerable interference in the private sector and as expropriation of something that was rightfully theirs. (It wasn't long afterwards that the notorious bumper sticker appeared in the West, threatening to refuse to sell oil to the Canadian "East," as "tax-grabbing Ottawa" was known in Calgary—*Let the Eastern Bastards Freeze in the Dark*.)

Although I've said I didn't hesitate to accept the challenge, my participation was not without its limitations. I told Trudeau from the start that I was not prepared to make a long-term commitment. I had neglected my own personal business affairs for too long already—but I agreed to take on the job of establishing the new corporation, recruiting a management team and getting it launched. This was made clear in the press release announcing my appointment.

I arrived in Calgary on a cold winter's morning just before the New Year, armed only with the Act of Parliament and my new mandate. I even had to finance initial expenditures out of my own pocket, pending receipt of the first tranche of funds from the government. But if the weather was cold, the reception I received from industry people was even frostier. Soon after I arrived, I addressed a meeting of industry executives, and the questions that followed were sharp and hostile. At one point I was openly jeered. Still, in the weeks that followed I took comfort from the fact that the many friends I'd made and colleagues I'd worked with in earlier years in Calgary remained amicable to me personally, to their great credit, despite their antipathy to a state petroleum company.

I immediately rented some rooms at the International Hotel and set up our first offices there until we located a recently constructed building nearby, where we became the main tenants. This gave us the right to name the building, and I chose Canada Place. The building was made of red brick and was soon derisively nicknamed Red Square.

My first task was to put together a core management team and board of directors that would command the respect of the industry, not an easy thing to do given the general hostility in the oil patch to Petro-Canada and the Liberal government. Immediately after my arrival in Calgary I received a call from a New York friend, David Mitchell, a protégé of the noted banker Siegmund Warburg who represented the Warburg firm in New York. He told me about an extremely bright and promising young Canadian, John Ralston Saul, who was just returning to Canada from the United Kingdom, where he had been living, and would, he said, be an ideal executive assistant to me. I asked David to send him along, and a couple of days later he appeared at my hotel offices in Calgary. He had no experience in the oil industry but was intelligent, articulate and resourceful. I hired him on the spot, though he knew there could be no guarantee of a permanent role—that would depend entirely on his performance.

He performed superbly. A quick learner and obtrusively curious about what others were doing and thinking, he soon established himself as an invaluable, though unconventional, member of my personal staff, helping me with a wide variety of the tasks and decisions that go into the establishment of a new enterprise. At times he caused me some problems with other members of our growing team, whose toes he frequently stepped on. His manner and lifestyle were those of a cultured aristocrat, which made him something of an eccentric in Calgary. He soon became known in the local restaurants for his fastidious taste, which few if any of Calgary's establishments were able to satisfy. John was not the type to remain an executive assistant for very long, but our period together during the early days at Petro-Canada formed the basis for an enduring relationship with him and later his partner, Adrienne Clarkson, a lovely and consistently creative and brilliant television personality, combining a cutting-edge intellect with a disarmingly candid manner and charismatic charm. John has since established himself as a successful author of works of political philosophy and has become something of an intellectual guru. He and Adrienne are among my closest and most supportive friends. As I write this, John and Adrienne have moved into Rideau Hall. An inspired choice. They will breathe new life and influence into the governor-generalship.

Michael Pitfield, who had taken an active interest in Petro-Canada, had introduced me to Wilbert "Bill" Hopper, assistant deputy minister in the department of energy, mines and resources. Hopper had played a central role in developing the government's plans for Petro-Canada and shaping its enabling legislation. He had a strong professional background in the industry and extensive private sector experience before he was recruited to the federal government by Jack Austin. I met with him in New York while winding up my UN assignment, and we got along well. Physically short, stocky and overweight, he exuded hyperactive energy, expressed enthusiastic commitment to the concept of Petro-Canada and had clear ideas as to how we should run it. I could see he had the potential to take over the leadership of the company in due course but was frank in telling him that, coming as he did from the government that created Petro-Canada, he would have to earn the confidence of the board and the respect of the industry for this to happen.

In the meantime he accepted that I'd be considering others for the CEO role but that he, as senior vice-president, would have the opportunity to demonstrate his capacities; I promised not to appoint anyone else to succeed me until he'd had a fair opportunity to do so. As we concluded our discussions after a long walk in New York, I told him that if my own instincts were correct, he would take over from me within two years, and in the perspective of time would be seen as the person who had really built Petro-Canada. He agreed to join me, and my prognosis was ultimately fulfilled.

I drew on my past relationships in the industry to recruit other key members of the initial team—Don Axford, former vice-president in charge of exploration for Mobil Oil; Don Wolcott, with whom I had worked at Dome; and John Godfrey, whom I'd met when he was one of the leading land negotiators for Imperial Oil. To head our financial and strategic analysis team we brought in one of the Ottawa bureaucracy's most creative and influential operators, Joel Bell, who combined a rare analytical genius and a prodigious capacity for productive and innovative work with an abrasive style that earned him the respect of those who worked with him, though seldom their affection.

Another of our early appointments was Douglas Bowie, whom I'd long known as an effective social and environmental activist. It was one of my innovations to appoint him our director of environmental and social affairs. As far as I know we were the first in the industry, and certainly first in Canada, to create such a position, and we encountered stiff resistance even within our own organization, both on the part of the professional staff and among the directors. Nevertheless, we insisted that each project had to be subjected to a rigorous environmental and social assessment and that this assessment would be given equal weight with economic and technical considerations in the approval process. Even with support from the chief executive, it took a lot of time and effort for this apparently heretical notion to be integrated into the culture of the organization.

One particularly difficult situation arose when the exploration people wanted to drill a well on what they regarded as a highly promising prospect in the Bylot Basin in Northern Baffin Island, which would have had an impact on the rich and vulnerable marine resources of the area. At a tense board meeting I was alone in insisting that in this case the environmental considerations had to outweigh the economic and technical case for drilling.

The board was incredulous, but I wouldn't give in.

"I'll stake my job on this," I said. "I could not live with myself if I had to be party to going ahead with this project."

I don't normally do things like this. In my view managers who have to do so aren't managing very well. But I saw that this case was different. Not just because the Bylot Basin was such a pristine environment, though that had something to do with it. It was more that I had to insert the fact of the environment into some very stubborn and resistant heads, to make them understand that environmental concerns had to be at the heart of our corporate ethos.

In the end I was able to kill the project, at the cost of a continuing resentment on the part of some board members. However, I'm pleased to say that to this day the pristine ecology and precious marine resources of the Bylot Basin have been spared.

Much of our focus, indeed, was in the northern frontier areas, where environmental and social impact would be especially sensitive. Accordingly, we gave high priority to establishing good relations with the native peoples there. We didn't regard this just as a matter of public relations; we were determined to establish real consultation and real co-operation. Both Douglas Bowie and I had good links with some of the native peoples through our previous activities. But we also knew that their trust and confidence could only be earned over time and would be based on what we actually did, as opposed to our statements, however good our intentions. This was never going to be easy, but it would be worthwhile.

Soon after we established ourselves in Calgary, I called a meeting of native leaders. One of them stood up at the start to point out the differences in the two cultures and the ways that native peoples and mainstream Canadians viewed economic development activities.

"I know you view natives as erratic and unreliable because we're unwilling to work on what you regard as a normal schedule," he pointed out, "whereas we follow nature's cycles. When the hunting and fishing are in season, we'll give it priority over routine work." He paused, grinned a little and added, "We native people think you're just as peculiar as you think us. You work around the clock all year just to be able to spend a couple of weeks living like we do all the time."

By then Hanne had become my full-time partner. She volunteered her expertise as an interior designer to give Petro-Canada's headquarters in Calgary an ambience that was attractive and distinctive without being ostentatious, as she had done with the UNEP headquarters in Nairobi. And she did the same with our impressive log house that dominated the eight-thousand-hectare ranch that I bought on the outskirts of Calgary, with a beautiful view of the Rocky Mountains. Despite its proximity to Calgary, it was a nature reserve, and we took special pleasure in exploring it on horseback.

Hanne had always had a great interest in and affinity for native peoples. When she was with me in Nairobi our home was always a gathering point for the most interesting people, many of them local Africans and not members of UNEP; it was through Hanne that we developed an especially close friendship with Wangari Maathai, then a university professor, who later headed a grassroots tree-planting organization and became internationally known as a very effective and radical environmental leader. Hanne soon made friends with members of the several native groups in southern Alberta, particularly from the Sarcee Reserve near us. She became a special friend and supporter of Chief Smallboy, who had established himself in the wilderness area in the Rocky Mountain foothills with a small number of followers who wanted to continue their traditional way of life. Our Rocky Mountain ranch home became popular with our native friends, who occasionally intruded into my own tightly planned schedule by arriving without notice.

Hanne has a great heart, a lively, effervescent personality and a forthright, open manner, combined with a deep and sincere interest in those she regards as disadvantaged. The same qualities that enable her to establish relationships of trust and friendship with many people, however, do not automatically endear her to everyone. There were occasions when her candour and her challenges to the conventions of the frontier culture of Alberta did not go over well. Her concern for the underprivileged was manifested in many ways. At Christmas, for example, she would organize a traditional dinner for hundreds of street people and other needy individuals in downtown Calgary.

The combination of Hanne's activities and my environmental interests made us somewhat suspect in the Calgary establishment circles that we inevitably moved in but were not really a part of.

By early 1977, Petro-Canada had become a significant, though still controversial, presence in the industry. Its position was given a substantial boost by the acquisition of the Canadian subsidiary of Atlantic Richfield, which I negotiated with its chief executive, Robert O. Anderson, one of the great men of the industry, over breakfast at the Links Club in New York. It brought to Petro-Canada a going concern with extensive production and land holdings and a highly experienced and competent team of managers. Once they got over the shock of realizing they had been taken over, and by a government corporation at that, most of them remained and formed the core of Petro-Canada's professional and operating capability.

I was satisfied that Bill Hopper was well prepared to succeed me as president and chief executive officer and that he had indeed won the confidence of the board. I therefore relinquished these posts, remaining as an active, though part-time, chairman. About the same time Prime Minister Trudeau appointed me chairman of the International Development Research Centre, which I'd earlier helped to create under Mitchell Sharp. Bill Hopper's elder brother, David, was still there, so I had the rare opportunity of serving as chairman at the same time to two members of one exceptionally talented family.

By the late 1970s, the IDRC had established itself as one of the most effective institutions in the development community, specializing in supporting the growth of scientific and technological capabilities in developing countries. As chairman I had no executive or management functions, my primary responsibility being to chair board meetings and provide the principal link between management and the board. But the position also enabled me to keep in close touch with the international development constituency that was of such importance to me, and when I travelled abroad it was always useful to have the IDRC connection.

The time had come, after several years of engagement in full-time official positions, to return to private life. I needed to rebuild the base in business that was essential to the independence I was determined to retain, the independence that made my international commitments possible. I also had quite a few non-governmental affiliations that I had not been able to attend to very well during my period at Petro-Canada, concentrating as I did on trying to make the corporation a good example of how resource development could be carried out in an environmentally and socially responsible way.

But I didn't want my business interests to let my international environmental activities wither on the vine, so I made sure I had the opportunity to refurbish these relationships, mostly by taking a more active role in some of the many organizations I was affiliated with. These ranged from the International Institute for Environment and Development in London, which I helped to reshape following the Stockholm Conference (I had recruited to its presidency Lady Jackson, better known as Barbara Ward); the World Wildlife Fund International, where I was one of two vice-presidents during the first part of Prince Philip's tenure as president; Resources for the Future; the Rockefeller Foundation; the Rockefeller University; the Aspen Institute for Humanistic Studies; the Dag Hammarskjöld Foundation; the Institute of Ecology of Padjadjaran University in Indonesia; Canada's North-South Institute; the Society for International Development headquartered in Rome; the Canadian Executive Service Organization, which I helped to establish; and the World Economic Forum, also in Geneva. It took a good deal of time and energy to service all these organizations responsibly, of course, but I found that there was considerable synergy between each organization that enabled me to contribute to what I had learned in the others. And I have always made a practice of resigning from organizations when I felt I could no longer make a necessary contribution to them.

I have long struggled with my tendency to take on more responsibilities than I can reasonably handle. When I periodically try to put some aside, I disappoint friends and colleagues, but I believe there are few instances of my failing to live up to my commitments while serving on a board. I try to prepare myself well for every meeting, but this imposes heavy pressures on my time, which I have learned to manage fairly well. Out of necessity I have developed a rhythm in my life that helps me to focus fully on each item, even if only for a short time. I have found that I can do a great deal with my time if I don't try to do everything at once and concentrate on the issue at hand. Thus, while I continue to take on more responsibilities than many think reasonable, I find I can manage them.

As I'd found at Petro-Canada, there was still a high degree of mistrust and even hostility between the environmental movement and industry. I saw my role as a bridge between the two, but I found that it made me suspect in both worlds. In industry I was often seen as a flaky idealist, yet I was criticized by some of the more extreme elements in the environmental movement for my links with industry.

At one environmental meeting I was attacked personally by a representative of Greenpeace, who accused me of selling out the environmental movement through my relationships with business.

I always welcomed such challenges and the opportunity of responding to them, so I said, "You accuse business of being the source of most environmental evils and call for it to change. But how can you expect it to change if at the same time you denounce those people with an environmental commitment and skills who work within business?" Then I asked him pointedly, "Could you tell me how you got here today?" I knew he'd come from another city.

He was surprised at the question and hesitated. "By plane and then by car," he said.

"So you use the products of the very multinational corporations you condemn, and no doubt in your day-by-day life you use quite a few others. So you, like all of us here who live in this society, are caught up in the processes and excesses at the root of its problems. You are trying to change the society from within, and so am I. And those of us who decide to work in or with business are trying to change business from within."

I never tried to hide or fudge my position—quite the contrary. I made a virtue out of necessity by actively seeking opportunities to debate the issue in both the business and environmental communities. My core argument—and something I have come to believe passionately—was that we needed to develop a positive synergy between our economic and environmental needs. It's through our economic life, I argued, that we affect the environment, and it's only through changes in economic behaviour, particularly on the part of corporations, which are the primary actors in the economy, that we can protect and improve the environment. This change in turn opens up new business opportunities and provides a sounder, more durable basis for our economic future. Once you get around short-termism and limited economic horizons, it's possible to see that a protected, nurtured environment is actually good for business. I made the case with all the powers of persuasion I could muster, but it was not an easy sell in either community. There were many controversial projects under way, and the principal focus of public attention remained the many instances of conflict between the two points of view.

It was always going to be a long haul. I knew that.

Just after I left Petro-Canada I was confronted with the need to make a decision on whether I was ever going to enter into national politics. It was certainly not on my agenda at that point.

I had flirted with the idea before. Anyone active in public life goes through this sometime, and I'd been forced to at least think about it a decade earlier, just after Pierre Trudeau had become prime minister. In July 1969 I'd been visited in Ottawa by a delegation from the York West constituency represented by Robert Winters, who had been beaten by Trudeau in the run for Liberal Party leadership and had decided not to seek re-election. They were looking for a new candidate. I wasn't really tempted. I recognized that politics was the route to the highest levels of public service, but my principal interest had always been in policy and in the substance of issues, and I felt no particular attraction to the hurly-burly of the political scene. Also, my interests and aspirations were primarily in the international area.

I did discuss the matter briefly with Trudeau. "You really don't need me now," I said. "If you ever do, I'd be interested. If I was ever to make the move into political life, it would be then."

Apparently he remembered, for when I was approached in the early summer of 1977 by the party's key strategist and "rainmaker" Keith Davey and two other leading Liberals—my old friend Jim Coutts, who was then secretary to Prime Minister Trudeau, and Heather Peterson, vice-chair of the Liberal campaign—to become the Liberal candidate in Scarborough in Metropolitan Toronto, they reminded me of what I had said. The need, they argued, was now. The strong public support for the Liberals that had swept Trudeau into power had waned, and they needed new blood in preparation for the next election.

At first I told them no. I'd decided not to go into politics, I said. "In any event the timing is bad for me. I've just gone back into private life and need time to rebuild my affairs, and I've just taken on some new responsibilities." I had just committed a substantial portion of my resources to a major interest and leadership role in a u.s. company, AZL Resources Inc. I didn't want to relinquish my new-found freedom so rapidly and did not see how I could back away from the new responsibilities I had assumed to my bankers and other investors.

But they pushed the point. If I was ever to demonstrate my support for Trudeau, this was the time to do it. They were persuasive. In any event, they pointed out, the matter would be decided very quickly, as the election was to be held in the fall. If, as I expected, I didn't win, I could go on with my business, having done my duty for the Liberal Party.

In the end I agreed and became one of "three new star candidates," at least in the media's view, the others being John Evans, former president of the University of Toronto, and Doris Anderson, noted journalist and women's rights activist.

I was immediately plunged into a life very different from anything I'd experienced before. This wasn't, I can say frankly, my finest hour. I wasn't a natural politician; my skills are largely in persuasion, argument and synthesis of ideas, not in the highly charged rhetoric of electoral politics at the local level. There was a positive side: I was gratified by the people who rallied to support me in various ways, and I enjoyed the interaction with the public. But I was somewhat overwhelmed by the schedule put together for me by my organizers, all of it necessary to the nitty-gritty business of getting elected: a constant round of speeches to community groups, lurking at strategic street locations and bus stops to greet and meet people, coffee parties and visits to individuals and groups whose support could contribute to my prospects.

I shouldn't have been surprised that the constituents of suburban Scarborough didn't have the same interests or priorities that I did in the areas of the environment and international affairs. They were fine people—professionals, tradespeople, small-business owners, blue-collar workers, many of them at the middle and senior levels of their organizations, and educators. But as former speaker of the u.s. Congress Tip O'Neill once put it, "All politics are local," and my constituents' priorities were parochial, their focus being the direct impact of government policies on them. My speeches on the environment went over like so many lead balloons. They wanted to hear my views on the very local and the very here-and-now. I particularly remember a woman who was adamant that she'd never vote for me unless I could ensure that the snow would be cleared away rapidly from the road in front of her house. When I explained, mildly, I thought, that this was a local and not a federal responsibility, she became abusive.

Things weren't even smooth in my own party. When I was asked to become the Liberal candidate, I was told by the party manager that a prominent member of the local Greek community, John Tsopolis, had already announced his candidature, but that they had arranged for him to withdraw. He hadn't, however, yet done so, and it soon became clear he was holding out for an alternative, a promise of some government appointment or other. The matter had still not been resolved to his satisfaction by the time of the nominating meeting, so he insisted on presenting himself and making a statement. He was somehow lured off the platform, and I found out later he had been escorted out of the hall through the back door by party organizers. This caused me a good deal of consternation and embarrassment and was understandably the subject of much media criticism.

As it happened, the election was postponed when polls indicated some slippage in Liberal support. In one sense that was a relief. But the uncertainty about the election date complicated my life, and I was concerned at having to commit myself to a prolonged campaign. It was turning out to be a difficult period for me. For one thing I was in the midst of formally separating from Pauline, and my bank had made it clear that if I withdrew from AZL Resources, which I had financed with a substantial loan, they'd withdraw their support. I went to Trudeau and told him of my dilemma. He was understanding and graciously offered to relieve me of my obligation to run.

I regretted disappointing him and those who had supported me, but felt it was best to opt out while I still could and while there was still time to nominate another candidate. The media, of course, didn't buy it or any of my given reasons for pulling out. They gave widespread coverage to a civil court action I had been involved in in the United States some time before, suggesting that it had embarrassed me out of politics, despite the awkward fact (for them) that the case had been dismissed with no adverse consequences or implications for me. Later the paranoid right went in quite another direction, assuming I'd dropped out because I'd discovered I could exercise more power as a shadowy, unelected manipulator of public policy at the international level. I wasn't sure whether to be irritated or flattered.

Thus ended my brief political career and one of the most frustrating episodes of my life. Nevertheless, it did enable me to get the political option out of my system and—as always—I learned a great deal from the experience.

In 1978 I purchased a package of properties, mostly small farms with some seven kilometres of beachfront, scattered along the southern

Caribbean coast of Costa Rica from Cahuita to near the Panama border. The purchase came about as a result of a visit I'd made to Costa Rica the previous year on the invitation of the president, Daniel Oduber, who'd invited me to lecture on "The Role of Small Countries in the World." Oduber was rightly proud of his country's commitment to conservation and of the new national parks they'd created. At his urging I visited the parks, and I fell in love with the natural and unspoiled beauty of the coast.

The president told me some of the land was at risk from poor development. It had been purchased by an American doctor who had fallen into financial difficulties and needed to sell. It was beautiful land, then totally undeveloped, with access only by sea or trail. The national parks authorities were eager that it be purchased by someone who would care for it responsibly.

"What can I do to help?" I asked.

Well, I was so impressed that I bought it on impulse. Thus began a long association with Costa Rica, which has become one of my favourite places and still figures prominently in my life.

I was now paying more attention to rebuilding my private business interests and non-governmental activities—I knew that with my private affairs in good order, I could more easily take up opportunities for public service in the international field when and if they arose.

My main vehicle was a company called Stronat Investments, which I had formed together with Paul Nathanson, who had inherited the fortune his father had made as a pioneer in the movie distribution business and had built it into control of a number of companies including Famous Players and Odeon Theatres in Canada and major interests in the United States, mostly in the film and entertainment business. He had been introduced to me by Paul Martin and had become one of my best friends. He was a true eccentric and a financial genius who combined one of the most original and fertile intellects I have known with astute judgment and a shy, retiring nature that kept him at a distance even from his friends and those who ran the companies he controlled. One of the more interesting, and productive, things we did was to join with the financier Andy Sarlos, a uniquely creative person and another financial genius, to make a bid for Abitibi-Price, one of the country's largest pulp and paper producers. The management, which was closely tied to the Toronto establishment, successfully resisted our overtures, but we did well financially. Paul Nathanson and I had earlier joined in acquiring control of one of Toronto's largest real estate developers, Yolles and Rotenberg; now we sold it and formed a new company, Rostland, led by Kenneth Rotenberg, who had run Yolles and Rotenberg so successfully. It undertook a number of major real estate projects in Canada and the U.S., including development of the Sun Life headquarters in Toronto and the redevelopment of the Arizona Biltmore Hotel in Phoenix, one of the world's great hotels, originally designed by Frank Lloyd Wright.

The U.S. subsidiary of Rostland, AZL Resources Inc., was based in Phoenix. For the next while, therefore, I moved the primary locus of my business life to Arizona. I never intended to live or put down roots there, however: the physical setting was attractive and life was pleasant, but it had no emotional appeal to me.

AZL Resources owned some 1 million hectares of ranchland in the southwest U.S., and it was while touring these properties that I came to the San Luis Valley in Colorado to see the company's Baca Grant Ranch. Hanne and I felt an instant affinity with the place. The San Luis Valley is one of the largest mountain valleys in the world. The floor of the valley, at an altitude of some two thousand metres, is flat and arid and surrounded by mountains, some of them towering a further two thousand metres overhead. Baca Grant was one of the historic ranches of Colorado, dating from a grant by the King of Spain to Maria Luisa Cabeza Vaca (later anglicized to Baca), who had accompanied the Spanish explorer Coronado on his expeditions to what was then Spanish America. The ranch dominated the northwest end of the valley, including the peak of the highest mountain, Mount Kit Carson, and a corner of the sand dunes, an extraordinarily picturesque piece of desert nestled at the base of the mountains, which had been made into a national park. During the gold rush days of the 1800s, the area had seen one of Colorado's most active and controversial mining booms. The village of Crestone, which now has fewer than a hundred inhabitants, was a thriving and boisterous mining town, and the Baca Grant Ranch adjoining it attracted a small army of prospectors panning for gold in the streams and digging along the front of the mountains. One particularly rich lode became the Independence Mine, for a time one of Colorado's most prolific producers.

The place had a colourful and sometimes violent history. At one point the ranch's owners claimed all the mineral rights, and a nasty conflict arose when they tried to expel the miners as squatters. Eventually the u.s. Supreme Court upheld their title, and with the help of marshals brought in from Denver they forcibly ejected the miners from the land. It is said that seventeen marshals were shot in the process, which left a permanent residue of bitterness and resentment toward the ranch owners—permanent enough, we found, that we inherited some of it. Some of the evicted miners established a new town just outside the boundary of the ranch, which they defiantly called Liberty.

I purchased the site of Liberty (which had become a ghost town) for Hanne and brought it for the first time under common ownership with the Baca Grant, but that didn't help. When we moved into the old ranch house, we were seen as just the latest heirs to privilege and therefore inevitably in conflict with the community. Relations hadn't been helped by the earlier actions of the company, which had attempted to develop a large piece of land at the base of the mountains carved out of the ranch, a project that had proven a gross economic failure and a threat to the ecology of the area. As soon as I could, I put a stop to the development and returned most of the undeveloped land to the ranch. And we tried to give the development area a theme and character more in keeping with the rare natural beauty and tranquility of the area, seeking to make it an attractive venue for spiritual, cultural and ecological activities.

I saw AZL as a vehicle for demonstrating in practical terms my commitment to sustainable development, as well as for extending the business into the international arena.

AZL Resources had made a modest entry into the minerals and oil and gas field by separating the mineral and petroleum rights from its ranch properties. But it seemed to me the best prospects for building an important position in the oil and gas business were international, particularly in the developing world. Many of the countries badly in need of economic development also had major potential. Around this concept we formed a new company, International Energy Development Corporation, and put together an exceptionally competent and experienced management team headed by one of the ablest oil executives I know, Nordine Ait-Laoussine of Algeria, who had been chief operating officer of their national oil company, Sonatrach.

Under Nordine we assembled a small but experienced professional team that included Keith Huff, former international exploration manager for Exxon, and Frank Parra, whose extensive experience in the industry had included a period as secretary-general of OPEC. For a time we were joined by Alastair Morton, who had been the head of the United Kingdom's national oil company and went on to chair the Channel Tunnel Company. We also put together an impressive group of international investors who bought into our vision, including the Swedish automobile company Volvo, a Canadian independent, Sulpetro, the Kuwait Petroleum Corporation, Kuwait's national oil company, and the Arab Petroleum Investment Corporation, established by the Arab governments as a vehicle for investment in the industry. We located our corporate headquarters in London and our operating base in Geneva, and I moved to London to oversee the corporation as its chairman.

We found that developing countries welcomed the prospect of partnering with us. It helped that they knew and had confidence in Nordine and some other members of our management team, as well as some of our main shareholders. It also gave them relief from over-dependence on the majors. Accordingly, we assembled a portfolio of promising projects, in Oman, Sudan, Angola, Ghana and also a major position in Australia. Some of these required substantial investments, and to keep up with the need to provide its share of the capital was well beyond the means of AZL Resources. We therefore accepted an offer of merger from Tosco Corporation, the largest independent refiner in the United States, which was seeking to develop its own sources of international oil supply.

Coincident with this, with the help of my experienced and

resourceful vice-president of finance, Bill Holt, I rearranged the interest of my private holding company, Strovest, in AZL by exchanging our AZL position for control of a Swiss company, the Société Générale pour l'Énergie et Ressources (SOGENER), through another Swiss company that we had acquired, Crédit Immobilier.

The marriage with Tosco was short-lived. The collapse of oil prices and some untimely investments by Tosco precipitated a major crisis; the company's bankers effectively took control of the company, forcing the exit of its visionary and creative CEO, Morton Winston, and the sale of assets not directly related to its core refining business. This included most of the AZL assets.

It had been a condition of our deal that my group exchange their AZL shares for shares of Tosco, making us one of the largest shareholders of that company, and that I play an active role in its management. Now the value of our Tosco shares was virtually extinguished, and this was reflected in a massive reduction in the share values of both Crédit Immobilier and SOGENER. It came as a major financial blow to me, wiping out most of the capital value I had built up over the past several years. But I took some satisfaction in the fact that the public shareholders of AZL Resources had all received cash for their shares in the Tosco transaction, and at a price more than three times their market value, when we had come into the company. The crisis also meant the effective end of the partnership that had created International Energy Development Corporation. The other partners, in varying degrees, with the exception of the Kuwaitis, were also hard hit or discouraged by the severe downturn in the oil business. As a result they accepted an offer by Kuwait Petroleum Corporation to take over the company and use it as a principal vehicle for its own international operations. This brought to an end one of the most interesting episodes in my own career in the oil and gas business. Paradoxically, some of the properties we had assembled turned out to be real winners, and we would have done very well had we been able to maintain our interest in them.

All through this period I'd kept in touch with events in Canada. Among other things, I'd been following the fate of the Canada

Development Corporation, which I'd helped create. The CDC had always been, I thought, an interesting hybrid—created and controlled by the government while given the mandate to operate as a private sector corporation. But now I became aware that my friends in the Trudeau government had become increasingly estranged from Tony Hampson, CDC's chief executive officer. I'd been the one who originally introduced Hampson to the CDC—I'd recruited him to work with me at Power and then saw him move to the CDC after it was formally set up by Walter Gordon.

In the summer of 1981, while on a visit to Tokyo, I had a call from Allan MacEachen, then minister of finance and deputy prime minister, asking me if I'd be willing to take on the role of chairman of CDC at the forthcoming annual meeting. It seemed an appropriate role in light of my original involvement, and I agreed. Unfortunately, and to my surprise and embarrassment, the government had not done its homework and had failed to make its intentions known to the board and management of CDC. Despite the presence of no fewer than three deputy ministers on the board, they had claimed that they had no idea what the government was intending and had gone ahead and appointed one of their members to the chairmanship. So when I showed up for the annual meeting in Winnipeg, I found myself in the middle of a major brouhaha, with Tony Hampson leading the charge against me.

The prime minister, determined to prevail, arranged to have the government's proxies, representing control of the corporation, made out in my name and encouraged me to vote the entire board out if necessary. I felt this would be counterproductive and instead worked out a compromise in which I became vice-chairman.

This sorry incident prompted the government to re-examine its holdings of other Crown (state-owned) corporations of a commercial nature. As a result, in 1982 it established the Canada Development Investment Corporation (CDIC), to which it transferred controlling interest in CDC as well as several other government-owned corporations. I consulted closely in this process with Michael Pitfield, Clerk of the Privy Council, and was subsequently asked to take the lead in setting up the company as its chairman and in putting together the board and management. At my suggestion it established its corporate headquarters in Vancouver, where I moved from London in January 1982. Trudeau was good enough to ask me to suggest what minister I would like it to report to, and I was pleased when he acted on my suggestion that my long-standing friend Jack Austin, by then a senator, be the minister responsible. We recruited Joel Bell from Petro-Canada to be the president and CEO. Having now direct responsibility for the controlling interest in CDC, I became active in its affairs. Also included in the CDIC portfolio were De Havilland Aircraft, Canadair, Telesat, which had a monopoly on international telecommunications from Canada, and El Dorado Uranium. We quickly initiated a series of measures designed to inculcate in these companies a commercial culture and system of accountability that would prepare them for eventual privatization.

CDIC by its nature and structure offended conservative sensibilities, and it was the target of strong criticism from the Conservative opposition in Parliament, which threatened to dismantle the company if it got to power. I persuaded Prime Minister Trudeau to allow us to appoint as vice-chairman a prominent Montreal business leader, Bernard Lamarre, who I felt would have the confidence of the Conservatives. This proved prudent. When the Tories under Brian Mulroney swept the Liberals out of office in 1984, Sinclair Stevens, who had led the charge against CDIC in opposition, became the minister responsible and summarily fired Joel Bell as its CEO.

I'd taken pre-emptive action. Immediately following Mulroney's election I had called him to say I'd resign. One of the most important roles of the chairman of a Crown corporation, I told the new prime minister, was to act as the link with the government as principal shareholder. He should, I insisted, be in a position to appoint to the position someone who had good access to and the confidence of his government. I slipped in the suggestion that Lamarre would be a logical successor, as he was already in place and knew the company well. I was pleased when Mulroney decided to appoint him, and we parted on congenial terms. Later, I was even more pleased to hear back from a mutual friend that Mulroney had called the way I handled the matter a "class act." Lamarre's presence enabled the government to decide soon that CDIC was, after all, a useful vehicle for managing and privatizing government investments of a commercial nature. Accordingly, they kept the corporation and used it for this purpose.

After our marriage in February 1981, Hanne and I continued to make Baca our main and favourite home. When Tosco had been forced by its banks to sell off its non-refining interest, I put together a group to bid on the Baca Grant Ranch, and our bid succeeded. The first person I invited to join me was David Williams, whom I had first met in Calgary when I was a young upstart competitor to a company he controlled in Alberta. To the chagrin of his partners he had made peace with me, and out of this we developed one of the most enjoyable and durable friendships of my career. He was wise, experienced and visionary, and we shared many common interests. I made a habit of consulting him and comparing notes on our various plans and activities. I found that he already knew a great deal about the Baca Grant Ranch and the immense groundwater reservoir that underlies it. And he was actively pursuing a number of water development prospects in the western United States designed to help meet the growing water needs of the West. Then, at lunch one day in Vancouver, Sam Belzberg—I had known him since my early days in Alberta, and he had since become a well-known financier and entrepreneur—asked me what I was doing. I told him about our Baca project, and he immediately offered to provide the financing. I had never before done business with Sam, and I told him that I intended to put together a group of equal partners with none in a dominant position. I said I would be pleased to have him as one of them, and he agreed. I then discussed the matter with my friend Jim Wolfensohn, who had only recently set up his own investment advisory firm. He explained that he had all his capital tied up in it at that point but introduced me to two friends of his who had previously worked for him and had set up their own private investment company, RRY Partners. They agreed to come into a partnership they formed for this purpose, Natural Resource Partners LP, bringing with them a bright young associate, Alex Crutchfield, who became a prime mover in the project. We formed a new company, First Colorado

Corporation, to acquire the ranch, and a subsidiary, American Water Development, to develop its water potential.

From my previous association with the ranch through AZL Resources I had concluded that if we wanted to protect our water rights, we would have to develop them or they could be claimed by others. Water is a major issue in the U.S. Southwest, and the laws governing its ownership, development and use are unique products of scarcity of water and early struggles over water rights. In some fundamental respects they no longer make sense, but they're so deeply entrenched that any move to revise them inevitably arouses strong resistance that is more emotional than logical. One basic principle that actively encourages waste and inefficient use of water is the "use it or lose it" one, which means that the owner of water rights will lose them to the extent that the rights are not put to constructive use. However rational this may have been in the early days of agricultural development, it clearly makes no sense in an era of water shortages and environmental vulnerability.

My interest in the water went beyond it being just a good business. I saw development of the water as an exceptional opportunity to apply my sustainable-development principles on a real-life scale, before we came into control of the ranch.

After a hotly contested battle the U.S. government had won the right to take groundwater from the substantial aquifer underlying the valley. They had "condemned" 38,000 acres of the Baca Grant Ranch and were draining its water into a canal constructed along its boundary. Their primary purpose was to help fulfil a deficit in Colorado's long-standing obligation to supply water to California and Mexico through the Colorado River system. The water development also had a significant economic potential that would enable us to maintain and protect the remainder of the ranch, as ranches in themselves were a losing proposition. By the time we arrived in 1983, this Closed Basin Project was well advanced. Others were already moving to stake their claims to "our" water under the use-it-or-lose-it rule. Our lawyers suggested that we had a good basis for claiming an exemption from the Colorado Water Law, since our rights were included in the original Spanish grant, before the state came into existence. But we knew it would be unwise to rely on this opinion; we had no real option but to develop our rights.

Our initial proposals were based on local use of the water for a variety of purposes—irrigation, a brewery, greenhouses and so on. The application immediately drew the hostility and active opposition of most of the people in the valley. There was wild speculation that I intended to export the water to Canada. A cartoon in the *Alamosa Courier* showed a caricature of me with a big maple leaf on my chest and a straw in my mouth sucking up the water from the valley. That I was not only an outsider but a foreigner compounded the suspicions of the local people and fuelled the rumour mill. I made determined attempts to enlist the participation of the local community—visiting influential leaders, holding and attending public meetings. People were surprised when, on a visit to the valley, Governor Roy Rohmer, who was a friend, singled me out for recognition at a public meeting in his honour, but I had cautioned him against compromising his political position in the valley by endorsing the project. I had hoped, somewhat naively as it turned out, that by working with the local community we could make it a model of sustainable development that would produce important benefits to the valley. My persuasions fell largely on deaf ears. Even those who were sympathetic to my proposals—and they were quite a few—were coerced into silence.

To a degree the community suspicions were not ill-founded. There was a growing estrangement between me and my partners in the venture, except for David Williams, whose staunch support and sound judgment were immensely helpful to me until the exigencies of his own financial affairs required him to sell his interest. Initially, my partners had all given at least passive support to my plans for the project, which I had insisted from inception had to be an example of environmental and socially responsible development. But it soon became evident that their real interest was in maximizing the financial benefits—the potential profits, after all, were very substantial. This meant moving the water out of the valley into the more profitable markets of the front range area of Colorado or south to California.

The estrangement deepened when I followed through on a promise I'd made at the beginning—that any profits I made from the project would be put to public purposes. I donated my interest to the
Fetzer Foundation, whose objectives were in keeping with the goals
and values that Hanne and I were committed to. The foundation,
headquartered in Kalamazoo, Michigan, had been set up and was
still run with an iron hand by John Fetzer, a highly successful media
entrepreneur who combined an egocentric view of the universe and
a tough, domineering manner with a deep interest in spiritual issues.
On his visit to Baca he had spoken enthusiastically about making
Baca a major pillar of his foundation and supporting the development there of the kind of spiritual and ecological community that
Hanne and I were striving for. We thought our common goals
would be advanced by contributing our interest in the companies
that owned the Baca properties to the foundation, which had much
greater capacity to ensure their realization. As a member of the
board and chairman of the investment committee of the foundation, I continued to represent it on the board of American Water
Development. But my partners were unhappy about this, worrying
that it would strengthen the prospect of injecting my soft environmental and spiritual ideas into the development. Additionally, one
of them was a fundamentalist Christian who strongly disapproved of
the support we had been giving to non-Christian religious groups.
They increasingly asserted their control of the company, particularly
after Williams departed, moving it more and more in a direction
that I felt was not only incompatible with my goals and values but
was also not likely to succeed.

I began to feel that the ultimate failure of the project was not
only inevitable but desirable.

When I saw the way things were going, I recommended to Fetzer
that the foundation sell its interest. The board took my advice,
and realized $2.5 million for the foundation. I promptly resigned from
the company and severed all ties with it. I wrote a letter to the local
newspaper advising them of this and explaining that the reason was
that I was no longer in a position to ensure that the project would be
developed in accordance with my original assurances to the people

of the valley. However, the antagonism and distrust had grown so much that many saw this as a ruse and a tactic, and continued to consider me the sinister power behind the scenes.

Ultimately, the Water Court, a special feature of the legal system in Colorado and some other southwestern states set up to adjudicate water disputes, rejected the company's application to export water from the ranch and assessed costs against the company. The Appeals Court upheld the decision, and the company had to be liquidated at a loss, which I believe was close to $20 million, to the remaining partners. Although I was pleased to have withdrawn from the company well before this, I was sorry that my former partners had taken such an ill-conceived path to a costly failure.

The African Famine

I N 1984 the rains failed in the Sahel. Again.

Dry years were nothing new, not on the arid southern frontier of the Sahara. The rains had been failing on and off for centuries, for millennia, as far as anyone knew. Once the Sahara itself had been verdant and lush, home of hippos and pink flamingos, but long ago the swamps had begun to dry up, and the sands of the Great Erg pushed relentlessly southward.

The hardy rural people of the Sahel—the Sudan, southern Ethiopia and Chad—had long ago learned to cope. There had never been much help from outside, not under the old Malian or Kanem Bornu empires, or under colonialism, or in the brief period since independence. The people had been forced to learn the brutal truths of self-sufficiency in an arid land: they would live and die by their own efforts. Sometimes the droughts were accompanied by famines, and whole communities perished. But some survived, and over the centuries they had learned to cling to their existence by maintaining their own stores of grain and carefully husbanding their seeds and precious water supplies.

So they could survive if the rains failed. They could survive even if the rains didn't come the following year either. But when the rains failed in 1984 it was after sixteen straight years of meagre rainfall. It was too much.

First the stored grain disappeared. Then the livestock, the people's most precious possessions, died or had to be killed or sold. The people sold their few remaining tools for food. Then they resorted to eating the precious seed grain. When that was gone and the wells were reduced to puddles, they had no choice but to abandon their homes to look for help.

Thousands and thousands of desperate families trudged along the dusty roads of the Sahel, starving and suffering people making their way to urban centres and makeshift relief camps.

At first hardly anyone outside the Sahel noticed. Most of those affected were rural peasants and villagers remote from the main urban areas, and their plight received little global attention. It wasn't until BBC television cameras alerted the world to the dimensions of the great human tragedy unfolding that the world began to pay attention. They focused attention initially on Ethiopia, where conditions were particularly acute, and virtually overnight the tragic human drama that the world had largely ignored up till then became prime-time news everywhere. A remarkable demonstration of the positive power of television. Many thousands of people had already perished along the refugee routes, and the cameras showed the grim evidence—pathetic piles of bones picked over by vultures. Those who survived told poignant stories of aged parents and, in some cases, children they'd been forced to leave behind or who had died on the terrible journey. The human agony brought into the homes of millions of people by television stirred hearts and consciences throughout the world and gave rise to an outpouring of compassion and generosity, accompanied by an upwelling of public pressure on governments and international organizations to take urgent action.

It soon became apparent that the crisis was much greater than in Ethiopia alone. Much of sub-Saharan Africa was similarly afflicted. The United Nations estimated that some 200 million people in twenty African countries were severely affected by the drought and related famine conditions. The survival of 30 million was at imminent risk.

It was against this background that in early January 1984 I got a phone call from Bradford Morse, administrator of the United Nations Development Program. The UN secretary-general had just put him in charge of setting up a special Office for Emergency

Operations in Africa to galvanize and lead a concerted UN effort to mobilize relief for victims of the famine engulfing so much of sub-Saharan Africa. He couldn't entirely set aside his responsibilities at UNDP and required assistance.

"Will you join me, Maurice? I need your help. It's urgent. It must be done at once."

I said I'd call him back.

If I was to go, I'd have to go immediately. How could I? I had business responsibilities, businesses to run that depended on me. The portfolio of interests we had assembled through our private company, Stronat Investments, needed active attention. While we had competent people running most of them, some were at a critical point, and I felt it would be risky to leave them. But in truth, how could I not? That night I put my personal affairs and the global crisis in the balance, and when I reflected on the awesome human dimensions of the challenge and my long-standing affinity with Africa, I knew I'd have to try. In the morning I telephoned Brad and told him I'd do it, and the same day I was on my way to New York.

Later that evening at UN headquarters I joined Brad and the small team he had already begun to assemble under an experienced UN official, Charles La Munière. They were huddled in an intense discussion of how best to proceed. I was immediately caught up in their sense of urgency—we all realized that the lives and the hopes of many thousands of people in Africa depended on our ability to respond rapidly to their needs. We couldn't afford to talk very long. We had to act.

What a tangled problem it was! There were already dozens of separate relief efforts under way. The United Nations Disaster Relief Organization (UNDRO) simply did not have the capacity to rise to a challenge of these dimensions. The UN High Commissioner for Refugees, the World Food Program and Unicef were already on the front lines of the relief effort, as were OXFAM, the Red Cross, Save the Children, CARE and many other private agencies. Ethiopia had its own relief organization, which was well led and quite effective, and similar organizations existed in most of the affected countries, though most of them had limited capabilities and were not geared to cope with crises like this. Relief supplies on the ground in most places had been exhausted, available finances used up and the capacities of the organizations in the field stretched to the limit by the time the world community awakened to the unfolding tragedy. At that point the challenge took on a new dimension, as people from all parts of the world responded generously to Africa's plight. The problem became one of matching the responses from thousands of different groups, organizations and places to the needs of Africans in as many thousands of locations, some of them in remote areas not accessible to rail or road traffic. Relief supplies came in many forms, many of them in kind, without the finances required to transport and deliver them, and some were not well suited to meet priority needs. In many cases too many of the same kinds of supplies were being sent to some destinations, and little or none to others. As a flood tide of relief supplies moved toward Africa, ports were congested, trucks and aircraft in short supply, railroad tracks and bridges in disrepair and roads in many cases virtually impassable.

It was already clear that only the UN could respond to the formidable challenge of co-ordinating the flow of relief supplies, ensuring that they matched actual needs on the ground and managing the planning of logistics for receiving, transporting and distributing them.

On January 11, 1985, I became executive co-ordinator of the Office for Emergency Operations in Africa (OEOA), which Brad Morse had set up a month earlier. It was designed to be an exceptional, ad hoc operation, to mobilize and deploy the resources and capacities of the entire UN system and to provide overall leadership and co-ordination of the international relief effort.

Alas, UN turf rivalries intruded even here. Paradoxically, the one organization that proved least co-operative and useful was the organization set up to deal with such emergencies, UNDRO, which had been overwhelmed by the immensity of the problems and angrily resented being bypassed by the creation of OEOA.

In New York the "high command" was composed of the heads of the principal UN organizations and agencies. We set up a two-part administration system for staff. There was a small cadre of dedicated officials in New York, never many more than twenty at the headquarters level, who were responsible for co-ordinating with governments and non-governmental agencies, for identifying and anticipating needs, for mobilizing resources and for planning deployment and distribution, as well as for identifying and dealing with bottlenecks and special problems. They worked around the clock, ensuring that the people in the field received the support and the supplies they required and the means of getting them to those in need.

In the field we used the established network of UN field offices, with a resident co-ordinator in each country. Most of these people performed heroically.

We were especially fortunate in the fact that the secretary-general's special representative in Ethiopia, Kurt Jansson, was already there and had rapidly established himself as the leader of the relief operations. He had been appointed by the secretary-general before our body was even constituted, and because he was a person of exceptional ability and courage, he'd rapidly won the respect of the Ethiopian government and the proliferating number of people from other governmental and non-governmental organizations, many of whom were not always responsive, to put it mildly, to UN leadership and co-ordination. At first Kurt was sceptical of our intervention and even our existence; he was worried we were just more bureaucrats to get in his way. But we soon forged an effective partnership, and he came to see us as his principal ally in obtaining the support he needed to do his job on the ground. With our help he was able to override and cut through bureaucratic constraints, both from headquarters and from Ethiopian officials.

This was not always so easy. Ethiopia was at the time suffering not only from famine but from war. The country's government, while quite effective in many respects, was a military dictatorship headed by the ruthless and tough-minded president, Haile Maryam Mengistu. Relief operations were severely complicated by the conflict with Eritrea, which was fighting for independence from Ethiopia, and the province of Tigray, which was fighting for a higher degree of autonomy. For Mengistu and his Derg government, military operations took precedence over humanitarian and relief needs, and we suspected many relief supplies were missing, diverted to the military.

Kurt Jansson asked for my help in dealing with the problem, which was severely compromising our relief efforts. With a personal appeal to President Mengistu, I was able to obtain his agreement to most of our requests. The trade-off was my commitment to deliver more than a thousand trucks, which would be turned over to the Ethiopians after their use in relief operations. I found Mengistu to be well informed, incisive and coolly civil in his manner. He made it clear to me that he felt he was misunderstood and not sufficiently appreciated by the West, particularly the United States, and would welcome better relations with the U.S. and other Western countries. This was no doubt an important motivation in his agreeing to our request, but at least it enabled us to keep the relief supplies moving.

In Sudan, the situation was in some ways even grimmer, partly because the government had at first denied that the famine situation was serious and insisted that they were able to deal with it. The efforts of the UN and other donor agencies to mount major relief activities were neither encouraged nor facilitated. As a consequence the UN had not appointed a special representative there.

On the other hand the government of Sudan had been willing to accept the flow of over a million refugees from Ethiopia and to co-operate in the establishment of several camps to accommodate them. This denial at home and acceptance of foreigners inevitably led to tensions between the refugees, who were receiving international assistance, and local residents, who were themselves suffering from famine. Eventually the Sudanese government acknowledged that it did indeed have a severe famine to contend with and, with some reluctance and hesitation, began to be more open to international assistance. To complicate matters the government was not well organized to deal with the situation and frequently frustrated rather than facilitated the international efforts. When I arrived for my first visit, the relief effort was in a state of disarray. Some organizations were doing effective work, but there was little co-ordination, and prospects of being able to mount the kind of large-scale relief that clearly was required were not promising. Fortunately, I was immensely helped and guided by a wise and experienced former foreign secretary of Sudan who knew his country well, Francis Deng.

I arrived, in fact, to encounter a mounting crisis. The water supply had failed at one of the refugee camps—a large one, holding some eighty thousand desperate people—but neither the provincial nor the central government had allowed the refugees to be moved. Under those conditions the people couldn't be expected to survive more than a few days. I flew out to the area and persuaded the provincial governor to give his permission to make a new site available. Returning immediately to Khartoum, I met with President Gaafar Mohammed al-Nemery. He was a tough man, an army colonel who had taken over in a coup, and who ruled Sudan for sixteen years with an iron hand. Flexibility wasn't in his vocabulary.

At first he was recalcitrant. The main problem was the unwillingness of the provincial governor to agree, he said.

"But I have the consent of the governor," I said.

He shifted ground. His government was encountering strong resistance among their own people to establishing new campsites. "I just can't afford to make a new location available."

"The result," I said, "will be a major human tragedy," and then I backed into the threat, "a tragedy that will receive world-wide attention. But if you are the instrument for averting the tragedy, I'll make sure you receive full credit for it."

He caught the implication quickly enough. If he didn't agree, the blame for the tragedy would be levelled at him, and along with it, international condemnation. After some haggling, therefore, he agreed to the new camp.

But I knew it wouldn't be enough to carry away verbal assurances. My word wouldn't cut me any slack with his officials after I left him, and I needed urgent and prompt attention and action. I therefore pressed Nemery to put the agreement in writing. He was nonplussed —dictators are not used to being issued conditions, especially in their own offices. But after some hesitation he called in his secretary, and I waited while the document was completed and signed.

My UN colleague was very nervous. To my surprise I found that he had never had a direct conversation with the president before, having seen him only on ceremonial occasions. While the drafting was under way and Nemery was consulting his officials, he kept nudging me. "You can't speak to the president like that!" He was very much surprised and visibly relieved when we were able to take a congenial leave of the president and walk out with his signed order.

It worked, too. The order galvanized the government, and we were able to proceed immediately with making the new campsite ready and arranging to move the endangered refugees to it.

A few weeks later I was with one of our convoys as it moved slowly along a dusty road in western Sudan. We were heading for another temporary refugee camp, yet another of the many we had heard were severely overtaxed, supplies dangerously low. The plain was treeless, parched, and it was hard to see much through the cloud of fine rust-red dust churned up as we ground through the desert. The heat beat down relentlessly, searing, scorching, reflecting off the dust and the metal of the trucks, prickling the skin like a thousand needles. The camp was still some way off, and I wasn't expecting to see anyone out there in that searing hell, so it wasn't until we had almost gone by that I noticed two or three hundred people sitting in little clusters in the dust by the side of the road. There was nothing else there, no village, no huts, no trees, no shelter, no water, just the people. It couldn't by any stretch be called a "camp." And, indeed, the Sudanese officials with whom we were travelling protested that we shouldn't stop because they were merely people, not an official "relief centre."

But clearly, relief centre or no, the people were in desperate need of help. They were mainly women, the elderly and children, with a few scattered possessions on the ground next to them, pathetic bundles and scraps of clothing. There was no sign of food or water.

I overrode the protestations of the officials, insisted that we stop and commandeered a truck loaded with bags of meal, ordering the men to drop off a bag for each cluster of people.

Our vehicle had stopped close to a woman with two small children. She sat on the ground, watching us with a transparent mixture of hope and anxiety. Emaciated as she was, she was beautiful and dignified. She was watching us, only partially shielded from the burning sun by a tattered scrap of cloth held up by two sticks.

The men finished their work and clambered back into the truck. As it began to pull away, I saw that somehow the woman had been missed. Perhaps her little family group had been too insignificant to be noticed. I saw the silent anguish on her face as she watched the truck drive away, but she made no protest. She stared after the retreating vehicle, her anguish succeeded first by despair, then by resignation.

I could not leave that way; for her and her children it would clearly be a matter of life or death. I had our driver catch up to the truck and make it return. After it had dropped a bag of meal at her feet, she told us through an interpreter that her husband and two other children had died along the route. She and the two babies had had nothing to eat for several days, many days, how many she couldn't remember, there were too many to remember. . . . She told her story carefully, slowly, as though it were a legend to repeat to the children, then she rose to her feet and with tears in her eyes pressed into my hand a small object carefully wrapped in a piece of paper. It proved to be an egg, smaller than a hen's egg, which she had been saving for her children. She wanted me to have it.

I have never been so moved or so confused. What could I possibly do? It was unthinkable, utterly unthinkable, to take the gift. But it was also unthinkable to affront her by refusing it—her dignity was the one thing the world had not been able to strip from her, and to refuse would have been an act of gratuitous cruelty.

In the end I took the egg, and through much tactful diplomacy on the part of my Sudanese colleagues was able to give it back to her—for her children, as I made sure they told her. It would be a special treat for them before I left.

As the convoy drove away, I looked back. Her head was bowed slightly, staring down at the bag of meal. There was no sign of the small paper parcel. She had secreted it away.

Whenever anyone asks me the "why" of my long life of public service, whenever anyone asks why I continue my optimism in the face of what seems like gathering anarchy and imminent ecological catastrophe, whenever anyone questions the utility of foreign aid or the politics of relief, whenever anyone, someone who should know better, demands in a fit of post-modern Western anomie why they should bother to "fix the unfixable," the woman in the western Sudan desert comes to mind, a woman who miraculously preserved the human gift of generosity in the face of unspeakable privation. That precious egg, wrapped so carefully in its torn scrap of paper, has become for me a metaphor for the largeness of the human spirit. In the face of that memory, pessimism becomes an act of betrayal.

The media coverage in the Western world of the famine was extensive, and public interest was therefore high. But nothing grabbed attention more than the initiative of the British rock star Bob Geldof and his makeshift Band-Aid organization. Through concerts and relentless exhortations, Geldof and others raised awareness of Africa's needs—and raised a significant amount of support in cash and in kind. Geldof also inspired a parallel effort in the United States in which a number of pop stars—including Harry Belafonte and Michael Jackson—joined in a concert that produced a best-selling record, *We Are the World*. It raised a total of some $100 million, which was dispensed through a charity set up especially for this purpose, USA for Africa.

In the total scheme of things, the practical support that the stars produced for the victims of the African famine was relatively modest—much more modest, in point of fact, than the visibility and credit they received would indicate. Still, they were important —they ignited and sustained public engagement. And the experience made me realize what a precious and invaluable gift is their ability to engage mass attention and influence public attitudes and behaviour.

Because of my role with the UN I became very close to the USA for Africa organization and later served on its board. This was something of an experience. Individually—to put it delicately—the stars of the entertainment world are often more to be enjoyed at a distance than admired at close range. On a board of directors it was worse. The clash of rampant egos made for stormy and chaotic relationships. Dealing with them was a task that few could undertake and even fewer carry out successfully. This impossible job fell to two people who were themselves exceptional personalities: Ken Kragen, the Hollywood agent who put the group together and then kept it focused, and the canny, innovative social activist Marty Rogol, a veteran of the Ralph Nader campaigns. Rogol ran the disbursements and put together a small but highly effective organization designed to ensure that the funds raised were used in the most efficient way. The group co-operated closely with our UN office in doing so, without in any way abrogating the independence or identity of USA for Africa. I developed a high regard for Marty Rogol, which has led to an enduring personal and professional relationship.

During the summer of 1985, relief supplies seemed to be flowing adequately, but even with the help of the pop stars, public interest eventually waned, and news of the famine dropped from prime time. Closer to the catastrophe than the media, we understood it was not over. There was yet another crop failure in northern and western Sudan, and we knew a recurrence of acute famine conditions could be expected within months. It was coming, and to deal with it we had to make a special effort to mobilize funds and supplies in advance. But how? We badly needed somehow to stimulate public interest again.

I turned to an old friend, Bill Moyers, one of the ablest communicators I knew, and one of the finest people in the communications business. He had done an interview with me in the early days of UNEP, which had received high ratings, and he had used the occasion to bring his wife, the administrator in the family and now his manager, and two young children with him. I know he had thoroughly enjoyed the experience and it had been a success for him professionally, too. We took them on safari, and this shared experience enabled us to get to know and appreciate them. I proposed to Bill that he bring a crew to the Sudan and follow me around for a week. I promised that we could expose him to some dramatic human-interest stories that would surely be worthy of coverage. I knew him well enough to be sure that his own instincts and values would impel him to give the proposal a sympathetic hearing, which he did. But he was also an experienced professional. He'd have to sell it to the brass at CBS, he explained. If he could get the interest and support of his superiors, he'd do it.

I was delighted when he reported that he had the green light, and we took off for Sudan together.

For ten harrowing days we travelled through the Sudanese countryside. It was painfully evident to all of us—very much including Bill Moyers and his crew—that people struggling to recover from the effects of the previous drought would be devastated by its imminent recurrence. The dispatches that resulted were television at its best. So powerful was the reportage that CBS News used Bill's pieces from the Sudan in prime time on five successive nights, something of a record, and he later received an Emmy for his work.

Even better than an Emmy, though—and I know Bill agrees—was seeing that his efforts had the effect we had hoped for. The programs revitalized public interest, and we were able to mobilize the support necessary to prepare for the latest round of drought.

This meant we had helped prevent a natural failure from turning into the human tragedy of famine for hundreds of thousands of people.

And yet, and yet . . . the lessons to be learned from famines are tough ones. In the long term, what did all this co-ordinated, generous, passionate outpouring of help achieve? The principal lesson is that though droughts are inevitable, famines are not—famines result from human failure and apathy leading to ecological breakdown. In both human and economic terms, it really makes no sense to wait until the magnitude of avoidable deaths and suffering attracts public attention, thereby evoking a generous response. Better by far to undertake development programs in advance of climate failure. Such programs would make it possible for people affected by droughts to develop sustainable livelihoods, making outside generosity unnecessary. This is one case where what is best in human terms is also the most economical use of scarce resources.

Unfortunately, as we see over and over, the world's response is usually short-lived. It is not translated into the longer-term support required to avert future tragedies.

Which means—of course—that they'll inevitably recur.

The safety of the planet and its human populations needs—demands —long-term planning, far-sighted thinking. Under our current system, how is this to be achieved? The UN, to me, has always been part of the answer. But I had long ago ceased being naive about the UN; the competing interests of contending nation-states could not be altogether escaped, even there. Nor could pettier motives. Petty politics and small-mindedness constantly interfere with the UN's work. The aftermath of the famine was not untypical.

When we established the OEOA, Brad Morse and I had pledged to phase it out when its principal task had been completed. We didn't want it to grow into just another UN organization. We envisaged transferring its experience and capabilities to the permanent parts of the UN already responsible for these matters. Surprisingly, the Red Cross and other major private organizations (which are usually sceptical of UN efforts) appealed to the secretary-general to maintain the OEOA. But we went ahead and phased it out in the fall of 1986. Alas, the organization that could have learned most from our experience, the UNDRO, remained as aloof at the end as it had been at the beginning, and when we offered to turn over to them the information system that had been so critical to the success of our efforts, they refused even to come in and examine it.

This tragic famine was a cogent reminder of the interconnectedness of human affairs with nature's processes. There could be no more compelling example of the need for sustainable development and the devastating consequences of failure to follow a sustainable development pathway. The degree to which the famine that afflicted sub-Saharan Africa was the product of ecological breakdown was made horribly clear to all of us involved in it. Overgrazing by cattle and goats and the cutting-down of scarce trees in the relentless search for firewood turned productive but fragile lands into near desert. The onslaught of drought, combined with the overcropping, meant the loss of topsoil through erosion, and afterwards, even when the rains came, many areas could not be returned to productivity, particularly with the meagre resources available to peasant farmers who had lost everything. In effect, ecological breakdown turned what would have been a temporary crisis into the permanent loss of productive land and displacement of the people who had always depended on it. Man's failure compounded nature's failure. It was a stark reminder of the ugly effects of ecological degradation.

That was a harrowing and emotionally draining time. As I moved from one stricken area to another, I was in close and daily contact with people who were suffering and dying. Particularly poignant were the children, helplessly wandering in search of vanished or dead parents, or mothers and fathers carrying the bodies of their dead or dying children, their faces gaunt from starvation and sorrow. One family remains burned in my memory. The father, mother and three children arrived exhausted at one of our camps just as we got there, after a four-hundred-kilometre walk. A hundred kilometres from the camp the children had simply collapsed, unable to go any farther. And the mother was too weak to continue carrying one of them. So the father went on, carrying one of the children and leaving the other with the mother. After walking a few kilometres to a place where he could with some safety leave the older one, he would return for the mother and the other child. This prolonged the journey and suffering. It is hard to imagine the determination, the will and the love that enabled them to complete this heroic journey. And when I saw their emaciated condition, I wondered how they could possibly have made it. There were others who didn't make it. Their own parents had to be left behind to face certain death, and two other children died along the way. Those who finally reached the camp were desperate for food and water, but as they staggered into camp they were told that supplies had run out.

We got there just in time. We knew that more supplies were on the way and turned our own food supply over to them.

But how few we could help! And how many they were!

Astonishingly, astoundingly, most of them kept their spirits up.

Whenever we moved through the crowded camps, we were accosted by throngs of eager children holding up the palms of their hands. At first I thought they were begging for assistance. But it was simply a gesture of friendship—they wanted to establish a bond with us by pressing the palms of their hands to ours. I was ashamed of myself for having so misread this gesture of human solidarity, and Hanne and I pressed palms with hundreds of them.

As I moved among these desperately poor but incredibly dignified people, I knew I was sharing their world without in any real way being a part of it. Despite all the rhetoric about every person being part of the same human family, the worlds we live in are so very different and so very far apart. My experiences of the Depression in Manitoba gave me an affinity with their suffering, and as I looked into the eyes of so many bright and hopeful young people, I saw reflected there images of myself in my childhood. But at the same time I was now living under conditions of privilege and affluence that were utterly foreign to them. How could this happen and what could I do about it? What prospects did these young people have for a better life, and how could I contribute to it?

The African famine experience made me confront and rethink the great questions of human existence. What is the source and the purpose of life? Why do unfairness and injustice exist, and why do they so often seem to prevail? The Christian doctrine is that we'll be rewarded for virtue or punished for sins committed. Why do so many people experience hardship and suffering that are disproportionate, out of any rational relationship to sins they may have committed in this life, while others enjoy benefits impossible to equate with any visible acts of virtue? How to square this with observation and experience—how to reconcile it with the dreadful sufferings of so many thousands of little children?

Universalist expressions of religious belief have always attracted me, as I have always seen that the innate spirituality of people, and the common values they share, are the essential foundations for a more peaceful, co-operative world. On the other hand, the emphasis on the differences in belief has made religion one of the principal sources of division and conflict. I sense a continuity in our spiritual life paralleling that in the physical world: our physical bodies consist of elements that have always existed; they come together to give us our distinctive identity as human beings during our lifetime but return to the "dust from which we come" after we die. So the spirit that resides in our individual souls emanates from the universal spirit, becomes incarnate within us during our lifetime, to be then subsumed into the universal source. Personally, I feel more at home with this notion than with the prospect that we go after death to "heaven" or "hell" as individuals or are continuously returned as reincarnations. But I am prepared to live with the mystery while being awed and challenged by it.

I have found the development of my inner spiritual resources one of my most constant challenges, and my connection with the cosmic forces that shape all existence has become central to me. Building the spiritual and moral dimensions of my life has not been easy, but the experiences are both enriching and exhilarating, and none more so than my experience with the African famine.

CHAPTER 9

The Run-up to Rio

I
N THE LATE EIGHTIES, after the African experience, I once
again made Colorado my headquarters, spending as much time
as I could at our home in Baca, which I always found spiritually
nourishing, and making my office in Denver, which I found a convenient place to develop my interests in American affairs and politics. I soon became quite active, particularly through the Western
Regional Council, an influential body consisting of the governors,
senators and leading businessmen from the eighteen western states.
I was introduced to it by Jim Poirot, who then headed CH2M Hill, a
leading environmental and water engineering firm that was our
technical adviser for the Baca Grant Project. The driving force in the
Western Regional Council was DeeDee Corridini, who went on to
become the mayor of Salt Lake City.

Through the council I was involved in making representations
to both the administration and Congress in Washington on issues
affecting the U.S. West. Water and related resource issues figured
prominently on the agenda. In light of the active interest I took in
these matters—though I was still a Canadian citizen, but with a green
card to allow my residence in the U.S.—I was soon made chairman
of the committee. It proved an interesting opportunity to meet a
wide range of American political leaders and public officials and get
to know something of the political dynamics of the U.S. as seen from
the western states.

I had come to know Richard Lamm when he was governor of Colorado as an attractive, charismatic leader with a disarmingly warm and congenial manner. When he decided not to seek another term, I was one of the many who rallied to support Roy Rohmer. Through him I became involved in fundraising for the Democrats in Colorado. He then drew me into the national fundraising effort for the 1988 presidential campaign. This gave me some fascinating insights into the exotic world where finance and politics intersect in the United States. I made a personal contribution of $100,000, which brought me into the privileged circle of top supporters with access to George Dukakis and other leading Democrats. I was made a trustee of the Democratic National Committee and invited to contribute to their foreign policy platform, which introduced me to Madeleine Albright, Dukakis's foreign policy adviser. I was surprised at the degree of involvement I was able to have as a Canadian citizen; this never seemed to inhibit my acceptance into the inner circle of Democratic politics, presumably because I had long been quite active in American business and policy circles. After the presidential campaign was over, and Dukakis had been decisively beaten, *The Washington Post* included me in a list of what they described as the ten top supporters of the Democratic Party.

George Bush was now president, and his advisers presumably clipped the *Post*'s piece, because I was told it was trotted out as evidence of why the u.s. should oppose my appointment in 1990 to head the secretariat for the UN Earth Summit in Rio, scheduled for 1992. In the end they went along with my appointment, but only because Bush himself, whom I had come to know and like when he was American ambassador to the UN, in typically gentlemanly fashion indicated that I was okay, that I should be regarded as acceptable to the u.s. And this despite the fact that he couldn't have known that I had also helped to raise funds for the Republican National Committee, out of friendship with some key Republicans. My attitude toward u.s. politics has always been generally bipartisan.

As was my custom, I didn't let my involvement in politics and business interfere with my active interest in international life. I resumed an advisory role with the United Nations and continued to be active in the World Economic Forum, the World Wildlife Fund International and the Aspen Institute for Humanistic Studies. And for a brief period I became president of the Better World Society, on the invitation of its chairman, founder and main benefactor, Ted Turner.

The way it came about was characteristic of the disarmingly unconventional style of this creative media genius—a true American original. I had never met Turner, and my curiosity was aroused when in the summer of 1981 I received a phone call from his office. He was going to be in Denver for a board meeting and would like to meet me for lunch.

We met at the restaurant in the Embassy Suites in Denver, and I was immediately taken with his ebullience and animated charm. Over lunch he told me of the Better World Society and his aspirations for it as a non-profit organization designed to use the media to create awareness of and support for some of the principal international and humanitarian causes that were at the centre of my own interests.

Then, midway through lunch, he abruptly put down his knife and fork and got down on his knees on the floor. He looked up at me with his hands folded in the manner of a supplicant.

"Maurice," he said, "I'm down on my knees to you because I want you to become president of the Better World Society, and I beg you not to say no."

To say that I was nonplussed would be putting it mildly. I looked around covertly. Not unnaturally, we had become the focus of attention for the other patrons of the restaurant, who were doing their best not to stare, and failing. The attention didn't faze Ted a bit, and after that I could scarcely say no.

It wasn't just the dramatic way he issued the invitation, either. I was very much attracted to his purposes in establishing the society— to develop programs for television on important issues of public interest, particularly the environment, nuclear disarmament, bridging East-West Cold War tensions, population and matters of special concern to developing countries. These were, of course, issues I had always been passionate about, and I shared his sense of their importance. His television holdings were obviously important—television was the most powerful communications medium, but it had always been difficult to obtain the commercial sponsorship required to produce good-quality programming. Ted made the facilities of Turner Broadcasting and CNN available for Better World Society projects, often at very significant cost to him, even when the result was a loss of advertising support and sponsorship at a time when his television interests were struggling to achieve financial viability.

He had already assembled a star-studded board of directors for his Better World Society, including former Norwegian prime minister Gro Harlem Brundtland and former U.S. president Jimmy Carter. It was an educational and stimulating experience for me, and I formed a great admiration for and warm personal rapport with Ted. This survived his disappointment at my need to leave as president when I took on a new responsibility as president of the World Federation of United Nations Associations, headquartered in Geneva, where I felt I could be more useful at that point.

Other people I met during this period included the actress Shirley MacLaine, who introduced us to one of her closest friends, a very different personality but a woman who shared many of Shirley's down-to-earth qualities and values. This was Bella Abzug, a former member of the U.S. Congress, who was one of the most indefatigable and effective campaigners for women's rights and other liberal causes. In my work in the UN I came to know her as a relentless but constructive critic. She became a senior adviser in my role as secretary-general of the Earth Summit and later was an honorary member of the Earth Council until her unexpected death in 1998.

Others included Laurance Rockefeller and his wife, Mary, whom I got to know after Hanne sparked his interest in the spiritual activities she was undertaking at Baca. I met Robert Redford through my environmental friend Terry Minger, who had a close relationship with him. Terry wanted us to meet because we shared an interest in the environment, and Redford invited me to Sundance, which he was developing as a major resort and conference centre.

Afterwards he asked me to serve on the board of directors of the Institute for Resource Management, headed by the noted Arizona conservationist and former secretary of the interior Stewart Udall. Udall agreed with me that business leaders should be brought together with environmentalists and similar interest groups, and Redford's institute arranged meetings around controversial issues with a view to helping to develop a co-operative approach. It was obviously a purpose I could readily subscribe to, and indeed the institute did some good work.

Redford himself proved as distinctive and colourful a personality as those he portrays in his movies. He's a creative man and has many of the eccentricities that so often accompany genius, attributes of character not so easy for others to live with. At my first Sundance meeting, I was surprised, for example, that he never showed up. He was, after all, both chairman of the meeting and its host. My surprise turned to some irritation when I saw him skiing by, completely ignoring the meeting that he had invited us to. However, I soon learned to overlook what in less committed people would have been seen simply as bad manners. In his own way Bob Redford has done a great deal for the environmental movement and continues to do so.

When I moved back East I found it difficult to remain active in the Institute for Resource Management. Bob wasn't too happy with me when I resigned, but though I don't see much of him these days, he seems not to have held it against me.

At the end of 1988, I moved from Colorado, making my home and headquarters in Ottawa. I conducted my personal and business interests from there, as well as my increasingly active advisory role with the United Nations Development Program. I also renewed my close association with friends in the Canadian political and business communities.

Whenever I could, in speech after speech, at seminars and meetings and conferences and committees, I kept hammering away at the ideas that had emerged after the "Founex" process for the Stockholm Conference, which I had come to see as critical to our survival: sustainable development, the intricate interconnectedness of economics, development and the environment. I called the synthesis *eco-development,* but the term *sustainable development* was what caught on.

It was validated in its turn by the World Commission on Environment and Development, headed by Gro Harlem Brundtland, and of which I was a member. The commission's report in 1987, *Our Common Future,* made a compelling case for the positive integration of the environmental, social and economic dimensions of development through sustainable development, calling it "the only secure and viable pathway to the future of the human community."

The report of the Brundtland Commission gave new impetus to the movement. It also highlighted the limited progress that had been made since Stockholm and made some important recommendations to be considered—and hopefully acted on—by governments. It occurred to me that the twentieth anniversary of the Stockholm Conference in 1992 would provide a good opportunity to give new impetus to the environmental movement in the context of sustainable development and to stimulate the attention and action of governments.

The Swedes were enthusiastic about hosting Stockholm 2, and the General Assembly accepted the idea and at its session in December 1989 formally mandated it as the UN Conference on Environment and Development (UNCED). However, other countries, notably Brazil, wanted to host the conference, and Sweden graciously bowed out, accepting the political premise that it would be appropriate this time to hold such a meeting in a developing country, conceding that Brazil had a strong and persuasive claim.

In the summer of 1989 I'd received a call from Lucien Bouchard, then minister of the environment in the Mulroney cabinet, inviting me to meet with him. I knew him only casually and was curious about the meeting, which took place in his office. We had a congenial discussion of current environmental issues and Canada's interest in the forthcoming UN conference. Then Bouchard cut to the chase. "Would you be willing to have Canada put your name forward for the post of secretary-general of the conference?"

I was totally taken off guard. This was the last thing I had expected, particularly from a government I was not close to. Of course, I had a deep interest in the conference and wanted to do everything I could to contribute to its success. But I felt strongly that it should be used to bring on a new generation of leadership. I expressed these sentiments to Bouchard, making clear my deep appreciation of his proposal. But through our discussion, it became evident that putting my name in the ring at this early stage, before the General Assembly had even made its final decision about the conference, could produce some leverage for Canada while at the same time making it more difficult for others to promote alternative candidates for reasons that had more to do with politics than qualifications. On this basis I agreed. So Bouchard proceeded to obtain the necessary approvals from the prime minister and his cabinet colleagues, which resulted in my becoming Canada's candidate. At the time I did not really aspire to the job or believe I would end up with it. But I felt that having Canada present me as a candidate could contribute to ensuring that a suitably qualified person would be appointed.

In December 1989 the General Assembly made its decision to convene the conference in June 1992 and accepted Brazil's offer to host it. In February 1990, before the Preparatory Committee for the conference had met and elected its chairman, Secretary-General Javier Pérez de Cuellar called Canadian UN ambassador Yves Fortier and me to his office and told us that he had decided to appoint me as secretary-general of the conference.

Thus I returned to a new full-time role and a memorable new episode in my UN career.

One formidable candidate for chairmanship of the Preparatory Committee emerged—Tommy Koh of Singapore. Koh was a legendary figure in the UN. His masterly chairmanship of the Law of the Sea Conference while he was ambassador of Singapore had produced agreement on one of the most difficult and important treaties ever negotiated under UN auspices. He was well versed in environmental matters, an interest of his since the Stockholm Conference, where I'd come to know him well. He was a consummate negotiator and one of the most attractive and congenial personalities I've met in my international life, the kind of person who would be a prime candidate for virtually any international post. I was therefore delighted when he easily won election as Preparatory Committee chairman at its first meeting in March 1990. He'd been put up as a candidate of the South, but he was held in universal esteem.

In my opinion his rare combination of professional and personal qualities proved key to the success of the conference. His uncanny ability to produce innovative solutions to what seemed like unresolvable deadlocks, his clear understanding and relentless pursuit of the primary goals and his rare blend of good humour and toughness saw us through many difficult moments when the fate of the conference hung in the balance.

Managing the Preparatory Committee was far from an easy task, and perhaps only a Tommy Koh could have brought it off. The committee was much too large. The conference had generated so much interest that the entire membership of the UN, plus non-member states, were on the committee—about 175 national delegations in total.

A committee that large needed to be managed and guided by a particularly experienced and skilful "bureau" consisting of vice-presidents and rapporteurs. This political team had to be drawn from all the main regional groupings composing the membership of the UN. Here again we were lucky. This kind of political process seldom results in the election of the best-qualified candidates. In this case all the individuals proved to be dedicated and competent, and of particular importance, they worked well together under Tommy Koh's leadership in a process that went smoothly. Ambassador Bo Kjellen of Sweden reclaimed his country's role in the conference and became one of its most influential and respected leaders after being elected chairman of Working Group I on Biodiversity, Biotechnology, Desertification, Soil Erosion and Related Issues; Dr. Bukar Shaib, a respected and experienced scientist and former minister from Nigeria, became chairman of Working Group II on Oceans, Fresh Water and Toxic Wastes; Dr. Bedrich Moldan, a leading environmentalist and former minister of the environment for Czechoslovakia, was elected head of Working Group III, dealing with issues that cut across the other subject areas, including the crucial issues of organization and finance. Ahmed Djoglaf of Algeria, who was not well known at the time but had impressed me as one of the brightest and most promising younger officials involved, was elected to the important role of rapporteur.

But if election of the bureau went relatively smoothly, agreement on the agenda and the rules of procedure proved much more difficult—a portent of even more severe difficulties to come. The debate was fractious and occasionally acrimonious, and only Koh's relentless chairmanship was able to secure agreement, and even that only after an all-night session ending at six in the morning of March 17, 1991.

With this agreement, though, we were well and truly launched, and I was able to turn my attention to building a secretariat and developing our management plan.

The secretariat was to be located in Geneva. I was pleased because so many of the organizations and agencies on whose co-operation we depended were located there, and I knew the city well. The historic buildings the Canton of Geneva gave us weren't always everything we would have wished in practical terms, but the location did enable us to develop a sense of identity and esprit de corps.

One of the worst features of the UN, in my view, is its personnel policies and practices, which always favour politics, both governmental and internal—some amazingly petty—over competence. Take "equitable geographical representation," which means that the secretariat has to reflect a "reasonable balance" of nationals from countries of each of the main political regions. Though in individual cases this was not intended to take precedence over qualifications for the job, in the highly politicized environment of the UN it often proved to be the determining factor in appointments. In our case, we also needed to ensure gender balance and some competence in each of the official languages of the UN. And all this for a small staff of forty. In my long experience of the UN I have always respected and honoured these requirements and believed very much in them in principle; but the practice often created frustrations and problems for me in my own recruitment process. In the final analysis, however, I was always able to achieve an equitable geographical balance in my staff without making significant concessions to quality. There was only one disappointment this time. I'd wanted at least half the professional staff to be women and had lined up enough qualified candidates. Unfortunately, I was unable to persuade some of them to join us, and we fell short of the 50 percent target I had set. Still, we were able to achieve a higher percentage of women in senior posts than in the UN as a whole.

I frequently had to ward off governments, many quite insistent that I accept the candidates they put forward. I wouldn't budge. I was determined to get the people I wanted—and needed. These sponsored candidates weren't all useless, either. Mexico, for instance, put forward one of its ablest diplomats in New York. But I still demurred. I knew which Mexican I wanted—the dynamic Alicia Barcena, formerly Mexico's first undersecretary for the environment and now director of their National Institute of Fisheries. She agreed to come and, as I'd predicted, became one of the most productive members of our team. Her experience in marine issues and her negotiating skills proved especially valuable.

The secretariat I assembled was of exceptional quality by any standard, particularly considering that many of them were leaving satisfying and lucrative jobs for essentially part-time work—with no assurance of resuming where they had left off. Clearly, the prospect of participating in a process that was both unique and historic was sufficient motivation.

Our task was daunting. We were faced with an impossibly broad range of complex issues, many interlinked and overlapping, and out of these we were supposed to develop a process that would make the conference work. How to distil from all this a manageable number of themes and issues—"manageable" in the sense that an international conference could reasonably be expected to take action on them. And action, too, that would meet the high expectations that had been set for the process.

Maybe, I concluded, it wasn't possible. I knew the UN well. Everyone could easily agree in principle that our work should focus on a few priority areas, but each government had its own view of what the priorities should be. So I couldn't see how it was feasible to limit UNCED to a few key issues.

But more than not possible, I didn't even think it was desirable. "After all," I argued, "the environment–development relationship is itself not a question of focusing on single issues. What we need is not to deal with issues piecemeal but to find a new, systemic and integrated way of dealing with a broad range of issues, all of which interact to shape our common future."

Over and over in committee and in long discussions with individual team members I made the same point: the answer to focusing the "outputs" of the conference was not to select a range of single issues, no matter how compelling. "No, we must devise a new approach to co-operative management of the entire system of issues."

Much easier to say than to do. Our secretariat was in real terms just the servant of member governments, which exercised their authority through the Preparatory Committee. The four PrepCom meetings themselves lasted a total of ninety-eight days, and there was consultation with and among governments in between, but there was no mechanism for them to provide direction to the secretariat, which was expected to carry most of the workload. The budget didn't help much. It was modest, providing limited funds for our substantive work.

So I knew we'd need more resources—and more people. It was essential to add to our own core team in Geneva. I therefore set about building an extensive network of people and institutions, designed to give us access to the best expertise in each field and to the guidance and support of experienced and influential policy and political leaders. It was this ad hoc network of the best and the brightest that in the end made the process possible.

As a result of endless consultation and advice, we decided to recommend to the Preparatory Committee that the conference be designed to produce a Declaration of Principles, which I proposed should be in the form of an Earth Charter, and a Plan of Action, which came to be called Agenda 21.

So far, so ordinary. The Earth Charter would reaffirm and build on the Declaration of the Stockholm Conference, IUCN's Covenant and similar statements that have emerged from other international processes, setting out basic principles to guide the conduct of nations and people toward each other and the Earth. Agenda 21, on the other hand . . .

All UN conferences are expected to produce plans of action, and most of them are just filed away and forgotten. I wanted ours to be different—a new form, one that would enable the many issues included in it to be addressed on an integrated basis. It should be designed to guide the world community along a sustainable development pathway to the goals, targets, priorities, allocation of responsibilities and resources necessary to determine the future of our planet. It should therefore incorporate provisions for monitoring progress and for periodic review and revision.

But no plan is meaningful unless it can actually be implemented. Thus, the key cross-sectoral issues of financial resources, technology transfer and the institutions to oversee them would have to be dealt with. And so I set out six areas around which to organize the work of the conference.

First, conventions on such topics as biodiversity and climate change would be negotiated separately, and the conference itself would provide the forum for confirming agreement to them and providing for their signature; second, the Earth Charter would set out the basic principles for the conduct of people and nations toward each other and the Earth to ensure our common future; third, the document called Agenda 21 would provide concrete measures for implementing the Earth Charter principles; fourth, financial resources—measures for financing the actions provided for in Agenda 21, and in particular for ensuring access by developing countries to the additional money required to integrate environmental practices into development policies—must be made; fifth, there must be technology transfer, ensuring developing countries access to environmentally sound technologies on an affordable basis; and sixth, there must be measures for strengthening existing institutions, notably UNEP, and the machinery to enable environment and development issues to be examined at the policy level.

I also set out the basic philosophy underlining and motivating my approach. A viable balance between environment and development factors doesn't mean just adding environmental protection clauses to development agreements. It means a fundamental change in our economic life and behaviour. I used energy as the most dramatic example. The changes demanded in our patterns of energy use and transport to bring about the fossil fuel reductions needed to head off climate change would require a concerted global effort to improve energy efficiency in all sectors and a transition to alternative forms of energy that are more environmentally friendly. For example, there should be greater incentives and support for research and development on new energy sources and storage options, such as electric batteries and hydrogen to power motor vehicles.

Industrialized and developing countries would have to change the way they deal with each other, I said. Continuous confrontation is counter-productive. Resource flows to developing countries must no longer be seen as "foreign aid." Supporting the development of developing countries, and particularly arresting the vicious cycle of poverty that is as destructive in environmental and human terms as it is morally repugnant, must be seen as a sound and necessary investment in the future of our planet.

Once the core of our secretariat had been put together and was functioning well, I left most of its day-by-day management to others. All over the world organizations and institutions were formulating ideas and initiatives designed to support the conference. Just keeping track of them was task enough, but we had also to give them all a sense that their contributions were welcomed and appreciated and then somehow arrange actually to use them. We tried to encourage as much of the preparatory work as possible to take place outside the secretariat, but inevitably many meetings had to be held in-house. Every day there was a stream of visitors—ambassadors and officials of governments, representatives of important organizations and agencies. They all had to be seen, briefed and listened to.

I concentrated my own efforts on our network of relationships. I knew that was the only way we'd ever get the substantive contributions our work demanded and the only way to build a broad constituency of support for the conference itself.

In particular, I set out to build a group of "eminent advisers." I managed to recruit Noboru Takeshita, former prime minister of Japan, Margaret Thatcher, former prime minister of Great Britain, Miguel de la Madrid, former president of Mexico, Jimmy Carter, former U.S. president, Lee Kuan Yew, former prime minister of Singapore, former French prime minister Michel Rocard, and former Commonwealth secretary-general Shridath Ramphal. Each one required a personal meeting and in some cases a good deal of persuasion. Not all were noted for their environmental commitment or their confidence in the UN. But I was determined that the conference be seen not solely as a meeting of environmentalists but as an important political event supported by a broad spectrum of influential political leaders. There is no question that this impressive group of advisers helped very much to give credence to this concept of the conference.

On the technical level the International Council of Scientific Unions, through its executive secretary Julia Marton-Lefèvre, gave us access to a broad range of scientific expertise. Lane Kirkland, president of the AFL-CIO in the U.S., provided a link with the labour unions. The IUCN (now called the World Conservation Union), the distinctive organization including both governmental and non-governmental members, was especially active in extending their co-operation.

I also knew it was vital that we draw on the immense variety of resources and interests of the world's NGOs. Again we were lucky. On our own staff was the exceptionally talented NGO leader from Ecuador, Yolanda Kakabadze. She somehow managed the impossible task of orchestrating our relationships with this vitally important community, ensuring that their concerns and contributions were channelled into our work process and—even more important—inspiring their confidence. Complementing her work within the secretariat was Warren "Chip" Lindner, an American lawyer who had devoted his life to environmental causes. I wanted as many NGOs in Rio as possible, but so many had expressed interest—and had become involved—that I knew we couldn't accommodate them all at the conference. So I devised another formula. I encouraged Chip Lindner to bring the NGO community together in a "parallel event" in Rio; this would be linked closely with the official conference while enabling extensive NGO participation in the conference itself. Chip was then running the Centre for Our Common Future in Geneva, which he'd set up after his role as secretary of the World Commission on Environment and Development to co-ordinate follow-up of the commission. He certainly had the kind of commitment, network of relationships and organizing skills that fitted him well for this assignment.

But we took some flak from other NGO leaders for anointing him in this way. It's never easy in the NGO world to translate a broad common interest into actual co-operation—there are as many personal and institutional egos in the non-governmental community as there are in officialdom, and if anything they're even more fractious and divided. The consensus Chip put together for a Global Forum was fragile and from the beginning fraught with continuing controversy. Many times, right up to the conference, it seemed on the point of coming apart. But Chip's persistent efforts and relentless drive ultimately prevailed, and the Global Forum that resulted became one of the most important and successful features of the Rio experience.

I was particularly determined that the planet's indigenous and traditional peoples have a role in the conference. I use *indigenous* for those cases, mainly in the Americas, Australia and New Zealand, where the aboriginal societies have been largely overcome by immigrant populations, *traditional* for those countries where the population's ethnic roots are local, such as Japan, but where minorities continue to follow their ancient ways of life despite the fact that the majority has opted to build a modern society. The two groups have much in common, and are often lumped together under the *indigenous* rubric.

Hanne shared in particular my interest in traditional societies, and developed a deep affinity with the native peoples of Canada and the United States. For the Rio process, she became my unofficial ambassador in developing relations with the communities of traditional

peoples around the world and in helping to arrange for their participation in our preparatory work and the conference itself. With her
help we recruited as our secretariat adviser an Argentine Indian,
Beatriz Schulthess, who had been actively involved in the attempts
to obtain recognition and support for native peoples at the international level. Traditional and indigenous peoples share common
interests and concerns, but they are far from a united community,
and the many differences and rivalries that divide them often make
them difficult to deal with. Our experience was no exception.
Nevertheless, we were able to provide for the presence of some
of their most influential leaders at Preparatory Committee meetings, and they were very visibly present at Rio, where their concerns
received a great deal of attention and support, particularly from
other NGOs.

Money was a constant problem. Most of these activities had to be
financed outside our budget, for the UN had given us almost no funds
for these "extras." So fundraising became a part of our task. We were
given our first real boost when the prime minister of Sweden, on
my first visit to Stockholm, offered to contribute $3 million—before
I even asked. We owed gratitude for the money, I knew, to a quiet,
unassuming and remarkably innovative Swedish official, Bengt
Säve-Söderbergh, his country's undersecretary for development co-
operation. Only two days before I left for Stockholm, he'd discussed
our situation with me over a glass of wine at my favourite hotel in
Geneva, the Hôtel d'Alleve. In that brief time he'd been able to
swing his government into action.

It got us off to a great start, and we were able to use it to elicit
funding from a number of other governments.

But we also needed to tap private sources, including wealthy individuals, foundations and corporations—though of course we had
to be careful that accepting corporate money wouldn't compromise
the values represented by the conference.

One of the first people to volunteer his services, on a pro bono
basis, was Benjamin Read, formerly U.S. undersecretary of state and
the first president of the German Marshall Fund. Thoughtful, modest

and wise in the ways of the diplomatic and political world, he inspired confidence and the trust of all who knew him. I proposed to him that he set up a non-profit foundation to mobilize private funds. He proceeded to set up the Eco-Fund, which became an indispensable vehicle for raising and deploying money in support of the conference.

One of my best decisions was to invite the Swiss industrialist Stephan Schmidheiny to become my principal business adviser and undertake the formidable task of mobilizing the participation and support of the business community. Schmidheiny, a quiet, thoughtful and deliberate person with a clear concept of what sustainable development meant, has a strong commitment to giving a practical effect to it in his business life. As one of Switzerland's, and Europe's, wealthiest and most successful industrialists, he had the capacity to engage the attention and respect of other business leaders.

Schmidheiny wasted no time. At his own cost he established an office and set about recruiting other business leaders into a new organization, the Business Council for Sustainable Development. Within a short time he'd brought in fifty-eight chief and senior executive officers of major international corporations and undertaken an intensive program of consultations and study that yielded one of the most influential reports to the conference. That document, called *Changing Course*, became a best-seller and was printed in several languages.

A mark of the quality I so much admired in Stephan Schmidheiny was his response to a provocative question put to him by a Greenpeace representative in the Palais des Nations in Geneva when he presented *Changing Course*.

"Aren't you and the other authors of this report yourselves running polluting companies?" the Greenpeacer demanded.

"Yes, we are," Stephan said candidly, with complete equanimity and no apparent irritation. "And we're all committed to reducing our pollution levels and environmental impacts."

The next creative idea—this one from the senior secretary/special assistant I'd brought with me from Ottawa, Dorothy Sitek—was to create a special Swatch watch for the conference. Fortunately, Stephan Schmidheiny was at that time a major shareholder and board member of SMH, the company that makes Swatches, and he introduced me to the high-spirited and innovative head of the company, Nicolas Hayek, the Swiss-Lebanese engineer who had invented the Swatch and used it as the basis for rejuvenating the Swiss watch industry.

Hanne joined me in a drive to his headquarters in Bienne, where we met with him and his wife, Marianne. He took us on a tour of the factory, explaining volubly along the way how he'd come to take over the company and develop the Swatch as the most successful new product that the Swiss industry had produced in our times. He was also bubbling with ideas for new products and initiatives, including development of a small, fuel-efficient automobile. From someone less creative and successful this might have seemed a wild idea, but from him it seemed a stroke of genius—why not, indeed, combine the expertise of the watch industry with that of the automobile industry to produce an environmentally low-impact mini-automobile for use in urban areas? And indeed Hayek has since produced such a car, the Smart Car, in partnership with none other than Daimler-Benz.

It didn't take Hayek long to accept the challenge of producing a special-edition Swatch for our conference. He'd give the Eco-Fund five Swiss francs for each one sold, and he devised an ingenious marketing program that was launched in the General Assembly Hall of the United Nations, followed by a gala evening. It resulted in sales of over a million of the special-edition Swatches, a record for the company, and produced a substantial fund for our purposes.

Meanwhile, international negotiations were proceeding separately on the Conventions on Climate Change and Biodiversity, and strong efforts were being made to establish a negotiating process designed to produce a Convention on Forestry. They were all extremely important issues and for that reason highly controversial.

Was—is—the earth warming? Our human activities, particularly the burning of fossil fuels, produce a real threat to the Earth's climate system. And does that really matter? Scientific consensus was lacking. There were scientists who said yes, others who said no, and still others who merely said, "Data inconclusive." A vigorous debate was kicked off by a report from the Intergovernmental Panel on Climate Change (IPCC), then chaired by the noted Swedish scientist Bert Bolin. This panel consisted of a broadly representative international group of leading scientists, and their report had produced compelling, but still not conclusive, evidence that emission of carbon dioxide and other "greenhouse gases" from human sources was changing the filtering mechanism of the atmosphere. This, the report said, was likely to produce a warming of the Earth's climate, accompanied by increasing climatic turbulence.

The group couldn't, of course, be absolutely sure. The science had not advanced to the stage of certainty, nor could the nature or the consequences of the prospective changes be predicted with any degree of accuracy. But it was also clear to me that if we waited for certainty before acting, the process would be too late to reverse.

Why wait? Even if, by happy chance, the scientists were unduly pessimistic—something I didn't believe—the actions called for would be good for the planet and the environment anyway. Indeed, I argued over and over, many preventative actions could be taken on a "no regrets" basis—they were eminently justified in economic terms. A useful example was the substantial improvement in energy efficiency and conservation that was already feasible using existing technologies.

The stage for the climate change negotiations was set by a conference convened in Toronto in October 1988. At this conference governments pledged first to stabilize their carbon dioxide emissions by the year 2000 and then to achieve a reduction of 20 percent from 1990 levels by 2005. This was a modest enough target—much too modest, according to environmental organizations. It would constitute only a small first step toward the kind of reductions that would be necessary, and was clearly achievable in economic and technical terms. Even so, the political will was just not there. Sadly, not only were the Toronto targets not met, but most industrialized countries, including Canada, continued to increase their emissions afterwards.

As they had been in Stockholm, North-South splits on the issue were a constant source of acrimony. Developing countries came into these negotiations with a great deal of reluctance. They were united in insisting, as they had on other issues at Stockholm, that it was a problem created by the industrialized countries and was primarily theirs to solve. The North must not only reduce their own emissions but must make money and technology available to the developing countries.

Early on it became evident that all we could expect by the time of the conference would be agreement on a "framework" convention, a kind of convention for a convention. Substantive provisions, including targets, would have to be negotiated later.

This was extremely disappointing. But in light of the unresolved controversies between North and South, and even among the more developed countries, it was clearly not going to be feasible to reach such binding commitments by the time of the conference. A breakdown of negotiations would have set back the process, probably for years. It was indeed only through the political impetus provided by UNCED that agreement could be reached even on the framework convention. This in itself marked a historic milestone in the development of international law, as it was clear from inception that it would involve some very fundamental changes in industrial civilization. To paraphrase Iraqi president Saddam Hussein, not hitherto known as a social philosopher, climate change is shaping up as the "mother of all environmental issues." True, this convention did not go nearly as far as I and many others would have liked, but at least it set up a process for continuing negotiations. Thus, change would be incremental. Such protocols didn't demand the signing of another major convention, though of course each protocol would require the approval of parties to the convention. This is how progress is made in forging new international law.

The search for a treaty on biological diversity, or biodiversity, was even trickier. To some degree this was because the concept itself was vague and difficult to explain. And partly because the most biologically diverse regions on Earth—the great tropical rain forests—are in the custody of developing nations. In these negotiations the North-South divide was sharp.

Still, the very fact that governments were prepared to consider a treaty on the subject underscored the emerging sense of the importance of living organisms—plant, animal, insect and bacterial life—not only as individual species but in their complex, systemic relationships within the world's great ecosystems. There was a growing realization that these systems were not just exploitable resources but the very life-support systems of the planet. Even on the popular level, people were beginning to understand that "jungles," as they had so long been called, were not just impenetrable places filled with a bewildering array of life forms, many of them inimical to humankind, but repositories of life itself—and a source, among other things, of unique and irreplaceable genetic resources and of many invaluable pharmaceutical and medicinal products. And now this precious reservoir was at risk.

In conventional economics these great forests were valued only for their timber or seen as obstacles to be cleared for agriculture. Economists have always simply taken as a given their vital role in global environmental integrity (for example, their critical role in the carbon cycle). These are therefore "free"—services with no economic value attributed to them. Thus, there has been no economic incentive to save them.

In reality, however, it is global economics that has been hopelessly skewed—what is "free" really isn't. Biological resources have real economic value, and "environmentalism," by extension, is not some touchy-feely love of nature but prudent and conservative fiscal planning.

Economics, therefore, was at the heart of the North-South split on the issue. In the North the chemical and pharmaceutical companies have used their virtually free access to the resources of the tropical forest areas as a source of basic genetic material. Biotechnology has allowed them to manipulate this material to produce high-value-added products, but because the raw materials were "free," they've never felt any obligation to share part of the added value with the developing countries where the material originated. Now, developing countries were insisting that their sovereign control over these resources be recognized and that they share in the benefits arising from their commercial utilization, in principle certainly fair and responsible but requiring some very basic changes in current practice. The more industrialized countries, notably the United States, were equally insistent that their companies have free access to these resources, while at the same time demanding protection for the intellectual property rights that arose from their investments in research and development.

Related to this was the perennial issue of financing. Developing countries were united in their demands for "new and additional" financial resources. Rich countries must recognize, they insisted, that the biodiversity they were being called on to protect provided a valuable service to the world community and must be accorded economic value.

If climate change and biodiversity were difficult, a forestry convention proved impossible. Even a framework convention proved out of reach, despite universal acknowledgement of the importance of the world's forests and the need to ensure their conservation and sustainable development. But the differences between developing countries and more developed countries proved too deep and intractable. The best that could be achieved would be an "authoritative, non-legally binding statement of principles on forest management," and even that evoked some of the toughest and most divisive negotiations of the entire Rio process. In the end all that could be managed was an inventory of problems and differences, which basically marked out the agenda for future negotiations that have thus far made only limited progress toward establishing a formal negotiating process for a forestry convention. The importance of conferences like UNCED is that they provide political impetus and a specific target date for the completion of negotiations on issues like this, which otherwise tend to lag.

The issue generally, but somewhat inappropriately, known as "desertification" was a particular concern of a number of developing countries, notably those of northern Africa, vulnerable to recurrent, devastating droughts, large-scale degradation of arable land and loss of soil, as we've seen. To spearhead this issue in our secretariat and to act as my special representative for Africa, I was fortunate in enlisting the services of an exceptionally skilled African, Arba Diallo. The former foreign minister of Burkina Faso and permanent representative of his country to the UN, he had also had extensive field experience with the United Nations Development Program Unit dealing with the Sahel region, where desertification was a major issue. He was well known in the region, and his knowledge of its problems was encyclopedic. Diallo's efforts were reinforced by the work of another key secretariat member from the region, Alemneh Dejene, who made an important contribution to the process, as well as to the chapter on the subject in Agenda 21.

Having put this issue on UNEP's agenda during my tenure as executive director, I had been disappointed that despite the vigorous efforts of my successor, Mostafa Tolba, UNEP had only been able to make modest progress toward mobilizing action on this issue. I felt that UNCED provided the best opportunity of giving the process strong impetus and lent it my full support. But our most effective support came from Swedish ambassador Bo Kjellen, who in his capacity as chairman of Working Group I of the Preparatory Committee used his formidable influence and diplomatic skills to engineer a compromise. The United States and a number of other industrialized countries had strongly resisted the proposal, arguing that desertification was a regional problem that need not be addressed at a global conference. But Kjellen was finally able to get them to sign on, however reluctantly, to a proposal by the Preparatory Committee that UNCED recommend to the UN General Assembly that it mandate an intergovernmental negotiating process to seek agreement on a desertification convention. Again, not as much as we had hoped, but nevertheless a major step forward. On this basis the team of Bo Kjellen and Arba Diallo were able to lead the drive that resulted in completion of the Convention to Combat Desertification in June 1994.

The second meeting of the Preparatory Committee held in Geneva in March and April 1991 continued the sharp differences between developing and more developed countries. G-77 representatives were unrelenting in their three key demands: an insistence on "new and additional financial resources," a demand for free or at least concessional terms for transfer of technology, and a commitment by the more developed countries to reduce their pressures on the environment through changes in their patterns of production and consumption, thus leaving "space" for the developing countries to grow.

The United States in particular took a hard line, supported to varying degrees by other more developed countries, which shared some of the major American concerns but were pleased to let the u.s. be out front in asserting them. Some of the key members of the u.s. delegation, particularly its head, "Buff" Bohlen, were torn. They had a difficult brief that they were not themselves very happy with, but they still did a loyal and effective job in arguing the u.s. position.

George Bush, who had earlier said he aspired to be the "environmental president," was surrounded and besieged by right-wing ideologues, including his own chief of staff, John Sununu, who vehemently opposed any concessions that might impose limitations on u.s. economic interests or the American lifestyle. Their influence persuaded President Bush not to commit himself to attending the conference, though we knew his absence would undermine its credibility and impact. The hard line was reinforced by a policy analysis from the influential right-wing Heritage Foundation, which asserted that meeting the demands of the developing countries "could affect profoundly America's economic growth, productivity and international competitiveness."

Although at times the divisive and rancorous exchanges made me wonder if agreement could ever be achieved in time for the conference, we did in the end make some progress in Geneva. Most important from our point of view, the Preparatory Committee agreed to my proposals to concentrate the agenda on the six theme areas I had proposed earlier, and gave us the authority to begin drafting the Earth Charter and Agenda 21. It also agreed, with the reluctant acquiescence of the United States, to demands by G-77 that eradication of poverty be recognized in the program for the conference as an important objective of sustainable development.

Among the many personalities who participated in one way or another in the Earth Summit process, two in particular stand out— Jacques Cousteau and Ted Turner.

I'd long been a great admirer of Cousteau and had enjoyed and been inspired by his television programs and books. I first met him during preparations for Stockholm, though he didn't participate directly in the conference, having a low regard for governments and correspondingly low expectations that they'd take necessary action. But he was personally friendly to me and gave me some sound advice and moral support. He both inspired and cautioned me with his strong and on the whole pessimistic views about the state of the environment and the prospect of reversing the ominous trends he saw.

After I took on the responsibility for UNCED, Cousteau came to Geneva to see me and made it clear that he felt that the conference presented a rare, and perhaps last, opportunity to rally world opinion and governments to take the kind of actions he had long been espousing. He said he intended to make a film designed to help, and I assured him of my full co-operation. At a later stage, when we were meeting in New York, he interviewed me at some length, and his camera crew followed us through the corridors and the conference hall of the UN.

Unfortunately, he didn't complete the film for distribution before he died, though I'm sure it's still in his archives. It could still have real significance as history, perhaps even more as current affairs commentary. Cousteau's devoted and energetic widow now heads the Cousteau Society and is the custodian of his legacy, and it is she who will decide the uses of the uniquely rich resource represented by his film library.

One of my most important challenges was how to ensure media interest and coverage of the conference, and of course Ted Turner was critical here. I knew his commitment to the environment was unique among his media peers, and it was later to be dramatically evidenced in his $1 billion gift to support UN programs and purposes.

I still needed a leader to take on the vexed question of those "new and additional resources" demanded by the developing countries.

The argument about these resources and where they were to come from permeated virtually every aspect of preparations for the conference and at times threatened its breakdown.

This wasn't so surprising. Most donor countries were going through periods of austerity and resisted major new responsibilities. The United States in particular was reducing its foreign aid budget and was adamant that it would not sign on to anything that required an increase in these expenditures. Canada had much the same basic position (though in the typical Canadian way the delegates dressed it up in positive rhetoric and let the u.s. do the heavy hitting). A few of the Europeans, among them the Nordics and the Dutch, continued to meet their commitments, but overall the European Union was notably reluctant to take on anything new. Certainly the leadership I had hoped for wasn't forthcoming.

The best prospect, therefore, seemed to be the Japanese. Although they had done better in recent years, they still lagged far behind in the percentage of gross national product devoted to development assistance. The Japanese had a strong interest in the environment and had recently been asserting more leadership in international affairs. So I saw in them the logical candidate for leadership on these issues at UNCED.

I'd already met Noboru Takeshita, the former prime minister, when he was one of its longest-serving and most influential finance ministers and governor for Japan at the World Bank when I was acting in that capacity for Canada. He was said to be skilful at devising new sources of government revenue, and had been responsible for the establishment of Japan's Environment Protection Agency. Of all the Japanese politicians, he was regarded as the leading political supporter of the environmental movement. I arranged to meet with Takeshita during my visit to Japan in 1991.

He received me with characteristic Japanese politeness in his modest office and listened with interest to the case I made.

"Your country," I argued, "should take the lead, not just in global environmental co-operation but in its financing." I pointed out that the environment and sustainable development were a natural area for leadership by Japan, based on its impressive record in bringing its own environmental problems, particularly air and water pollution, under control. The environment, through UNCED, I added, presented an opportunity for Japan to assert a leadership role in international affairs, one it was particularly suited for.

I then appealed for his help and advice, referring to his own domestic environmental record and his reputation as a financial innovator. He was obviously encouraged that I knew his reputation, but nevertheless didn't leap to agree. It took time and patience within the Japanese political system to arrive at a decision, he said. I was pleased. At least he hadn't said no.

I thought I'd stretch my luck and moved the matter ahead a notch. Perhaps, I suggested, he might help to arrange and chair a meeting in Japan of eminent persons on the financial issues facing UNCED?

He modestly demurred. He just didn't have enough experience to undertake such a role, he said. Still, he asked me to write him, setting out my proposal in greater detail. He also said he would consult Prime Minister Toshiki Kaifu, his protégé, and other political and business leaders.

During the same visit I met with Kaifu, who had obviously talked to Takeshita, as well as with other ministers and senior officials. At a breakfast meeting organized for me by Keidanren, Japan's powerful industry association, I presented the case for international leadership by Japan in the field of environment and sustainable development based on Japan's own domestic experience, its technological achievements and the commitment of its ministry of international trade and industry to a long-term program of developing and marketing environmental technologies. Parodying the title of a book then popular in Japan, *The Japan That Can't Say No*, I suggested that it might now be timely to go a step further by saying yes without waiting for the United States and other industrialized countries to make the first move. They listened with what seemed to be respectful interest, but I had enough experience with the Japanese to know that their real reaction would only become apparent in time. After some further correspondence on the subject, I made another brief visit to Tokyo, during which Takeshita confirmed that he would accept my invitation to chair the conference on the condition that we would undertake the substantive preparations for it and ensure participation of a suitable group of "eminent persons." He also said that he would want as co-chairmen Kaifu, who had recently left the prime ministership, as well as Gaishi Hiraiwa, whom I had first come to know as chairman of the world's largest electric utility, Tokyo Electric Power, and who was at the time chairman of Keidanren. He also made it clear that while he would sponsor and participate in the meeting, he would expect me to take principal responsibility for chairing the proceedings.

My alliance with Noboru Takeshita was one of the most important among the network I developed on the road to Rio. Some, like him, I enlisted; others volunteered, including some I could make little use of, not so much because they had nothing to offer as because a small secretariat like ours was limited in the amount of help it could actually use. Through one of my friends and key advisers, Jim MacNeill, former secretary-general of the Brundtland Commission, I had been introduced to a brilliant and somewhat mercurial Indian journalist, Pranay Gupte, who became a senior media adviser to us at our New York office and later ran the conference newspaper, *The Earth Summit Times*, which has subsequently evolved into *The Earth Times*.

We had to find financing for Gupte outside our budget, and he located a source of funds from a prominent New York labour lawyer, Theodore Kheel, to whom he introduced me. Kheel volunteered to help in financing Gupte's efforts and other initiatives designed to elicit public and political support for the conference in the United States. He was so quiet and unassuming in manner that initially I didn't expect too much from him. But he proved one of our most valuable allies, and his many imaginative and practical ideas greatly helped us, particularly in rallying u.s. support. For example, he was a close friend and the attorney for the noted artist Robert Rauschenberg, whom he persuaded to create an original painting for us, which evolved into our official poster and produced considerable revenue. Later Kheel arranged for signs advertising the conference to be placed on municipal buses in several cities and for advertisements in movie houses inviting people to urge President Bush to go to Rio.

He also took over the task of promoting and disseminating the "Earth Pledge," which I had produced. This led to his forming the Earth Pledge Foundation as a non-profit organization. He gave some significant financial resources to continue his non-profit environmental activities after Rio.

I also had a good deal of help from corporate leaders, including my friend Jim Wolfensohn, who had maintained an active and supportive interest in the environment throughout his highly successful career in the financial world. Don Keough, president of Coca-Cola, whom I had met at Davos, and his senior vice-president, Alex Malaspina, offered to help us by making some of their senior marketing and public relations people available to us, as well as the services of the public relations firms that assist them. Since no organization has a more sophisticated capacity for marketing, this was a gift indeed, and in putting this at our disposal, without seeking any credit or attribution, they did for the conference what we could never have done for ourselves. Thus were the key messages promulgated throughout the world.

This in turn attracted major media attention—far more attention than we could ever have generated through UN channels. As a direct consequence the attention helped persuade political leaders and an unprecedented number of media and civil society representatives to attend the conference itself.

By the time of the third preparatory meeting, held in Geneva in August 1991, our work had progressed well, but as the meeting began, it became evident that there had been little progress toward agreement on the issues that divided North and South, particularly on that difficult question of new and additional financial resources and access to technology.

In intergovernmental negotiations it's not uncommon for dramatic movements—breakthrough movements—to occur only after long, tough and divisive negotiations. But there are also occasions when important progress is made by the tacit acquiescence of the parties without crystallizing a formal agreement. This proved to be the case during our third session, when delegates signalled their acceptance of the basic framework of Agenda 21 by focusing on its particulars. Virtually every issue proved to be controversial, and in most cases the controversy had its roots in the continuing demands of developing countries for access to additional money and technology. But everyone at least agreed on the notion itself.

By the end of this Preparatory Committee session, therefore, we'd entered the home stretch. We had an acceptable framework for the conference, quite well-developed proposals in respect of each of the key issues, though little agreement at the political level on the most difficult of them.

Was this enough? When I first undertook the job of managing the conference, I'd known that the prospects of breakdown and failure were very real. I had said as much to friends and colleagues. I was determined from the start that if the conference couldn't be a real success, I'd see that it was not just a failure but a spectacular failure—that might show the world community the seriousness of the issues that the survival and well-being of the entire human species depended on. The worst result would be a failure presented as a success. In the end, of course, it wasn't so easy to determine.

As the countdown progressed, more and more attention was focused on the issue of whether President Bush and his senior advisers would attend. I made periodic visits to the White House, and President Bush always received me congenially. He explained that he'd like to come, but there were strong domestic pressures on him not to do so. On what grounds? That his presence would give credence to the kind of demands being made on developed countries that the U.S. could not accept. Finally he invited me to lunch, together with Boutros Boutros-Ghali, who had by then become UN secretary-general, and announced that he had decided to attend the conference.

I expressed my appreciation and added, only half joking, "We should thank you, Mr. President, for the long delay in making your decision. It has provided the basis for so much media speculation, and that has focused a great deal of attention on the conference."

The final meeting of the Preparatory Committee, held in New York in March 1992, was marked by the same North-South differences that had divided previous sessions. But also in evidence was a general awareness of the importance of the conference to the future of the world community and the United Nations, and the tragic consequences of a breakdown and failure. This created a strong will to bridge remaining differences, without, however, reducing the intensity of participants' presentation of their positions on the issues.

It had become clear by then that it wouldn't be feasible to obtain agreement on the kind of Earth Charter I had proposed, and I had to reluctantly concede this to Tommy Koh when he insisted we'd have to settle for a lesser document, a "Rio Declaration," which went a great deal further toward an Earth Charter than it would have without the skilful and even coercive leadership of Koh. While a good deal of progress was made on many of the issues in Agenda 21 and the Declaration, the G-77 were still unwilling to agree to the text that had been negotiated without more concrete assurances from the developed countries on the issue of financial resources. Japan and European donors made some positive statements about their willingness to provide such resources but made no specific commitments. The U.S. held firm in its resistance to any language that would commit it to providing additional financial resources or to changing the American lifestyle, which President Bush had said was "not negotiable."

The meeting entered its final stages still deadlocked on the financial issue.

But then the astute and influential ambassador of Pakistan, Jamsheed Marker, speaking as chairman of the G-77, finessed the issue. He indicated that developing countries would accept an "acknowledgement in principle" that new and additional financial resources would be forthcoming, leaving the particulars to be worked out in future negotiations.

This elicited a positive statement from the head of the U.S. delegation, Buff Bohlen.

"There is no question that developing countries and countries in transition must have new resources," he declared. "I would like to make it absolutely clear that the United States is committed to working with other industrial countries to mobilize new and additional resources for a new partnership."

This was not exactly an explicit commitment, but it had the effect of clearing the way. An agreement finally came together after intensive negotiations that began on the final day of the meeting and continued till six o'clock the next morning. Tommy Koh, always quick with the gavel, left the bare minimum amount time for action on each issue and prodded the weary delegates to a positive result.

There were, of course, many key issues still unresolved. Only six weeks were left before the conference itself, and I knew the prospect of resolving them during the two weeks in Rio was not promising. In my mind, therefore, there was a very real possibility of a dramatic breakdown. It became imperative to use the remaining period for informal negotiations that would offer some hope of reaching agreement at Rio. This lent special importance to the meeting of eminent persons we had convened in Tokyo in mid-April 1992, with a stellar group, including senior business people and a clutch of former presidents and prime ministers.

It proved to be a constructive meeting, producing the Tokyo Declaration, which stated, "New and additional financial resources should support the processes of fundamental change which the transition to sustainable development requires." It made a strong case for the industrialized countries to be forthcoming in providing such resources, as well as an "appeal to Japan," along with other industrial countries, to assert their leadership at the Earth Summit and "to indicate with some specificity their support for global environment and development co-operation."

The Earth Summit

A ND SO IT CAME TO THIS: the summit to save the world. Would it succeed, or would it fail? Or, perhaps worse, would it do neither?

I arrived in Rio de Janeiro the week before the conference with my wife and most of the members of our secretariat. The very congenial and co-operative mayor of Rio de Janeiro, Marcelo Alencar, had made available a splendidly appointed mansion in beautiful park-like surroundings in the city, which he urged me to make my personal headquarters. I hated to disappoint him, but if I stayed there I'd use a lot of precious time travelling to and from the conference. Accordingly, I persuaded him that it would be best to use it for some of my eminent advisers, former presidents and prime ministers, for whom it would be especially well suited.

Meanwhile, I installed myself in a small suite in a modest but perfectly adequate hotel on a beautiful stretch of beach within easy access of the conference centre. It proved a good choice, not the least because I wasn't constantly exposed to the delegates and media people who swarmed around the lobbies of the luxury hotels, where most of the dignitaries stayed.

The Brazilians provided me with a chauffeured limousine, and a second car with security people followed me everywhere. I accepted all this with reluctance as a necessity in the circumstances, but asked them to reduce the number of armed guards surrounding me and to limit their visibility.

Once, just after I'd installed myself in my offices at the conference centre, I came in followed by three soldiers in battle dress with machine guns.

"Do you really need this kind of security?" a reporter demanded.

I just smiled. "They're really here to get the negotiations going," I said.

Many of the delegates also arrived early, to continue their informal negotiations. No breakthroughs resulted, but there is no doubt that these informal sessions helped set the stage for advancing the negotiating process at the conference.

Before the conference itself, there were other duties to perform, some of them more pleasant than others.

For example, a world conference of indigenous peoples had been convened for Rio and held just prior to UNCED proper. It attracted representatives of indigenous and traditional peoples from virtually every region of the world, in all their incredible variety and colour. Their exotic costumes and distinctive songs and dances proclaimed their diversity, but they were nevertheless entirely united in their basic messages to the conference: maintain respect for the sacredness of Mother Earth and for aboriginal cultural and spiritual traditions; curtail the exploitative practices that were desecrating the Earth's resources and intruding into the habitats and livelihoods of traditional peoples; and see to the introduction of justice and equity in redressing the oppressive policies and practices that deprived them of their livelihoods and dignity.

I'd been invited to address them and to participate in the opening ceremony, where these messages were solemnly promulgated in a multiplicity of languages by a number of eloquent spokespeople. It was moving, but there were awkward moments too. The speeches were followed by a traditional pipe ceremony. I've always been fastidious about personal hygiene and never even drink from a glass used by someone else. Smoking a pipe that had passed through several mouths before it reached mine made me wince. I kept—almost literally in this case—a stiff upper lip and passed the pipe on as hastily as I could without offending. (Religions—and customs—are alike here: I'd had much the same feeling some years earlier when I was obliged to drink from a common cup at a communion service at the Episcopal cathedral in New York.)

Another especially interesting event held outside the conference but in conjunction with it was a Sacred Earth Gathering of Spiritual Leaders, which Hanne had taken the lead in organizing. The message they conveyed to the conference was similar. The changes in behaviour and direction called for at UNCED must be rooted in the deepest spiritual, moral and ethical values, the gathering declared. We must reinstate in our lives the ethic of love and respect for the Earth that traditional peoples have retained as central to their value systems and revitalize the values common to all principal religious and philosophical traditions. I spoke at one of their sessions and felt a deep affinity with its purposes, which I referred to in my own opening statement to the conference.

For me, both these ancillary conferences helped to put what we were trying to do at UNCED into a deeper ethical context. This wasn't just politics as usual, just another conference. We were really trying to illuminate the more hopeful, ethical and sustainable pathway to the future of the Earth and its peoples. It was a humbling feeling.

On Wednesday, June 3, 1992, the day we had waited and worked so long for finally arrived. There was a buzz of excitement among the thousand or so delegates who filed into the plenary assembly hall for the opening ceremonies. My own excitement was mixed with apprehension, as I knew only too well the many difficulties we still had to resolve in the less than two weeks that had been allocated—most of it in the seven days of meetings prior to the arrival of heads of government for the final summit portion of the conference.

The main conference hall was crowded. All of them, I'm sure, shared my sense that their presence there was a historic milestone, not just for them but for their people, and through their people for the planet. The very fact that they were there signalled a victory of sorts. But I knew it could turn to ashes if the delegates failed to resolve the key issues on which agreement had still not been reached It's normal, after all, at great conferences of this kind for most issues

to have been resolved by informal negotiations preceding the
event itself. Usually, the issues left open are those for which agreement seems assured and that need only the stamp of approval from
the head of each government, and only a few that require special attention, are left to be negotiated. In this case, it wasn't so; an unusually large number of issues remained to be resolved. And the UN
practice that agreement should be by consensus didn't help matters either. In effect, this convention gives every country a veto and
is all too frequently used to frustrate the will of the majority. The
net effect is to weaken proposals that would have gained majority
support in a tabulated vote.

In the plenary hall, delegates were busy greeting each other,
finding their seats and settling in when I joined Secretary-General
Boutros Boutros-Ghali on the dais. It was the moment we had been
waiting for, and the room was tense. The secretary-general called the
conference to order and began his opening address.

When it was over, he moved so swiftly to the business of the
meeting that no one had time for applause. I was embarrassed and
applauded enthusiastically myself, hoping to get the crowd going.
They didn't. No one joined me, and it soon became evident that
I was merely interfering with the secretary-general's remarks. He
glared over at me and then pressed on with the business at hand,
announcing to general applause that President Fernando Collor of
Brazil had been nominated as president of the conference. This
was hardly a surprise—at UN meetings it is customary for the
host country to nominate the president, and delegates had already
reached agreement on this and other nominations through prior
consultations.

Collor then took the podium. His opening statement was something of a surprise, so candid was he about Brazil's environmental
problems, including those affecting the Amazon. At the same time
he strongly articulated the position of the developing countries on
the issue of new and additional financial resources.

It was then my turn to give my opening statement. I'd had some
help with it from Anita Gordon, then the enterprising producer of
CBC's *Quirks and Quarks* radio program and an ardent environmentalist.

She'd prodded and pushed and shaped, but the main messages were those I had been articulating for years.

As I finished, I was given a standing ovation, much to my surprise —such enthusiasm is most unusual in official meetings, where everything is measured to a fare-thee-well. It was also considerably embarrassing. The contrast with the silence that had greeted the secretary-general's speech was evident, particularly to him, and he didn't even try to conceal his resentment. It got us off to a rocky start.

Our relationship didn't improve as the conference went on. At a later point, when Prime Minister Kiichi Miyazawa of Japan was prevented by a last-minute domestic crisis from coming to Rio, I arranged for him to give his address by satellite television. So as not to set a precedent—always important in UN circles—his address was to be made in an "informal session" immediately following the formal adjournment of the plenary and then presented by the head of the delegation at a formal session so it could be entered into the records of the plenary. I'd already cleared the notion with President Collor, who was my "boss" for the time being (once the secretary-general had handed the conference over to him, our role as a secretariat was to serve the conference and him as its titular head). I didn't really need Boutros-Ghali's approval but briefed him in any event, as I tried to do with all important matters.

He was furious and brushed aside my attempts at explanation.

"I will not allow it," he said crisply, ignoring my admonition that the president had already approved it.

I replied with a crispness that matched his own, "You're the secretary-general and my boss. I'll do what you say. But I'll do it only under the most severe protest, as you are wrong." With his staff watching apprehensively from a distance, I said curtly, "Good night, Mr. Secretary-General," turned and walked out on him. I can't recall ever treating a superior like that, but then I've never been treated that way by a superior either. For me it was the low point of the conference.

We patched things up a bit the next morning. I sat alongside him on the dais, and he was somewhat conciliatory. He didn't apologize but explained that he had been tired the previous evening. It was important for us to get along, so I responded in kind. "I was tired too," I said. Then I added, "You can always count on me to serve you loyally—but I've got to be able to speak frankly with you. I'll carry out your orders, but if we don't agree I expect at least to have the opportunity to explain the reasoning behind my views." At that point I had already yielded to his instructions and arranged with President Collor and the Japanese to cancel Prime Minister Miyazawa's speech by satellite. It was a disappointment to the Japanese and to me, and something of a setback to the conference itself.

For the remainder of the conference the secretary-general and I were civil and correct with each other but little more. Despite this inauspicious start, however, we later repaired our relationship and ultimately became friends. And toward the latter part of his term I even went to work for him again.

In the conference's organization, principal responsibility for substantive discussion and negotiation was given to the Main Committee. Unanimously, and appropriately, Tommy Koh was selected to chair it, continuing the work he had so ably carried out as chairman of the Preparatory Committee. The only other committee formally constituted by the conference was the Credentials Committee. As a result of pre-conference consultations, a total of forty vice-presidents were elected, representing every region and sub-region. Everyone wanted to get in on the act.

A bureau of that size is clearly unwieldy if it is expected to deal with all the issues affecting the business of the conference. Invoking his usual style and skill, Koh orchestrated a series of informal consultations, selecting the people he regarded as most appropriate to lead negotiations. And there were many of them. The results of these informal negotiations were then fed into the Main Committee, where they were often subjected to intense debate, particularly on the part of those who had not participated directly in the informal consultations and negotiations. In many cases Koh had to send them back, and sometimes, to try to break an impasse, he made a change in the person he had designated to lead the negotiations. Thus on the particularly knotty finance ones, he asked Rubens Ricupero, who had recently become Brazil's finance minister, to handle it, and he was able to engineer a compromise. While it really satisfied no one, it gave the Group of 77 the basis for claiming that they had won a commitment of "new and additional resources" while being sufficiently ambiguous on this point that the more developed countries did not feel bound by it. Subsequent events made clear that developing countries were right to be disappointed with it.

My office was located conveniently near the back entrance to the plenary hall, so I could move in and out of the conference readily. And I had to do so frequently as most heads of delegation and many others wanted to see me. I had to balance these visits with my primary responsibility of overseeing the conference proceedings and dealing with various crises that arose. Some were less serious than others, some rather graver. Typical of the "ordinary" crisis was an urgent appeal from the Canadian delegation (which, I was pleased to see, included my old friend Paul Martin Jr., then the opposition critic on the environment). They had been frantically seeking an appropriate office where Prime Minister Mulroney could meet with President Bush—his own office being inconveniently located for this purpose. The solution was simple: I simply vacated my office and let him use it while I took my place on the podium, where I was expected to spend a reasonable amount of my time anyway.

We'd arranged a number of side events to the main conference, and the most popular proved to be speeches and press conferences given by Jacques Cousteau and Ted Turner. There were a good many such side shows, both within the conference complex and outside it.

With members of my secretariat assigned to each of the committees and negotiating groups, I received constant feedback about what was happening, and I intervened on many occasions when that seemed useful or necessary. The negotiations themselves were, of course, the responsibility of the delegates. In practice, however, we had a significant influence on the process, helping to overcome differences and heading off compromises that would in our view weaken or distort measures we felt were especially important.

Compromises are, naturally, necessary for any process of negotiation to succeed. Most of these left the fundamentals intact, but some seriously diminished our prospects for both the Earth Charter and Agenda 21, thus diluting the overall results of the conference. The Vatican, for instance, led the charge against provisions for limiting population growth; and the United States, in addition to its resistance to any promise of new money, persisted in its refusal to accept any language calling for changes in patterns of production and consumption—that is, anything that would in their view jeopardize "the American way of life."

Another failure was on energy. The oil-producing nations, led by OPEC members, were unrelenting in their resistance to the inclusion in Agenda 21 of provisions that might constrain the use of fossil fuels. At one point I met privately with the Kuwait delegate and some of his OPEC colleagues, all of whom I knew well. I reminded them of my own involvement in the oil and gas industry and pressed them to modify their position. It would be, I contended, to their political advantage and ultimately in the best interests of the oil industry to acknowledge the importance of the issue and affirm their willingness to co-operate in finding acceptable resolutions. I went so far as to suggest that because the overwhelming majority of members were on the other side of the issue, it might even be necessary to make an exception to the normal consensus procedure and call for a direct vote. It didn't work. In the end they refused to retreat.

I couldn't help contrasting their recalcitrance with the leadership shown years before, when Sheikh Zaki Yamani was masterminding Saudi and OPEC oil policies. At that time the Saudis loudly proclaimed that petroleum was too precious a commodity to use wastefully, and they advocated conservation measures as well as the development of alternative fuels, accompanied of course by higher prices.

June 5 was the twentieth anniversary of the opening of the Stockholm Conference.

It was a somewhat sobering day. Looking back at Stockholm, and in particular reviewing my speech at the opening of that conference, I was struck by how much of it was still directly relevant to the issues on the Rio agenda. The degree of awareness and knowledge of the issues had expanded greatly, and the geopolitical landscape had been transformed by the end of the Cold War and breakup of the u.s.s.r. But the principal issues, especially those that divided North and South, were echoes of the differences that had emerged at Stockholm—so much so that my opening Stockholm speech, with suitable alterations to reflect the time and place, could have been recycled for Rio. It was disappointing to realize how little progress we had made in twenty years.

The Global Forum of NGOs that accompanied the Rio conference had an exuberance and circus-like quality that made it a much more lively and colourful place than the primary one. It attracted thousands of participants and visitors, and at any given moment a variety of events were under way—seminars, discussion groups, presentations on every conceivable environmental subject, and serious drafting sessions, which produced a series of NGO "treaties" (informal agreements negotiated just as seriously and hotly as the formal agreements being negotiated by governments). The controversies and differences among participants were no less intense or divisive than those in the official conference, but they too produced broad consensus on many of the issues, though naturally of a much more radical nature than reflected in the agreements of governments.

The number of NGOs finally accredited to UNCED was some 1,450. Most of them were from the more industrialized countries, but the number of developing country NGOs was much higher than in previous conferences, mostly because we had set up an NGO Participation Fund to help finance their involvement. We'd also made some effort to get governments to include NGOs in their official delegations, and in fact some 150 NGO representatives had been sent that way.

Women too were strongly represented both in the delegations and in the many women's organizations accredited. The most visible leadership was provided by the Women's Environment and Development Organization (WEDO), led by the dynamic and colourful Bella Abzug. She had also been instrumental in involving women's organizations and driving the focus on women's issues through the preparatory process.

I was disappointed that youth groups were not better represented despite the special efforts we had made to get them there. They had been encouraged by our secretariat, but even those that appeared were not as well organized as others. Still, they had as significant a presence and impact at Rio as they had during the preparatory stages, and the conference paid special attention to youth issues.

The Global Forum proved to be a great success and an indispensable and influential companion piece. One of its most enduring effects was to develop a broad constituency for NGO and citizen follow-up after the conference.

As heads of government and heads of state began to arrive for the summit session that was to be the climax of the conference, the pressure to complete negotiations escalated. No delegate wanted his leader to show up to participate in a process that might fail, so their motivation was high. This pressure, along with the inspired leadership of Tommy Koh and his team, finally produced agreement on the two issues that were last to be settled, finance and forestry principles— settled, that is to say, for purposes of UNCED but far from being resolved more fundamentally.

In respect of new and additional financial resources, I have already referred to the compromise negotiated by Brazil's skilful and persuasive Rubens Ricupero, which was further modified in plenary sessions extended until the very end of the conference. The final text included acknowledgement that implementation of Agenda 21 "will require the provision to developing countries of substantial new and additional financial resources," and that "grant or concessional financing should be provided according to sound and equitable criteria and indicators and call for use of all available funding sources and mechanisms, including multi-lateral development banks and funds as well as pledging innovative financing means and debt relief." But it contained no binding commitments.

I'd realized from the start that the financing issue was going to be the most difficult one to deal with, and the key to the success of the conference. I didn't really expect that there would be a major breakthrough to increase Official Development Assistance (ODA), but I wanted to use the conference to make an emphatic case for "new and additional financial resources" beyond the traditional sources of ODA.

At an OECD meeting in 1991 I'd initiated the proposal for the establishment of an Earth Increment beyond existing ODA. I'd also suggested that a good starting point would be to include it as an additional component to the replenishment of the World Bank's International Development Association (IDA) "soft" loan program for the poorest developing countries, then being negotiated. I was pleased when the World Bank president, Lewis Preston, took this up and advocated it in his speech to the conference in Rio.

I also encouraged the efforts of Mohamed El-Ashry on behalf of the newly established Global Environment Facility (GEF), which he headed. The organization of GEF is innovative, consisting of a tripartite sponsorship of the World Bank, the United Nations Development Program and the United Nations Environment Program, serviced by a small core secretariat, which uses the administrative support of all three organizations. In principle the partners are equal, but the World Bank obviously carries the most weight. Thanks to the stellar leadership of El-Ashry and the confidence he has earned in both donor and developing countries, the GEF has become one of the most effective development finance organizations, with influence well beyond the relatively modest resources it deploys.

Originally, GEF was a means to find support for the financial arrangements agreed to in the Montreal Protocol on Substances That Deplete the Ozone Layer, and in the UNCED process there was a great deal of controversy about whether it should also be used to generate monies for developing countries under the climate change and biological diversity conventions. Developing countries themselves were highly suspicious and insisted on changes to get around the weighted voting that governs the World Bank and gives donor countries much of the power.

In the end, though the GEF negotiations were not carried out within the framework of UNCED, they were very closely related and figured prominently in the agreed text of the Financial Resources and Mechanisms section of Agenda 21.

The Forest Principles adopted by the conference were a meagre substitute for an agreement to mandate a formal negotiating process to produce a convention, which a number of countries and most NGOs

had called for. The principles it set out were useful but largely reiterated those already generally accepted, and in some respects they
also reiterated existing guidelines of organizations like the International Tropical Timber Organization (ITTO), the Food and Agricultural Organization (FAO) and the World Bank, all of which were
themselves regarded as inadequate. Some urged that the continuing
negotiating process be taken out of the United Nations. However,
up to the time of writing this, there is still no agreement on even beginning negotiations on a convention inside or outside the UN. It
was a failure that will cost the world community dearly.

The summit session itself consisted primarily of speeches by
leaders of delegations, with priority to those who were heads of state
or government. This was not as simple as it sounds. To accommodate in two days speeches by heads of all 178 delegations presented a
formidable challenge. We needed to confine each person to a maximum of seven minutes—and this with people who were not used to
having their speeches checked by timekeepers—and some who were
notorious for speeches that went on for hours. Cuba's Fidel Castro,
it was well known, was one of these—he'd been known to speak for
up to six hours on occasion.

I went to see him myself. Fortunately, I'd known him for some
time in both my Canadian and UN capacities and felt I could be both
frank and good-humoured.

"Mr. President," I said, smiling, "you're a great speaker, but you're
also known for your long speeches. I'd be very grateful if you could
assure me that on this occasion you will confine yourself to no more
than seven minutes."

He readily and very congenially agreed to do so. When he
walked to the podium to deliver his speech, he looked up at me and
held up the fingers of one hand—five minutes, he signalled, no
more, and he grinned. And indeed, he spoke under his allotted
seven minutes, his speech receiving more applause than any other.
I even observed George Bush applauding. True, at the time he was
speaking to the person beside him, and his applause might have
been more automatic than appreciative. If he'd thought about it,
he'd likely have sat on his hands. No U.S. president wants to be

photographed for the u.s. media applauding Castro. Some photo-ops are better ducked.

Without doubt Bush's presence was appreciated and added significantly to the importance of the conference. I believe he would also have liked an opportunity to demonstrate leadership, but the ambivalence of the u.s. position on the issues unfortunately made that impossible.

President Bush was naturally sensitive about the lambasting he was taking from the media about American "negativity"—an irritation exacerbated by the respect, not to say deference, the media were showing to his political opponents, senators Al Gore and Tim Wirth, who were both on the congressional contingent of the American delegation. The president had asked someone to find out if Gore would be in the room when the president spoke at Rio. The implication was clear: he'd better not be.

This was an easy one to field. I simply said that Gore was a member of the u.s. delegation, and it was up to the United States to decide which members of its delegation were allotted the limited number of seats in the plenary hall at any point in time.

When the day came, I had a visit from both Gore and Wirth. They were distressed that their own delegation had denied them seats. This I could fix: I quietly arranged for them to be seated as my special guests.

Alas, my quick fix of the situation almost blew up in my face when Prime Minister Mulroney, in total innocence of all this, spotted Al Gore in the hall, greeted him enthusiastically and drew him over to say hello to President Bush. Luckily, the president was diplomatic enough to hide his surprise and irritation.

There were many high points for me. Among them was the speech given by the woman responsible for so much of the progress that had been made to develop the concept of sustainable development and build support for it, Prime Minister Gro Harlem Brundtland of Norway, who spoke at the opening of the conference as chair of the World Commission on Environment and Development. Malaysia's Prime Minister Mahatir made full use of his speech to present in strong but reasoned terms his case for making industrialized countries accept primary responsibility for the environmental problems that they had largely created and, if they expected developing countries to join them in global environmental action, provide the additional resources and access to needed technologies. And he chided them for their hypocritical approach in criticizing Malaysia and other countries for their alleged environmental sins. But the speech that moved me and other delegates most was delivered by Severn Cullis-Suzuki, a twelve-year-old Canadian, daughter of the noted environmental journalist/scientist David Suzuki, whom I had invited to speak at one of the final plenary sessions. "Parents used to be able to comfort their children," she admonished delegates, "by saying, 'Everything is going to be all right; we're doing the best we can and it's not the end of the world.'" But, she went on, "You can't say that to us any more. Our planet is becoming worse and worse for all future children. Yet we only hear adults talking about local interests and national priorities. Are we even on your list of priorities? You grown-ups say you love us, but we challenge you to make your actions reflect your words." It was a cogent and moving reminder that the real beneficiaries of our work at Rio, and the victims of our failures and neglect, would be our own children and those who follow them.

Two of the most important events at Rio took place outside the main plenary hall, where the Conventions on Climate Change and Biodiversity were opened for signature. The United Nations Framework Convention on Climate Change was, appropriately, presented by President Collor of Brazil on June 4, 1992, and during the next ten days it was signed by representatives of more than 150 countries, in each case in a brief ceremony that provided a photo opportunity.

Corresponding arrangements were made for signature of the Convention on Biological Diversity, and more than 150 countries signed this as well, with the notable and ominous exception of the United States. The u.s. had cast something of a pall over the conference when it announced a few days before that it would not sign this convention, primarily because of the strong objections of its business interests to the provisions dealing with biodiversity and the demand of developing countries for access to biotechnology on preferential terms as well as the sharing of intellectual property.

On the first day of the summit portion, Thursday, June 12, President Collor hosted a lunch for heads of delegations, after which they all posed for a historic photograph—more heads of the nations of the world than had ever before been assembled in one place. Then they wandered into the conference room with the big oval table, and I began the speech I described at the beginning of this book.

As I sat on the dais during the last plenary session on June 14, with one ear open for any gems in the final speeches of delegates, I reflected on what we had really accomplished. And then, on the Friday night before the closing day of the conference, I stayed up all night agonizing over my last statement. The problem was not so much finding the words—here once again I had the persuasive guidance and cajoling of Anita Gordon—but deciding what position I would take.

On the positive side, UNCED had, among other things, enlisted thousands of organizations and tens of thousands of people in its preparatory process and stimulated interest in and awareness of environmental and sustainable development issues beyond anything that had ever been achieved before; it had assembled in Rio an unprecedented number of world leaders, civil society representatives and media; had produced agreement on two historic conventions, the one on Climate Change and the other on Biodiversity; had adopted the Rio Declaration on Environment and Development; and had approved Agenda 21, an encyclopedic document of forty chapters setting out the basic framework for a comprehensive program of actions. These would provide the basis for a new global partnership for sustainable development, enabling the world community to make the transition to a secure, sustainable and equitable future. And if it fell short of an Earth Charter, well, it represented some significant progress toward this goal and remains open-ended and dynamic. It is far from perfect, but the fact that it had been negotiated, word by word, and agreed to by virtually all the governments of the world, most of them represented at the highest levels, gives it a unique degree of authority.

And hat wasn't all. The conference had also led to the mandating by the UN General Assembly of a process for negotiating a Convention to Combat Desertification, not an insignificant achievement. And it had provided strong support for extending the mandate of (and mobilizing finances for) the Global Environment Facility.

It had also incorporated into its framework a close and continuing interaction between the official conference and the even larger People's Global Forum organized by Chip Lindner. What was different about the Global Forum from the role NGOs had played at previous UN conferences was that they not only criticized and helped influence what was going on in the official conference but concentrated on committing themselves to action on these issues through a series of "treaties" negotiated at the forum. In the course of this they formed many alliances for co-operation following the conference.

Was all this enough?

On the minus side: the Declaration of Rio, Agenda 21, the Agreements on Financing, Technology and Institutional Measures, as well as the Framework Conventions on Climate Change and Biodiversity had all been diluted in the process of achieving consensus. On key issues like population, energy, forests, and production and consumption, Agenda 21 was weakened to the point that it had far too little real "bite." Also, the Conventions on Climate Change and Biodiversity were only frameworks, leaving the tough, substantive issues to the future.

I knew that I could use my closing speech to declare the conference a failure. This would make me a popular hero among environmentalists, but it would be an awesome responsibility to take on. And would it be right?

Despite the deficiencies and disappointments, all in all I felt the balance sheet reflected a good deal more progress than most people had thought possible. It would have been unrealistic to expect that a single conference, even at the summit level, would "save the world." Rio was never seen as the end of the road, but rather as an important milestone. Rio provided the road map for the journey ahead.

I summed it up in my mind: what had been agreed did represent substantial progress on many critically important issues, and it would be tragic to lose that momentum. If governments were prepared to implement the agreements that had been reached, and to continue negotiations on those matters on which the agreements of Rio were inadequate, there was a reasonable chance that the public interest and political impetus generated by Rio would carry the process forward. If I declared the conference a failure, with the whole world looking on, would not this kind of signal risk jeopardizing the progress we'd made? And without any real assurance that such a declaration of failure would prod the world's nations into action?

In the end I decided to say exactly what I thought—and made the statement without a text, using a few notes I had scribbled in the small hours of the morning.

After Rio, the Earth Council and the Environmental Movement

A S THE CAPTAINS AND KINGS DEPARTED, Hanne and I hosted a gala party in the home of a Brazilian friend for our staff, advisers and special friends. The mood was warm and celebratory; whatever our doubts about the real results of the conference and how events would unfold in the future, we all felt a sense of relief (at the lifting of the huge organizational burden) and exuberance (at how well the event had gone off).

Afterwards, Hanne and I spent a few days alone at a beach resort south of Rio, where we were able to relax and begin thinking about the future.

Too much had happened at UNCED for me to just let it go. The more I thought about the prospect for implementation of its results, the less I thought it sensible to depend only on governments; I could see how easily governments, caught up in the serial crises in the management of a modern state, could shunt the conference's

recommendations into bureaucratic corners where they would neither bother anyone nor achieve much. As the preparations for UNCED
had proceeded, I had become increasingly convinced that its ultimate results would depend to a great extent on the actions of non-
governmental organizations and citizen groups, what we now more
generally refer to as "civil society." So many thousands of local and
grassroots groups had emerged, in developing countries as well as
the more developed ones, and I could see the urgent need to provide
them with better links to each other and to the policy and decision-
making processes that affect them.

During the latter part of the preparatory period I had begun test-
ing an idea on some of my friends and colleagues. The notion was
to set up a new global, non-governmental body—which I called an
Earth Council—with the goal of activating and servicing a network
of NGOs and citizen groups committed to implementing the results
of the Earth Summit—co-operating rather than competing with
existing organizations. It was to focus especially on grassroots and
community-level organizations in the developing countries that had
little access to external resources or international ties. I found a great
deal of interest and some strong allies. Among them were Martin
Holdgate, director-general of IUCN, Julia Marton-Lefèvre, executive director of the International Council of Scientific Unions, and
Maurice Williams, president of the Society for International Development, all of whom agreed to join in sponsoring this initiative.
I also had strong support from Gus Speth, then president of the
World Resources Institute, who had indicated his willingness to
serve as president of the Earth Council when it was established,
Gordon Goodman of the Stockholm Environment Institute, Ashok
Khosla of Development Alternatives in India and quite a number
of others.

Part of my idea was to locate the new organization in the developing world. I wanted to make a clear exception to the vast majority of
international NGOs, almost all headquartered in, and dominated by,
the more developed countries. Costa Rica seemed to me an obvious
choice. I already had connections there, and it was recognized as an
environmental leader. I didn't know the current president, Rafael

Calderon, but I remembered that in one of his first speeches as president he had called for the establishment of a "new ecological order." When I did meet him, he expressed strong interest in having the Earth Council headquartered in Costa Rica and extended his support.

At a meeting arranged for the purpose in Rio, President Calderon and I announced that the Earth Council would be established in Costa Rica. In this, at least, one aspect of the next phase of my life had been launched.

My principal task as chairman of the new body was to put the legal and financial structure of the council in place and to recruit its members.

During the early period I took an active interest in the council's affairs, particularly in making sure it had the money it needed and in orchestrating the extensive process of consultations to select the members of the council. Money is never easy to come by, but here we had a head start. The Eco-Fund still had a considerable sum remaining, mainly from sales of the Earth Summit Swatch. Much of this money had come in after the Earth Summit was over. We'd always intended to use it to help implement Earth Summit initiatives, and the Earth Council was the ideal vehicle.

We had set up a democratic electoral process, inviting some ten thousand non-governmental organizations to nominate candidates to the twenty-one-member council. Having set up this process to function democratically, I could hardly override it. The rejection of my friend Stephan Schmidheiny, who had so effectively led the participation of business in the Earth Summit, caused me great embarrassment and anguish.

Nevertheless, the electoral process we had set up did produce a quite well-balanced council, with representatives of every geographical region and various sectors of society, including youth and indigenous peoples, nearly half of them women. We also established a category of honorary members: we invited a number of eminent persons to express their support for the council by joining it.

The Earth Council had been set up as a new and somewhat different kind of NGO, one that would work in partnership with others, particularly grassroots organizations that lacked connections to international organizations. We were very much assisted by some of the key NGO leaders and others who had joined us in setting up the council and, to varying degrees, were prepared to co-operate in its programs. A number of these who had been members of the Earth Council's Organizing Committee became its Program Advisory Committee, which was then reconstituted as the Earth Council Institute, the operating component of the council.

Its chair was Maximo Kalaw, who had set up the Green Forum in the Philippines and was one of Asia's most effective and influential NGO heads. He had taken the lead at the Global Forum in Rio in the extensive negotiating processes that produced the NGO "Treaties."

The first meeting of the Earth Council, where a number of honorary members participated, was in San José, preceded by a meeting of the Earth Council Institute. The meeting produced a series of program recommendations to the council.

Spirits were high and discussions were lively, but it took some time for the group members, drawn from diverse backgrounds, to really understand and appreciate one another. For example, Emile van Lennep, the eminent Dutch economist, a former minister in his country's government and secretary-general of OECD, who had been one of my most active and effective senior advisers at UNCED, came to me after the first session. He was irritated at the interventions of some of the others, notably the New Zealand Maori leader Pauline Tangiora and Nigerian chief Bisi Ogunleye, each of whom spoke passionately for constituencies and points of view that Emile, as a product of Europe's conservative political/intellectual/diplomatic establishments, considered "off the wall" and "not professionally sound."

I reminded him that the Earth Council reflected the real world, where such viewpoints, whatever one might think of them in conventional and professional and policy terms, nevertheless were representative of the attitudes and interests of many people, perhaps the majority in the world. It was precisely the intention of the Earth Council to provide a forum for real dialogue and interaction among people representing this diversity.

I was pleased to see how quickly and graciously Emile and others adapted to this notion and began to enjoy the interaction with those representing other worlds.

At the first meeting the council accepted the recommendations of the Earth Council Institute and strongly endorsed the mission of the council "to support and empower people in building a more secure, equitable and sustainable future" and mandated it, in doing so, to "help to build on and improve co-operation among and between components of civil society in ways that add value to, rather than compete with, the activities of others."

There were many ways of doing this. Among them the Earth Council undertook to help set up many National Councils for Sustainable Development, whose task was to help governments and civil society co-operate in implementing the Earth Summit's Agenda 21. Another important endeavour was to encourage support for a body called the International Council for Local Environmental Initiatives (ICLEI), whose purpose was to help cities and towns throughout the world develop their own Local Agenda 21, based on Rio's global agenda.

Other aspects of the Earth Council's work included helping indigenous peoples relate their spiritual traditions and value systems to the movement for sustainable development and creating an "ombudsman" function to help redress environmental injustices and resolve disputes.

That the council's headquarters were in Costa Rica made it easier to be especially active in Central America, and it was a strong supporter of the movement by the governments of the region to establish a Central American Alliance for Sustainable Development, the first of its kind in the world.

Not long after the establishment of the Earth Council, Costa Ricans elected a new president, José Maria Figueres Olsen, son of José "Pepe" Figueres Ferrer, revered as the father of Costa Rica's democracy and the person who had, in an extraordinary stroke, abolished its army. The young Figueres was a slight, wiry, handsome, highly intelligent and suave product of West Point who had lived most of his recent years away from Costa Rica.

I hadn't known him before but met him a couple of times during the campaign and was impressed with his lively intelligence and his effervescent enthusiasm as he articulated a stream of ideas, many of them his own. I was encouraged to hear of his avid commitment to sustainable development, which I later came to understand was not merely a political issue for him but a deeply held personal conviction. He was well briefed on the Earth Council and assured me that he would be fully supportive if he became president.

He was more than true to his word. At his inauguration the Earth Council was accorded full diplomatic status, and I was allotted one of the best seats in the house. The following morning he took the unusual step of convening a National Forum on Sustainable Development and asked me to be a principal speaker. The audience consisted of the entire cabinet and other leading Costa Rican political, business, academic and civic personalities, as well as the diplomatic corps and other representatives of the international community. Figueres made it clear that sustainable development was to be the cornerstone of his administration's policies, that he intended "to make Costa Rica a living example of sustainable development."

Figueres soon extended his leadership of the sustainable development cause to the Central American region; it was he who persuaded the other countries of the region to join him in the Central American Alliance for Sustainable Development. The Earth Council was quite involved in the process, and I was asked to give my views and advice at a meeting of the region's presidents. Afterwards, I developed a close relationship with Figueres and provided support wherever I could, particularly with the World Bank, the u.s. government and some of my friends in the business community. For his part he maintained a deep interest in the Earth Council and was generously supportive of it throughout his term as president, both with his own time and attention and in the material and policy support of his government.

Our headquarters site, too, came through Figueres's efforts. He persuaded the government-controlled electric power company to give us a well-situated parcel of land, which was supplemented by a gift from the neighbouring landowner, Evangelina Aguiluz de Gonzalez, the matron of one of Costa Rica's most distinguished families. Our own needs for office space were modest, and so we planned an Earth Centre, designed as a model of the latest sustainable development techniques and technology. This was not only to exemplify the purposes and values of the Earth Council but also to generate some revenue for it by incorporating office, commercial and residential space and a unique "edutainment" centre into the complex.

President Figueres had a shrewd eye for financing initiatives. He helped us, for example, by inviting us to co-operate with Costa Rica in its initiative to develop "certified tradeable offsets" (c.t.o.s) of carbon dioxide emission credits. These credits were generated through joint implementation agreements with CO_2-producing parties and were in essence simple, if still rather controversial. They worked this way: Costa Rica would set aside, or agree to reforest, specific tropical forest areas, which would otherwise have been destroyed, to act as sinks to absorb and offset CO_2 emissions produced elsewhere, usually by companies in countries like the United States, where the cost of abating or offsetting emissions would be much higher. This difference created an economic value that could provide a source of cash for Costa Rica while reducing the cost to the source of the emissions. In essence, the innovative system designed by the Costa Ricans, the first of its kind, would enable emission credit certificates, and bonds secured by them, to be issued.

At that point the Earth Council had entered into a co-operative relationship with one of the world's leading experts on financial instruments, Richard Sandor, president of Centre Financial Products (now called Environmental Financial Products), who had pioneered the development of "emissions trading" on the Chicago Board of Trade and agreed to join us in supporting and advising the Costa Rican government on their initiatives. For emission offsets to have any value, of course, an agreement must exist between the government of the country purchasing the credit and the government of the country providing the offset; this agreement enables the purchaser to obtain credit against its obligation to meet prescribed emission levels in its home country. I was to have more to do with these emission credits later.

During the Christmas season in 1995, Figueres volunteered an arrangement that promised to provide substantial funding for our Earth Centre project. He proposed and subsequently brokered an agreement between Costa Rica's National Parks Foundation and the Earth Council, which made the Earth Centre project an entry point to Costa Rica's national parks system, and thereby enabled it to share the proceeds of the four million tonnes of CO_2 emission credits that the Costa Rican government contributed to the partnership. Valued at $10 a tonne—much below the actual cost of abating emissions—it could produce some $40 million.

During this period the Earth Council also entered into strategic relationships with a number of organizations that were committed to sustainable development but felt they could benefit from our knowledge, advice and extensive constituency. One of these was the World Tourism and Travel Council, for whose industry, the world's largest, the environment is obviously an indispensable resource. Another was the International Road Transport Union, which the Earth Council helped to devise a sustainable development charter based on Agenda 21. Co-operation of a different sort has been established with Australia's Olympic Co-ordinating Authority, which is constructing the facilities for the Sydney 2000 Olympics; under this agreement the Earth Council is monitoring the authority's environmental performance in relation to the commitments it made in order to obtain the Olympics.

For centuries the dominant attitude toward the natural world was that it existed for the benefit of humankind, to exploit as we saw fit. "The world is made for man, not man for the world," Francis Bacon wrote four hundred years ago, and there was no one to contradict him. Even in the last century the natural world has been treated with a carelessness that seems criminal. It required only manipulation by industry and science to provide an endlessly increasing flood of benefits for the humans who inhabited it. The notion that the biosphere was itself vulnerable seemed merely absurd.

Environmentalism as a Western political phenomenon arose from the water, air and noise pollution associated with, and indeed caused directly by, the Industrial Revolution, together with increasing urbanization and its consequent increased living densities. People began to demand healthier living conditions, including better sanitation and air quality.

In America in the 1840s and 1850s, Henry David Thoreau dramatized the damaging effects on the human spirit and the nature of the encroachment of industrial and urban life into the wilderness areas of New England. George Perkins Marsh of Vermont, in his monumental book *Man and Nature: The Earth as Modified by Human Action* (1877), documented the systematic and pervasive impact of human activity on nature and how it reverberated to undermine human welfare. It sounded the alarm that "man is everywhere a disturbing agent and wherever he plants his foot, the harmonies of nature are turned to discord." His insights that humans inflict damage on themselves by damaging nature has become a basic premise of modern environmentalism.

From the beginning there have been two dominant and sometimes contradictory trends driving the conservation and environmental movements. One is the romantic, spiritual view that nature is God's creation and that we, as good stewards, have a responsibility to preserve it for its own sake. The other, more pragmatic, utilitarian view is that it is in our interest to protect nature and conserve its resources as they provide the basis for our own economic interest and quality of life. In my own view both approaches have validity, but they come into conflict when there is a trade-off—as there so often is—between the immediate economic benefits from exploiting a resource and the need to sacrifice a unique piece of nature. Two remarkable pioneers of the American conservation movement exemplified these schools of thought. John Muir, a businessman turned mystic and naturalist, championed the preservationist approach of protecting wilderness areas for their own sake. As a co-founder of the Sierra Club he had an undiluted commitment to nature that remains central to the ethos of the organization, still one of the most effective and influential of the environmental movement. By contrast to Muir, Theodore Roosevelt brought a scientific and pragmatic approach to the cause of managing his nation's natural resources to ensure that they served the interest of all the people and of future generations.

In his excellent book *A New Name for Peace*, the former *New York Times* environment correspondent Philip Shabecoff documents cogently the early development of the environmental movement and the emergence of a number of voluntary associations, the precursors of the plethora of NGOs that characterize today's movement. England was the home of one of the first of these: the Commons, Open Spaces and Footpath Preservation Society was established in 1865. In 1888 the Fog and Smoke Committee was created as a citizens' movement to ameliorate urban air quality. In the U.S., Teddy Roosevelt, before he became president, joined a number of other wealthy sportsmen to form the Boone and Crocket Club to counter the wanton slaughter of bison and other big game animals, which were then in danger of extinction.

My own environmental credo, which is a synthesis of the romantic and spiritual with the pragmatic and utilitarian approaches, was shaped by my experience, but also by the inspiration I derived from these pioneers. While I was still active in the mining and prospecting business, I was very much influenced by a book by the geologist Harrison Brown, called *The Challenges to Man's Future*, in which he traced the relationship between human needs and the availability of natural resources. Then Rachel Carson's *Silent Spring* had a great impact on me, as it did on so many of my generation, and expanded my awareness of how the industrial civilization I was deeply involved in was undermining the natural resources and life-support systems that the human future ultimately depended on.

NGOs played a major role in putting the environmental issue on the political agenda in the 1960s, and in 1969 helped prod the UN into accepting Sweden's proposal to hold the first global environmental conference. They also made a significant contribution to its results.

The Stockholm Conference itself had an important impact on the NGO environmental movement, too. The heightened awareness and controversies that it gave rise to stimulated an immense wave of citizen interest. The proliferation of environmental associations and the mushrooming of the international movement from Stockholm through Rio took place in the context of a massive shift of power and influence in this area from governments to civil society. The social philosopher Lester Salamon, in a thoughtful article in the summer 1994 edition of *Foreign Affairs*, compared the emergence of a strong and influential civil society in the latter part of the twentieth century to the rise of the nation-state in the nineteenth.

None of this is static. And the shift is going both ways—the environmental movement has become more conscious of development issues, but the reverse is true also: organizations primarily concerned with development are broadening their own activities to include the environment. Even organizations devoted to social issues, like the Boy Scouts, the Girl Guides, human rights and feminist organizations and indigenous people's groups, have all to varying degrees recognized the relevance of sustainable development to their interests.

And even the approaches to sustainable development keep changing. At first the concept was seen mostly as an interaction between the environmental and economic dimensions of development; now it is common also to include the social dimensions of development. Many NGOs retain as their primary focus one of the three components—the environmental, the economic and the social—but now generally relate it to the broader idea of sustainable development. An example is the Sierra Club. Even Greenpeace, the largest and best known of the activist extreme of the movement, now makes sophisticated policy recommendations to governments and international organizations and has even begun to dance with business, engaging in attempts to resolve issues previously irreconcilable between the two solitudes.

What has emerged is an intricately connected global environment and sustainable development movement. Crudely, it can be said to consist of six principal categories of organizations.

1. Large, well-established organizations that work both nationally and internationally, often through counterparts in other countries created on their initiative and with their support

These include the traditional pioneers of the environmental movement—the Sierra Club, the Audubon Society, the National Wildlife

Federation, Friends of the Earth, the Environmental Defense Fund and the National Resources Defense Council, all originating in the United States and drawing most of their support and influence from their American constituencies. There are fewer such organizations in other countries, and their influence is more limited. I've already mentioned the Commons, Open Spaces and Footpaths Preservation Society in Britain, but there are others in Canada, Europe, Australia, Japan and developing countries. Most of these were initially committed to conservation, but as understanding of the broader, systemic nature of environmental issues has grown, they have enlarged their focus to include first the environment and now sustainable development.

2. Organizations that are principally international in their purpose and character

Foremost among them is the International Union for the Conservation of Nature and Natural Resources (IUCN), now known as the World Conservation Union, which uniquely combines in its membership both governmental and non-governmental organizations, including nature protection bodies, scientific research organizations, natural history societies and, in its early years, even a few hunting organizations. Founded in 1948 as the International Union for the Protection of Nature, it was first headquartered in Brussels. Now based in Gland, Switzerland, it has a membership that consists of 74 national government members, 105 government agencies (such as the U.S. Environmental Protection Agency) and more than 700 non-governmental organizations (ranging from Friends of the Earth and Wetlands International to the Wildlife Clubs of Uganda). In total the members of IUCN make up a global network of 895 institutions and organizations representing people from all walks of life, working toward the common goal of nature conservation. The union's mission is to influence, encourage and assist societies throughout the world to conserve the integrity and diversity of nature and to ensure that any use of natural resources is equitable and ecologically sustainable.

The IUCN is genuinely international in character rather than being an international extension of a national organization. Its diverse membership allows it to work at all levels of the environmental debate, from the local and community to the national and up to the global level.

When I was involved in IUCN, my principal contribution was to broaden their base of financial support, recruit new leadership and begin a program of Conservation for Development through which IUCN's conservation ethos and expertise became more concentrated on issues and practical programs of particular interest to developing countries. There was considerable resistance from traditional conservationists in its membership, but the changes that resulted have immensely extended IUCN's influence and effectiveness in developing countries, as well as bringing to it new financial and political support.

Early in the life of IUCN it became clear to some of its founders, particularly Sir Peter Scott, the eminent British naturalist, that an organization of professional conservationists was not well geared to raise financial support from private sources. Sir Peter formed the World Wildlife Fund, with help from a galaxy of notable people— the legendary Belgian-Swiss banker Louis Frank, the British advertising mogul David Ogilvy, the Swiss conservationist and member of the founding family of one of Switzerland's leading pharmaceutical companies, Luc Hoffman, the South African industrialist Anton Rupert and Prince Bernhard of the Netherlands. They built WWF International into a formidable fundraising enterprise that has now become operational itself and independent from IUCN, though the two still have close relations.

Of all the NGOs in this group, perhaps the most influential is Greenpeace, which originated in Canada on the initiative of Mac-Taggert Cowan. Greenpeace has become an internationally known environmental "brand name," mostly through its dramatic confrontational tactics designed to draw attention to issues ranging from French nuclear tests in the South Pacific to Shell Oil's plans to dispose of a North Sea oil platform by sinking it in the deep ocean.

As the principal "prosecutor" of the environmental movement, Greenpeace has never been much of a conciliator. Recently, however, it has done some constructive, though less well-known, work in developing credible, professional policy input into a number of international negotiations. It has also proven inventive in other ways, especially in pushing "green" solutions to problems. One of its causes was to promote the use of refrigerators free of fluorocarbons. Even at its most provocative and contentious, I believe, Greenpeace has played an invaluable role in publicizing issues and rallying political support.

Though Conservation International, a relative newcomer in the field, is very much an American product, both in its origins and its culture, it has, under the leadership of its dynamic founder, Peter Seligman, developed a broad, international dimension with local affiliates and partners in many developing countries. It has become increasingly an international rather than a purely American organization.

3. Community, grassroots and special-purpose organizations, many of them linked through a series of loose networks and coalitions

These include many thousands of organizations and citizen movements in developing countries and in the former Soviet Union. One of the best known is Kenya's Green Belt Movement, led by the dynamic scientist turned environmental activist Wangari Maathai. Some seven hundred of these organizations are members of the Environment Liaison Centre International based in Nairobi, which was established on my initiative to facilitate relationships between NGOs and UNEP. Elsewhere, the European Environmental Bureau, which acts as an umbrella organization for NGOs within the European Community, has been effective in dealing with some important European and broader international issues such as transboundary pollution.

But such organizations, which have co-ordination as their primary function, face inherent difficulties in trying to develop common positions and common action programs. Their memberships are, to put it politely, fractious in the extreme and represent a wide diversity of interests and viewpoints.

When I set up the Earth Council with the co-operation of a number of friends and collaborators in the movement, it was to serve a wide and diverse constituency. We planned to become a facilitator of partnerships and co-operative actions rather than reaching common positions.

It's difficult to estimate the total number of organizations, citizen groups and movements that have emerged in the developing countries. Many of them are informal, very specialized or local in their interests. The same is true in Eastern Europe and the former Soviet Union, where the local manifestations of severe pollution and environmental damage gave rise to ecology clubs and action groups close to those sources. They were never organized into coherent national movements but nevertheless played an important part in the grass-roots ferment and discontent that contributed to the demise of the Communist regimes in these countries.

Such groups continue to strive to organize local action and political support. But their efforts are severely constrained, both by lack of money and because the disintegration of their economies has pushed environmental concerns to the margins.

Helping to mobilize greater external support for these movements has become one of the highest priorities of the environmental and sustainable development community.

4. Policy and scientific research institutes working in the environment, natural resources and international development fields
Again, these are predominantly American organizations, though there has been encouraging activity in other countries, including the developing world. The most prominent of these are also the most effective, I believe—though I readily acknowledge I'm not completely objective, since I've had close ties to them all. These are the World Resources Institute in Washington, D.C., where I was until recently chairman, Sweden's Stockholm Environment Institute, of which I am still chairman, the International Institute for Sustainable Development in Winnipeg, Manitoba, which I served as a board member, and the London-based International Institute for Environment and Development, where I also served as a member of the board.

The earliest policy institute in the field, and a highly influential one, is Resources for the Future, of which I was also a board member. It was established in the United States, initially to undertake research on important natural resource–related issues, and has since expanded its scope to include the broader fields of environment and sustainable development.

There are many others. In Germany, the Wuppertal Institute has become a leading influence in the field of energy and the Keil Institute of World Economics in the field of economics. In Pakistan, the Asian Institute for Sustainable Development was formed by Mahbub ul Haq, one of the most brilliant and innovative leaders of the sustainable development movement, who helped me greatly in the run-up to Stockholm. He and his wife, Khadija ("Bani"), were the most remarkable and effective team in the field. In recent years Mahbub became especially known for the creation of the UNDP's *Human Development Report* and the Human Development Index, which measures the performance and quality of life in individual countries in terms of the actual impact on people. His tragic and premature death in 1998 robbed the world community of one of its most visionary and influential development leaders.

Academies of science have also become important contributors to scientific and policy research, notably the Swedish Academy of Sciences and national academies in the United States, Russia, China and many other countries. The International Council of Scientific Unions in Paris, which is the world organization of scientific academies, has become an actor in this field.

Universities have also been significantly involved in research in both policy and technical areas.

Of a somewhat different nature is the WorldWatch Institute, founded shortly after Stockholm by the American agricultural scientist turned journalist Lester Brown. He is one of the most influential gurus in the field, universally respected as a committed and effective advocate, though some regard WorldWatch reports as good journalism more than good science. A few of Brown's views are considered overly extreme and even alarmist by other professionals, particularly his predictions of an impending food crisis. But the WWI is in a class by itself as the principal non-governmental source of information on and analyses of environment and sustainable development issues.

When I headed the United Nations Environment Program, we became one of its first supporters.

Other useful data can be found in the *World Resources Report*, produced by the World Resources Institute in co-operation with UNEP, the *World Bank's World Development Report* and *Mahbub ul Haq's Human Development Report.*

5. Organizations primarily concerned with other issues that now have important environment/sustainable development dimensions
These now include parts of the trade union movement, which had been traditionally apprehensive about and in some cases actively hostile to environmentalism (and in fact still is on many local issues) but has now become much more constructively engaged. Lane Kirkland, then head of the AFL-CIO in the United States, became an active member of my group of eminent advisers.

6. "Local initiatives," which generally involve a combination of local government support and citizen action
Driving these initiatives has been a unique organization, non-governmental in character but composed primarily of representatives of local governments worldwide. I have already mentioned ICLEI—the International Council for Local Environmental Initiatives —which was established under the aegis of the International Union of Local Authorities, a direct result of the impetus provided by the Earth Summit. From its headquarters in Toronto, under the able leadership of its secretary-general, Jeb Brugmann, ICLEI has fostered the adoption by some three thousand cities and towns around the world of their own Local Agendas 21, based on Rio's global Agenda 21. These agendas have demonstrated both the political importance and the practical efficacy of addressing global issues at the local level and represent perhaps the single most hopeful development in the implementation of the results of Rio. This is the reason I have, both personally and through the Earth Council, tried to be especially supportive of ICLEI.

Where does business fit into this scheme of things?

Like trade unionism, business and industry have been ambivalent in their approach to the environment and sustainable development.

At the time of the Stockholm Conference there was still a deep suspicion of environmentalism among business leaders, and only a few brave souls swam against the current, like Ian MacGregor, the chairman of the Environment Committee of the International Chamber of Commerce, who became supportive of our efforts to engage business more constructively in the environment movement. In 1990 the International Chamber of Commerce adopted a Business Charter for Sustainable Development. After the Earth Summit it joined with Stephan Schmidheiny's Business Council for Sustainable Development to form the World Business Council for Sustainable Development, which has established a strong constituency of business leaders committed to sustainable development and led the way in demonstrating its practical applications and benefits. Some business leaders, like Sir John Browne, chief executive officer of British Petroleum-Amoco, have been among the most influential advocates of sustainable development. Others are still reluctant, and in some cases recalcitrant, as can be clearly seen from the industry-financed campaign in the United States to undermine support for acceptance of commitments to reduce greenhouse gas emissions under the Climate Change Convention. This has its counterpart in Canada, where some industry leaders, notably R. B. (Bob) Peterson, CEO of Canada's largest petroleum company, Imperial Oil, have based their opposition to any moves to reduce CO_2 emissions more on prejudice and their own corporate interests than on the kind of scientific and rational risk assessment they employ in their business decisions. Indeed, this prompted me to remark in response to a question during a press conference that in the fossil fuel industry, "not all the fossils are in the fuel." Fortunately, historical precedents such as the resistance by some business leaders of the time to the movements to ban the slave trade and child labour with grim warnings that they would be disastrous for the economy, show that the more enlightened views are those that prevail. And ultimately, what is good for society is good for business.

In sum, the environment and sustainable development movement comprises a vast number of individual actors and organizations, large and small, local and global. For some, saving the environment and achieving sustainable development are their principal purposes. For others, this objective complements their primary purposes. And in some cases, particularly with business, their interest is more a matter of public relations and image than of deep commitment. Some are linked through regional organizations and National Councils for Sustainable Development. UN organizations, and most notably UNCED, have served to bring NGOs together, demonstrating that collectively they could have a formidable influence on the policies and negotiations of governments. So have UN conferences, such as those on population in Cairo, on women in Beijing, on social development in Copenhagen and on habitat in Istanbul.

There is no question that NGOs play the central role in building and sustaining both the public awareness and the political will that are required for action on these issues. But as yet they have not been able to establish a permanent framework within which they can concentrate their efforts. The Earth Council is helping. It and other organizations are using the Internet to provide civil society throughout the world with access to the information necessary to build a sense of common purpose and co-operative alliances. Indeed, such alliances are, in my view, the wave of the future—and the Earth Council is well positioned on the leading edge of this wave. And the Stockholm Environment Institute is also taking the lead in demanding a system-based environment and development network.

It's difficult to make an accurate count of the total number of citizen action and non-governmental initiatives in the developing countries. As I recounted in the previous chapter, there were more than a thousand NGOs officially registered for the Earth Summit. Several thousand more were not registered but participated in the accompanying Global Forum. The UNDP Human Development Report for 1993 indicated that in the early 1980s one estimate suggested that NGOs touched the lives of about 100 million people in developing countries—60 million in Asia, 25 million in Latin America and some 12 million in Africa. In 1993 the figure was nearer 250 million, and rising, but that was only one-fifth of the 1.3 billion people living in absolute poverty in developing countries. Fourteen hundred NGOs are now accredited to participate in the UN Commission on Sustainable Development.

The global recession in the early nineties caused some setbacks in the movement. But public response to particular issues like climate change make it clear that the environmental ethos has become deeply rooted in the consciousness of a majority of people. The public backlash in the U.S. at the attempts by the right-wing Republican-dominated Congress to roll back some of the environmental legislation of recent years testifies to the underlying strength of the public commitment to the environment, even when it may be temporarily overshadowed by more immediate concerns with the economy and employment.

In a thoughtful review of the state of the movement in America in his book *A Moment on the Earth*, the journalist Gregg Easterbrook suggested that environmentalists have been too pessimistic, that there has been much more progress made in dealing with environmental concerns, particularly in the United States and other industrialized countries, than most environmentalists have been willing to admit. He made a strong case for incentives rather than regulation. But even as he did so, he also acknowledged that things have become better largely because of the environmental movement and the impetus provided by legislation.

Civil society, clearly, is ready for the changes that are necessary for its own long-term survival. And its principal instruments, the NGOs, are becoming more sophisticated and skilled in using the latest information technologies, particularly the Internet, to amplify the message and leverage their influence.

A Matter of Energy: Running a Power Utility

THE RETURN TO GENEVA AFTER RIO WAS, naturally enough, an anticlimax. We had to begin the process of scaling down and then phasing out our secretariat; by the end of July it was mostly done, and we'd bade farewell to many of the colleagues who had shared what was for each of us one of our greatest human experiences. I'd agreed to stay on until September with a small core staff to prepare the report of the conference for the forthcoming General Assembly session and other necessary cleanup activities.

In mid-July 1992 I had a call from Stephen Lewis, with whom I'd developed a close friendship when he was Canada's ambassador to the UN at the time I was working in the Office for Emergency Operations in Africa. He prepared me to receive a phone call from Ontario's new premier, Bob Rae, hinting that the call would have something to do with the search for a new chief executive for Ontario Hydro.

I'd known Rae for a long while—he was a teenager when I occasionally visited with his father, Saul, one of the stars of Canada's diplomatic service.

Of course, the idea was attractive—the chance to run, and therefore to shape, one of the continent's huge public utilities (and one of its primary generators of nuclear power). Ontario Hydro was a massive and monolithic utility company with plenty of problems of its own and would be a massive challenge for anyone. But for an environmentalist it could also be seen as an opportunity actually to practise sustainable development, and in one of the largest companies in a field that was central to the issues I had been dealing with at Rio. I knew many of my friends in the environmental movement wouldn't understand—for them, nuclear power was a devil only slightly less sinister than soft coal (or, for some, even more so)—but I'd be prepared to risk their displeasure if I thought it would really give me the opportunity to put my sustainable development principles into practice. So the prospect that Stephen Lewis dangled before me was tempting. How could I do it?

Premier Rae duly phoned me shortly thereafter and made his pitch.

I told him I was flattered, but I'd thought about it and couldn't see how I could take it on. I explained that I needed to give my attention to my business affairs, which had fallen into bad shape during the time I was preoccupied with UNCED. I wasn't exactly broke, but I was no longer in a position to exercise the independence I always needed, and so I had, once again, to rebuild that. I also needed to devote time to the follow-up of UNCED, particularly the development and nurturing of the Earth Council. Maybe, I suggested, a more appropriate role for me might be as non-executive chairman. I could then help recruit a new chief executive.

Rae said that though he understood my position, he would like to explore ways of resolving my problem rather than accepting the fact that it would make an insurmountable barrier to my taking on the job. Hydro, he explained, was experiencing great difficulties and would need my full-time commitment. We agreed to meet to discuss it further, which we did at a restaurant in Toronto. I was interested to listen to him. He'd grown into an intelligent and experienced political leader, but the New Democrats he led had been vaulted somewhat unexpectedly into office when the governing Liberals frittered away a majority government. In Ontario Hydro, Rae faced one of his major challenges.

He badly needed a new chairman who would also be chief executive. The board and management of Ontario Hydro were determined to protect it from the kind of changes they feared that the new "socialist" government would try to force on them. And the whole internal culture of Hydro, as I was to find out, was resistant to change and particularly change from the outside, including the owners. Hydro's whole organization and cost structure, and its commitment to the continuing expansion of its nuclear-power generating capacity, had all been geared to its forecasts of a continually increasing demand for electric power. It had always been thus at Hydro, and the organization was ill prepared to deal with the severe recession then afflicting Ontario's economy and the consequent declining market. Typically, the corporation had reacted to declining revenues by increasing its rates. It had trimmed some of the extra staff it had built up in anticipation of continued expansion, but most of the fat remained. Customers were balking at the rate increases, and important industries were abandoning their plans for expansion in Ontario, some threatening to move out altogether. Criticisms of Ontario Hydro were persistent and universal. Failure to deal with the problems immediately would further damage the province's economy, already reeling from recession.

The controversy around Hydro had been exacerbated when the board, appointed by the previous government, named a CEO without consulting Rae's government. The government promptly retaliated by exercising its right to appoint a new chairman, Mark Eliesen, who up to then had been deputy minister of energy for the province. His appointment, and the precipitous increase in remuneration it gave him, were widely criticized, and after a short and stormy period he resigned to become president of BC Hydro, thus creating the vacancy that Rae was now seeking to fill.

"If you take it," the premier told me, "you'll have unfettered executive power and full political support."

Rae had shrewdly laid out the very conditions I would find challenging, and my appetite was whetted. But I still didn't see how I could do it. It would be a formidable full-time executive responsibility. The small oil company Baca Resources (now called Cordex Petroleums Inc.), of which I was the principal shareholder and to which I had guaranteed a bank loan, was on the brink of insolvency. Some of my close friends had invested in it, and I simply could not let it go under. I had also been pursuing plans to establish an environmental technology company. I'd need three months—at least—to put my business affairs on an even keel and ensure that they'd be well managed if I had to absent myself again. But there was no guarantee I'd do it in such a short time.

I also reminded the premier how important it was to me to leave room in my life for my environmental and sustainable development interest, and how much I wanted and needed to follow up my work at the Earth Summit. Here again he reacted shrewdly. He shared my commitment to the environment and sustainable development, he said. "I'd regard the continuation of your environmental work as an important part of your responsibilities at Ontario Hydro. It would be a contribution to the province, which the government would be pleased to encourage and support."

By the end of the dinner I was still reluctant, but half persuaded. "If I can, I will," I told him. "But for the moment, I just can't commit. I have to leave the matter open."

He agreed. "But only until October at the latest."

And on that note, we parted.

I began immediately to work on organizing my affairs and thinking through how I might accept the premier's offer. When I moved back to Toronto from Geneva in early September, I canvassed a variety of possibilities. At the urging of my friend Andy Sarlos, I discussed my situation with Peter Munk and his partner, Joe Rotman. Munk I'd known for some time; he'd become one of Canada's most influential business leaders. Rotman I knew only through his reputation as a successful businessman and a generous supporter of public causes. I told them in confidence of Bob Rae's offer and my concern that it was too soon for me to lock up my personal interests again. My business was already beginning to improve, but I still worried that it would be premature for me to take on the Ontario Hydro job.

Both of them stressed to me how important Ontario Hydro was to the province's economy and made it clear that I should not forgo the opportunity to do a service to the province. Typically, being the kind of men they are, they also offered me the kind of tangible support in my business activities to give me confidence that I'd be able to resolve my problems.

On this basis I was able to advise Premier Rae that I'd accept his offer and worked out the particulars with his quietly efficient and savvy deputy minister of energy, George Davies. The announcement of my appointment was greeted with mixed reactions. Some were complimentary about me personally but sceptical about whether I was the right person for the job. Fortunately, my appointment couldn't take effect until I'd appeared before the appropriate legislative committee, which was in early December. This gave me more time to work on my business affairs. It also enabled me to undertake an intensive study of Ontario Hydro so I could make a quick start when I took up the role in December 1992, after surviving the legislative hearing.

We rented an apartment on the waterfront in Toronto and began to look around for a country retreat somewhere between the city and Ottawa—my son Fred and I both lived in Toronto, but my other children were in Ottawa, and I wanted a place accessible for all of them. I've always enjoyed rural living and have usually been able to arrange to have either my main home or a second one in the countryside. This time it wasn't so easy. My cash position was tight, and I knew I'd have to settle for something modest.

We were about to commit ourselves to an old log house by a brook in a beautiful spot near the town of Cobourg—which had the additional attraction of having been the home of my paternal grandparents, who had moved to Manitoba from there—when Fred came across a place in the Kawarthas near a village called Buckhorn. It had qualities I liked, including its own private lake, Lost Lake. There were several log and wood buildings and many trees. Everything was rundown, but the basic structures were sound, and the property itself was a gem: constituting its own mini-ecosystem surrounding the lake, isolated from neighbours yet readily accessible to the village. Best of all, I was able to take it over with a very modest outlay. We've gradually refurbished it, and it's now my favourite retreat, my principal home and the gathering point for our family.

The more I delved into the state of Ontario Hydro, the more I became convinced that the crisis it faced was severe and fundamental. It was a classic example of a company that had long been so dominant in its field that it had developed a strong internal culture resistant to effective oversight or to necessary change.

I put my nose down and plowed into the masses of material I'd asked for. The fact that I'd had some experience in the electric power industry at an earlier stage of my career, when I was president of Power Corporation, gave me some background to draw on, and I had had considerable experience since then in other aspects of the energy business, primarily oil and gas. I have an analytical bent, which was useful, and I soon saw that critical information was missing. Nowhere in all that mountain of paper were the basics to assess how different parts of the corporation were performing. I asked for the figures showing our capital investment in each area of the business and their revenues and costs. I focused especially on the nuclear plants, which accounted for most of our generating capacity and most of our debt. The answer I received, rather sheepishly, from our financial vice-president was, "This isn't the way the corporation's accounts have been kept. It will take some time to dig out these figures." I told him to get to work on it immediately, but in fact it was almost a year before the figures were produced. They showed that some $28 billion had been invested in Hydro's nuclear facilities, and the best estimate of their current value was something in the range of $15 billion. The good news was that this was largely offset by the fact that our other generating facilities, principally the hydroelectric power plants, had been written down to the point that their current value would come close to offsetting the huge writedown of our nuclear facilities.

I was astonished. Why had the board of directors, which over the years had included some of Canada's most prominent business leaders, not insisted on being given this kind of information, so essential to sound decision making? How could they do their job of guiding the company's management without the necessary information? The shocking answer was that they had not.

It had taken the current economic recession to reveal the fundamental weaknesses of Hydro, but those weaknesses were not new.

They had their origin in the history of a company that contained in its management some of the best professionals in the country—indeed in the entire electric power industry—and on its board some of the province's most eminent people. Despite all this eminence and all this brainpower—or maybe because of it—management had become arrogant. They had learned to outwait their political masters, at least those they did not approve of. The rest they either co-opted or avoided. It wasn't so much a conspiracy by devious people as a culture of blind conviction—a classic case of the best of people who thought they knew best and as a result became blinded to some pretty obvious realities.

Chief among those was their assumption that past boom times would continue indefinitely. Their analysts had projected that future demand would increase on the upward trend they had followed in past years. Hydro had thus embarked on a massive program of expanding nuclear generating facilities and transmission lines to meet these projections, stubbornly adhering to them despite mounting evidence that they had become entirely unrealistic.

My analysis of our cost and revenue projections showed me that unless something changed drastically, matters would get worse: rates would have to be increased again, and quite steeply.

In professional and technological terms Ontario Hydro was still unquestionably an industry leader, but its culture was dangerously out of sync with reality. The ethos was still that of a monopoly, which could expect to meet higher costs by raising rates indefinitely. This situation was reinforced by the anomaly that Ontario Hydro was its own regulator, receiving the "advice" of the Public Utilities Board but not subject to its control.

Even during the recession, despite some staff reductions, Hydro's costs had still not been brought under control. Management seemed to have assumed that the reductions in demand for electricity were purely temporary, and there would be a return to business as usual—an almost perverse response. Open markets and competition were heralding the demise of the monopolistic structure that had characterized the industry; technological advances were making it feasible to generate power competitively in smaller and more efficient

co-generation units, and a new contingent of independent producers were demonstrating that economies of scale no longer dictated
that consumers must rely primarily on mega-generating plants for
their power supplies.

One of my chief concerns in this analytic process was to understand how we had become disproportionately dependent on nuclear
generation for the province's power supply. It was clear that the
corporation had made an early move into nuclear, and that its commitment had become deeply entrenched in the corporate culture
and accepted by successive governments and the public. Nuclear
advocates had dominated management, and there'd been scarcely
any opposition from successive provincial governments and their
board appointees. But there were some vocal critics in the environmental and non-governmental community—notably Energy Probe.
When I analyzed their positions, I was impressed with many, but
certainly not all, the points they had made.

Bob Rae's NDP government was cast in a different mould from
those that had preceded it. It came into power with a strong commitment to the environment and was from the beginning concerned
about, if not hostile to, Ontario's disproportionate reliance on nuclear
energy. One of its first acts had been to declare a moratorium on the
further development of nuclear.

This upset of Hydro's nuclear establishment was underscored by
my appointment. My credentials as an environmentalist and the concerns I had expressed publicly about nuclear energy over the years
deepened the sense of estrangement from the seats of power that our
nuclear enthusiasts were feeling. In retrospect it's clear that they
developed a siege mentality, designed to insulate the nuclear business of Hydro as much as possible from the threats they perceived
from both the NDP government and the new management. In fairness, they were for the most part good people; they saw themselves
as "keepers of the sacred flame" of nuclear power.

I soon developed a close rapport with, and reliance on, Al Kupcis,
who had only recently been made president and chief operating
officer. He'd first made his mark in the corporation's research and
development department, and his professional skills, his talent for

management and sound judgment inspired the confidence of all who knew him. For my part I was grateful that he was not captive to the dominant ethos of the corporation. As it turned out, he shared, and indeed helped to shape, my analysis of the corporation's problems and needs. He also helped me select from the senior and middle management ranks of the company a team of the brightest and ablest younger people, who themselves believed in the need for change and had the knowledge and experience of the organization to develop a specific program of change.

To chair this inside team I recruited a tough-minded, experienced outsider, John Wilson, who had headed the management consultancy practice of one of Canada's leaders in that field, Woods Gordon. A forthright, no-nonsense man, he brought to the team a disciplined and analytical mind, honed by vast experience dealing with organizations undergoing change. His somewhat crusty temperament put some of our people off. But our restructuring team was high-spirited and not easily coerced, and members soon developed respect for him.

John and I had our differences, though we resolved them amicably. The most important was my insistence that we invite a senior representative of each of our unions to join the team. John was opposed, but I pushed him. I knew we'd never implement any radical change without the co-operation of the unions, and they'd be much more likely to go along if they were on the inside. Later he was gracious enough to concede that it had been a good thing to do.

I set a daunting deadline of sixty days for the completion of the restructuring team's work. "In that time," I said, "I want specific recommendations of specific changes in organization and structure, which will give effect to the new premises that the corporation must adapt to."

They met their deadline, and though I didn't go along with all the recommendations of the team, I did use their report as the basis for the changes that I proposed to the board.

The actions we took were drastic and far-reaching—a massive program of cost reductions to halt spiralling rate increases, reduce Hydro's indebtedness and effect a fundamental restructuring of the organization to make it more businesslike, more flexible and more responsive to customer needs. We committed to freezing rates in real-cost terms for the balance of the decade, reduced staff by more than 30 percent, cut operating and administrative costs by $600 million and slashed the capital expenditure program by $13 billion. We wrote off "soft" assets and cleaned up the balance sheet.

These measures were designed to launch the corporation on a long-term program of debt reduction, stabilizing and even modestly reducing some rates. Even with very slow growth and our self-imposed rate cap, we'd reduce the $35 billion debt by about $8 billion over five years. In our restructuring we organized the corporation into semi-autonomous, strategic business units and separated transmission and distribution from the generation side of the business. We created an electricity exchange and developed transfer pricing among our business units to duplicate competitive conditions in an internal setting. We embarked on an hourly spot-market experiment to develop experience with competition among other Ontario generators, and prepared for the opening up of Ontario's electricity market. We undertook a series of measures to inculcate a performance-oriented culture within the corporation, establishing corporate performance measures and a related executive compensation system.

My personal support staff has always been essential to sustaining my highly activist management style. I have taken care to select them, rapidly released those I knew either could not measure up or were not willing to make the commitment it required. And I have always been well served.

To lever my own time and energy and take care of the large amount of correspondence, internal and external, that I always liked to handle myself, I needed the very best of secretarial and administrative back up. In Phyllis Pandovski, the senior secretary I had inherited from my predecessor and decided to retain on a conditional basis, I soon found I had a rare gem.

During this same period, the Public Utilities Board was continuing an apparently endless series of hearings on the whole question of power generation in Ontario, including interventions by environmental and other special-interest groups funded by Ontario Hydro.

The hearings, which had begun before I came into Hydro, had produced a vast amount of material but had taken a good deal longer and involved greater expense than had originally been contemplated. That they had not yet produced a report and wouldn't be able to do so for several months posed a dilemma for us. We didn't want to delay our urgently needed reforms—but how could we go ahead while hearings were continuing on much the same subject?

Accordingly, we proposed, and the government agreed, that the hearings be terminated. In return we promised to consult the analyses, viewpoints and insights the hearings had produced, and we did.

The fact that the utilities board had influence but no real control over Ontario Hydro was always a source of tension between the two organizations, and this became evident in the board's often peremptory treatment of Hydro officials who testified before them. The difficulty was brought into focus when we decided not to seek a rate increase for 1994. Our lawyers advised me that if we weren't trying to put up rates, then legally we didn't need utilities board hearings. I was delighted. The hearings had become an annual ritual, when board members and intervenors could bring up many other Hydro-related issues, and there was no precedent for not holding them. On the other hand, if we had let the hearings continue, we would have had to present our restructuring plans, and this would inevitably have delayed them interminably; in all probability they would simply not have been implemented, or only in a much diluted form.

So we cancelled the hearings. As a result, paradoxically, the most extensive program of transformation in Ontario Hydro's history was carried out more rapidly than anyone thought possible, without prior review by the Public Utilities Board, something that I don't believe could have happened in any other jurisdiction. In this case I think it worked to the advantage of Ontario Hydro and the province, but I don't believe it's right in principle that the monopoly supplier should also be the regulator. I made my position on this clear in my public statements, to the disappointment of some of my more traditional colleagues.

Next, I turned my attention to the unions.

My insistence on bringing union representatives in on the reform process worked, to a degree. Nevertheless, they strongly objected to the sheer scale of the staff reductions, and to a number of other measures they thought might weaken their power. They were also suspicious that the division of the corporation into business units might be a step toward privatization and segmentation of the labour force. They therefore vehemently resisted our proposals to have each of the business units deal separately with the unions in negotiating agreements. The Power Workers Union staged raucous demonstrations on the grounds of the Legislature and appealed to the public in a series of advertisements, always featuring photos of their president, John Murphy. Despite this, my personal relationships with John and his principal colleague, Peter Kelly, were generally civil and even friendly.

Hydro's workers had pay and benefits that were the highest in the province and among the highest in Canada. And that wasn't the only cost. In their various contracts they'd succeeded in imposing severe restrictions on the rights of managers—to a degree, in my opinion, that made effective management extremely difficult. (Which is not to say that managers were always right. On the contrary. The union members seldom had the same professional qualifications, but they often had more practical savvy.)

They'd gone along, albeit reluctantly, with our reform program, but the negotiations were bruising and had left tensions. Now we had to prepare for the next round of contract negotiations. We were determined to hold the line on wage levels and benefits and, indeed, to seek some concessions in light of the company's precarious financial position. We knew it would not be easy, and we were right: the negotiations were tough, occasionally degenerating into bitterness.

As the deadline for the expiry of the existing contract neared, tensions escalated. At one point John Murphy attempted to shift the focus of negotiations to the government, but Premier Rae held tough, insisting that Murphy negotiate with us. Nevertheless, during the final days of the negotiations, a government mediator was assigned to facilitate them. Then, much to the apprehension of my colleagues and advisers, I responded to Murphy's insistence by involving myself directly in the negotiations. We narrowed the gap considerably but were still short of agreement on important issues, especially the union's insistence that we not make further staff reductions.

Late at night, when tempers were short, one of my senior colleagues could no longer suppress his indignation at some of the positions being taken by the union's team. He particularly objected to the rough and unfair language. He angrily insisted that they stop.

This wouldn't do. I leaned over and quietly, but visibly, restrained him. Then I did something I rarely do with colleagues: "Shut up," I said.

Later I explained to him that I'd learned from my diplomatic experience that one should never show anger in a negotiating process, except as a deliberate tactic. When you feel real anger, it is important not to let it show—visible anger is a sign that you're losing control and weakens your negotiating posture.

At that point I suggested to the premier that it was time for him to intervene and call us in, which he did. He made it clear to both sides that we must come to an agreement. The stick he carried was that the government could seek legislation to prevent a strike and provide for compulsory arbitration, something neither side wanted.

On the final evening I gave orders to start the process of shutting down our nuclear plants, something the unions hadn't believed we were prepared to do. It would indeed have been a drastic step, but would also have precipitated a situation that no government could allow to happen again.

I carried on the negotiation on a one-to-one basis with Murphy in a small hotel room. The mood finally improved when I suggested to him something the union had long aspired to but had not made a sticking point in the negotiations—membership on the board of directors.

"This could be an important step forward in relations between the union and the corporation," I said.

I think it was, in the end, that critical extra element needed to enable us to bridge the gap that separated us on the other issues. I continued to insist that Hydro could not tolerate wage increases—

that there would be no real security for the employees unless the corporation itself was secure. Restoring financial integrity had to be our priority. In the end Murphy went along.

The turnaround was dramatic. After experiencing the largest loss ever, over $3.5 billion for 1993, we achieved our largest profit ever in 1994, while managing small reductions in rates for many customers for the first time in more than thirty years. And this has enabled rates to remain frozen ever since, a real bonus to the Harris government, which claims credit for an achievement they inherited from Bob Rae.

I was also determined to focus our corporation on a strategy for sustainable development and "eco-efficiency" in the production, transmission and use of energy and in the prevention, reduction and recycling of wastes. I decided to declare this commitment by changing the statement of our corporate goal from "To be a world-class energy company which provides energy and services essential to the prosperity of the people of Ontario," to "To make Ontario Hydro a leader in energy efficiency and sustainable development, and to provide its customers with safe and reliable energy services at competitive prices." I realized that most of the members of the management committee and the board of directors were sceptical, but I pressed for the change, realizing that if I was ever to get it through, it would have to be then, before my honeymoon period had elapsed.

My strategy was accepted, with various degrees of enthusiasm, by my colleagues and with what I sensed was a reserved acquiescence by a silent majority of our people. Some of my board argued that though sustainable development and energy efficiency were noble goals, we should make our changes first and worry about strategic orientation afterwards.

"No," I said, "the changes we're making provide a unique opportunity to integrate sustainable development and eco-efficiency practices into our whole organization. We must get out of the habit of thinking of them as 'add-ons.' To be effective, they must be pervasive. They will, in fact, contribute significantly to the goals of our change process."

Energy efficiency, of course, had to be one of our primary objectives. On the initiative of the Rae government, Hydro had already embarked on a major program designed to make its customers more energy efficient, offering substantial financial subsidies as an inducement. This was derided by some of the corporation's traditionalists —how could it make sense to help our customers reduce their use of electricity? Especially at a time when we had a large surplus capacity and were experiencing declining revenues? But in my view, helping our customers reduce their costs by more efficient use of electric power offset the effect of the large rate increases we'd inflicted on them and made them more competitive at a time when their businesses were suffering. And this would make it more likely that we could retain them as customers over time.

But subsidies couldn't, and shouldn't, go on forever either. We needed a longer-term plan, and to devise and implement it I had brought in John Fox, who had recently led one of the most successful programs of energy conservation for the large California utility, Pacific Gas and Electric. He was given the difficult task of overhauling and strengthening the program while phasing out the direct subsidies we had been offering.

In 1993 we commissioned one of Canada's most respected environmental leaders, Jim MacNeill, whom I had known since Stockholm Conference days, together with his colleague David Runnalls, to develop a sustainable development and energy efficiency program.

Their report was an eye-opener. It identified many instances of wasteful practices and unnecessary environmental impact, some verging on horror stories, attributable to carelessness or neglect and a lack of environmental awareness or sense of responsibility. But they also found that many Hydro employees themselves, purely out of environmental concern and public-spiritedness, had sometimes taken steps to prevent or remedy environmental damage—despite lack of encouragement, and sometimes even lack of support, from their superiors.

The MacNeill–Runnalls report was the subject of a lively discussion at the board, which endorsed it in principle, without explicitly approving some of its more controversial recommendations. These, it was agreed, would be brought back to the board on a case-by-case basis at a later stage. This, nevertheless, provided me with the degree of board sanction I required to put the recommendations into practice.

One of the most shocking facts to emerge from this report was the extent to which Ontario Hydro had been ignoring in its own operations the energy efficiency measures it was pushing its customers to adopt. The corporation was at the same time its own best and worst customer—"best" because Hydro used in its internal operations more electricity than its biggest single customer, the City of Toronto; "worst" because we didn't charge ourselves for it. As it was treated as a "free good" within the organization, there was no incentive to save electricity—indeed, there was a strong propensity to waste it. To rectify this we instituted a system of charging all managers for the electricity consumed in the operations they were responsible for and holding them accountable for meeting energy efficiency standards. We thus began practising what we had been preaching.

It was indicative of the degree to which the nuclear culture had taken over Ontario Hydro that there were no effective control and reporting systems in place to enable top management, the board of directors or the government to hold the nuclear organization accountable. It was true for the whole organization, but it was much more important, and more dangerous, for the nuclear division to be beyond control. This was because of the disproportionately large amount of the company's capital that was invested in nuclear, its heavy reliance on nuclear power and the high standards of safety that had to be met to ensure against the ever-present risk of accidents and the deferred costs of decommissioning and waste disposal.

Particularly surprising was the absence of any special mechanism at the board level to monitor and review nuclear safety. To rectify this we put in place a Nuclear Safety Committee, strengthened the Environmental Committee and provided for joint meetings of these two important committees from time to time.

We also exposed our nuclear operations to review by an independent panel of nuclear utility experts from the United States, who had no difficulty finding room for improvement. Similar deficiencies were criticized by Canada's Atomic Energy Control Board. These were the subject of intense discussion by senior management and the board, which mandated strong measures to remedy them. Generally, these various reports gave our nuclear operations overall passing grades, but they were a matter of serious concern to me and to the board. We didn't want just a passing grade. We were insistent, and I was determined, that our staff reduction and cost cutting would not impair the measures we were taking to maintain the highest possible safety and environmental standards. We were constantly assured by nuclear management that the measures we were taking would indeed achieve this, and the oversight now provided by the Nuclear Safety Committee improved my confidence that this was being done.

Nevertheless, I remained uncomfortably sceptical that we were getting the full flow of reliable and candid information on our nuclear operations that we expected and needed. In consultation with Hydro president Al Kupcis, I decided we had to replace the division's top management, and we did so. In light of what has since come to light about the fudging of information about lapses in nuclear operations, it is obvious that we should have done it sooner and that even replacing the division's head was not enough.

Ontario Hydro had always designed and constructed its own nuclear plants. As a consequence the nuclear division was dominated by a large engineering and construction organization, which in turn dominated the orientation of the entire corporation. As the need to construct new facilities was pushed into the indeterminate future, we had to radically scale back this part of the organization and transform the whole division from one that was construction oriented to one that was primarily operations oriented. In fact we simply abolished the Engineering and Construction Division altogether, a severe blow to the corporation's nuclear establishment and its morale.

Nuclear power is a highly complex, skill-intensive business. It takes a great deal of time to give nuclear operators the training they require. Indeed, there is a special bond of mutual interest and dependence between them and the corporation. There is no external pool of people in Canada for Hydro to draw on to replace its nuclear operators; and as Hydro is by far the largest nuclear operator in Canada, there are very few places nuclear operators can go if they leave Hydro.

Nor is it easy for people without the necessary expertise to discern problems. We had to rely on existing systems—the regime of control and accountability we had established, the independent reviews of the Atomic Energy Control Board, peer review of external experts and the integrity of nuclear managers and operators. Subsequent events have demonstrated that this confidence was not justified. The nuclear organization had systematically put the most positive gloss, even in some instances to the point of suppressing information, on incidents they feared might be used by its critics to undermine confidence in nuclear power. The softness and lack of discipline that permitted this was entrenched in the habits and culture of the organization. I have no doubt that most of Hydro's nuclear people are honourable and responsible, and that those who participated in withholding or distorting information to management honestly believed that they were doing so in the higher interest of protecting the reputation of our nuclear power and, in doing so, Ontario's energy future.

The high price that Hydro and Ontario paid for this became starkly evident years later, in 1997, when the report of a team of American nuclear experts that had been brought in by Kupcis revealed the degree of deterioration of its nuclear facilities. The report recommended shutting down seven plants, representing 17 percent of Ontario Hydro's generating capacity, and introducing a vigorous program of retraining. As a result Kupcis fell on his sword and resigned the presidency, taking responsibility in the Japanese fashion. Carl Andognini, who headed the American team, was put in charge of Hydro Nuclear.

Since then, there has been some progress in improving performance of the nuclear plants, and one of those that were shut down, at Bruce, is being put up for sale to private operators who would put it back into production. But the nuclear issue is still far from being resolved. Massive amounts of money will have to be spent—far sooner and in far greater amounts than was originally provided for in the depreciation accounts of the corporation. When the politicians and the public actually face spending these amounts, there's bound to be an intense new debate on the role of nuclear power in Ontario's energy future.

With the changes well in place, I turned my attention more and more to the longer-term issues: the future of the electric power industry in Ontario and Ontario Hydro's role in it. We prepared a paper setting out various options for the future and used it as a basis for a series of consultative meetings with various stakeholders—the municipal utilities, large consumers, business leaders, non-governmental organizations and native peoples. These evoked great interest and lively dialogue. The fact that we had taken the trouble to consult this way was appreciated even by those who were highly critical of Hydro.

The financial insights we now had, together with our continuing analysis of supply alternatives, convinced me that there was still no single source of electricity both environmentally benign and economically viable. I concluded, therefore, that the best approach was to develop a mix of sources designed to reduce our reliance on nuclear, and—in the short term, at least—move to natural gas as our primary source of fossil fuel energy.

I also saw natural gas as a logical complement to our own product, electricity. Not only is gas the most efficient fossil fuel for generating electric power, but it also provides a competitive alternative to electricity for many of its uses at the consumer level. I had expressed to Bob Rae my disappointment that I came to Hydro too late to try to engineer its acquisition of Union Gas, the second largest natural gas distributor in Ontario, when it had become available.

One scheme that appealed to me was for Ontario Hydro to make a massive purchase of natural gas. This would have allowed Ontario Hydro to control, at least partly, its own energy source. It occurred to me that we could make such a purchase in western Canada of gas not yet connected to pipelines and therefore available at prices that would make it a good investment. For less than $3 billion, roughly the cost of retubing one nuclear reactor, we could acquire a very large gas reserve that would contribute significantly to our long-term security of supply. True enough, we were currently in surplus of supply, largely nuclear, but it was vulnerable to disruption in the event of accidents or safety problems. An investment in natural gas would provide an important reserve and secure future supplies. It would surely be a better investment than refurbishing nuclear plants, because natural gas in the ground would increase in value, while investments in aging nuclear plants would depreciate significantly. Bob Rae was attracted to the idea, but it was much too exotic to sell to a cabinet facing an early election.

I also concluded that we should foster the development of smaller, decentralized hydroelectric co-generation and renewable energy sources, even though we knew it would be some time before they would replace nuclear or fossil fuels for our base-load power supply. We should also accelerate our commitment to energy efficiency and conservation, intensifying our research and development efforts aimed at fuel cells and other promising energy technologies, on which our researchers had already made significant progress.

I arranged to present the alternatives to Premier Rae and his senior colleagues on the Policy and Planning Committee of cabinet. We got their attention, all right, but with an election in prospect in the near future, they weren't about to act on issues so fundamental and potentially controversial.

Because of my international interests I naturally paid special attention to Hydro's international role. The corporation had for some time been selling its services through a division called Ontario Hydro International, and I felt we had a unique opportunity to expand this role. After all, the demand for electricity in developing countries was increasing rapidly, and Ontario Hydro had, both within the corporation and in recent retirees, a supply of skilled and experienced people. An export market for our skills and technologies would open up opportunities for engineering and other consulting firms and suppliers, all of whose domestic markets had been severely affected by the cutbacks in Ontario Hydro.

It became evident to us after more scrutiny that we'd do better abroad if we could actually invest as well as sell our services. We therefore took some steps in this direction. For example, we invested $30 million in a partnership with Hydro-Québec and Power Corporation of Canada in establishing Asia Power, to exploit opportunities in China and other parts of the rapidly developing Asian market. We also acquired a 25 percent interest in the distribution company supplying electric power to much of the city of Lima, Peru. These moves proved highly controversial, both within the government (despite the strong support of Bob Rae) and with various Hydro stakeholders. The amounts we intended to commit were a trivial percentage of our total assets, but public and political opinion in Ontario was dubious about it nevertheless. I didn't really understand why. Why shouldn't one of Ontario's principal industries open up new markets at a time when the domestic economy was faltering? Ontario Hydro had a surplus of the kind of skills that were in demand and the province had launched an export drive. The parochialism the opposition expressed was disappointing.

A particularly interesting expression of Ontario Hydro's international outreach was its membership in the E-7 group of utilities in the G-7, the world's industrialized countries. Canada, uniquely in the group, was represented by its two principal utilities, Ontario Hydro and Hydro-Québec, because both were among the largest.

My first meeting of the group was to be in Tokyo, and in my briefing papers I discovered that the main agenda item was to be a statement endorsing the merits of nuclear power. Through Rod Taylor, then our "sherpa" (a term used to describe the person responsible in each organization for preparing the meetings), I made it clear that I would never endorse such a statement and strongly urged the group to focus on the sustainable development of energy. After some resistance this was eventually agreed.

The heads of these great utilities, with budgets larger than those of many countries, were powerful figures in their own right, yet the meetings were carefully scripted by officials to prevent "surprises." This meant there was no real dialogue and no real exchange of views. This, I knew, was very much in the Japanese tradition: staff always prepared the statements to be made by their senior representatives at such meetings—and expected their bosses to adhere to them. They also insisted that they be given copies of what the other parties were going to say in advance. On this basis a meeting is hardly necessary, except for the social aspects. In any case I insisted on a period of free-for-all discussion, and our Japanese hosts apprehensively agreed. It was fruitful and energizing, and the group decided to accept the format for future meetings. I was also pleased, if somewhat surprised, at the positive response to my proposal that we take the lead in committing ourselves to sustainable development. We decided to hold a special conference on the subject in Cologne, in conjunction with the regular E-7 meeting to be held there in 1996.

Not everything was smooth sailing. I knew it wouldn't be—the chairman of a public utility going through a fundamental reinvention of itself was bound to be living in a fishbowl, with every move subject to scrutiny and criticism. Just after I assumed office, I saw how acerbic some of that criticism was going to be. I had been given a handcrafted birchbark canoe at a dinner held in my honour by the Canadian Executive Service Organization (CESO). When it came time to deliver the thing, I checked the dimensions of my apartment and found there was no way I could squeeze in a full-size canoe. Having no other place to put it, I asked people at Hydro whether they had any storage space they weren't using. Sure, they said, an abundance. I offered to pay an appropriate storage charge, but they said it wasn't necessary—the space wasn't otherwise being used. To my great surprise and chagrin, this soon became an issue in the media—I was accused of using company premises for personal storage. I soon moved the canoe to my country house in the Kawarthas, but the incident continued to be raised against me by my critics.

Another outburst of righteous indignation followed a revelation in the Toronto *Globe and Mail* that I had charged Hydro some $700 for limousine costs during the inauguration of President Clinton and Vice-President Gore in Washington in January 1993. The rest of the costs of the trip—several thousand dollars' worth—I'd absorbed myself, but my staff persuaded me it was right to charge a portion to the company, since my Washington relationships would be useful to Hydro. So I did. I appreciate that $700 seems a lot for a limousine service—conjuring up fat-cat images of sleek black limos with uniformed chauffeurs—but this one was very modest. By the time I decided to attend the inauguration, the prices of normal limousine services had skyrocketed. Through the very helpful secretary of Robert McNamara, I was put on to some college students who were renting their own car, using it to make some money for themselves. I've always made a habit of living modestly, even when travelling on expense accounts, yet here suddenly I had the image of a big spender living luxuriously at Ontario Hydro's expense. I should have known better. In fact I, and Ontario as well, I believe, got good value from this as the new vice-president singled me out at one of the gala parties that followed the inauguration, calling attention to my presence and the fact that I was from Ontario.

An incident of a different kind brought home to me the consequences of initiatives that run counter to public perceptions and attitudes.

All electric power utilities were being driven to seek ways of reducing or offsetting their carbon dioxide emissions in light of increasing evidence of the role of CO_2 in affecting global climate. Of course, by far the best way would be to reduce emissions at source. But there are limits—you can't eliminate them all. Consequently, a number of U.S. utilities, as well as one of Canada's best-run private utilities, TransAlta, were undertaking projects in developing countries to use the CO_2-absorptive capacity of tropical forests to offset CO_2 emissions much more economically than could be done in their own country. (I mentioned this subject in the previous chapter.) I didn't know it at the time, but Ontario Hydro was exploring such a project in Costa Rica. It was still at a preliminary stage, not yet rating the attention of senior management.

It reached me soon enough, and dramatically enough. A news story announced that Ontario Hydro was buying a piece of rain forest in Costa Rica and pointed out that this was a country I had close ties to and where I owned some land. The clear implication was that my personal interest had somehow to be related to Ontario Hydro's plan.

The news was greeted with consternation by the Ontario government. The minister asked that I quickly renounce any such intention.

My response was measured. I would certainly make it clear, I said, that no decision had been taken and also that it had absolutely no relationship to my own holdings in Costa Rica, which were far removed from the site of this project.

On the other hand I saw here a chance to explain why and how these projects—known as joint implementations—actually work, that they are, in fact, a recognized, though still controversial, means of using the resources of developing countries, including their tropical forests, to offset with cash CO_2 emissions from sources in the northern industrialized countries.

I was widely attacked, of course, and the incident has often been dredged up since as evidence of my own soft and eccentric environmentalism. In fact, the practice has since become widely accepted as a response to the challenge of climate change. But at the time, the Ontario public was clearly not ready for it; nor was I ready for the lambasting I received.

I was not able to be very active in international affairs or business when I was at Hydro, but I didn't lose touch with everybody. A very good friend with whom I maintained contact was Jim Wolfensohn. He had continued to turn in a stellar performance in the financial community, but his long-standing interest in a major public service appointment was still very much alive.

I was at my home at Lost Lake when Jim phoned me on a weekend in May 1995 to tell me that he'd just had a call from President Clinton asking him to be the U.S. nominee for the presidency of the World Bank. The campaign to get him nominated, which I'd played a part in, had been a long one and I was delighted for him. Of course he accepted.

Once installed as president, Jim invited me to become his senior adviser—the first appointment he made. I told him I needed no official role and would be pleased to give him whatever help and advice I could on an informal basis. But he insisted on making it official, and I soon became established in an office at the bank on a part-time basis, as I continued with my responsibilities at Ontario Hydro.

Jim gave me a wide mandate to look into any issues that interested me, and I in turn gave him advice on many matters confronting him. He had strongly committed himself to strengthening the bank's leadership in environmental and sustainable development matters, and I focused a good deal of my energies on helping him shape the bank to do this effectively, against the same kind of institutional resistance I had experienced at Ontario Hydro.

I soon realized that one of the best contributions I could make to be supportive of Jim in his new role was to get to know his colleagues and to help them work with him. Overall, he had a strong and experienced group of professionals to choose from in reshaping his senior management team. But most had come up through the ranks of the bank, had the qualities of professional excellence and internal political skills that enabled them to move to its top ranks and at the same time were products of its culture and steeped in its ethos, which might be summarized as "the Bank knows best." In the best of the professional tradition, they were eager to serve their new boss. They were excited at his vision and enthusiasm but often found it difficult to accommodate his management style. This and internal resistance to change made the process inside the bank slower, more complex and more difficult than the very positive sense of change that Jim projected to his external constituency. He soon chose three of the ablest and best bank veterans as managing directors—Gautam Kaji of India, Caio Koch-Weser, a German who had been brought up in Brazil, and Sven Sandstrom of Sweden—and I developed a high regard for and good relationship with each of them, as well as with other members of Jim's team. It is a testimony to the quality of that team that since then his dynamic vice-president of external relations, Mark Malloch-Brown, has been appointed administrator of the United Nations Development Programme, and Caio Koch-Weser has been tapped by the German government as state secretary for finance.

The new directions Jim set for the bank were enlightened, visionary and imperative, and are now beginning to be followed.

His major focus was on changing the basic ethos of the bank to make it a development leader rather than merely a lender, to move it closer to its clients by establishing offices with real decision-making authority in virtually all client countries, and to forge partnerships with business, foundations, other development and policy institutions and NGOs. He sent managers for training at the Harvard Business School and other leading management schools, and reoriented its formidable intellectual and policy capabilities in the economic, social and environmental fields that are directly relevant to the bank's mission to make "knowledge" a central feature of its mandate.

All this has been disruptive and controversial, as change always is, but there is no question that it is transforming the bank radically. Jim has already succeeded in creating a much more visible and positive public image for the bank and in disarming some of its most vocal critics, particularly among non-governmental organizations. They respond not only to Jim's refreshingly candid and open style, but also to the important substantive initiatives he has taken to make the bank more sensitive to the social, human rights and ethical dimensions of development, strengthening its commitment to reduction of poverty, to the environment, to sustainable development and to leading the attack on the pernicious issue of corruption. He has articulated a new and more comprehensive approach to development that requires all these factors to be included in the bank's assessment of its own financing policies and priorities. And he has opened up the bank to consultations and partnerships with other key actors—private foundations, the corporate world and non-governmental organizations. Thus Jim Wolfensohn's bank now projects the image of a new, more innovative, enlightened and responsive world leader in the field of development. But inside the bank, the process of change has been more traumatic and less popular, even to the point of outright resistance in some cases. The internal stresses this has created have still not worked their way through, but now, unanimously elected to a second term, he will have the opportunity to complete his revolution. Already, however, it is clear that the bank will never be the same, and Jim Wolfensohn has made impressive progress toward effecting the kind of fundamental changes required.

There were many interesting parallels between Ontario Hydro and the World Bank. Both were large organizations; both had been long accustomed to being dominant in their field and able to attract the brightest and the best of professional staff; both had developed strong and self-protective internal cultures that were sophisticated in resisting criticism and deflecting the influence of the board and shareholders. Virtually all those in senior management positions in the World Bank joined as young professionals and moved up through the ranks, with little experience of the world outside. Much the same had been true of the professionals in Ontario Hydro. Both clearly needed to change if their organizations were to continue to survive and lead in a world very different from that at the time of their inception.

I'd always made it clear to Bob Rae that I'd undertake to resolve the crisis at Ontario Hydro and try to put the corporation in shape to meet its future challenges but that I had no intention of staying any longer than necessary. By December 1994, I was confident that the new policy and management structures we'd put in place were capable of accomplishing what was necessary and that Al Kupcis had the qualities and the commitment to take on the primary executive leadership. Accordingly, with the agreement of Rae, I yielded my CEO responsibilities to Kupcis, while retaining an active oversight role as chairman and reverting to a dollar-a-year salary.

An election was called for June 1995. The crisis that had made Hydro so intensely controversial had been brought under control, and I didn't expect the utility to become an important election issue. Still, I prepared to make the new government aware of Hydro's vulnerabilities. When Mike Harris and his Conservatives surprised the pundits by pulling ahead of the Liberals in the home stretch and winning the election, I sought an early meeting with the new premier, with whom I had developed a friendly, though not close, relationship. I urged him to allow us to make a presentation to his cabinet of our analysis of Ontario Hydro and our case for the need for expeditious action by the government.

Hydro had not been a part of their election platform, he replied, and it would have to wait.

I soon found I didn't have anywhere near the access to the new government that I had had with Rae's. This was understandable enough, but I was concerned. The principal role of the chairman in Crown corporations is to act as a bridge between management and government, and therefore it requires a person with close ties to the government and the full confidence of it. I was clearly not such a person. Harris, when I told him this, didn't demur, and my resignation became effective in late November 1995.

I was then able to spend more of my time at the World Bank, on my work with the Earth Council and, finally, pay some more attention, long overdue, to my private business interests.

CHAPTER 13

Rio+5: Successes and Failures

A FTER THE EARTH SUMMIT WAS OVER, some of the participants—and some of the media—had asked a stark, deceptively simple and apparently even simplistic question: did we save the world at Rio?

The answer, even at the time and much more clearly in retrospect, was no. But what *had* we done?

By 1997 I was immersed in the process of helping Secretary-General Kofi Annan reform the UN (more about this later), but I never forgot Rio. The third anniversary of the Earth Summit had come and gone, and so had the fourth, and it was always in my mind. The fifth was almost on us, and despite the demands of the UN, I was inevitably caught up in the process of reviewing what had happened—and not happened—since the captains and kings had dispersed to their corners of the Earth. How far had we come? How difficult the road ahead? Who were the laggards? Who was in the vanguard? How could we help? Whom could we enlist? Did we need dramatic formulations and pronouncements or a series of small, incremental steps—or both?

To review the progress and assess the prospects, the Earth Council, together with a host committee of Brazilians and other partner organizations, planned a forum that came to be called, simply, Rio+5, whose theme was "moving from Agenda to Action." The notion was to draw together representatives of civil society (NGOs and grassroots organizations) whose task would be to assess how well the nations of the world had implemented the Earth Summit's recommendations and requirements. One of the major impediments to more progress is the fact that many of the organizations and individuals working for sustainability in their own communities and sectors continue to work largely in isolation from one another. We wanted to help them overcome this isolation by exchanging experiences and establishing new alliances so their successes could be multiplied and they would have a sense of being part of a world movement. We also hoped that recommendations would emerge that we could take to the meeting of the UN Commission on Sustainable Development in New York in April and the special session of the UN General Assembly that followed in June.

The man who really helped us organize Rio+5, was an ebullient and influential Brazilian, Israel Klabin, who became co-chairman with me of the International Organizing Committee and who also served as the chairman of the Brazilian Host Committee. Klabin, a former mayor of Rio de Janeiro, had grown up in a wealthy Brazilian family but had chosen to devote his life principally to charitable and public service activities. A brilliant man, he has a passionate commitment to the environment. With his help we secured the backing of Brazil's President Fernando Cardoso, who agreed to be honorary president of Rio+5 and to give a keynote speech to the assembly. Klabin's role was not without controversy. Many of the leading representatives of the NGOs, always prickly about their independence, bridled at the prospect of participating in a process dominated by Klabin, who they didn't think was sufficiently respectful of their crucial role. There were many tense and anxious moments.

In the end, through the leadership of an exceptionally talented and committed Brazilian, Katia Maya Drager, the conciliatory efforts of Klabin himself and the soothing role of the Earth Council's executive director, Maximo Kalaw, a workable alliance was formed. It remained shaky, but it did hold together and deliver the goods.

The invitees were as broadly representative as possible of stakeholders with expertise and involvement in sustainable development action. National Councils for Sustainable Development (about a hundred had been established since the Earth Summit) constituted a primary constituency for the forum. There were also community-based organizations, local authorities, business and industry, science, technology and research institutes, NGO networks, financial institutions, UN development agencies, environmental organizations, private investors, philanthropic organizations and educational groups. We asked them to review their own experiences and to submit papers as background for the forum and as a contribution to the overall fifth-anniversary review process.

Parallel with this, Rio+5 partner organizations co-operated to set up a series of national and international multi-stakeholder consultations, producing as they did so more than seventy special-focus and eighty national and regional reports. These provided a rich source of information about progress or lack of it in implementing the Earth Summit agreements. Thus, Rio+5 was not simply another meeting, but an attempt to produce new alliances for action among civil society stakeholders and stimulate renewed impetus to action on the part of governments and intergovernmental organizations.

Rio+5, which took place from March 13 to 19, 1997, was a raucous and sometimes chaotic meeting with a lively, colourful and diverse group of more than five hundred participants from around the world. The fact that it had to deal with a broad range of issues in a relatively short period of time dictated a hectic pace and produced results that varied greatly from group to group — near breakdown in some cases to real breakthroughs in others. It was a frustrating experience for some of the more professional and experienced NGO leaders, who felt it was not sufficiently orderly. But we had deliberately concentrated on bringing to Rio representatives of developing country NGOs and grassroots organizations who did not normally get to international conferences, and we gave them a great deal of freedom in managing their events and meetings. This was admittedly risky, and we paid a price for it with some of our supporters; but we also won many new friends who appreciated the fact that we had not precooked the conference for them.

Though the results of Rio+5 were uneven, they made, in my view, an important and much-needed contribution to re-energizing and refocusing the efforts of the civil society participants and to keeping the pressure on political leaders to carry out their commitments. In any case, that was the message I took back with me to New York in a statement I made to the ministerial session of the UN Commission on Sustainable Development on April 8.

"The good news," I told the meeting, "is that there is a great deal of good news; the bad news is that there is not nearly enough of it. The world community has still not made the fundamental transition to a development pathway that will provide the human community with a sustainable and secure future. Environmental deterioration continues, and the forces which drive it persist."

The primary need pointed out at Rio+5 was to find better ways of translating the agreements reached at Rio into effective action at local, national and sectoral levels. These "ways" would include a legal framework, fiscal and budgetary mechanisms, communication and educational programs. How to do this? Despite the lack of a concluding report, a number of recommendations filtered out of the deliberations. I give them here in one gulp, since they're all facets of a complicated but integrated process: that the UN and governments lend practical support to the civil society Earth Charter process; that governments support the formation of multi-stakeholder mechanisms to develop Local Agendas 21; that governments strengthen National Councils for Sustainable Development, which would link to local initiatives as well as lead to regional and global co-operation; that regional forums and councils be encouraged; that better and more open means should be found to funnel money to local and national groups working for sustainability; that new funding be found to help developing countries make the necessary transitions; that the Global Environment Facility be replenished at a higher level with an expanded mandate; that the UN and its members move beyond UNEP to build a truly effective world environment organization with more effective monitoring, assessment and early-warning functions; that the UN make sure all relevant stakeholders take part in debates leading to international accords and their implementation; that industrialized countries agree at the forthcoming meetings of the Parties to the Climate Convention to reduce their carbon dioxide emissions by 20 percent from 1990 levels by the year 2005; that corporations be more accountable to the communities where they operate, as well as to society generally; that governments move to set up a global framework for regulation of international capital flows; and that governments reorient their incentives and subsidies to eliminate unsustainable development practices and to encourage sustainability.

"Some of these," I told the Commission on Sustainable Development, "are fairly easy to get under way—demanding little more than an affirmation by bodies already preconditioned to do so. But others would be much more difficult and much more contentious. A few —such as the demand for global capital-flow regulation, and the somewhat pious notion that corporations should be 'accountable' to the societies where they operate—would indicate a radical change in outlook and would be fiercely resisted by those vigilant to any putative limitations on national sovereignty.

"Much of this was exhortation on all too familiar themes. As one who has worked for so long to move governments to take more action on these issues to try to improve the public awareness and support of such measures that political action requires, I share the general frustration that things have moved so slowly. But I have always refused to be defeated by it. Rhetoric is not sufficient, but it is also not without its value. The rhetoric of political leaders is certainly no substitute for action; but it is often an essential prelude to action and the commitments that leaders make at the level of rhetoric can be invoked to pressure them to act and to hold them accountable. After all, the messages of the great religions have not yet produced a perfect world, but it is still important that they be repeated continually to set the standards and goals to aspire to. We have only been working for fundamental environmental change for a relatively short period, and overall there has been significant progress. We must view slow progress as a reason to continue and strengthen our efforts, not to abandon them."

The special session of the UN General Assembly in July 1997 was noteworthy more for the fact that it attracted so many world leaders than for the progress they had to report. The results were clearly disappointing, because what governments had actually done to follow through on the agreements of Rio was in itself disappointing. But the presence of some sixty heads of government demonstrated that the issues addressed at the Earth Summit continued to have a good deal of political life and served to focus renewed attention on them.

Reforming the UN

I N   T H E   F I R S T   F O U R   Y E A R S following the Earth Summit, I
hadn't been directly involved with the UN but had kept in touch
with some of my friends there and had a good sense of what was
happening—and not happening. One of the "not happenings" was
the United States' frosty attitude toward the secretary-general.

Part of the problem was that the U.S. felt that Boutros-Ghali
hadn't moved fast enough to reform the UN. To boost his campaign
for a second term, Boutros-Ghali wanted to demonstrate clearly his
commitment to reform. And so, through a mutual friend, in July
1996 he asked if I might be responsive to an approach from him to
assist him with his reform efforts.

As usual in these circumstances, I didn't hesitate. "Of course," I
said, "I'll always respond to a call from the UN secretary-general."

He followed up with a phone call to me at the World Bank and
came right to the point. He was determined, he said, to develop a
program of accelerated reforms for the UN.

He invited me to the house he had rented for the summer in Con-
necticut. We spent the entire day together. His wife, Leah, joined us
for lunch, but otherwise we were alone.

The discussion went well. Boutros-Ghali confided in me his
willingness to accept a compromise—a two-year term instead of
the usual five. Then he dangled the bait: become his deputy, with
the prospect of succeeding him for the remaining three years. "I'm

prepared to give you my full trust and confidence and a primary voice in major decisions, including the appointment of senior officials."

I didn't need to think about it very long. I had formed a high regard for him and I very much appreciated his confidence. I said I was prepared to work with him through the balance of his term without any commitment to a possible future role. I knew, in any event, that it was not something that could simply be arranged between the two of us and not a likely prospect. Although my name had been mentioned on a number of occasions as a possible candidate for the secretary-generalship, I had never seen it as a realistic prospect or aspired to the post as a goal of my service to the UN. I knew if it were to happen it would only be through a combination of events possibly leading to my emergence as a compromise candidate. Thus, I never entered into a campaign for the job, and on those occasions when I was asked by friends if they could submit my name to the Security Council, I always demurred. This time the Africans were strongly supporting a second term for Boutros-Ghali and had made it clear that if he were not re-elected, they would insist that the second term he had been denied go to an African, because all previous secretaries-general had served two terms. In my view this was most reasonable. And even then, to me and others on the inside at the UN, Kofi Annan of Ghana was clearly the best and most likely choice in this eventuality.

Boutros-Ghali and I arranged to meet again, this time in New York, for several hours alone in his office, which no doubt set off the ever-active gossipmongers among his staff. At that meeting I agreed to become special adviser to the secretary-general and to go to work immediately, designing a reform program and strategy. Right afterwards I called Jim Wolfensohn at the World Bank. I wanted his advice and also his permission to take such time away from my bank responsibilities as would be necessary. Boutros-Ghali also spoke to him about it.

In August I quietly went to work on the thirty-eighth floor of UN headquarters. I knew I needed some help, particularly to pull together and evaluate the vast amount of material on UN reform and restructuring that had already been produced. These reform studies and recommendations had become something of an industry, and the fact that actual reforms had thus far been minimal was not for lack of ideas but for lack of political will and a sufficient degree of consensus among member governments. That the United States had taken the lead in the drive for reform didn't help generate enthusiasm for it, and in fact made the G-77, among others, more resistant rather than less. The u.s. was pushing cost savings, staff reductions and greater efficiency (the whole fashionable "downsizing" rigmarole), and developing countries were suspicious that the net effect would be to weaken the UN in the very areas of greatest importance to them, principally economic and social development.

It wasn't only the G-77 who were irritated. Even the u.s.'s usual OECD allies, themselves very much in favour of reform, resented the hard-edged American tactics. It was, after all, the u.s. that had accumulated more than $1 billion in arrears in meeting its financing commitments to the UN, which kept the organization in a continuous state of near-bankruptcy.

The u.s. administration was pressing hard for reform on the one hand, and on the other working with the Republican-dominated Congress for a way to pay down the arrears. But this got tangled in the extreme demands made by the right-wing Republicans, led by Senator Jesse Helms, who had a long record of hostility toward the UN. The radical reforms they demanded, accompanied by benchmarks prescribed by the u.s., went well beyond what was politically acceptable to other member governments. Some were not even within the authority of the UN General Assembly or the secretary-general.

Meanwhile, the rumour mills had been busy, and many names for the secretary-generalship were put forward, though none formally. I was pleased and encouraged when it appeared that Kofi Annan was indeed emerging as the front-runner. His candidature gathered momentum when the government of his home country presented their favourite son as a formal candidate and went to work to rally support for him.

Annan certainly had the right credentials. He had spent virtually his entire professional career in the UN and was universally respected and well liked. The u.s. had already made it clear that Annan was their favourite African. This was a mixed blessing, given the circumstances—the mere fact of American favour diminished his support among others. Also, while he spoke decent French, he was not a francophone, which set the French against him. But in the end the French yielded. On November 19, 1996, the Security Council unanimously voted to recommend to the General Assembly that Kofi Annan become the next secretary-general of the un. The General Assembly less than a month later unanimously approved.

While the arguments about the secretary-generalship had swirled about the un, I had beavered away preparing a statement on reform, and I gave it to Boutros-Ghali, who had intended it as the basis for the reform program he would carry out in his second term. But he kept delaying its presentation until time ran out, and he never used it. It probably wouldn't have made much difference to the final result.

I'd known the new secretary-general for more than twenty years and dealt with him in several of his earlier capacities in the un secretariat. I liked him very much and had developed a high regard for both his personal and his professional qualities. We were not close exactly, but we had a very friendly and congenial relationship. In the closing days of Boutros-Ghali's stewardship, when speculation had linked both of our names to the job, I had a frank discussion with Kofi Annan about this in my World Bank office in Washington. I shared the view that he'd be the front-runner if Boutros-Ghali faded, and I knew I was at best a long shot. In that meeting Kofi and I agreed, if you like, to agree. We both knew that the political dynamics that would decide the issue were well beyond the control of either of us. Whatever the result, we could count on each other.

Despite all this cordiality I hardly expected him to want me to continue going ahead with my assignment on reform. Kofi knew the inside workings of the un better than I did, and I anticipated that he'd want a different sort of person to work with him on reform. We talked on the phone immediately following his election, and he made polite comments about wanting my help, but I didn't take this as an invitation to join his team. Nor did we meet in person before he assumed his office on January 1, 1997. Shortly after his election he left for Ghana, to a hero's welcome home. I was therefore somewhat surprised when on his first day in the office as secretary-general he telephoned me and asked me if I could come to New York right away to discuss my future role. I did so, and he told me of his plan to launch a major reform program immediately and invited me to lead it, working directly under him.

I said I'd be pleased to do so, but I had three points I wanted to clear up first. I ticked them off.

"First, I'll be starting afresh. I want to terminate the contract I signed under Boutros-Ghali. I should be appointed to my new responsibilities by you, the new secretary-general. Second, I want to make it clear I'll not be a candidate for any permanent appointment, including the post of deputy secretary-general [which he wanted to establish]. Third, I need to be able to speak frankly and openly with you whenever I have views to offer."

He readily agreed to all three points, and I found myself appointed executive co-ordinator for UN reform with the rank of undersecretary-general and chairman of a newly constituted Steering Committee for Reform made up of the most senior UN officials.

I went to work immediately in the same office I'd already been using, and the work I'd done under Boutros-Ghali enabled me to get off to a fast start in designing the reform program.

The first task was to lay out the dimensions. I have always had the habit of working on paper, dictating into a mini-cassette recorder to produce drafts that I can then review and massage. Whenever I embark on a new project, I like to set out in memorandum form the basic elements and structure of the project. There are inevitably many blank spaces and holes, of course, but it helps me organize my own thoughts and elicit the input of others. So I moved quickly to prepare a memorandum outlining a proposed structure, not so much for the reform but for the reform process, including a preliminary plan for the contributions we would need from sources inside and outside the UN.

I began to recruit a small staff, paying attention as usual to the variety of skills and experience and geographical, gender and linguistic balance required to work effectively in the UN. I was fortunate that Miles Stoby, a former ambassador of Guyana to the UN, with whom I had worked closely in the past when he had served so well as secretary of UNCED, agreed to become my deputy.

We had no separate budget, so we had to draw all our staff on secondment from other parts of the UN. We had no trouble doing this, since the secretary-general had made it known that he'd put his considerable weight behind our requests—and as a consequence we never had to rely on his direct intervention. We put together a superb team, which was strongly reinforced when a Columbia University professor and international affairs expert joined the Secretary-General's Office.

A supernumerary member of our team who volunteered his services was an old friend, Sir Ronald Grierson, an eminent British financier and industrialist who had also served in a number of high-level government positions and, at an earlier stage in his career, had worked with the United Nations Economic Commission for Europe. With a razor-sharp mind, a galaxy of connections and an immense reservoir of energy and experience, he proved to be a great asset to our team. He soon earned the esteem of all my colleagues and became something of a mentor to the group.

Not everyone loved my appointment. Madeleine Albright, by then secretary of state in President Clinton's new administration, was cool. In her first visit to Kofi Annan after he became secretary-general, she said, "We're pleased you're moving ahead with reform, but why appoint Strong? We have a high regard for him, but you already have competent people in place to do the reform job."

By "competent" she really meant American. And indeed there were exceptional Americans who could do the job. Indeed, a highly competent and experienced American, Joseph Cannon, undersecretary-general for management and administration, had already initiated a significant reform process, but Kofi needed to show early on that he wasn't in the Americans' pocket and that reform wasn't going to be solely an American show—he'd run his own. He also realized that a reform program driven too much by the U.S. would not fly with others.

It was an important statement. It's always difficult to predict how a person will react to the responsibilities and realities of high office, and there had been questions about Kofi. He was liked and trusted by almost everyone, but even some of his supporters wondered aloud whether such a "nice guy" could make the tough decisions required. This incident—and a few others like it—demonstrated that he has what it takes. If he goes on like this, he promises to be the best secretary-general ever and the right person to lead the UN through a period of crisis and transformation.

The most visible and dramatic manifestation of the very different leadership style he has brought to the secretary-generalship was his courageous and dramatic trip to Baghdad in 1998, when he succeeded in persuading Iraq's Saddam Hussein to allow the UN Weapons Inspection Team to resume its work and enable the U.S. and its allies to pull back from the brink of the air attacks that they were about to mount on Iraq. Despite the fact that Hussein later let him down by expelling the UN team and precipitating a resumption of air strikes, Annan's achievement established his stellar status on the world stage and signalled the transformation his leadership had effected in the public image and political efficacy of the UN. The fact that he has disappointed the U.S. on a number of issues since then has largely brought his honeymoon with the American political leadership and public to an end, but at the same time it has disabused others of their suspicions that he was too subservient to the U.S., and this has given him a much broader political base.

In fact, my high expectations have been more than validated. Kofi Annan has become the greatest asset of the UN, and his leadership is the best hope for its future. And in carrying out his own reform program he has substantially improved management and cost effectiveness. While this certainly has not solved all the UN's problems, it has provided strong direction at a time when, despite his efforts, there has been a continued erosion of political support for some of the UN's traditionally most important activities, principally peacemaking and peacekeeping. With the withdrawal of its inspection team from Iraq and the embarrassing revelation that the U.S. had used its participation in the inspection team to carry out intelligence for its own purposes, giving credence to Saddam's earlier allegations, the UN's role in Iraq has been seriously undermined.

The UN has found it virtually impossible to enforce the peace agreement it negotiated and was monitoring in Angola. Its role in the Balkans has been a sporadic and limited one. And it played no real part in the negotiations over Kosovo. Resolution of the conflict in Liberia did not involve the UN; nor did it have a role in the attempts to make internal peace in Sierra Leone. And in the development field, in which the developing countries continue to look to the UN for strong leadership, its capacity has been eroded by reductions in the support it received from member nations. The initiative has shifted to the World Bank, given the strong new leadership that Jim Wolfensohn has brought to that institution.

Kofi invited me to go along with him on his first visit to Washington after assuming office. I already knew most of the members of the new Clinton cabinet, and I was interested to see how warmly they and the president welcomed the secretary-general. Clinton was particularly cordial. He made it clear he was committed to paying up the U.S. arrears and had positive words for Kofi's clear commitment to reform. He was candid in explaining his problem with the U.S. Congress, where the Republicans had maintained their majority in the recent election, and suggested that the secretary-general cultivate direct relationships with key congressional leaders, particularly Senator Helms and Newt Gingrich. His views on the house speaker were particularly interesting. He painted a surprisingly positive picture of the controversial Gingrich as a highly intelligent and competent person with a much greater degree of interest in the kind of issues that the UN deals with than might be apparent.

Our reception on Capitol Hill was a lot less cordial. We visited with Helms and members of his Foreign Relations Committee, with Gingrich and with the Senate majority leader, Trent Lott, and others. While the secretary-general was received civilly (and in most cases it was obvious that people warmed to him personally), they were all forthright and frank. Congress had the final say in paying up, and there'd be no money unless the reform process met certain U.S. expectations. They demanded not only radical reforms but reductions in the American share of both the UN's regular and peacekeeping budgets.

The secretary-general, for his part, was polite but firm. I was greatly impressed by the way he put the UN's case. The United States, he reminded the Congressional leaders (who sometimes forgot), was only one member of the UN. There were 184 others whose views needed to be heard and agreement obtained.

I know this made an impression on Gingrich, because he made a point of referring to it in his remarks to the press following the meeting. Kofi had also impressed the crusty leader of the Senate Foreign Relations Committee, Helms. "I like that fellow," Helms said to me after the meeting, as we walked along a corridor. Kofi might not have changed many minds, but he had clearly changed the mood.

Management skills and experience receive little or no weight in the highly politicized process of selecting a UN secretary-general. It should be no surprise, therefore, that past secretaries-general have not been noted for their management of the organization, and indeed have usually had little interest in it and very little time to spend on it. Kofi Annan is a welcome and timely exception, having received an advanced degree in management at MIT and served in key management positions within the United Nations before becoming secretary-general. He was, therefore, the ideal person to take the lead in the reform process.

It was against this background that we devised what we called a two-track approach to the reform program. Track One consisted of those reforms that the secretary-general could carry out within his own authority and for which he felt there had already been sufficient consultation, so that they could be implemented immediately. This included the single most radical restructuring of the secretariat that has taken place since inception of the UN, bringing together some thirty departments, funds and programs into five executive groups. These consisted of the UN Development Group and similar groups for political and security affairs, economic and social affairs, humanitarian affairs and human rights.

Kofi announced the Track One measures on March 17, 1997, and received a generally positive reception. He also undertook to present his Track Two suggestions by July. This was a formidable challenge for our small team; other studies on reform that were purely advisory in nature had normally taken at least a year, usually more.

Track Two addressed issues that required at least some degree of sanction by governments, as well as those reforms of a more fundamental nature that are solely the prerogative of member governments. On these matters, which included revisions to the UN Charter and an overhaul of the UN's agenda, the secretary-general could make only recommendations, and even this was seen by some governments as an unwelcome intrusion into their prerogatives. The most far-reaching and radical reforms would be an enlargement of the Security Council (which no longer reflects the world political reality), and the reassessment of various countries' financial obligations (which in practice meant dealing with the American demand to pay less). Our reform program noted these two issues but did not address them, as they were already the subject of intense negotiations among delegates.

We had already decided, too, not to address issues specific to the specialized agencies of the UN—the World Bank, the International Monetary Fund, the Food and Agricultural Organization, the World Health Organization, the United Nations Educational, Social and Cultural Organization and others. Each of these has its own treaty-based constitution and governing body and is not subject to the authority of the UN secretary-general. He does, however, chair the Administrative Committee on Coordination (ACC), composed of the heads of these agencies. They meet twice a year "to ensure co-ordination," but cynics view the ACC as a forum where the members seek only to protect their individual autonomy and avoid, at all costs, being "co-ordinated." This, I have found, is somewhat exaggerated, though there is a good deal of truth to it.

Kofi Annan had also asked me to help him identify candidates to succeed the current executive director of UNEP, Elizabeth Dowdeswell, and her counterpart as executive director of Habitat, Wally N'Dow, both of whose terms expired at the end of 1997, and to review the future of the two organizations. I had, not surprisingly, quite a few ideas of my own about the changes that needed to be made and had already called for "the establishment, based on UNEP, of a much strengthened world environmental agency with a status and influence equivalent to that of such international agencies as the World Trade Organization." Still, we left specifics out of our reform process, as we felt it would be best to give the new leadership of the two organizations an opportunity to take part in developing plans for their future.

It was clearly not feasible in the five months that we had to develop our reform proposals to pay equal attention to every issue. We therefore decided to concentrate on those with a sufficient body of data and analysis already assembled on which to base our recommendations. Annan had often made the point that reform was not a one-shot effort but a continuing process. Two examples of issues that we felt we should skip were information technology and the environment.

I've long thought that the UN should give highest priority to improving its capacities to collect, evaluate and disseminate information that bears on the major global issues on its agenda. It's true the UN has already spent large amounts of money on computers and information-processing hardware, and true also that its Office of Statistics is highly respected as the best source of reliable numbers on many matters of global interest. But it has proven extremely difficult to find a common framework to make better use of both capital and human resources. We decided not to deal with this problem extensively, mostly because a major study was under way when our reform program was launched. Now that this study has been completed, it is important that the issue be given greater priority. It is the most important tool that the UN has at its disposal for dealing effectively with the manifold functions it seeks to perform for the world community.

The situation was somewhat different with the environment. The special session of the General Assembly called to review progress in implementing the agreements reached at the Earth Summit in Rio de Janeiro took place while our reform work was under way, and we didn't think it appropriate to anticipate or pre-empt the results. A change in the leadership of UNEP was scheduled for the end of the year, and the Governing Council of UNEP had set up a Special Ministerial Committee to consider key issues bearing on its future. So we decided to propose the establishment of a task force to consider how the environment issue could be more effectively dealt with in the UN, and UNEP's role.

In December 1997, when the secretary-general appointed Dr. Klaus Töpfer, formerly Germany's minister of the environment and chairman of the UN's Commission on Sustainable Development, to succeed Elizabeth Dowdeswell as executive director of UNEP, he also gave him broad responsibilities for oversight of Habitat, the human settlements organization of the UN, and made him chairman of the task force.

Kofi Annan had entrusted me with the preliminary discussions with Klaus, one of the most respected and influential leaders of the world environment movement. I was convinced he was the right person for the job and worked with him in developing the terms of reference and recruiting the membership of the task force, then stepped back to serve as an ex officio member of it. Although its report was not as radical as some had hoped, it made sound and sensible recommendations for the strengthening of UNEP, and of its relationships with Habitat and the other organizations and agencies of the UN that have important environmentally related activities and responsibilities. The report made a number of recommendations for strengthening UNEP's leadership and co-ordination role and re-establishing it as the principal forum for ministers of the environment. Recognizing the current low level of political will for radical change, the writers did not deal with proposals for upgrading UNEP's status to that of a specialized agency, merging it with the World Meteorological Organization and the International Oceanographic Commission to establish a new world environment organization with responsibilities for integrating environmental and Global Commons issues. Such changes are yet to come.

A problem I wrestled with during the whole process was the role of non-UN and non-governmental organizations.

There has been a quantum multiplication of the extent and importance of what we now term *civil society* in all the major issues on the UN agenda. In my own UN roles, in the Stockholm Conference, UNEP, the Office for Emergency Operations in Africa in 1984–86 and the Earth Summit, I made special arrangements to make sure civil society organizations took part, despite resistance from some quarters in the UN itself. It's now become conventional wisdom, though not accepted by all, that the UN must reach out more broadly to civil society, provide it with much greater opportunities for effective participation in UN deliberations, and establish ongoing operational relationships with organizations that share common interests and concerns. In many cases these organizations now have much larger budgets and more extensive management and field operational capabilities than their counterparts in the United Nations. And in order to exercise its leadership, the UN must command their confidence. They must therefore be regarded and treated as full partners of the UN in the areas in which they have substantial interests and information, rather than as subordinate actors, as they have so often been viewed in the past.

Kofi has a deeply felt commitment to strengthening the UN's relationships with civil society. And he strongly supported our reform team in consulting widely with civil society organizations and their leaders. The strength of this commitment was reflected in his reform program, despite the reservations of some governments that regard such organizations in their own countries as part of the opposition. Highlighting this was his call for the holding of a People's Millennium Forum parallel to the special millennium session of the General Assembly. This would give visibility and practical effect to the fact that the UN Charter itself emanates from and begins with "We, the people . . ."

One of the most controversial of the secretary-general's proposed reform measures, and one that he felt very strongly about, was the establishment of the position of deputy secretary-general. He saw this as someone with whom he could share some of the complex and demanding responsibilities of his office, which really had become too much for one person to handle. This wasn't exactly welcomed by the UN establishment, including the various undersecretaries-general, who disliked the prospect of interposing a deputy between them and the secretary-general. Some governments shared this concern. There were also political worries. The G-77, for example, feared that the appointment of a deputy from the North might serve to dilute the authority of "their" secretary-general. They suggested that such a deputy might have to be elected by the General Assembly and raised the notion that the secretary-general and deputy might in future have to run as a combined slate.

After intensive formal negotiations these issues were resolved by providing that the deputy secretary-general position would be integrated into the office of the secretary-general and would derive its authority solely by delegation from the secretary-general, without any separate and distinct mandate of its own. This enabled the governments to agree that the appointment would be made by the secretary-general without requiring election by the General Assembly.

Kofi and I often talked about who should serve in this essential role. After deciding not to pursue his efforts to recruit Gro Harlem Brundtland of Norway or the UN high commissioner for refugees Sadako Ogato, he discussed with me the other possible candidates and then asked me, "What do you think of Louise Frechette?"

My impulsive reaction was, "That's a great idea." I explained that though I didn't know her well, everything I knew suggested that she'd make a first-rate prospect. As one of Canada's ablest public service executives she had established an exceptionally good reputation during her term from 1992 to 1995 as Canada's ambassador to the UN. Subsequently I discreetly checked with some friends who knew her better, particularly Bob Fowler, an old friend and confidant who is now Canada's ambassador at the UN. Louise had succeeded him as a deputy minister of national defence in Canada. I reported back to the secretary-general positively. He made her the offer at a breakfast meeting in Ottawa. She accepted and has already more than validated Kofi Annan's inspired choice of her and the confidence he has invested in her. That she brought to her new job the experience of having presided over a major program of restructuring and cost reductions in the Canadian National Defence Department and Armed Forces equipped her well to assume from me the responsibility for the ongoing reform process in the UN.

Louise took over my role as chairman of the Steering Committee on Reform and also moved into my office on the thirty-eighth floor of the UN tower. I have retained my link with the UN as a senior adviser to the secretary-general and an ex officio member of the reform steering committee. But I have stepped back from direct involvement in the process, confining myself to providing occasional advice to the secretary-general and his deputy. I have been greatly impressed at the way Frechette has moved smoothly, quietly and authoritatively into her new role. Proof of her success is the respect and confidence she now has inspired in the senior echelons of the UN.

The Department of Public Information, with or without reform, could hardly be blamed for the bad press the UN had been receiving before the reform process began, particularly in the United States. Their media attention had focused on the continued campaign of criticism of the UN in Congress and by the UN's traditional right-wing enemies. I wanted to fix this, if I could, or at least get out the positive message of reform. There's no question that the UN's best friend among media leaders over the years has been Ted Turner. Not only had he provided valuable air time on the Turner television networks for positive features on the UN, but he had also produced and aired many programs on UN-related causes, including the environment, nuclear disarmament, the promotion of East-West rapprochement during the Cold War period and the need for better understanding and support of developing countries.

I knew Ted had a long standing interest in the role of religion in conflict, and I was not really surprised when I received a call from his office that he urgently needed to talk to me.

His staff connected me to him in his car, and in his usual staccato and exuberant style he said, "Maurice, now that the Cold War is over, religion is the main source of conflict in the world. Why can't we get leaders of the world's main religions together at the UN? They could make a commitment to peace that would hopefully influence their followers. I'll make sure it gets good television coverage."

I told him I thought it was a good idea.

"But it probably can't be done as an official UN conference," I said. "The UN could provide encouragement and support, though."

I agreed to take it up with Kofi Annan and get back to him. The secretary-general was very receptive. With his support, the Interfaith Center of New York, in co-operation with a number of other religious and spiritual organizations, is now planning to hold a major Summit of Religious and Spiritual Leaders for World Peace to convene at the UN in the year 2000.

Ted's other current concern was climate change and greenhouse gases. It wasn't long afterwards that I had a call from Barbara Pyle, whom I have often described as Ted Turner's "secret weapon"— although her talents are no longer so secret. She told me that she, Ted and Jane Fonda, his wife, were extremely concerned about the public campaign being mounted by U.S. industry to dissuade the administration from agreeing to specific targets and timetables for reduction of greenhouse gas emissions at the forthcoming meeting of the Parties to the Climate Change Convention in Kyoto in December 1997. This cynical and deceptive campaign was designed to make the point that the whole notion of climate change was a plot against the U.S. way of life and promoted the UN as the main villain in the piece. The campaign was based on so much misinformation and outright untruths that even some industry leaders distanced themselves from it. Barbara Pyle reported that Ted was so upset that he insisted that CNN not run its advertisements, though he could not sustain that position for long. She indicated that he wanted to mount a counter-campaign that would present the climate change issue in a more positive and objective manner. She thought that it would be useful if the UN secretary-general could make encouraging noises.

Of course I shared these concerns, so I discussed the idea with the secretary-general and suggested that he write Ted Turner and invite him to come to New York to discuss it. I followed up with Ted, and he said he'd be in New York to receive an award and give a keynote address to the annual meeting of the UN Association, and this would be the best time for him to meet with Kofi.

When he came to my office just prior to his meeting with Kofi, he was in an exuberant mood. "Maurice," he announced, "I've decided to give $1 billion in support of UN causes and programs. What do you think of that?"

I was flabbergasted, of course. Neither Kofi nor I had considered actually soliciting money from him for the UN.

He was bubbling over with enthusiasm. "On the plane I began thinking. My net worth increased by about $1 billion since the first of the year, and before I got too used to it, I should give it away to a foundation that would support UN causes. And Jane is in total agreement."

I stared at him for a while, but I could see he was absolutely serious, and when I recovered my breath I knew that this could be a very important moment for the UN. I excused myself to break in on the secretary-general and tell him what to expect in his meeting with Ted Turner. He was just as astonished and delighted.

I escorted Ted into the secretary-general's office, where he repeated his decision to make a $1 billion gift. He made it clear it was not meant as a contribution to the UN's budget and most certainly should not be seen as making up for the arrears in the U.S. government's contributions. He wanted it to support the secretary-general's reforms. The priorities would be worked out between the UN and a new foundation. The foundation would be set up to attract other contributors, and he offered his own services to take the lead in encouraging other such contributions.

"I don't want my billion to be an endowment, only spending the interest. I want you to spend $100 million a year over a ten-year period."

Whatever this meeting had originally been about, those purposes had now clearly been superseded. Kofi Annan was quick to realize the importance of the gift, not only as a source of new financial support for the UN but as a demonstration of confidence in and commitment to the UN on the part of one of America's best-known and most influential personalities. This dramatic gesture, the largest single charitable gift in U.S. history up to then, would make the point with the American public that if Ted Turner was prepared to make such a commitment to the UN, there must be something good and worthwhile about the organization, after all.

What particularly pleased me was the extremely positive chemistry between Kofi and Ted, two very different personalities with shared values and goals. This augured well for the relationship between the UN and the new foundation.

Naturally enough, the gift received wide media attention in the U.S. and throughout the world. Most of it was positive, but inevitably there were some suspicions about his motives, and speculation that he wanted to exert undue influence over the UN. Even in the UN itself there were a few who tended to look this gift horse in the mouth.

Of course, it was subsequently necessary to work out a detailed agreement between the UN and the new foundation, all of which took time and involved some difficult moments reconciling the requirements of U.S. law for charitable foundations with the policies and procedures of the United Nations, as there were no real precedents for this kind of relationship. In the end the UN agreed that the name be the UN Foundation. In addition, a separate non-profit organization was set up, the Better World Fund, with the same board of directors and administration. This fund was seen as a means of supporting activities that could be undertaken in an entity separate from but related to the UN Foundation. Ted invited me to serve as a board member of both foundations, and Kofi Annan readily agreed. Ted then moved quickly to appoint as the president of the foundation Tim Wirth, a former congressman and senator from Colorado who was serving as U.S. undersecretary of state for global affairs. He and Al Gore had been the primary champions of environment and related issues when they served together in the U.S. Senate, and they remain close friends and confidants. Tim was an inspired choice for the job and moved quickly to translate Ted Turner's vision into reality as an innovative and effective ally of the UN.

The initial board of the foundation consisted of Ted as chairman, Tim Wirth as president, Andrew Young, former mayor of Atlanta and U.S. ambassador to the United Nations, and me. The first meeting was held in January 1998, and it has now been expanded to give it a much more international character with the inclusion of Graça Machel of Mozambique, since married to Nelson Mandela; Ruth Cardoso, an eminent sociologist and also the wife of President Cardoso of Brazil; Muhammad Yunus of Bangladesh, who developed that country's Grameen Bank, which has become a model for providing small loans to poor farmers and grassroots enterprises; and Emma Rothschild, a noted British policy researcher and social advocate.

On the UN side the secretary-general established a new office, the UN Foundation for International Partnerships, reporting through the new deputy secretary-general. I was pleased when he decided to appoint to head this office my good friend Miles Stoby, who had done such a fine job as my deputy for UN reform, and also to give him a well-deserved promotion to the level of assistant secretary-general. In his private conversations with me, Miles made it clear that though he saw this new role as an important opportunity, he looked at it as a relatively short-term assignment to get the new foundation launched, after which he would hope to go back to the UN mainstream. He did so somewhat earlier than anticipated, when the secretary-general offered him the challenging responsibility of co-ordinating preparations for the UN's Millennium Assembly. I was taken by surprise when Ted insisted that I become chairman of the Executive Committee, the Finance Committee and the Nominations Committee. I responded that these responsibilities should be spread around and that I would vote against this proposal. But Ted brushed aside my reluctance.

In any new enterprise there is always a period of trial and error, and the new foundation has not been exempt from this. Nevertheless, the partnership between the UN and the foundation is off to a promising start, and already the foundation staff is devoting a good deal of attention to attracting support from other sources.

The secretary-general's reform program became the centrepiece of the General Assembly session in 1998. The president of the assembly, Ukraine's foreign minister, Hannadiy Udovenko, decided that the reform program would be debated by a Committee of the Whole, and that he'd chair it. It proved to be a sound decision. Udovenko, a stolid, dour, though good-humoured person with a great deal of experience in the United Nations, presided over the deliberations of the committee and the many backroom, informal consultations with a combination of firmness and accommodation, which enabled him to contain and defuse a number of controversies that threatened at several points along the way to derail the process. The Pakistani ambassador, Ahmad Kamal, a man of well-honed and brilliantly dexterous diplomatic skills, mounted a vigorous attack on the proposal to integrate the UN secretariats responsible for disarmament activities into a new Department of Disarmament. In doing so, he moved agilely from assertive criticism of virtually the entire range of reform proposals to a disarmingly charming and good-humoured embrace of the program, if only it would accommodate his concerns on disarmament.

Developing countries now account for about two-thirds of the total membership of the United Nations, and approval of any significant issue requires their support or acquiescence. Although there are great divergences of interest among these countries, which makes it very difficult to concert their positions on many issues, they share a political interest in maintaining at least a semblance of unity. This they invoke to ensure that their position can prevail when they see their broader interests and principles at stake. The position of the G-77 is generally reinforced by the support of China, which, while reserving the right to act alone when its interest requires it, normally aligns itself with the group.

Most members of the G-77 were deeply suspicious of UN reform, and the lack of progress on reform had been largely due to their resistance. They particularly saw the drive for UN reform as a response to demands by the United States and the desires of other major contributors to the UN to reduce costs and thus reduce their own contributions. There was also concern that reform would produce staff reductions and fewer opportunities for nationals of their countries. But now, in Kofi Annan, they have a secretary-general who is one of their own and in whom they have confidence. This confidence is well placed. Our reform team was especially sensitized to the concerns of the G-77. We met frequently with the chairman of the G-77, Tanzania's ambassador Daudi Mwakawago, a quietly astute and knowledge-able man whose skilful leadership of the G-77 made an indispensable contribution to keeping the General Assembly deliberations on track and enabling a final consensus to be reached that accommodated the principal concerns of developing countries. But it was not until the final hours of the General Assembly that agreement was reached on a resolution that broadly endorsed the reforms undertaken by the secretary-general on his own authority. The assembly responded much more tentatively to his recommendations for the more funda-mental reforms that could be undertaken only by member govern-ments; the best it could do was to keep them on the table and ask the secretary-general to provide further information.

So Kofi Annan got a vote of confidence for his secretariat reforms. But there was no commitment by member governments to move ahead with the more fundamental reforms that the secretary-general had recommended and the UN sorely needs. Nor was there any real progress toward agreement on the key issues of enlargement of the Security Council—which the U.S. was resisting—and revising the formula for assessing the financial contribution of members to the UN—which the U.S. was pressing for. Still, it did represent by far the most substantial and far-reaching reform of the UN at the sec-retariat level that had ever been effected. And the fact that the driv-ing force was Kofi Annan signalled a major revitalization of the leadership and influence of the office of the secretary-general.

Nevertheless, as I write this, I have to confess to a sense of real disappointment that the political will on the part of the govern-ments that "own" the UN is at a low ebb. While it is gratifying that the secretary-general's reform program has somewhat muted, if not satisfied, the critics of the UN, notably in the U.S. Congress, it has also given rise to an attitude of complacency and tiredness on the part of the United States and most other governments in moving ahead with the reform agenda set out by the secretary-general.

The good news about his reform program is that virtually all the measures he undertook to carry out within his own authority either have been implemented or are well under way. The bad news is that there has been virtually no progress on the more fundamental proposals that he made to member governments, which only they can decide. Although there will be a special millennium session of the General Assembly, there seems little prospect that it will agree to initiate the kind of fundamental reform process Kofi Annan proposed. The People's Millennium Forum to be convened in conjunction with it will undoubtedly be more venturesome. Louise Frechette's strong and determined leadership of the process is keeping it very much alive, but it is not easy for the secretariat to press on with reform when there is little drive for it on the part of governments.

Managing the World without World Government: The New UN

Looking beyond the current reluctance of governments to confront the need for the kind of fundamental changes in the United Nations envisioned in Secretary-General Kofi Annan's reform proposals, what kind of a "new" UN would I like to see in the twenty-first century? More particularly, what kind of a UN will the world need? Will it—should it—evolve into a world government, as some propose and others fear?

Let me make my own position clear: world government is just not on; it is not necessary, not feasible and not desirable.

This is not to say that we can aspire to a world without systems or rules. Far from it. A chaotic world would pose equal or even greater danger. The challenge is to strike a balance so that the management of global affairs is responsive to the interests of all people in a secure and sustainable future. Such management must be guided by basic human values and make global organization conform to the reality of global diversity. The cause-and-effect relationships that determine the way our policies and actions interact to create our future are systematic in nature, and therefore must be managed systemically.

Many pressures bear on political leaders, as they seek both to be effective and to retain support at the national level. Notwithstanding the drawbacks of nationalism, however, the history of even this century encourages us to believe that from the very best of national leaders can come the very best of internationalism. Today, a sense of internationalism has become a necessary ingredient of sound national policies. No nation can make progress heedless of insecurity and deprivation elsewhere. We have to share a global neighbourhood and strengthen it so that it may offer the promise of a good life to all our neighbours.

As the need for more of what I call "co-operative governance" increases, paradoxically, there is an increasing mistrust of government in all its forms and a growing reluctance to entrust governments with more power, authority and control over resources. There has been strong support for right-wing calls to "get governments off the backs of the people" and to reverse the trend toward ever bigger government that has characterized the post–Second World War period. This has been especially evident in the United States, but there is a similar trend in other Western countries and more recently in some developing countries.

A parallel push is for reduced support for international organizations, nourished too by strongly voiced fears that they're likely to subvert national sovereignty and, indeed, represent a movement toward world government. This fear—not to say paranoia—has been greatly exaggerated by extreme right-wing elements in the United States, which in turn have had a disproportionate influence on the U.S. Congress. Such fear has undoubtedly contributed to the American retreat from its financial commitments to the United Nations, as well as from its support of other international organizations.

I know these right-wing paranoias well, having been something of a target for them. Unable to convince the free citizens of the world to buy into world government, I am trying to sneak it in through the back door via regulations, bilateral and multilateral charters, supranational agencies and so on. There is just enough here, a small kernel of fact, to convince a mind prone to belief in conspiracies of the truth of the accusations. I have already said we have to devise and accept global regulations that would impose constraints on our actions for the purpose of maximizing our long-term freedoms. On the other hand, let me be direct: the fear that international organizations represent a creeping movement toward world government may be understandable, but it is simply not valid. Indeed, the idea is both dangerous and counterproductive, to the extent that it undermines the principal instruments that governments must use to co-operate for the protection and benefit of their own citizens.

At a time when even the strongest national governments are experiencing difficulties and constraints on their capacity to perform the duties already entrusted to them, establishing a central world government would compound the problem, not solve it. What is needed instead is an improved system of international agreements and international law and more streamlined international organizations to service and support the co-operation among governments and other key actors that will be required.

The United Nations, the Bretton Woods institutions and the many other regional and specialized international organizations that now exist provide the basic elements for such a system. Of course, they need continuing reform, restructuring, rationalization and re-orientation to make them more effective and more efficient and prepare them for the enlarged functions they will be called on to undertake in the period ahead. But even more than this, they need revitalized mandates and a renewal of the political and financial support that is essential for their effective functioning. This will not be possible without a much broader understanding and more positive appreciation of the role of the United Nations and other multilateral organizations and their relevance to the issues that affect the lives and prospects of individuals.

Creating a much closer link between people's interests and local concerns and the larger global issues that these international organizations deal with is one of the principal challenges we face in revitalizing support for global co-operation. Better understanding of the local–global connection is essential if we are to develop the will to act on global risks. For example, the attitudes and behaviour of individuals toward the use of fossil fuels give rise to the emissions of carbon dioxide and other greenhouse gases through which humans affect the filtering mechanism of the atmosphere, and that in turn affects climate and human well-being.

These basic considerations provided the philosophical under-pinnings of the United Nations reforms undertaken by Secretary-General Kofi Annan, which I was involved in. But, as the secretary-general has frequently made clear, reform is not a single event but a continuing process. And it is a process that must be embraced by all international organizations.

There is very limited understanding, and much misunderstanding, about the nature of international organizations. They are not governments but the servants of governments, and lack the basic attributes of governments.

In democratic societies local, state and national governments are elected directly by the people and are accountable to them. They have taxing and borrowing power to raise the revenues and capital required to act as mandated by their people. National governments have their own military establishments.

The United Nations has none of these features. It was created by national governments, which are its members, provide and control its finances and determine its functions and activities. It cannot tax or borrow and has no source of revenue independent of governments. The UN has no military forces or capacity of its own to carry out missions mandated by the Security Council or to enforce its decisions. It has no direct relationship with the people of its member countries, despite the fact that the preamble to the United Nations Charter begins with "We, the people . . ."

The UN is therefore totally dependent on its member governments, can only undertake activities that they agree to and only to the extent that the same governments provide the wherewithal. Because member governments frequently fail to supply the funding and military support to carry out the decisions, the UN becomes a scapegoat for delinquent governments.

There is another important difference between the United Nations and governments. In nation-states, the various departments (finance, foreign affairs, and so on) are an integral part of government, subject to its overall control and direction. Not so in the United Nations. The specialized agencies of the United Nations, such as the World Bank, the International Monetary Fund, the World Health Organization, the Food and Agriculture Organization and the United Nations Educational, Social and Cultural Organization, are the international counterparts of the related departments of national governments, but they are not integrated into the central body of the United Nations. Each has been established through a separate international agreement among the governments that become members of the organization, and these generally, but not entirely, parallel the membership of the United Nations. They are therefore autonomous organizations within the extended United Nations family, or "system," but each reports separately to its own governing body, consisting of the governments of its member countries, and is financed separately by them. They are loosely grouped within the framework of a United Nations Administrative Co-ordinating Committee (ACC), chaired by the secretary-general, but the central body of the UN has no real control over them. Of course, this compounds the problems of managing the UN, particularly at a time when so many issues are interrelated and require more and more co-operation.

The relationship between the UN and the World Bank requires resolution. Originally, the World Bank and the IMF kept aloof from the UN and resisted any attempts by the UN to influence them, but there was an implicit division of labour between the UN and the bank in the development field: the UN Development Program was the principal provider of technical assistance, and the World Bank of capital, to developing countries. The mandate, structure and political nature of the UN lends itself more to dealing with normative rather than operational issues, whereas the World Bank is much more geared to operations. Normative issues include the setting of internationally agreed standards and regulations, whereas operational activities involve the actual implementation of these. These distinctions have become increasingly blurred as the World Bank has undertaken more and more functions of a normative nature and the UN has broadened its operational activities. Now, with the leadership of Kofi Annan at the UN and Jim Wolfensohn at the World Bank, relations between the two organizations have never been better, and this opens up the prospect of movement to a more effective division of labour and co-operation between the two.

Rationalization, restructuring, co-ordination, consolidation and even in some cases elimination of UN programs are clearly called for. But all this can be done without transforming the UN into a world government.

1. Apply the principle of subsidiarity

I am a great believer in the principle of subsidiarity—that government is most effective and should be carried out at the level closest to the people its decisions affect. Many of the powers and functions that national governments have taken on in recent years could be more logically and effectively performed at the state, local or in some cases regional levels. In most Western countries there has already been a significant movement in this direction. By the same token more and more of the responsibilities and functions of national governments require international co-operation for treaties, conventions and agreements. Rather than an abdication of national sovereignty, such involvement represents the voluntary exercise of sovereignty, in concert with other national governments, to manage together issues that individual governments cannot manage effectively on their own.

Under the principle of subsidiarity, there are a number of activities performed by the UN organizations and agencies that in today's context could be better or more appropriately handled by other regional and special-purpose organizations, including those of a non-governmental nature. In other cases it makes more sense for the UN, as the only world organization with a global membership and mandate, to provide the framework for actions by national governments and others.

It's not easy, though, to devolve issues away from the UN. Thus far it has proven virtually impossible to remove an item from the agenda of the UN General Assembly. At last count the agenda for the 1999 UN General Assembly includes 166 specific items, which have accumulated over the years. Many of these could be removed either by closing off the issue or transferring it to another organization, but each one remains the special interest of one or more member governments, often allied to the units in the secretariat that service the item. Revising the agenda was built into Kofi Annan's reform proposals, but it remains to be seen whether member governments will take up what is clearly a sensitive subject.

2. Define the "boundary conditions" that should prescribe global priorities

What should remain on the UN agenda? I believe the issues that should be accorded highest priority at the international level are those that can have a major effect on the security, survival and well-being of the entire human community or major portions of it. These centre on what I call the "boundary conditions," by which I mean establishing the outer limits that humankind as a whole must respect to protect us all from major risks to our common future—and, of course, to realize major opportunities that cannot otherwise be achieved. It is these "boundaries" that the world community needs to accept and to find ways of managing co-operatively.

Even agreeing on where the boundaries are is difficult, never mind finding ways of enforcing compliance to regulations that affect them. Nor is it easy even within nations to regulate the individuals and corporations and organizations affecting and affected by the definition of boundaries.

Initially, agreement on such boundary conditions should be limited to a small number of areas—those with the highest degree of potential risk, which call for early action. This would be my "starter list":

1. Strictly controlling the manufacture and use of nuclear, biological and chemical weapons of mass destruction. Much progress has already been made on this issue since the end of the Cold War, but there is still a long way to go before the world community can ensure itself against this form of self-destruction.

2. Limiting the amount of carbon dioxide and other greenhouse gases from human sources that can be allowed to build up in the atmosphere.

3. Limiting the destruction or compromise of the earth's biological resources.

4. Limiting the discharge or transport by any country of hazardous and noxious substances that can inflict damage beyond its borders.
5. Limiting a country's intrusion into or undermining of the security or economy of other countries.
6. Defining the extent to which a government can suppress human rights or commit violence against its own people without justifying redressive action on the part of the international community.
7. Protecting the global commons—the oceans, the atmosphere, the Antarctic and outer space.

Most of these issues are already being addressed, and many aspects are included in international agreements or are the subject of continuing negotiations, but not on the focused, concerted and systematic basis that is necessary if they are to be managed successfully.

The growth in the number of nation-states and in the range and complexity of the issues requiring international co-operation will dictate major changes in the existing multilateral organizations. The task of revitalizing and reshaping multilateral institutions remains one of the principal challenges we face for the new century.

The changes must go beyond the improvements in management and efficiency that have been the principal objectives of the reforms to date. Governments must re-examine the division of labour among international organizations with a view to reducing areas of overlap. A more systemic relationship among them is necessary, enabling them to deal better with the increasing number of issues requiring the involvement of more than one organization.

The central bodies of the UN—the General Assembly, the Security Council, the Economic and Social Council and a refurbished Trusteeship Council—need to function as the principal political forums of the world community at the global level. They should therefore concentrate on those issues that are global in nature or importance, or require global context for national, regional or sectoral action. The UN should be prepared to divest other issues to the regional or special-purpose organization best suited to deal with them.

The UN would then give priority to its primary role, which is negotiating, articulating and ensuring enforcement of international legal agreements, providing the oversight and support needed to deal with multi-faceted issues, and focusing attention on and mobilizing appropriate responses to threats to the peace and security and well-being of the human family or major portions of it.

Security will remain a major preoccupation of nations and of the international community. But it's not realistic to expect security to be achieved through a single global security pact. More plausibly, we should build on the existing patchwork of multilateral and bilateral security arrangements. That way we could realistically achieve a global system based on a series of regional security agreements guaranteed by the international community through the UN. Each of the agreements would be individually negotiated by the countries of the region.

Growing threats to the Earth's life-support systems present more danger to the future of life than the threats we face from conflicts with each other. I contend, therefore, that the basic concept of security must be enlarged to accommodate this new reality. Movement in this direction was given credence by a speech in 1996 by then U.S. secretary of state Warren Christopher:

> In carrying out America's foreign policy, we will of course use our diplomacy backed by strong military forces to meet traditional and continuing threats to our security, as well as to meet new threats such as terrorism, weapons proliferation, drug trafficking and international crime. But we must also contend with the vast new danger posed to our national interests by damage to the environment and resulting global and regional instability.
>
> As the flagship institution of American foreign policy, the State Department must spearhead a government-wide effort to meet these environmental challenges. Together with other government agencies, we are pursuing our environmental policies—globally, regionally, bilaterally and in partnership with business and non-governmental organizations. Each of these four dimensions is essential to the success of our overall strategy.

Environmental security may still be a somewhat vague and distant concern on the part of the public, but awareness of its implications has been stimulated by recent signs of climatic turbulence—including the major changes in weather patterns attributed to El Niño, the devastating ice storms in New England and east-central Canada, the pervasive air pollution from forest fires in Indonesia and the devastating economic consequences of the depletion of some of the most important commercial species of fish, to name but a few instances. Unfortunately, such problems are likely going to get worse and more frequent. And they will, I submit, make environmental security a central issue on the agendas of people and governments in the twenty-first century.

If the UN is to provide the principal forum for an integrated, systemic approach to major global issues, member governments will need to change the way they approach the UN. They will have to integrate all national power blocs and interests and develop a cohesive approach to international matters. Such mechanisms already exist in most governments—cabinets, for example. It's just that they are seldom invoked at the international level, whether in the UN or in the wider multilateral community.

UN resolutions and exhortations can't change this, can't force national ministers of finance, for example, to participate in UN deliberations on economic and development issues. Only governments can do that. And if they don't—as is currently the case—UN decisions and resolutions just won't have the commitment by governments that they require for implementation and enforcement.

The WTO has become one of the most active and influential negotiating forums increasingly favoured by governments to deal with a range of trade-related issues that in many cases are directly relevant to the traditional functions of UN organizations. The fact that the WTO was established outside the framework of the UN has clearly weakened the capacity of the UN to deal with some key global issues, including environment, on a systemic basis, and closer co-operation and interaction between them is essential if both are to carry out their respective responsibilities effectively within a rational global governance system.

The UN does have the Administrative Committee for Co-ordination, which is designed to provide for co-ordination at the level of the secretariats of all UN agencies and organizations, but as I have pointed out, each of the specialized agencies has its own governing body reporting directly to member governments, and so co-ordination at the secretariat level too often does not rise much above turf protection. And the WTO is not a member. Given these constraints, secretariats do a surprisingly good job of co-ordination in many areas. An essential element in the movement to effective governance is to provide for the involvement of civil society actors—business people, scientists, non-governmental organizations—in co-operative management of issues in which they are prime actors. Kofi Annan's initiative in calling for establishment of an inclusive "issue management system" as part of his reform program is a promising step in this direction.

But only governments can make the changes required to effect real co-ordination, and this means that they need to change the ways that they use and direct international organizations.

Other non-governmental forums are becoming more and more important and influential, notably the World Economic Forum. Its annual meetings in Davos, Switzerland, attract a galaxy of world political, business and intellectual leaders. And its series of summit meetings in each region bring together a similar array of local leaders. Unlike the governmental forums, these gatherings do not produce formal resolutions or decisions, nor do they seek consensus. But they do provide an opportunity to work out informal agreements and strike deals as well as influence the attitudes and actions of world leaders. And as decision making in the UN and intergovernmental organizations with worldwide membership becomes more difficult, there will inevitably be a tendency for negotiations to be conducted and decisions made in smaller groups of a more informal nature. These informal processes can and should be closely linked to the formal processes of the UN and other intergovernmental organizations. It is encouraging that Secretary-General Kofi Annan has recognized this and initiated a process of co-operating with non-official organizations like the World Economic Forum.

It was my hope that the secretary-general's proposal that the

General Assembly meet in a special millennium session in the year 2000 would provide a unique opportunity for world leaders to set a new course for the international community and the role of the UN in it. In December 1998, however, the General Assembly decided to convene a Millennium Assembly but not to use it as an occasion to address the need for the kind of fundamental change that the secretary-general referred to in his reform proposals.

The member governments' cautious, lukewarm response stemmed from their fear of opening a Pandora's box of contentious issues that they were not ready to confront. I'm convinced that opening it and confronting its issues is both necessary and inevitable or the UN will never be fit to help the world community meet the challenges of the twenty-first century.

Whether or not fundamental reform proves politically feasible in the foreseeable future, it is, I submit, inescapable if the UN is to become the centrepiece of the system of co-operative governance that is required to ensure a secure, sustainable and equitable future for the human community in the new millennium. First and foremost, the UN of the future must be built around the distinctive attributes that provide the base for its unique and indispensable capacity to meet the needs of the world community. Primary among these are

> its universal membership, which is open to all sovereign nations, including "mini-states"

> its global mandate, deriving from its charter, which mandates it to deal with a broad range of security, economic, social, humanitarian, human rights and legal issues

> its unique status as a global political forum, with no credible substitute for dealing with peace and security issues and for identifying and legitimizing new issues for the international economic and social agenda; development co-operation, human rights, the environment, population and women's issues are some examples

its value as the principal global forum for the development
and administration of international law; though only a
few issues require action to be taken globally, an increasing
number need a global context or framework for action by
national, regional, local or sectoral governments—for example, national governments and local authorities are naturally reluctant to impose environmental standards on their
industries for fear of saddling them with a competitive disadvantage vis-à-vis their international counterparts, and the
UN can help establish a level playing field

If the United Nations is to do these jobs with the degree of effectiveness that will attract the confidence and support of the world
community, its principal bodies must be refurbished, in my view,
along the following lines.

1. The General Assembly

This is the central political forum. One hundred and eighty-five
members include virtually all the world's nation-states, ranging from
those with very large populations and economies to the very small
and the very poor. The majority, some two-thirds of the members,
are developing countries, though some, like Korea and Mexico, have
recently graduated to join the club of the rich and the powerful—
the OECD. The dominance of the General Assembly by the developing countries, which for many purposes constitute themselves as
G-77, is often trotted out as evidence that the UN is skewed against
Western interests. Much is made, too, of the fact that mini-states
like Andorra and Nauru, with populations less than those of many
small cities, have the same vote as major ones like the United States,
Germany and Japan.

Overall, however, the developing countries account for some
three-quarters of the world's population and constitute a little less
than that in the membership of the UN and the voting power in the
General Assembly. Some may call this the tyranny of the majority.
I submit, on the other hand, that it could most appropriately be
called democracy.

The real question, then, is quite different. It is, quite simply, this: Will the major nations of the world be prepared to allow democracy to function at the global level?

It's difficult enough to reach decisions at the General Assembly. The difficulty is compounded by the practice that all agreements must by reached by consensus. This is not a constitutional requirement—it is not built into the UN Charter—but it has become normal practice, and member governments are usually very reluctant to depart from it. The result is that even the smallest countries have a de facto veto, which in turn means that important agreements are often held hostage to narrow special interests. In consequence, most agreements are reached only by reducing them to their lowest common denominators.

No legislative body can possibly function effectively if most of its important decisions have to be made by consensus. No democratic country could operate this way. The UN of the future should be no exception. Consensus should still be sought for major issues, but the practice of insisting on it should be abandoned.

The other change required to make the General Assembly more effective is to streamline its agenda, as mentioned earlier.

2. The Security Council

The body responsible for peace and security, it deals with issues of the greatest political importance, which generally means they are also the subject of intense media attention and public interest. It is the Security Council that effectively selects the secretary-general, though the charter says the General Assembly must approve.

The fact that the membership of the Security Council is small—fifteen in all—enables it to meet frequently and expeditiously and to deal with crises. It is clearly the most effective of the UN's deliberative organs, as well as the most powerful. For several years it was reduced to impotence by the rivalries of the Cold War, but it has now regained much of the authority accorded to it by the UN Charter.

Its composition, however, is a problem, continuing as it does to reflect the political power structure that emerged from the Second World War. It is effectively controlled by the five permanent members—the United States, Great Britain, France, Russia and China—while the other ten seats are filled after intensely competitive voting in the General Assembly.

The Security Council must be enlarged and reconfigured to reflect today's geopolitical realities, including the political and economic power of Japan and Germany, the more than tripling of the membership of the UN and the growing economic and political power of its developing-country majority. Thus far, agreement on changes has eluded the UN. But agreement is imperative if the Security Council is to remain the centrepiece of the UN's peace and security role; otherwise it will be in danger of being bypassed or marginalized. This thorny issue remains unresolved.

Still, it's important to keep trying. An effectively functioning Security Council will be needed to deal with the new generation of peace and security problems the world must anticipate in the twenty-first century. Continuing impasse will weaken the UN and undermine its overall effectiveness.

If reform efforts fail, the Security Council's authority and effectiveness will diminish, and political power will shift to the General Assembly. But that body is too large and too cumbersome to deal with issues that by their nature require expeditious action. The result would almost inevitably be that the real action would take place outside the UN altogether.

3. The Economic and Social Council

This council, ECOSOC, much less well known than the Security Council, deals with a range of economic and social issues of primary interest to the UN's developing-country majority. It promotes and co-ordinates the UN's economic and social development programs, which focus on alleviating poverty, fostering sustainable development and facilitating the more active and equitable participation by developing countries in the expanding global economy. It is the principal forum for dealing with globalization in its various manifestations—development, humanitarian, environment and gender issues, the spread of crime, terrorism and drug trafficking.

The council has never worked as well as it should. It is supposed to knit together the various departments, programs and agencies of the United Nations dealing with economic and social issues into some kind of coherent whole. But there is so much overlap, and so many departments have acquired so much autonomy, that leadership has been excessively difficult. Recent reforms have improved its functioning somewhat, but there is still much frustration among the UN's membership over the council's apparent inability to exercise any significant influence over the specialized agencies of the UN, particularly the World Bank and the IMF, which are so crucial to the council's mission. As I've pointed out before, the specialized agencies report directly to governments rather than through the United Nations; their constituency consists generally of influential government ministers, who themselves resist UN influence and who seldom attend council meetings. All of this further limits the council's capacity to lead. An encouraging recent development was the convening of a joint meeting of the Development Committee of the World Bank and ECOSOC, which has brought finance ministers and senior officials into direct dialogue with their counterparts in the UN. This is an important breakthrough that I hope presages a new era of consultation and co-operation between these institutions that, after all, serve the same master and share the same goals.

The Commission on Global Governance recommended that ECOSOC be scrapped and replaced with an Economic Security Council, which would become the central forum for economic and financial policy and related social issues. It would have the mandate and the capacity to provide oversight and guidance to the policies and programs of the specialized agencies, including the World Bank and the IMF. Like the Security Council, it would have a relatively small membership but one representative of UN membership as a whole. There are various versions of this proposal, but the essence of it is to create an effective counterpart in the economic and social field to the Security Council in the field of peace and security. But there is virtually no support for this proposal, and at least for the time being it must be considered dead on arrival.

A more modest alternative is to create an executive committee or similar body within ECOSOC itself, of a size and with delegated powers that would enable it to do much of the work. As the secretary-general recommended in his reform program, this could be accompanied by a merger of the governing bodies of organizations that report to ECOSOC (UNDP, Unicef, UN Fund for Population Activities and World Food Programme). This would greatly simplify the task of ensuring co-ordination and coherence in the economic and social programs of the UN. An interesting variation would be to have the executive committee of ECOSOC act as the governing body for these organizations, with sub-committees to give special attention to them individually.

Ideally, in a fundamental restructuring of the UN (which would require opening up the charter and the treaties from which the specialized agencies derive their mandates), a reconstituted version of ECOSOC could provide broad direction to the programs of all UN bodies in the economic and social field. But this would only be effective if governments required their representatives on the governing bodies of each individual organization to exercise their powers within the overall framework set by the UN body. This is something governments have never done on a consistent basis and unfortunately there is little sign that they are likely to change. But in a world where it is no longer feasible to deal effectively with issues sector by sector, it is essential that the UN "system" function in a much more integrated and co-ordinated manner. Only governments have the power to make this happen.

The Economic and Social Council is the sole body with a broad enough mandate to provide the political forum for issues that cut across institutional boundaries. Only when governments recognize the need for such a forum at the global level will they provide the support that will enable ECOSOC to perform its tasks effectively.

Such changes, of course, will come about only when necessity compels them. On this I remain an optimist. I think the absolute necessity of such a forum is already making itself urgently felt, so I have to believe that the political will for change will in the end emerge.

4. The Trusteeship Council
As I've already said, this is a body that invites reinvention, and I've earlier sketched in some of what I think should be its functions. In

essence, a new Trusteeship Council would provide a forum—*the* forum—through which the nations of the world would come together to exercise their collective trusteeship for the integrity of the global environment and the global commons—the oceans, the atmosphere, the Antarctic and outer space. It is self-evident that these commons transcend national boundaries and can only be managed effectively through co-operation. There is no doubt they will move increasingly to the centre of the international agenda in the next century, and it's essential that the UN be much better prepared to deal with them. Kofi Annan's reform proposals have already suggested such a move.

5. Regional organizations

Most UN organizations and agencies have a regional structure, and in some cases, for example the World Health Organization, these have a high degree of autonomy. The most important regional entities of the UN itself are the regional economic commissions, which have made an important contribution to the UN and the regions they serve. For example, the UN Economic Commission for Europe was the only regional intergovernmental forum where representatives of both East and West participated during the Cold War. Since the end of the Cold War its function has become less important, and most of the work it now undertakes could be just as well handled by other organizations in the region. In other regions—Asia and the Pacific, Latin America and the Caribbean, and Africa—a case could be made that the regional economic commission of the UN could be merged with the functions undertaken by the other principal organizations rooted in the region itself.

There will be strong resistance to any such move by the organizations, as well as by many governments in their respective regions. But the need for stronger and more effective regional organizations, coupled with the advantages derived from rationalization and consolidation, will ultimately drive a review of these prospects and their costs and benefits. For the UN to yield its regional economic commissions to full autonomy and regional control would certainly be a wrench. However, stronger, autonomous regional organizations need not weaken the UN, as they could be accorded associate status and become the UN's principal partners in each of their regions. This would also enable the UN to concentrate on its central purpose and main comparative advantage as the world's principal global organization.

6. The secretary-general

Recall that the secretary-general is not merely an employee of the UN and its CEO. The UN Charter gives the secretary-general the status of an organ of the UN: his office is one of the sturdy legs of the UN. The Preparatory Commission for the United Nations that drafted its charter made the point that "the Secretary-General, more than anyone else, will stand for the United Nations as a whole. In the eyes of the world, he must embody the principles and ideals of the United Nations Charter to which the organization seeks to give effect." Over the years the authority of the secretary-general has been eroded by the tendency of member governments to micro-manage the organization. Kofi Annan's reform program and the strong leadership he has exercised have served to restore the authority of the secretary-general and clarify the division of functions between him and the General Assembly. And the new leadership and management structure he has set up, including for the first time a deputy secretary-general, can only strengthen his office.

What needs to happen—and I think the changes he has set in motion will make it happen—is a recognition that his role as the head of the entire UN system implicitly includes the specialized agencies. He needs greater political support for reshaping and redefining his role in this way. It's true that the secretary-general is chairman of the ACC, but this gives him little or no real authority over the heads of the specialized agencies. This is changing. Most agency heads, as well as many governments, now agree that much more co-ordination and co-operation are essential. Thus far the response to the changes he has suggested has been encouraging, but there is an inherent resistance to change in organizations that by their nature are committed to protecting their autonomy.

7. Financing

Financing of the UN is the single most serious manifestation of the decline in the political will to support it and has also produced a gradual deterioration in the capacity of the UN to carry out the functions that its members require of it. The United States, as the largest contributor to the UN's budget, and to the costs of the peacekeeping operations mandated by the Security Council, is also the biggest offender. Its arrears of over US$1 billion have still not been paid, despite the fact that the money represents a treaty obligation on the part of the United States. Payment has been held hostage by a single Republican congressman, who has insisted on making the appropriation of funds contingent on conditions relating to abortion; these are extraneous to the issue, would not be acceptable to UN members and manifest the low level of political commitment to the UN on the part of the U.S. It is also an ominous sign of the degree to which the world's only superpower, with the capacity to insist on the enforcement of international law and Security Council resolutions, is itself prepared to flout its legal obligations. It is a tribute to the often maligned and underestimated management of the United Nations, and in particular to the leadership of its current secretary-general, that the UN has been able to manage its way through this difficult situation. It has done this by substantial reductions in costs under Secretary-General Annan's reform program and by leaving unpaid funds owing to countries, including some of the poorest developing countries, that have provided troops for UN peacekeeping operations. It is ironic, and grossly unfair, that these poorest members should be in effect subsidizing the richest. I am sure that if the American people fully understood this situation, they would not tolerate it.

Whatever may be the resolution of the current financial crisis, it is essential that the United Nations' finances be put on a sound and sustainable basis if the "new" UN is to provide the services that only it can provide to the world community in the twenty-first century. There have been various proposals over the years for new means of direct financing for the UN and its organizations, agencies and programs—including the Tobin tax on international financial transactions, levies or charges on the use of the global commons, and other such stratagems that would provide funding to the UN and obviate reliance on the annual dues of its members. Indeed, one of the first things I did as executive director of the United Nations Environment Program was convene a study by the Brookings Institute, one of the most influential policy research institutions in the United States, on more direct and automatic means of financing global environmental programs. It still provides one of the best sources of reference for such measures. The study, *New Means of Financing International Needs*, by Eleanor Steinberg, was published in 1978 by Brookings Institute.

However, governments have consistently, and the U.S. most vehemently, opposed any new financing system that would accord the UN the equivalent of taxing power and relieve it of dependence on the direct contributions of governments. I believe this will change, indeed must change, over time, and the most likely prospect would be to put the costs of global environmental measures and protection of commons on something of a "user pays" basis.

Supplementing government support for UN development, humanitarian, environment and human rights programs with private contributions is a more promising prospect. Indeed, there are precedents for this in the public contributions that Unicef has long received for its work with children, and more recently Ted Turner's $1 billion commitment. There is a significant potential for increases in this kind of parallel private funding.

The centre of the UN's development programs, the UNDP, urgently needs to access new funding to maintain its leadership position in the field. Under its experienced and innovative new administrator, Mark Malloch-Brown, it is exploring new methods of accessing money from private sources—foundations, business and the public.

Another evidence of the unwillingness of member governments to permit the United Nations the right and the flexibility that most organizations have to manage their finances effectively is the denial of the right to borrow funds. It cannot even borrow to ameliorate the cash flow difficulties that arise from the practice of many members' delaying payment of their dues and the mismatch between the timing of the funds it receives and the need to meet its current costs.

A new, revitalized UN will not be possible if member governments continue to deny it the financial resources it needs, thus weakening its capacities and undermining its effectiveness.

The environment, human rights, peace and security, co-ordination of the international response to natural disasters and emergencies, and meeting humanitarian needs continue to be UN priorities. The new UN I envisage will focus on the political, legal and policy dimensions of these issues and less on mounting its own operations. Operations are not the UN's strong point. Many of the UN's most successful initiatives have been international operations that involved a variety of other actors—notably its peacekeeping missions, its response to the great African famine of 1984–86, and the major UN conferences that have shaped its agenda. These are essentially ad hoc operations in which the UN has used one of its most invaluable assets, its convening power, to mobilize both the skills and the financial resources required.

A new United Nations must be built around the best experiences of its past. It must shed the costly and bureaucratic baggage it has accumulated over the years and concentrate on its principal role as a global organization. It must become the primary source of objective, credible information on major global trends and issues. It must strengthen its capacity to provide early warnings of impending crises. Because crisis management relies on accurate information, the UN must avail itself of the extraordinary advances in communications. The secretary-general's reform program has given new impetus to this process.

Finally, perhaps for the first time, the UN will be enabled to ensure a safe, peaceful and productive life for all the nations of the world as we enter the much more complex, interdependent world of the twenty-first century.

Extending the Rule of Law Internationally

The rule of law is the key to the effective functioning of national societies; it is no different at the international level. In my view the codification, administration and enforcement of international law must become one of the principal functions of the United Nations in the period ahead.

This will not be easy—the rule of law implies enforcement and the punishment of transgressors. To date this has been possible only to a very limited degree.

Treaties affirming alliances to conduct and end wars are the most prominent features in the history of international agreements and are the precursors of international law. As industrial civilization has become increasingly complex and interdependent, there has been a proliferation of international, multilateral and bilateral agreements designed to deal with issues affecting all nations, such as trade, air transport, telecommunications, shipping and various product and labour standards.

The emergence of environmental issues has led to a whole new generation of treaties, conventions and "soft-law" agreements. These are designed to deal with a broad range of issues. In some cases they engage the interests of a group of nations, in others the entire world community.

The Declaration of the UN Conference on the Human Environment agreed on in Stockholm in June 1992 was a groundbreaking soft-law instrument that provided for limitations by governments on activities that might adversely affect the environment of neighbours or the global environment. But there have been other agreements concerning protection of the ozone layer, biodiversity, climate change, pollution of international waters, Antarctica, habitat and species protection, desertification, transboundary movement of hazardous products and wastes, and the peaceful use of outer space.

And what has all this activity produced? A plethora of hard-law instruments—treaties, conventions and protocols, binding on governments—as well as a great many soft-law instruments—declarations, statements and plans of action agreed to—which together provide a formidable set of ingredients for an international environmental legal regime.

But they do not yet constitute such a regime. They still consist largely of a patchwork of individual instruments, the product of a diverse range of political initiatives.

To complicate matters, each of the formal legal instruments is served by a small secretariat, each located and functioning separately and subject to direction only by the parties to the particular instrument they serve. The composition of these "parties" obviously varies significantly, so that each secretariat functions as a distinct entity, without any co-ordinating framework. In practice this means that co-ordination is difficult to achieve.

UNEP is, in my opinion, the organization best suited by its mandate and experience to provide the principal co-ordinating framework for the development and administration of international environmental law. Its Earthwatch monitoring and assessment functions serve to point out the need for new agreements and the revision of existing ones. It is also equipped to provide both substantive and administrative support for negotiating and administrating legal instruments.

The single greatest weakness of the existing international legal regime is the almost total lack of a capacity for enforcement. Enforcement is almost entirely dependent on the will of the strongest, usually the United States. If the U.S. doesn't agree with any international agreement, it will not be enforced. By the same token there is no way that the U.S. can be forced to comply with agreements against its will. Enforcement is therefore both inconsistent and unfair, reflecting the political interests, the will and the priorities of the power structure of the world community rather than the rule of law.

There is no question in my mind that the effective functioning of the world community in the period ahead will require the extension into the international arena of the same principles of law and justice that the viability of national societies depends on. One of the principal challenges of the twenty-first century will be to develop such an international legal regime from the miscellany of ingredients now in place.

To me the most promising and potentially important soft-law instrument is now being negotiated and discussed by people throughout the world under the auspices of an Earth Charter Commission established by the Earth Council and the Green Cross and now including many other organizations and movements.

A People's Earth Charter will derive its authority not from governments but from the broad support of ordinary people. And for this reason it is hoped that governments will give it their blessing and use it as the basis for adopting their own official version of the Earth Charter, both nationally and through the United Nations. The Earth Charter Commission intends to submit it to the United Nations in the year 2002 on the occasion of the tenth anniversary of the Earth Summit.

The latest version of the "benchmark" draft of the Earth Charter prepared by the drafting committee under the dedicated and skilled leadership of Steven Rockefeller, incorporates the following main principles:

1. Respect Earth and all life.
2. Care for the community of life in all its diversity.
3. Strive to build free, just, participatory, sustainable and peaceful societies.
4. Secure Earth's abundance and beauty for present and future generations.
5. Protect and restore the integrity of Earth's ecological systems, with special concern for biological diversity and the natural processes that sustain and renew life.
6. Prevent harm to the environment as the best method of ecological protection, and when knowledge is limited, take the path of caution.
7. Treat all living beings with compassion, and protect them from cruelty and wanton destruction.
8. Adopt patterns of consumption, production and reproduction that respect and safeguard Earth's regenerative capacities, human rights and community well-being.
9. Ensure that economic activities support and promote human development in an equitable and sustainable manner.
10. Eradicate poverty, as an ethical, social, economic and ecological imperative.

11. Honour and defend the right of all persons, without discrimination, to an environment supportive of their dignity, bodily health and spiritual well-being.

12. Advance worldwide the co-operative study of ecological systems, the dissemination and application of knowledge and the development, adoption and transfer of clean technologies.

13. Establish access to information, inclusive participation in decision making, and transparency, truthfulness and accountability in governance.

14. Affirm and promote gender equality as a prerequisite to sustainable development.

15. Make the knowledge, values and skills needed to build just and sustainable communities an integral part of formal education and lifelong learning for all.

16. Create a culture of peace and co-operation.

Of course, the Earth Charter will not in itself represent a solution to global problems. But that's not to devalue it. History demonstrates that documents like it have a significant influence over people's thinking and therefore ultimately their behaviour. And the process itself of developing it is important in educating people about their common interests and paving the way to common action.

The exercise also has another ancillary benefit. Collective behaviour tends to change private behaviour. Mere participation in such exercises tends to make people re-examine their personal lives, and leads them to consider actions they might take individually. They become more aware of how their own behaviour contributes to global problems—and how it can contribute to solutions.

The Changing Role of National Governments

What's the future of the nation-state? Will it—should it—just fade away? Will the idea of "national sovereignty" be tossed at last into the dustbin of history, a useful device now become obsolete?

Well, no . . . and yes.

The way we govern our own societies and the world community as a whole will, I am sure, be the central issue of the twenty-first century. Only by an effective system of governance will we be able to manage successfully the host of other issues that human survival and well-being depend on. I have already affirmed my own belief in the principle of subsidiarity—the idea that every function of governance should be carried out at the closest possible level to the people affected. Rigorous application of this principle would undoubtedly affect national governments most of all. They will need to yield jurisdiction over many issues to regional, state and local governments that are better able to deal with them, and they will also need to delegate more authority to international organizations, as cooperation with other governments becomes more and more necessary.

It is entirely possible that we will see a re-emergence of a modern version of the classical city-state of medieval and Renaissance Europe. We will also see ad hoc alliances, groupings of states into blocs (whether for trade, defence or simply mutual self-interest). None of this means that the nation-state as we know it today will just disappear. It will almost certainly continue to be the single strongest and most important level of governance, and the indispensable link between various levels and sectors of national society with the institutions and activities of the international community.

So nation-states will, and should, survive. But they will likely become smaller and almost certainly more numerous.

One of the apparent paradoxes of our time is that while nations are coalescing in trade, economic and, in the case of the European Union, political blocs, there is a counter-trend toward the fragmentation of existing nations. Important and distinctive (even if only in their own eyes) ethnic groups or regions are asserting their demands for autonomy or independence. But this is no paradox, really. In fact, these trends represent opposite sides of the same coin. It is becoming more and more feasible for smaller units to achieve the same kind of security and economic advantages that they currently obtain from being part of a larger nation, through membership in regional and global organizations. In such multilateral groupings they forgo sovereign powers largely in areas where they are not exercising them anyway, and attain a greater degree of identity and international status, so it should be no surprise that they move in this direction.

The European Union is an innovative governance structure that seems likely to provide a model that will influence others in the period ahead. It is neither a multilateral organization nor a national government. But it *is* a government—in the sense that its members, all of them national governments, have vested in it responsibilities formally and normally exercised by the governments of its member countries, together with the constitutional powers to carry out these responsibilities. While this represents an important divestment of sovereignty by the national governments concerned, it nevertheless enables them to continue to act as national governments, albeit with more limited jurisdictions, and each is still accorded in the international community the full status and the prerogatives of a sovereign nation.

I know from my own experience with the Earth Summit that there has been some difficulty in accommodating this new level of government in the traditional protocols accrediting governments to international organizations. Because of the importance of Europe, a formula has been developed to enable the European Union to participate in international meetings and to be accorded virtually all the rights of a single national government, at least on issues that require it to represent its members. But this still poses some problems, and these will be compounded when "Europe" proceeds with its plans to set up a Foreign Policy Directorate.

The unique constitutional structure of the European Union facilitates, though it is not designed to encourage, the separatist pressures that exist in a number of European countries. Some of these enclaves see membership in the European Union as an attractive means of having their cake and eating it too—obtaining international recognition as a separate nation while retaining the economic and other benefits of membership in a greater union. In some cases, as in Scotland and Wales, the separatist pressures can be accommodated by granting them a greater degree of autonomy within the nation, but the prospect of joining the European Union as full members could well lend impetus to the independence movements there and will certainly give them a greater degree of leverage.

Canada is wrestling with a new role for Quebec, whose nationalists now openly champion the cause of independence. As I wrote in my opening chapter, a regionalization of Canada need not be the end of the nation. A Canadian union modelled on the European Union could ultimately prove to be a viable alternative for Canada and deserves more serious consideration than it has yet received.

In Cameroon, the two English-speaking provinces have developed notions to separate from the six French-speaking provinces, a desire that has at least once been ruthlessly suppressed. And the bitter and persistent conflicts in the former Yugoslavia demonstrate that ethnic differences can drive the struggle for national identity and independence. The former Soviet Union became the Commonwealth of Independent States and then just Russia, and it is likely to fragment even further. Even in centralist China there are strong movements for provincial autonomy, not just in Tibet.

The United Nations now has 185 members, some of them microstates like Andorra, Monaco and Liechtenstein. The fact that they have full status in the Community of Nations is not lost on other groups, which can see that, if they were separate nations, they would be much more visible and possibly more viable. Quebec, for example, would be the thirty-second largest nation in terms of its economy if it were to separate—a useful reminder to Canadians that both Quebec and the rest of Canada could be viable separately by the standards of today's international community. The experience of Sweden and Norway is instructive. They were a single nation until 1905. Each has since developed a distinctive identity and role in the world, while remaining closely linked in many respects. Canadians might also reflect on the fact that both Sweden and Norway are smaller, in population and in the size of their economies, than either Quebec or Ontario.

It seems to me to follow logically from the basic principles of democracy that people should have the right to choose their own form of government and that this right should not be foreclosed just because history included them within the confines of a nation-state that they may now wish to separate from. I believe this is a legitimate right that is likely to be exercised more and more frequently in the future, and if it is not to produce destructive conflicts and anarchy, the process by which separation is legitimized by the international community must be guided by some accepted principles. These would need to include a requirement that the people seeking independence have the attributes and size to enable them to function as a viable nation, and separation would need to be effected through a democratic process consisting of at least two stages divided by a sufficient period of time to ensure that separation was not driven by purely impulsive or temporary moods and circumstances.

As a Canadian I would like to think that we will be able to rise to the challenge of accommodating Quebec's aspirations in a manner that provides positive examples for others. How sad it would be, after all, for Canada, which has been one of the most successful federal nations of the twentieth century, to enter the twenty-first century as a failed nation. We have thus far been very civilized in dealing with the tensions that the separatist movement in Quebec has engendered. But we must now become much more innovative and flexible or we may slide into a cycle of deepening division that could see civility and common sense overridden by emotion and prejudice.

The trend toward the creation of more nations will undoubtedly continue into the twenty-first century, and so will the trend to extend the agreements and institutions through which they co-operate to further their common interests. This will have important implications for the functioning and role of the United Nations and other multilateral organizations. On the whole, I believe that management of these new arrangements will be possible—but not easy.

The Emerging Strength of Civil Society— A New Sense of Global Neighbourhood

The running of our planet (I'm quoting from the report of the Commission on Global Governance here), "once viewed primarily as concerned with intergovernmental relationships, now involves not only governments and intergovernmental institutions but also non-governmental organizations (NGOs), citizens' movements, trans-national corporations, academia, and the mass media. The emergence of a global civil society, with many movements reinforcing a sense of human solidarity, reflects a large increase in the capacity and will of people to take control of their own lives . . ."

In the historical context what we now describe as civil society has always existed; indeed, people worked and lived together in family, communal and other informal groupings long before more formal structures of government were developed.

Civil society, in the current context, is one of those terms slippery of definition. While it's being used more and more often these days, it is still not widely understood. Indeed, there is a good deal of variety, and even some confusion, among those who consider themselves part of it.

In its broadest sense, of course, it encompasses all the sectors of society other than governments and thus goes beyond those organizations usually called NGOs. But some sectors—business, for example—hardly regard themselves as part of civil society. On the contrary, business usually sees itself as a distinct part of society or, often enough, as the core sector of society, and tends to look on NGOs as ideological opponents to its own free-enterprise notions. Business therefore keeps itself aloof and insists on maintaining its separate identity, with its own ability to intervene in the issues that especially interest it. This is changing, and there are many exceptions, but it is still generally true.

Civil society is therefore much more diverse and fragmented than governments and international organizations. This is of course one of its virtues, but it leads to difficulty in providing for the participation of civil society in the official processes of governance. Many civil society groups and organizations hold common positions on particular issues, but it's seldom feasible for them to present a united front. Sometimes the very number of small and often fragmented organizations inhibits agreement on common positions, and even governments that wish to accommodate their concerns have trouble doing so.

In some Western countries where NGOs have long had an important role, these processes have evolved to a point that they are working, if not fully satisfactorily, at least reasonably well. In countries like Japan and most developing countries, which don't have the same tradition of civil society involvement in governance, the movement from electoral democracy to participatory democracy has been much slower and fraught with a good deal of mutual distrust and controversy. In some countries the organizations of civil society have been seen by their governments as the political opposition—a view often shared by the organizations themselves. Thus any participation by civil society in the UN and other multilateral forums has to contend with the suspicion and resistance of some countries. As a consequence Western organizations or international organizations that are predominately Western in their origins and ethos take up a disproportionate share of international space. Participation by developing-country organizations has increased dramatically in recent years, but this imbalance continues to exist.

I've mentioned Lester Salamon's assertion in his *Foreign Affairs* article that the rise of civil society in the twentieth century can be compared to the rise of the nation-state in the nineteenth. This exaggerates the realities somewhat but it does underscore the growing importance of civil society movements, though they can never replace governments or be given the same status as governments. They lack, after all, the broadly representative character of governments. At least in principle, governments represent all people and all sectors in a particular nation; civil society organizations typically represent particular sectors or interest groups and have to varying degrees links with their counterparts in other countries.

It is no longer sufficient for the United Nations to provide civil society organizations only with opportunities to consult the UN and to provide their views on issues that the UN is dealing with. The long-standing practice of giving qualified NGOs consultative status with the Economic and Social Council has been useful but, as we realized in preparing the Earth Summit, is no longer adequate. For all practical purposes such status denies accreditation—and therefore participation—to the many citizen and grassroots organizations in developing countries, which are often, by Western standards, informal in nature and do not have the resources to qualify for accreditation or to be represented at UN Headquarters in New York. Thus, for purposes of the Earth Summit, I sought and obtained agreement to open up participation to all groups with an interest in the issues being considered. This resulted in the largest participation ever of civil society in a United Nations conference.

In addition, many civil society organizations today have financial resources and operational capabilities, particularly in the development, environment and humanitarian fields, that exceed those of the UN agencies and organizations operating in these fields. And collectively their resources and capacities vastly exceed those of the United Nations. Accordingly, the UN must move beyond consultative relationships with such organizations to real partnerships and operational co-operation. Secretary-General Kofi Annan's reform program provides an innovative mechanism for this in establishing an "issue management system," which includes key personnel and UN action.

To me, one of the most encouraging phenomena of recent times has been the explosion of non-governmental, citizen and grassroots organizations in developing countries, many of which are not linked with international counterparts. The environment and sustainable development movement, especially the Earth Summit, gave strong impetus to this development. National Councils for Sustainable Development were set up in more than one hundred countries as a direct result of the Earth Summit, which created a unique, though sometimes still tenuous, forum for bringing together government and civil society.

The People's Millennium Forum, proposed by Kofi Annan in his program of UN reform, provides, in my view, a unique opportunity to encourage this process. I hope that it will not be a single event but a whole series of events and processes, enabling the expression of voices of people throughout the world and stimulating the various elements of civil society to build a new set of alliances, which in turn will facilitate efforts to confront the challenges of the twenty-first century.

The horizontal links between civil society organizations and various official levels of governments need to be matched by a much closer vertical linkage, reaching from local government through provincial, regional and national governments to the relevant international forums. Each of these levels must be seen more and more as an integral part of the overall system of governance, and ways for them to interact and co-operate must be vastly improved and strengthened.

This is not going to be easy. Nation-states are notoriously prickly about anything that could be construed as challenging their sovereignty or limiting their freedom of action or authority.

One essential, I contend, is full transparency of information available to levels of government and the public. If central governments alone represent the nation, and if civil society participation is at their behest, as it is, this participation will be sporadic and unsystematic at best. It will therefore leave other levels of government frustrated, and even alienated, from international organizations. The UN and other multilateral organizations have to overcome this alienation. One of the most promising examples of a positive linkage between local and international action has been the proliferation of Local Agendas 21 in some three thousand cities and towns around the world, all of them based on the Earth Summit's Agenda 21. Another is the way local governments played an active and influential part in the United Nations Conference on Human Settlements, or Habitat, in Istanbul in June 1996, which raises the interesting prospect that this UN organization could be restructured to provide for the continuing participation of local authorities, and thus provide them with a UN "home."

As readers will have gathered by this time, I am a strong believer in the need to construct better networks of understanding and co-operation. The processes by which we manage our relationships— both horizontally, in engaging civil society with official levels of governance, and vertically, by creating closer links between the local, national and global levels of governance—are essential to the development of a more systemic means of managing our affairs. And I attach special importance to the need to "support and empower people in building a more secure, equitable and sustainable future," which is the stated goal of the Earth Council.

Of course, not all the organizations and activities of non-governmental sectors of society are "civil." While crime has always been with us, technology and the processes of globalization have vastly multiplied the capacities of criminal elements to undermine and exploit our societies. Organized crime has become highly sophisticated, both in the nature of the criminal activities it undertakes and in its ability to elude detection and accountability for its crimes.

Although reliable statistics are not available, it is now widely believed and probable that illicit trade, particularly in drugs, has become a major factor in world trade and produced immense profits that are laundered to enter the legitimate financial and trading system, leading to criminal control of legitimate enterprises and the subversion of the political process. Already there is strong evidence that some governments are closely allied with organized crime and dependent on its support. Such governments are increasingly infiltrating criminal organizations and influencing the legitimate business community.

And it's only going to get worse. I am convinced that international crime is emerging as one of the principal challenges of the twenty-first century, confronting nations and the international community with the need to mobilize their resources for an entirely new kind of war, in which the enemy is powerful, versatile and largely invisible. It is a war that no nation can wage alone, as organized crime is clearly highly adept at using the instruments of globalization to move people and resources across national boundaries. This is one of the challenges Kofi Annan addressed in his UN reform program. It is one that deserves high priority and universal support.

If the international criminal syndicates on the one hand and the multinational corporations on the other lead the way, why shouldn't civil society follow suit? There may be lessons to be learned from these organizations—their nimbleness, their resourcefulness, their fluidity of structure, their adherence to internal codes and rules. Civil society already has a significant international, even global, dimension, but as yet it does not function very effectively on this level. The civil society movement should now concentrate on extending its multi-national presence, and in doing so make an immensely important contribution to developing links between the local, national and global levels, providing a countervailing force for good and for shaping our common future.

CHAPTER 15

Can Technology
See Us Through?

SCIENCE AND TECHNOLOGY have made things better, and
by making them better have helped to make them worse.
Can they now help make them better again?

There is no question that science and technology have vastly
multiplied the human community's impact on the Earth's environment, on its life-support systems and natural resources. The dramatic advances in medical science and health care are fundamental
to this impact, and have led to population explosion. This in turn
has been accompanied by an explosion in the scale and intensity of
human activities.

Remarkably, the unprecedented growth in population has been
accompanied by an even greater degree of economic growth, all of
which has produced the richest civilization the world has ever
known, with more and more people enjoying a quality of life without precedent. What a tragic irony it is, therefore, that there are nevertheless more people mired in dire and debilitating poverty today
than ever, and a greater gulf between rich and poor. Bridging this
gulf, by ensuring more equitable sharing of the benefits our technological civilization provides and, in particular, by eradicating poverty,
poses the greatest challenge to the moral basis of our civilization—
and to its sustainability.

Technology has tended to exacerbate the gulf between rich and
poor. This of course is not the fault of technology itself but derives

from the fact that its benefits accrue primarily to those with capital and resources required to develop and employ it. Technology is also a primary source of environmental deterioration, but again this is not the fault of technology but of our misuse and mismanagement of it.

In the twenty-first century we'll have to confront the gross imbalances that are the inadvertent and largely unforeseen consequences of the ways we have used the awesome powers of science and technology. These imbalances will escalate to unmanageable proportions if we continue on our present path. The only way to redress these imbalances is to tackle them at their roots by changing the conditions that drive them. This is the central theme of the lessons I have learned from my own experience in life—the need to put in place a system of governance that will enable us to manage our relationships with one another and our impact on the Earth more effectively and equitably. This in turn is inextricably related to the need to conserve the resource base and life-support systems of the Earth that our life and well-being depend on. It follows from this, as I see it, that the transition to sustainable development is the indispensable key to the secure, positive and hopeful future that people everywhere aspire to. This is a challenge to our political will and capacity for social innovation and engineering, and we must make technology an ally if we are to meet this goal.

What are the prospects? There are some encouraging signs. For example, driven by its dependence on external sources of energy, Japan has employed technological innovation to reduce dramatically the use of energy and raw materials per unit of GDP.

And technology is also making it possible to effect major improvements in industrial efficiency. Technology created the addictive pleasures of the automobile. It has also led to impressive improvements in the efficiency of internal combustion engines and the fuels they use, which in turn has brought about significant reductions in CO_2 emissions. The relatively new science of industrial ecology promises even greater enhancement of industrial efficiency through the development of "closed-circuit industrial systems," with the waste products of one process used as raw materials for another. In theory at least, technology is now making it possible to foresee an industrial production system that could make much of what the world needs by processes that internalize and effectively eliminate all harmful wastes. We are a long way from this at present. But the technological achievements to date make it clear that the primary obstacles to a waste-free industrial system will be inadequate political will, institutional inertia and misplaced societal priorities.

The area that I am most familiar with is energy, through my experience in both the petroleum and the electric power industries. Energy, I believe, will remain at the centre of the challenge we face to build an industrial civilization that will be secure and sustainable in the twenty-first century.

We sometimes forget that energy, far from being scarce, is in fact the most abundant and pervasive element in nature. The constraint on energy supply is the extent to which nature has made it available in usable form, as for example coal and petroleum, and the cost of converting other resources into usable energy on a commercially viable basis. Until recently, therefore, the constraints on supply have been primarily a matter of cost. The need now to meet increasingly rigorous environmental standards has added another dimension to the issue of supply, which also in the final analysis equates to cost.

My experience at Petro-Canada and later at Ontario Hydro taught me that the process of cultural adaptation is much slower and more difficult than that of technological change. Even now, technology would make it possible to attain much higher levels of energy efficiency than are being achieved. The innovative environmental analyst Amory Lovins, who advised us at Ontario Hydro, estimates that energy use in North America could be reduced by some 70 percent without sacrifice of quality of life. A study conducted by the Electric Power Research Institute in the u.s. is more conservative, but nevertheless indicated that the country's energy needs could be met at 50 percent of current consumption.

The planet-wide worry about climate change—and the agreement reached by the Parties to the Climate Change Convention at their meeting in Kyoto in December 1997—have given new impetus to the drive for improved efficiency in the use of fossil fuels and to the development of alternative sources of energy to replace them. Technology is clearly the key to this transition. Collectively, cars are the largest single source of the carbon dioxide emissions, the main contributor to human-induced climate change. People are not about to give up their cars. The hundreds of millions of people in the developing world who have never owned an automobile and will soon have the means to buy one simply will not forgo the chance to acquire one, any more than those who already own one can be expected to give it up. Without doubt, then, the car population explosion will outpace the human one.

Accordingly, efforts to control CO_2 and other greenhouse-gas emissions even to the point of meeting the modest targets agreed to in Kyoto in 1997 must concentrate on reducing emissions from existing sources. Fossil fuels still account for some 68 percent of overall energy use, and so in the short term we must focus on improving the efficiency in the ways we use them and on developing alternatives. This must be one of our main priorities. The transition will not be made quickly or easily, but the risks—and costs—will be much greater if we don't move now.

Car makers are responding to the challenge. They know full well that the vast expansion of their prospective market will generate intense pressure for more regulation to cope with the massive problems of traffic congestion and air pollution that will inevitably result. They are seeking both to improve the efficiency of their engines and to develop alternative fuel systems, which reduce and in some cases eliminate emissions.

In my private business life the Technology Development Corporation, in which Stephan Schmidheiny is my partner, has invested heavily in a company, Quantum Energy Technologies, that is developing new, environmentally friendly fuel products based on a fundamental scientific breakthrough developed at MIT. This involves a new understanding of matter structured in extremely small particles —nano-technology.

As a member of the International Advisory Board of Toyota, I have been most impressed with the extensive capital and human resources the company is devoting to the issue—not just in improving the vehicles themselves, either. Toyota engineers are also designing means to integrate cars with other modes of transport into systems that make more efficient use of space, time, fuel, materials and capital.

Even with these and other efforts, the problem will not be easily solved, given the sheer magnitude of the car population and its concentration in already congested urban areas. All these measures will be helpful, but most of them are also costly, and the already congested cities of the developing world will be hard pressed to find the capital required. Thus, inevitably, automobiles will become more technologically sophisticated in response to these issues, and their environmental impact, at both the local and global levels, ever more controversial.

The major impact of the automobile will, of course, be felt locally and will need to be managed locally. But there is a direct link between motor vehicles as a local problem and the risks to the global environment. There could in fact be no better example of the link between individual behaviour, local action and protection of the global environment.

Some modest steps have already been taken in this direction. Ironically, the city of Los Angeles, which surely represents the epitome of the automobile culture, was also the first to impose limits on the use of gasoline-powered motor vehicles. This provided a strong incentive for car makers to develop vehicles that use alternative fuels.

Most major companies have produced their version of the electric automobile. True, the relatively high cost, the limited range and the limitations imposed by the weight and recharging needs of the batteries they use mean that they are still more expensive novelties than candidates for mass marketing. And they are no panacea: battery-driven electric cars eliminate emissions from the automobile itself, but they're still dependent on electricity and therefore on a conventional energy supply, so they displace emission problems rather than remove them. Toyota's new hybrid vehicle, using a combination of conventional fuel and a generator that runs on the movement of the car itself, promises important improvements in emission performance, though it is not a total solution to the problem.

The most widely heralded alternative to fossil fuels is the fuel cell. The technology itself is not new; it was first developed some 160 years ago by a gentleman in Wales who was also a judge. It is a leading contender in eliminating CO_2 emissions and substantially reducing those of other pollutants. The principal constraint to commercial use at this point is the high cost, which has limited the use of fuel cells thus far to specialized situations in which cost is not a major factor, notably in submarines and space vehicles.

There are other formidable problems still to be solved before fuel cells replace internal combustion engines. For example, hydrogen takes three thousand times the amount of space to produce the same amount of energy as gasoline. Nevertheless, progress is being made. Vancouver-based Ballard Power Systems has developed one of the most promising systems, an electric engine powered by fuel cells using a direct supply of hydrogen. Several car makers are taking it seriously. DaimlerChrysler has made a major investment in Ballard, and the company has co-operative arrangements with other automobile companies.

In the meantime, experiments continue on other alternative fuel systems. An important example of another alternative to fossil fuels that has actually been implemented on a large scale is Brazil's program of producing ethanol mainly from sugarcane. This industry, begun in the 1970s to reduce reliance on foreign oil, uses four million hectares of sugar plantations to fuel half of Brazil's vehicles while reducing CO_2 emissions each year by 18 percent. The government did at first provide financial incentives to make ethanol competitive and ensured its widespread availability through the mainstream distribution system. Some politicians in the South and Midwest u.s. were pushing for government incentives to produce ethanol from corn, but this, as well as Brazil's ethanol program, has lost momentum, mostly owing to low oil prices.

All energy sources require big investments.

As *The Economist* put it in 1998, "For most people, renewable energy used to conjure up thoughts of bearded vegetarians in sandals. No longer. Big energy companies are more interested in renewables than ever before. Compared with fossil fuels, renewables are becoming less expensive—and the spread of global greenery means that governments are backing them." The magazine quoted Cor Herkströter, chairman of Shell, as saying that "in 50 years, Shell could be 50% oil and 50% renewables."

Solar power offers one of the most promising prospects for extending the proportion of renewables in the energy economy. Significant advances in the technology of photovoltaics, which converts sunlight into energy, have already expanded its use and dropped prices by more than half. Photovoltaics have become cheap enough to be competitive in some areas that are not connected to the electricity grid. Wind power has done even better. Costs halved between 1990 and 1998; the technology has improved and the machines have got bigger, lowering capital and maintenance costs. As a result wind power is now just about competitive with fossil fuels in some local markets. In other markets, some of the time, biomass, geothermal, landfill gas and waste-to-energy can compete in price with carbon-based fuels.

The most exotic and seemingly far-out proposal to meet the long-term need for non-polluting energy envisages using the moon to collect solar energy. It would be concentrated on the moon into microwave beams and sent to Earth, where they would be received and converted into electricity from a variety of strategically located receptor stations. The notion was developed by a team headed by Dr. David Criswell, director of the Institute of Space Systems Oper ations at the University of Houston. I have checked it out with a number of experts, all of whom confirmed that the idea, which has been mooted for some time, may now be ripe to carry forward. The scale is awesome and the problems to be overcome are clearly daunting, but Criswell makes a persuasive case that it can be undertaken based on existing technology and the expertise acquired through the United States space program. The project would deliver net new energy to the Earth that is independent of the biosphere, would produce no CO_2 or other polluting emissions and have minimal environmental impact compared with other energy sources. Criswell's system has the capacity to generate electric energy equivalent to the entire current world oil production, using a land area on Earth equal to about 40 percent of the land area of Kuwait. It offers a perpetual, non-depleting resource as long as the sun shines and the moon remains in place.

And what about nuclear energy? It was once—before Chernobyl—seen as the ultimate answer to meeting the world's energy needs. I recall as a young man being captivated by the notion of "atoms for peace," in which the power of the atom could be harnessed to produce energy to meet society's needs. In Canada, as in the United States, France, Japan, Russia, the U.K. and some other countries, there was a major transition to reliance on nuclear power to accommodate growing economies in the post–Second World War period. Some environmentalists raised questions about nuclear safety and the unresolved issues of the disposal of nuclear wastes, but the public mood was generally positive, and governments were strongly committed.

However, the 1979 accident at Three Mile Island in Pennsylvania and the much more devastating one in 1986 at Chernobyl in what was then the Soviet Union called public attention to the potential for disaster with nuclear power and lent credence to the environmental and safety concerns so loudly and persistently proclaimed by its opponents. The uproar that followed Chernobyl, particularly, eroded political support for new nuclear power developments. The nuclear power industry has been under pressure in other areas, notably in Sweden, where the government decreed that existing plants would be phased out; and in France, which had been the primary champion of nuclear power, the new Socialist government has recently raised serious questions about the country's aging nuclear plants. The new German government has decided to call a halt to further development of nuclear power. In Canada, Ontario Hydro, which relies on Canada's distinctive CANDU nuclear reactor for some 60 percent of its base-load power, had to shut down, for safety reasons, seven of its nineteen reactors—17 percent of its existing capacity. It now faces difficult decisions as the high cost of rehabilitating these plants is bound to reignite the nuclear debate.

The economics of nuclear power have done more to impede its prospects than the pressures of environmentalists. The low prices of oil, coal and natural gas, combined with the high capital costs of nuclear power and the need to provide for the deferred costs of decommissioning and waste disposal, have made nuclear power an unattractive option. Even the advantage of being the only major energy source not producing CO_2 emissions hasn't yet given the industry a new lease on life.

There have been many improvements in nuclear technology, and it's now possible to construct safer, more compact plants that would reduce the risk of accidents or the consequences should accidents occur. This may form the basis of any significant expansion of the nuclear power industry. The economics of nuclear may be improved by the prospect of using weapons-grade plutonium freed up by the downsizing of Russian and u.s. nuclear weapons stocks. However, the political and environmental problems remain to be solved to the satisfaction of the public.

I think nuclear power will continue to have a place in our energy mix, but not as the primary source—unless of course there is a breakthrough in fusion research. Fusion—in which light nuclei join to form a heavier nucleus, releasing great amounts of energy—would be almost entirely self-generating, and could therefore be a safer and more acceptable alternative to fission. But most scientists believe it will be the middle of the next century—if ever—before fusion is a prospect.

On the present evidence it seems likely that new developments will be concentrated in four major areas:

1. Biotechnology and genetics

These sciences open up the possibility of engineering the basic elements that all plant and animal, including human, life is based on. In my capacity as chairman of the international panel charged with reviewing prospects for research in food and agriculture under the aegis of the Consultative Group for International Agriculture Research, I have been exposed to some of the implications of these prospects. On the positive side they include increasing agricultural production in food deficit areas and breeding species of plants that are naturally resistant to pests and make much more efficient use of water and fertilizers. The other side of the coin is that ownership of these new varieties will be vested in the organizations that develop them, principally private corporations, which claim intellectual property rights to the products of research they have funded. As a consequence, peasant farmers could find themselves having to purchase their seeds from multinational corporations rather than producing their own. It could also vastly accelerate the transition from land-based and labour-intensive agriculture to industrial food-producing systems, which could create immense social and political upheaval in developing countries like India, China, Pakistan and Indonesia.

Biotechnology also means we could breed animals to demand. For example, we could "design" cattle to increase both meat and milk production. Domestic animals could be cloned, to become living factories producing pharmaceutical products. These are controversial issues, as the public reaction to the cloning of the sheep Dolly in Scotland and the escalating tension between Europe and the United States (and Canada) over genetically modified foods makes clear.

These concerns deepen as the same genetic engineering techniques may be used to alter or tinker with human beings. The present political mood favours banning the cloning of humans, but experience indicates that when science presents new possibilities with such important implications, it is possible to regulate but not suppress them.

It's also probable that as the benefits of genetic engineering become more apparent, the public will demand access to them. Possible benefits include equipping people with the means to protect themselves against diseases and infirmities; producing organ replacements for transplants; and using technologies to improve health and prolong life. Without doubt, genetic engineering will be fraught with social, political and economic controversy.

2. Information and computer technologies
Progress in this field is so rapid that all we can confidently predict is that the future is unknowable and probably beyond our current ability to comprehend, let alone predict. It's likely that further

miniaturization of the computer chip will enable almost every product and service we use to be computerized. Video conferencing will be a standard feature of digitized telephones for most business and personal use, which will reduce the need for business travel. And in an increasingly congested world, virtual experiences and entertainment will be widely substituted for the "real" thing. The social and behavioural effects are hard to envisage, but there is an uneasy portent in a recent survey indicating that the majority of American children prefer spending time with their computers rather than with their friends—another clear sign that the blessings technology can bring us will be very mixed indeed.

3. Medical and health technologies

Developments in biotechnology and genetics have great potential to improve human health and lengthen life. Advances in digital technology and electronics will contribute significantly to diagnosis and treatment of many illnesses. The most important challenge, which will ultimately be met successfully, is a cure for cancer. Another is one for AIDS. Continued improvements will occur in preventing and treating diseases and in repairing injuries to the human body. All this will serve to relieve suffering and enhance the quality of life. Again, however, these changes will have profound social, political and economic consequences. Lower mortality rates and longer life-spans will mean more people living longer, in a world with population still climbing to critical levels. Although global population is likely to stabilize about the midpoint of the next century, current trends are producing a demographic shift of monumental proportions. In the more mature industrialized countries, the population is getting smaller and older, with a reduced proportion of productive people. In contrast, young people make up the largest single segment of the population of developing countries, where population growth is concentrated, creating huge and potentially unmanageable pressures to provide them with education, decent living conditions and employment.

Medical science also faces some ominous challenges, with no satisfactory solutions as yet.

Not long ago I chaired a meeting of leading world scientists. I asked them, "What do you think will be the major problems confronting society in the twenty-first century?"

To my surprise the majority response was the resurgence of traditional communicable diseases and the emergence of new strains. Not too long ago, before penicillin was discovered, a simple infection could be terminal. Since then, the development of a variety of antibiotics has enabled us to cure most infections, and we've become complacent about our ability to deal with them. But scientists now caution that new strains of bacteria are resistant to antibiotics; there is a real danger that these "superbugs" will overtake our ability to produce drugs to counter them. In addition, we've still failed to develop drugs to cure viral infections. Given the fact that the world is for all practical purposes a single community, the risks of a deadly epidemic or plague that could affect hundreds of millions of people is very real. Preventing this from happening or containing its consequences will be a central priority in the period ahead.

4. Automated and integrated industrial production systems
I have already referred to the prospect that future industrial production systems could "internalize" wastes and emissions, using waste products as an energy source for other processes. These closed-circuit systems will in all likelihood be fully automated, with robots replacing human workers. Japan has so far led the robotic revolution, largely out of awareness that they're facing an aging population with consequently few industrial workers available.

In Japan and those European countries with similar demographics, these systems can be a very positive thing; they allow those workers who are employed to be highly paid while relieving the country of the need to rely on immigrant workers.

Of course, for those countries where large numbers of people are unemployed, particularly in the developing world, the same reductions in the real workforce will be a severe disadvantage—first, because they lack the capital required to install automated systems, and second, because they'll need jobs for the huge numbers of people who will be seeking work.

The choices will be agonizing. If they are forced to maintain labour-intensive practices, wage rates will have to be kept low, which will retard their capacity to provide better standards of living for their people. Also, a failure to invest in the new technologies could reduce their competitiveness in the world markets that they depend on for their export earnings.

It's not impossible to find a way through this, to combine modern technologies with a greater degree of labour intensity. But it does underscore the challenge that developing countries face in competing in a world economy in which capital and technology are the principal sources of comparative advantage.

Can technology save us? No, yes and no.

We can use our human technological ingenuity to good advantage; indeed, we must. But we also need wisdom beyond the purview of the engineering schools. Technology can assist or hinder political solutions, but it is politics and its motivating values and priorities that are the keys to how we use technology to shape the human future.

CHAPTER 16

Avoiding Doomsday: A Program for Action

T HE FUTURE, I have argued, is in our hands. We have the ability to control our own destiny—and the responsibility to manage it. The timeframe in which we must act is very short. It is not that the demise of our civilization could occur rapidly but that the decisions and actions that would determine its ultimate fate are likely to emerge within the first part of the new century and particularly within the next two decades. Disaster is not inevitable. It is still avoidable if we effect the kind of "change of course" called for at the Earth Summit. Every year, every day, that we delay implementing change will make it more difficult to accomplish and less likely to succeed.

History catalogues the rise and fall of civilizations. But whatever decisions or events precipitated their demise, the consequences were limited primarily to the people and places concerned—and the world went on. If the citizens of Greece some three thousand years ago developed impressively advanced civilizations and destroyed their supportive natural resource base—well, it may have been ghastly for them, but the remainder of humankind was essentially unaffected. If Atlantis ever existed and if it disappeared in some terrible cataclysm, there was no enduring impact on the rest of humankind, other than in the curious minds of those who have speculated about its existence and its fate. Now, everything has changed. The consequences of local catastrophes are immediately transmitted to the rest of the world and can give rise to catastrophes on a global scale—and there is no safe haven. We can move away from the localities immediately affected, but we remain bound to our planetary home. The future is ours to make and our children's to inherit. And the Earth is our future.

It is in this larger context that I have always seen the environmental movement and its logical extension, sustainable development. The basic principles of environmental protection and sustainability must be fully absorbed into the ethos of our industrial civilization and into every aspect of our economic life and behaviour. Environmentalists have led by sounding the alarm bells but can do little by themselves to avert catastrophe.

So, to use one of Lenin's famous questions, "What is to be done?" If failure to change means self-destruction, as I have argued, how do we change? How do we acquire the will and the wisdom necessary to judge correctly? If the next two decades are the critical ones, how do we instil the proper sense of urgency? How, in short, do the shareholders of Earth Inc. (we, the citizens) persuade the board of directors (our political leaders) to act in the long-term interests of the company? Our politics is still based on opportunism, short-termism and parochialism. How to overcome that?

Could I, and my colleagues in the environmental movement, design a world politics—*pace* the right-wing conspiracy theorists—that would "fix" all our problems, a political version of the physicists' "theory of everything"? The answer, of course, is no. No humans have the right—or the wisdom—to attempt anything like it. But this is not to say we are helpless. The cumulative actions of individuals are, after all, the essential ingredients of politics, and change can be substantial and even radical without being directed from the top. There are many practical measures that can be taken, some immediately and others only over time, that will make things better.

Throughout this book I have indicated my own views on the kind of actions needed to effect the transition to the secure, sustainable and equitable development that will meet the hopes and aspirations of people in the twenty-first century. I dealt extensively with the importance of implementing, and continuing to build on, the Earth Summit's Agenda 21 and the accompanying Rio agreements. But let me also cite here some of the other key actions we can and should take to secure that future.

1. Promote the "greening" of the market system

The first thing to do is to use the current system.

Unreconstructed free-marketers criticize people like me as "loony environmentalists," because "doomsayers," as they also call us, have so often been wrong. And the reason for that, they suggest, is our under-estimation of the ability of human ingenuity, expressed through free-market capitalism, to solve problems as they emerge. So what, they say, if oil is a finite resource and will run out in the year twenty-something? By that time shortages will have driven the price up, which will create the incentive to develop an entirely new technology—which, no doubt, will be cleaner, more efficient and cheaper.

This conventional wisdom has been challenged by a new genera-tion of enlightened leaders in both business and government, who have realized that sound economic policies and business practices must integrate environmental and social considerations through sustainable development. This movement has been driven by the leadership and initiative of Stephan Schmidheiny, who, as I have already noted, was my senior adviser in mobilizing the participation of business and industry in the Earth Summit. It was the basic mes-sage of the book *Changing Course*, by Stephan and some fifty other senior executives of major corporations in their report to the Earth Summit. It called for fundamental changes in economic practices and behaviour based on a commitment to "eco-efficiency" in the use of energy and materials and in the prevention, disposal and recycling of wastes. And it made the case that this is good for business and the economy as well as for the environment. Stephan has since contin-ued to be a primary source of intellectual leadership in advancing eco-efficiency principles and, through his own companies and pri-vate foundations, providing impressive practical examples of sus-tainable development.

I believe that many of our hard-headed business people actually underestimate the stimulant effect of such necessary changes. The processes of adaptation required will create a whole new generation of opportunities for business that will, as in earlier times, more than offset the difficulties and constraints imposed on some sectors. One example already cited: automobile companies are competing vigorously to design engines and fuel systems that reduce emissions; there is a similar race to be first to develop better alternative fuels, and all this is stimulating new activity, new business and new markets.

Look at the innovative ways that have been devised to use the financial markets to reduce the costs of emission control through "emissions trading" and joint implementation agreements.

Provision was made in the protocol to the Climate Change Convention agreed to in Kyoto for both joint implementation, or "activities implemented jointly," and emissions trading, and though many of the important details remain to be worked out, it seems evident that these market instruments will figure prominently in the response to the need to curtail greenhouse-gas emissions.

The concept remains controversial. Environmentalists worry that their widespread adoption might enable industrialized countries and their corporations to dodge doing what they should be doing, which is to reduce their own emissions at source. This is a real concern, but it could be taken care of through a regulatory process.

There are benefits and hazards to reliance on offsets. A major benefit is that, as most of the emission offsets will occur in developing countries where costs are lowest, this system could lead to a very substantial new flow of capital to these countries. A hazard for developing countries is also implicit: what happens if they sell their emission rights now but later need the capacities they have already sold to offset their own emissions? This would increase their costs sharply over time. Of course, each country would be free to decide for itself the trade-off between immediate benefits and possible future costs, and on balance for most the advantages would probably outweigh the hazards, and would, I believe, drive their widespread adoption. But emission offsets will at best be only part of the solution, which must primarily be focused on reducing emissions at their source.

Emissions trading is an important manifestation of the global nature of both the environment and the economy. The fact that emissions originating in one country will be offset by measures undertaken in another will create transnational economic linkages of an entirely new character. These will add a new dimension to the process of globalization and require a degree of agreement and co-operation at the global level that is likely to go beyond anything yet envisaged.

But—and here's my main point—though governments must establish the policy and regulatory frameworks for emissions trading, the prime actors in developing and applying the agreements will be private-sector companies, financial institutions and individuals, and most of the capital involved will be private. This is particularly important as foreign aid is now in decline and private investment accounts for the principal flows of financial resources to developing countries. Accordingly, it is essential that we institute incentives and innovative financial mechanisms to ensure that private capital will support development that is sustainable. Only by the greening of private capital can we make the transition to sustainability provided for in Rio's Agenda 21.

2. Revamp subsidies

New sources of financing are important, but there is even greater potential in making better use of existing resources.

Governments of both industrialized and developing countries are spending vast amounts of money on unnecessary and counter-productive subsidies to various sectors of their economies. Often they are simply propping up unviable industries or, even more dubious, they are providing incentives for practices that are unsustainable in environmental terms, are unnecessarily costly and wasteful in economic terms, and run counter to the broad sustainable development objectives that most governments pay lip service to.

Subsidizing Unsustainable Development: Undermining the Earth with Public Funds, a recent study commissioned by the Earth Council, estimates that these "perverse" subsidies amount to at least $700 billion a year in the water, transport, energy and agriculture sectors alone. This surprising figure would be much larger if other sectors were included. It is estimated that developing countries subsidize their energy sector alone by an amount approximately double the total foreign aid they receive.

Governments have not been deliberately undermining sustainable development. It's only with our new-found knowledge of their impact on the environment and on incentives for sustainable development that we see how counterproductive they so often are. Subsidies almost always seem like a good thing at the time they are originally introduced, and then they tend to become entrenched in the system that they are a part of. Thereupon, those involved, particularly beneficiaries of the subsidies, almost invariably develop a vested interest in them and object furiously to their removal or reduction.

The Earth Council, through its Van Lennep Program on Economics and Sustainable Development, in co-operation with UN organizations and others, is undertaking the second phase of its major project on "perverse subsidies." This will provide further analytical evidence about their real impact and cost, and find alternatives that can provide a basis for advocacy of the changes required to deal with this widespread phenomenon, which is so costly in both environmental and economic terms.

3. Full accounting for environmental costs

In our modern, materialistic society, economics is the determining factor in decisions. Any proposed action that does not meet the economic tests we apply to it will be strongly resisted, even rejected.

It wasn't always so. The dominant values of many societies of earlier times—Rome, Greece, Renaissance Europe and Victorian England—were culture and the arts, and, yes, even the arts of war. Business played an important but supporting role.

And, even today, it isn't always so. There are many anomalies in the application of these high-toned economic principles. Take, for instance, one of the most important decisions made by any person: the choice of a life partner and then the decision to have children. There are exceptions, of course, but in most cases these choices are not driven by money. Indeed, by the economic criteria used to evaluate business decisions, there is no economic justification at all for having a child. Under the commonly accepted accounting practice of applying a discount factor to the projected future earnings of a project at current expected rates of return, the economic value of a child at birth would be less than zero. Raising the child to a time when he or she becomes productive will cost a great deal more and cannot be justified by any normal investment criteria.

The same kind of economics-be-damned attitude applies to the business of defence, the military. Nations have always been prepared to give their own security highest priority. When they perceive risks to their security, or sometimes to their ambitions, their commitment to building and maintaining their military capability overrides all other considerations. Recently, in peacetime and despite budget austerity in other areas, the u.s. Congress voted a military budget higher than that requested by the military itself.

We must reject the natural tendency to view the cost of transition to sustainable development as something that requires "new" funding. Thinking of it as new provides a handy pretext for the opponents of change to generate popular support—after all, in a period of financial austerity, no one wants to incur new taxes or costs. But we can't afford to view the environment and sustainable development as marginal issues to be dealt with when we can afford it. It is simply a matter of getting our priorities straight and making better use of existing resources.

We must take up the challenge of revamping and reorienting the existing fiscal, tax and policy system to internalize environmental costs and build in positive incentives to the kind of behaviour and practices by corporations and people that the transition to a sustainable way of life requires.

The over-exploitation of forests and fisheries, the depletion of soil and other renewable resources, the pollution of the air, water and the food chain, the pervasive undermining of human health—all these reduce the stock of natural capital that our economic survival and well-being depend on and impose huge costs on future generations. It doesn't take a genius to see that living off our capital in this way is simply not sustainable.

It is ironic that governments continue to subsidize the expansion and re-equipping of fishing fleets, exacerbating the incentives for overfishing that have already depleted fish stocks in a number of areas, including the rich Grand Banks fishing grounds off the shore of Canada's Atlantic coast.

Of course, the Earth is more than just another business. But by invoking business principles in managing the activities that shape the human future, environmentalists can turn business and the market into allies. I submit, therefore, that Earth Inc. must be managed in accordance with sound business principles, with full provision for amortization, depreciation and maintenance to ensure its sustainability.

The shifting of taxes, like changes in subsidies, will invariably be vigorously resisted by those most affected. This will certainly be the case with the higher taxes on fossil fuels that would be a necessary part of any such regime. Remember the widespread public anger that forced President Clinton to back down from his proposal of a modest increase in gasoline taxes in the United States—in the country that is not only the largest source of carbon dioxide emissions in the world but has much lower gasoline taxes than the other leading industrialized countries.

This means internalizing, in all investments and economic transactions, their full environmental and social costs. It means adjusting the system of incentives and penalties by which governments motivate economic behaviour in order to encourage sustainable development. It means eliminating or reorienting perverse subsidies. It means taxing those products and activities that are environmentally harmful and moving taxes away from those that are beneficial. This does not require that taxes be increased overall.

4. Accelerate the transition to environmentally sound energy

Energy, as I have said, is the essential in the environment–development nexus. Changes in patterns of energy production and use are thus indispensable to the transition to sustainable development envisaged at Rio. There can be no sustainable development without sustainable energy development. This means radical improvements in energy efficiency and conservation, combined with environmentally sound renewable energy sources.

The fossil fuels era is far from over. But the transition to the post–fossil fuels era must be accelerated by a combination of tough measures to improve efficiency in their use and to reduce the proportion of fossil fuels in the raw energy mix.

Strong incentives are needed to produce new alternative sources of energy. Hydrogen, fuel cells, solar and other renewable sources offer significant promise, and they all have a place in the energy mix of the future, though none at this point seems a likely candidate for the primary fuel. The energy crisis that drove up prices and spurred efforts to find alternatives to petroleum is behind us, for the time being. Low oil prices and abundant supplies have led to complacency for both the public and policy-makers. The result is a significant decline in research and development expenditures on alternative sources of energy, which could be an ominous portent for the future. I have proposed that OECD countries make a five-fold increase in their expenditures on research and development to improve the performance of existing fuels and find alternatives. I can think of no better investment in long-term environmental security.

As we have seen, the toughest opposition to higher prices has always come from the United States. In that freewheeling economy, even relatively modest increases in gasoline prices or taxes cause a public outcry and dire warnings from business leaders that higher energy costs will be ruinous to the economy. Never mind the evidence that the economies of Europe and Japan have thrived despite substantially higher energy prices.

But simply jacking up the prices is not the answer. All that will do is provide producers with incentives to produce even more. I believe that a special tax based on carbon content will be the best solution. The proceeds would be used to reduce taxes in other areas, which would encourage sustainable development.

Most electric power utilities today have some sort of demand-management program in place, and I believe we are just on the threshold of the potential savings such programs offer. However, there is a real danger that the incentives for demand management and energy efficiency may become victims of deregulation of the electric power industry unless specific provision is made to ensure their existence.

The 1993 report of the World Energy Council's Commission on Energy for Tomorrow's World starkly points out another problem— the shift of energy consumption from the industrialized to the developing world. It projects that within the next three decades the latter's share of worldwide consumption will rise to 55 percent from the current 33 percent.

While intolerable levels of air pollution and traffic congestion are putting the brakes on the unrestrained growth of automobile use in Los Angeles, Mexico City, Singapore and other large cities, the burgeoning economies of many developing countries are producing a veritable explosion in the population of automobiles—and therefore of CO_2 emissions. Though acid rain and its attendant health and environmental effects have curtailed the use of coal in many industrialized countries, it is now the primary source of energy for some of the largest and most rapidly developing countries, notably China and India.

The prospect of a massive increase in Third World energy consumption over the next thirty years underscores the urgent need for industrialized countries to take the lead in reducing greenhouse-gas emissions. We have to leave "space" for developing countries to begin to fulfil their own development needs without moving the total emissions beyond the danger threshold. Earth simply cannot sustain another traumatic round of undisciplined growth, a repeat of the unthinking exploitation that marked the first industrial revolution— and that, to an alarming extent, continues unabated.

The best investment the industrialized world could make in its own environmental security would be ensuring that developing countries have access to the latest state-of-the-art technologies and the financial means to employ them in all new energy projects. This could be done through a variety of financing mechanisms largely targeted at incentives for private investment to provide the incremental costs. I have suggested that the World Bank, the United Nations Development Program and the United Nations Environment Program, through the Global Environment Facility in which they all participate, take the lead in establishing a new Consultative Group on Clean Energy, patterned on the successful model of the Consultative Group on International Agricultural Research, as the principal instrument for mobilizing the financial and technological resources required.

5. Close the "knowledge gap"

Because today the products of science are the principal sources of added value and competitive advantage in the world economy, there are powerful attractions for corporations and private investors to invest in research and development for profit. As a result, an increasing proportion of all funds spent on research and development is made by private corporations; the portion invested by governments for public purposes has diminished. Academies of science, public research institutions, universities and the school system are the foundation of our knowledge society, and it is essential that we fund them so they remain the principal means to ensure that knowledge serves the public interest.

If "knowledge is power," knowledge is also money and, in today's economy, the primary economic resource. That's why the growing drive to convert knowledge into proprietary intellectual property is a mixed blessing. On the one hand it is necessary to reward those who carry out the research that converts into new products and services. On the other hand the commercialization of research and development imposes constraints on the free exchange of information, which has contributed so much to scientific progress. This will inevitably impoverish the overall fund of knowledge and cut off access to the products of research and development for those without the means to purchase them. This could especially disadvantage developing countries.

It is important that we support such countries in their efforts to extend their own scientific and technological capabilities so that they too can be generators of knowledge, especially in areas where they have a potential comparative advantage. According to the UNDP's 1999 *Human Development Report*, in 1993 only ten countries accounted for 84 percent of global R&D expenditures and during the past twenty years controlled 95 percent of the U.S. patents. More than 80 percent of patents granted in developing countries belong to residents of industrialized ones. If this continues—and there are few signs that it is likely to change soon—it can only lead to a widening of the knowledge gap between developing and more developed countries, with the consequent deepening of the gap between them in economic performance and wealth creation.

Developing countries also need to allocate a much larger proportion of their domestic resources to strengthening their scientific and technological capacities and to providing the kind of policy, institutional and professional conditions that are hospitable to science and its practitioners. Those who control the purse strings of international development assistance can make an important contribution to this process by devoting a much greater share of their diminishing budgets to the support of these efforts.

At the onset of the new millennium we live in a world of deepening disparities. How we deal with these will, I am convinced, be decisive in determining our common future. It is a world of unprecedented wealth as measured in financial terms. There are more rich people than ever, and the richest of them are richer than ever before. The 1996 UNDP report indicates that the assets of the world's 358 billionaires exceed the combined annual income of countries with 45 percent of the world's people. And yet everywhere the gap between rich and poor continues to grow. As world stock markets reach new highs, the ranks of the unemployed, the uprooted and the dispossessed also approach record levels.

During the recent recession and accompanying budgetary austerity, many governments in both industrialized and developing countries reduced their support for education and training. They will pay a heavy price for this. In developing countries education and social services, already starved of resources, have been further squeezed, often in favour of increased military expenditures. One of the advantages of an international system of security arrangements is that it would enable governments to reduce military expenditures and transfer the savings to the support of education and basic health care. Nothing would do more to improve the conditions of life and the future prospects for people in developing countries.

The science community has not always provided analysis and guidance on a basis that could be clearly understood and utilized by policy-makers and the public, who, in turn, have often ignored the voices of authentic science. Accordingly, I have been very encouraged by the recent initiative, led by the United States National Academy of Sciences, to form a consortium of leading academies of science from both industrialized and developing countries to provide authoritative scientific advice to policy-makers. This would be an important step forward in closing the other knowledge gap—between science and policy.

6. Move away from "foreign aid"

This might seem an odd injunction from one who has been involved in development assistance for so many years, but it is necessary.

Foreign aid played an important part in the rebuilding of wartorn Europe and Japan. And as it moved its focus to developing countries, many of them newly emerging from colonialism, it made important contributions in support of their efforts to pursue development and the prospect of a better life for their people. The results have been mixed but on the whole positive.

Many lessons have been learned, some of them not sufficiently heeded. The prime one is that for development to be successful, it must be homegrown, rooted in the political and economic management of each country, its social mores and disciplines, its policies and priorities, and driven by the shared aspirations of the people and their willingness to accept the attendant responsibilities.

Internationally, the era of foreign aid as we came to know it in the last half of the twentieth century is in any case coming to an end. No longer can it serve as a sufficient or satisfactory basis for the relationships between nations. There is a tiredness and frustration on the part of both donors and recipients—the donors because they see so much money being "wasted," and the recipients because they see it surrounded by so many restrictions and limitations and because they understand as well as anyone that a culture of dependence will never be a long-term solution. The institutions, both bilateral and multilateral, that are the principal purveyors of development aid will also recede in their importance and influence. Some will regenerate themselves as leaders of the movement for a much more complex and sophisticated system of relationships between developing and more developed countries, but others will inevitably wither away.

Resource transfers will, of course, continue to be a necessary feature of these relationships. But they need to be carried out within the framework of a broader set of measures including access to markets, to technology, to capital. Such arrangements would in many respects be the international counterpart of the measures undertaken within most industrialized nations to ameliorate disparities and ensure equitable sharing of both burdens and benefits within the society.

It is in wealthy countries' interests, therefore, to help where we can. Why?

For two reasons. First, because developing countries, which already account for some 75 percent of the world's population, will also account for an increasing share of the world's economic growth and potential for environmental degradation, as mentioned. Second, because developing countries are custodians of some of the most important and invaluable ecosystems on the planet, themselves vital to the environmental security of the human community as a whole. And they provide products and services necessary to the continued integrity and sustainability of the Earth's resource and life-support systems. This is particularly true of the great tropical forests of South and Central America, Africa and Asia, which contain most of the world's biodiversity.

The developing countries, which have the sovereign right to these resources, cannot be expected to bear the entire cost of maintaining them when it means forgoing the capacity to meet the immediate needs of their people. Therefore, the value of these resources to the world community needs to be recognized by having others bear a fair share of the costs of conserving them. This could be done through a special levy on products that use ingredients from these sources. Or it could be done more generally through the tax system.

7. Move to more flexible, incentive-based regulation

Where are the boundaries of personal space? What are the permitted intrusions of governments and regulatory authorities? We have accepted local, regional and even national limits to freedom of action. Consider now the notion of pan-national regulations.

I believe that the strongest single desire of all people is for future conditions that protect and support their children's lives and permit them to pursue their chosen interests and aspirations. Few would want government or anyone else to make personal choices for them, but most can accept certain limitations and constraints in order to be able to make these choices.

One of the clearest illustrations of this is the way we have accepted limitations on our use of the automobile. We must drive on the designated side of the road, stop at red lights, observe other traffic restrictions, obtain a licence to drive and ensure that our vehicle meets prescribed standards of safety and reliability.

I recall on an early visit to Buenos Aires being told of a controversy that was raging about whether traffic lights would be installed at main intersections. Some argued that this would be an intolerable infringement of freedom. But with the growth in the automobile population and in the hazards of driving in Buenos Aires, acceptance of traffic lights became inevitable.

In other examples, we have come to accept as normal the limitations on air travel, including the personal inconvenience, and to some the indignity, of being personally screened and searched before boarding aircraft. Television and radio, which we take for granted in our homes, and the supply of electricity, water and other services depend for their effective functioning on rules and regulations. Maintaining our personal health depends on standards of professional training and conduct and on the quality of medical services and of pharmaceuticals. If we counted up the number of constraints and regulations that govern our day-to-day lives, we would be surprised at how many we have come to accept and incorporate into our patterns of living in order to sustain community.

In short, regulation ceases to be a limitation but instead becomes a precondition of freedom. Similarly, as the process of globalization has created new dimensions of interdependence, there has been a need for a much greater degree of international co-operation and agreement to provide for harmonization of international regulations and standards. Driving this is the need to ensure that the people of one country are not disadvantaged vis-à-vis others and to provide for the effective functioning of the many activities and services that are by their nature international—trade, investment, air transport, shipping, telecommunications, disease control and the environment, to name but a few. In order to enjoy the benefits of these activities, a great deal more international co-operation will be necessary in the period ahead.

8. Provide more effective exercise of trusteeship over the global commons

What all the foregoing demonstrates is that we're not starting from square one in our efforts to deal with the boundary issues. The difficulty is that these issues are debated and considered in a variety of different forums, often with little connection. They are buried in a vast array of agreed principles, programs and measures and a broad assortment of declarations, action plans, legal agreements and soft-law instruments, which means they never get the concerted attention or priority they deserve.

Global commons issues are bound to be among the items at centre stage in the drive for more effective governance at the global level in the period ahead. After all, the oceans beyond national jurisdictions constitute some 70 percent of the Earth's surface; the Antarctic is in reality a global commons area; the high atmosphere and outer space, where human activities are increasingly extending, are the newest frontiers of the commons; and even the complex ecological life-support systems of the Earth itself have attributes of commonality. Management of these areas can only be carried out co-operatively, and we must devise a much better means of doing so. It is not necessary to confine responsibilities for these issues to a single super-agency. In my view what is needed is a global forum where such issues can be overseen, arrangements for their management negotiated, and to which various organizations and agencies undertaking activities that bear on these commons areas are accountable. It seems to me, as I have already noted, that a ready-made vehicle for providing this forum exists in the UN Trusteeship Council. Now that its original mandate to facilitate the transition of former colonies to independence has been fulfilled, it would normally be allowed to either wither away or disband.

9. Prepare for natural disasters and extraterrestrial threats

Natural disasters have always been a feature of life on Earth. Their recurrence cannot be prevented. But there is much we can do to anticipate such disasters, prepare to deal with them when they occur and mitigate their effects. The UN's humanitarian efforts, and those of private humanitarian agencies, are being focused more and more on anticipatory measures, particularly the development and improvement of the capacity to reduce the amount of human suffering, death and dislocation that such disasters incur.

It has also become apparent that environmental neglect and mismanagement contribute significantly both to the possible occurrence of, for instance, mudslides, avalanches and floods, and to their human and economic costs. Recent examples of this include the devastating consequences of Hurricane Mitch in Central America and the Yangtze flood in China. The Ombudsman program being initiated by the Earth Council, the IUCN and the UN University for Peace focuses particularly on the prevention of disasters that either result from or are exacerbated by human activities, such as the disruption and deterioration of watersheds in mountainous regions that control the flow of waters into the rivers originating in them.

Another factor that increases the human costs of natural disasters is the growing concentration of population in some of the areas where the disasters occur. Thus, while there is no reason to believe that the number of natural disasters is likely to increase in the period ahead, continued population growth in vulnerable areas is bound to lead to an escalation of the human and economic costs of any that do occur.

While people can do much to anticipate and ameliorate the consequences of natural disasters, we are much less well prepared to deal with risks that originate beyond the Earth, particularly collisions with asteroids. Evidence shows that such collisions have occurred in the distant past, causing extensive devastation, including possibly the demise of the dinosaurs. The prospect of future collisions is remote but nevertheless real. The development of space technologies and more sophisticated observatories have immensely increased our ability to detect asteroids that may be headed toward the Earth and perhaps to destroy them before they reach us. Certainly this would be a more sensible use of technologies developed for President Reagan's "Star Wars" project than purely military applications.

10. Rejoice in diversity and encourage it

In the final analysis, the structures through which people seek to manage their relationships with each other are the product of their history, their values, their aspirations and, yes, their fears and prejudices. It will be evident to any reader who has got to this point in the book that I have been placing heavy emphasis on greater co-operation among peoples and nations if we are to avoid the risks and realize the benefits of the new opportunities that will confront us in the complex world of the twenty-first century. But this is not to make a case for homogeneity. On the contrary. The diversity of human society is its most precious characteristic. Our challenge is to protect and enhance this diversity while co-operating in those areas essential to the sustainability, security and well-being of all human life, present and future.

I came to understand very early in my life that in nature the strongest and most resilient ecosystems are those that manifest the greatest degree of variety and diversity of species. It follows that a human society that sustains and enhances diversity will not only optimize freedom and quality of life but will also be stronger and more sustainable.

11. Encourage lifestyles of "sophisticated modesty"

I advocate using the benefits of technology to enhance the quality of life while reducing the effect on the environment. The effort to reduce one's own environmental impact is a continuing process of trying to break bad habits and to obtain the kind of services and products that will help accomplish one's goals.

Communications technology is a case in point. The rapid miniaturization of so many electronic products brings the great music, art and literature of the world into individual homes and enables us to communicate instantly with people throughout the world. Each of these advances significantly reduces the need to travel while providing unprecedented levels of nourishment for our intellectual, cultural and recreational interests. They also, of course, provide instant and almost universal access to pornography, violence, racism and misogyny, but on balance I think they're a force for good. (The same technology also supplies the means for us to censor pornography and violence when we have the will to do so.)

I don't pretend to be a paragon, but I have long made sophisticated modesty in living my personal goal. My home is not especially modest or small, as it is designed to provide a gathering point for all my family. Constructed of local logs harvested from fully mature trees near the end of their life, it is set in a virtually unspoiled wilderness area only an hour and a half from Toronto. We have clear, clean water and a natural ecosystem that provides a habitat for a variety of fish, birds, animals and, of course, insects. Heat and air conditioning are provided mainly by nature, through a ground source heat pump, and conserved by exceptionally good insulation. I own a car, but it's a fuel-efficient vehicle. I also use it sparingly, taking public transportation whenever I can. I'm conscious that I continue to have a much greater environmental impact than I would like in one area: air travel. My international involvement requires me to travel extensively, and for long trips there is simply no alternative. At least I try to limit my journeys to those I believe to be of the highest priority. Meanwhile, I am more and more using teleconferencing as a substitute for personal meetings.

12. Learn from those in "enclave communities"
One of the curious phenomena of modern Western nations resulting from the greater disparity between rich and poor is the protected enclave for the wealthy that the poor can't penetrate. This mimics,

in a way, elusive modern pools of capital, which can be withdrawn with remarkable speed from places its managers no longer consider safe. So-called gated communities for the rich are guarded by armed security forces. (The extension of this practice on a global scale may be seen in the struggle by rich countries to keep the migrant hordes of poor from crashing increasingly fortified borders.)

But "enclave communities" can be good as well as bad, can exist for socially positive goals as well as for negative ones, can become valuable laboratories of experience to teach others, as well as sources of spiritual strength in an increasingly fractious world.

This is hardly new. People seeking refuge from a turbulent and materialistic world have for many centuries formed monastic communities, many of them self-reliant. During the Dark Ages in Europe the monastic communities were the custodians of much of society's religious, cultural and artistic heritage.

Recently there has been a resurgence in the movement toward establishing such communities by secular as well as spiritual groups. One example I'm familiar with is the place where Hanne has played a leading role, with some support from me, in the San Luis Valley area of southern Colorado.

These are not utopias, and none of the people who live in them believe they are. They know well enough that in today's world it is not really feasible to insulate any community from either the natural or the human forces shaping our future. They can be a life-enriching experience, but the residents know full well that enclave communities can never be an option for more than a small segment of the population.

I also know from my own experience that such communities are not devoid of human prejudices and conflicts. Indeed, they can become hotbeds of rivalry and tension. But even in these cases they represent not so much an escape from the "real world" as an opportunity to experience it under conditions more congenial and sustainable than those outside. And I believe strongly that these communities can make an important contribution by setting an example of ways of life that can be pursued anywhere, anytime. I believe the movement to establish more of these enclave communities is likely to accelerate in the period ahead.

CHAPTER 17

And Now . . .

SINCE I FINISHED RESEARCHING, writing and editing this book, my life has continued very much in the same direction. I spend a great deal of time at UN headquarters, which has become something like a home to me. The security guards in particular treat me like family. After all, I started at the UN working with them. I continue my advisory role at the UN and the World Bank and, as an extension of Secretary-General Kofi Annan's reform program, have taken on responsibility for revitalizing a little known UN organization, the United Nations University for Peace. Established by international agreement on the initiative of then Costa Rican president Rodrigo Carazo, it was approved by the United Nations General Assembly in December 1980, with a broad and challenging mandate to "provide humanity with an international institution of higher education for peace and with the aim of promoting among all human beings the spirit of understanding, tolerance and peaceful co-existence, to stimulate co-operation amongst people and to help lessen obstacles and threats to world peace and progress, in keeping with the noble aspirations proclaimed in the Charter of the United Nations."

In my work for the secretary-general on UN reform I studied the constitutions of each of the UN organizations and was intrigued to find that the University for Peace had a unique status in that it was exempt from the normal reporting, administrative, personnel and other bureaucratic requirements. Like many other UN organizations, it did not receive financial support from the central budget, and the resources available to it were modest. Its programs were also on a small scale, limited primarily to Central and South America.

In fact, it has the character of a UN organization and the flexibility of a private foundation or non-governmental organization. It is also the only organization established by the United Nations explicitly to serve and support its peace and security goals, which were the principal reasons for the creation of the UN.

The University for Peace is situated on a beautiful campus on the outskirts of San José, the capital of Costa Rica. The choice of location was a logical one not only because of Costa Rica's role in having it established, but because it is the only country in the world to have formally abolished its army.

With the advice and support of UNESCO's director-general, Federico Mayor, I worked with the secretary-general and Nitin Desai, undersecretary-general for economic and social affairs and my former deputy at UNCED, to put together a wholly new council, the university's governing body. Consisting of only fifteen members—again a welcome exception to the much larger numbers in the governing bodies of most other UN organizations—the newly constituted council met in March 1999 at UNESCO headquarters in Paris and elected me its president. As it was also important to appoint a new rector as CEO of the university, I was given these additional responsibilities on an interim basis, pending recruitment of a more permanent rector. Since then the University for Peace has become my public service priority, and I have been spending a great deal of my time trying to put its house in order and developing a new strategic plan and program to relaunch the university. Already a number of promising initiatives are shaping up—both through establishing alliances with other universities, institutes and organizations with peace-related programs and establishing new programs in niche areas not occupied, at least at the global level, by other organizations. Using the latest distance learning techniques, it is now establishing a virtual global campus.

Peace-related organizations and programs are increasing in number throughout the world, and the many we have already contacted welcome our plans to fulfil the university's global mission by co-operating with them as partners, not as competitors. As the only truly international university mandated by the United Nations to grant degrees—the UN University in Tokyo does not have degree-granting powers—we are developing M.A. and PH.D. programs jointly with some leading universities and a network of co-operative alliances with others. Already we have undertaken, with the Earth Council, virtual classes through the Internet, with participation by universities around the world.

Of particular importance is the strategic relationship being developed between the University for Peace and the Earth Council (also headquartered in Costa Rica), which plans to move out to the university campus and share facilities and services as well as participate in programs related to the environment and peace. The University for Peace and the World Conservation Union (IUCN) have joined with the Earth Council in undertaking the new Ombudsman program designed to deal with the anticipation, prevention and resolution of conflicts, concentrating at first in the field of environment and natural resources, seen as one of the principal sources of conflict in the period ahead. The University for Peace has also joined with IUCN in developing a global centre to promote, facilitate and support the development of Peace Parks in transboundary and other sensitive areas. Peace Parks already exist in a number of areas—the first is the Waterton Glacier International Peace Park on the U.S.–Canada border between Alberta and Montana. It was the local Rotary clubs that proposed establishing the park in 1931. But there is no global body to accord these parks international status, establish common criteria and standards, exchange experiences and provide information and support for new Peace Park initiatives. Peace Parks for the most part involve transboundary co-operation between neighbouring states for their management, and often as well serve to protect areas of natural beauty and biological diversity.

Among the other programs now being developed are those that concern the military and peace, the media and peace, the moral, ethical and spiritual dimensions of peace (inner peace), development and peace, and governance and peace. It is envisaged that each program will be based on partnership with other organizations in its field to ensure full use of existing capabilities and expertise.

One of the most attractive features of this new role is that it provides the opportunity to forge new alliances with some of the people with whom I have worked closely in the past and whose friendship I value so much. Gerardo Budowski, whom I first met when he headed IUCN, ran the most successful program at the University for Peace before I took over and is now my vice rector. Martin Lees, a public policy entrepreneur par excellence, whom I first knew as one of the brightest stars of the United Nations, has taken on responsibility for program development at the University, assisted by Lucas Assuncao, who did such a good job as one of my key aides for the Earth Summit. Frans van Haren, the experienced and skilful Dutch diplomat has led the process of establishing the Ombudsman Institute. Mohammed Sahnoun, the senior Algerian diplomat who is one of the wisest and ablest people I know and a valued and constant source of counsel and assistance over the years, has become a key member of our Council and its Executive Committee; and Steven Rockefeller, who has led the process of drafting and promulgating the Earth Charter, has also become an active member of the University for Peace Council. I have been immensely encouraged too by the many others who have joined our new team and offered their support. It bodes well for this promising new venture.

For me this represents not only a challenge but a unique opportunity in this latter phase of my life to help establish an integrative institutional base for the international interests I have been pursuing for so long. Peace is the prerequisite for the achievement of all the other goals that the human community aspires to in the twenty-first century. Maintaining world peace and security was the principal motivation for the creation of the UN in the aftermath of the devastation of the Second World War. It continues to be at the centre of the UN's *raison d'être*.

I have also been working closely with Dr. Bruce Alberts, president of the U.S. National Academy of Sciences, to bring together some of the world's leading academies of sciences to provide objective, authoritative scientific advice to policy-makers. I see this as a particularly timely and promising undertaking that addresses a need that I have long felt is essential to the effective management of the largely science-driven activities shaping the human future.

I continue to be attacked in the right-wing media. One Internet article even led with the preposterous and extravagant headline "The First King of the World," making the now familiar allegation that I was at the centre of a global conspiracy to establish world government and undermine the sovereignty of the United States. I don't normally react to such criticism, but in October 1997, for the first time in my career, I launched a lawsuit, against the Southam Newspaper Group and the *Ottawa Citizen* for a scurrilous and inaccurate article on a front page. It was the kind of attack on my integrity that I could not ignore. I called Conrad Black, with whom I have had a long though not particularly close friendship. He was sympathetic but explained that there are limits to his interfering, as owner, in the editorial processes of his newspapers. I was fortunate that through my long-time friend, David Menzel, I was able to engage one of Canada's finest litigation attorneys to represent me in taking legal action. He negotiated a settlement that included an apology as well as a cash payment. Of course, apologies never get the same attention as the original articles.

I have become more active in my connection with Korea, in my UN role; I have developed a good relationship with President Kim Dae Jung in support of his "Sunshine" policy of working for resolution of the long-standing and deep-rooted conflict with North Korea, while responding with toughness and determination to provocative actions and threats from the North. Kim is a formidable man who has demonstrated remarkable qualities of leadership in dealing with the country's political challenges as well as its severe economic and financial problems. Whatever grudges he may bear against those responsible for keeping him in political isolation and subjecting him to torture and persecution over so many years have not been manifested in his attitudes and actions since he assumed power. On the contrary he has followed a policy of reconciliation within the country as well as toward North Korea.

Another role I have with Korea that is proving to be very interesting is as a member, with Henry Kissinger and Singapore's Lee Kuan Yew, of the International Advisory Board of the Korean Federation of Industries, which brings together the major corporations of Korea. Although I have no personal business interests in Korea, this relationship provides me with a unique window on the business and economic life of the country and how they mesh with its political processes. It also has enabled me to be helpful to them in several instances.

At the personal level, I passed the milestone of my seventieth birthday still feeling healthy and vibrant. I long ago decided not to make a sharp distinction between working and retirement, as I enjoy and seem to thrive busily doing what I like to do, which does not really seem like work to me. And I have always made a point of interludes of peace and withdrawal along the way. In a busy and noisy world it is important to have inner quietude, and while I have never fully achieved this, it is the key to my ability to deal effectively with a large number of activities and pressures. Starting each day with a combination of exercise and meditation, I withdraw for brief periods throughout the day and whenever possible have a nap after lunch. And I retreat for longer intervals whenever I can during the year rather than take a long period earmarked as a "holiday." My friends wonder why I seem to be unaffected by my extensive travels, but I have learned to develop a rhythm in the routine pattern of my life that, wherever I may be, helps me to adjust to changes of time zones and environments. I'm sometimes thrown a bit out of balance by my dependence on insulin to stabilize the diabetic condition that I have lived with for more than thirty years, but never long enough to really interfere with my normal life.

I continue a schedule of international speeches, conferences and board meetings planned for a couple of years ahead, but I still spend as many weekends as possible at my wilderness home. Indeed my most precious times are those I spend playing and conversing with my grandchildren, whom I'm very close to. I try to arrange my international travel around the times they can be with me. I have always remained close to my family, and their constant love and support has meant a great deal to me. One of the events I look forward to most each year is the annual reunion of my generation. My brother Frank and his wife Lois, my sister Shirley, and my youngest sister Joyce and her husband Dr. Roy le Riche join in at my Lost Lake retreat or our hometown, Oak Lake, for a vacation trip together. These are precious times when we enjoy nostalgic reminiscences, discuss family news and share plans for the future.

Some friends remark that I seem to be much too busy and should slow down, but my lifestyle suits me.

To suggestions that I should retire, I inevitably respond that I feel retired now in the sense that I am living the kind of life I want. And while my own efforts can do little in the larger scheme of things to "save the planet" from the ominous risks I fear it faces and help to bring about a better world, I still believe it is possible. So until nature calls a halt to my efforts, I will continue to do everything I can to help bring about the better world that is the finest legacy our generation can bequeath to our children, grandchildren and all who follow them.

And so my life goes on.

Selected
Bibliography

Chapter 2: The State of the Non-Union

Fromm, Erich. 1941. *Escape from Freedom.* New York: Farrar & Rinehart, Inc.

Malthus, Thomas. 1798. *An Essay on the Principle of Population.*

Meadows, Donella H., and the Club of Rome, 1972. *The Limits to Growth: A Report for the Club of Rome's Project on the Predicament of Mankind.* New York: Universe Books.

Soros, George. 1998. *The Crisis of Global Capitalism: Open Society Endangered.* New York: Public Affairs.

United Nations. 1998. *World Population Prospects (The 1998 Revision).* New York: United Nations.

United Nations Development Program. 1996. *Human Development Report 1996.* New York: Oxford University Press.

World Bank. 1997. *Global Economic Prospects and the Developing Countries.* Washington, D.C.: The World Bank.

———. 1999. *World Development Report 1999.* Washington, D.C.: The World Bank.

Chapter 3: Beginnings

Bailey, Ronald. 1997. "International Man of Mystery: Who Is Maurice Strong?" *National Review*, September 1997.

McAlvany, Donald S. 1992. *Toward a New World Order: The Countdown to Armageddon*, 2nd. ed. Phoenix: Western Pacific Publishing Co.

Chapter 5: The Levers of Business and the Corridors of Politics

Greber, Dave. 1987. *Rising to Power: An Unauthorized History of Paul Desmarais and Power Corporation.* Toronto: Methuen.

Head, Ivan, and Pierre Trudeau. 1995. *The Canadian Way: Shaping Canada's Foreign Policy 1968–84.* Toronto: McClelland & Stewart.

MacNeill, Jim, David Runnalls and John Cox. 1989. CIDA *and Sustainable Development: How Canada's Aid Policies Can Support Sustainable Development in the Third World More Effectively.* Ottawa: Institute for Research on Public Policy.

Morrison, David R. 1998. *Aid and Ebb Tide: A History of* CIDA *and Canadian Aid Policy.* Waterloo: Wilfrid Laurier University Press.

Morse, Bradford, and Hugh Wynne-Edwards. 1986. *With Our Own Hands: Research for Third World Development: Canada's Contribution through the International Development Research Centre, 1970–1985.* Ottawa: IDRC.

Randel, Judith, and Tony German (eds.). 1997. *The Reality of Aid: 1997/8: An Independent Review of Development Cooperation.* London: Earthscan.

Strong, Maurice F., and Jacques Hébert. 1980. *The Great Building Bee: Canada, A Hope for the Third World.* Toronto: General Publishing Company.

Chapter 6: Toward Stockholm

Carson, Rachel. 1964. *Silent Spring.* New York: Fawcett Crest.

Dubos, René, and Barbara Ward. 1972. *Only One Earth.* New York: W. W. Norton.

Forrester, Jay W. 1971. *World Dynamics.* Cambridge, Mass.: Wright-Allen Press.

Grey, Dodson, and William F. Martin. 1975. *Growth and Its Implications for the Future.* Branford, Conn.: Dynazar Books.

Meadows, Dennis L. 1974. *The Dynamics of Growth in a Finite World.* Cambridge, Mass.: Wright-Allen Press.

Meadows, Dennis L., and Donella H. Meadows. 1973. *Toward Global Equilibrium: Collected Papers.* Cambridge, Mass.: Wright-Allen Press.

Meadows and the Club of Rome. 1972. *The Limits to Growth.*

Stone, Peter B. 1973. *Did We Save the Earth at Stockholm?* London: Earth Island Press.

Strong, Maurice F. (ed.). 1973. *Who Speaks for Earth?* New York: W. W. Norton.

United Nations Environment Program. 1981. *In Defence of the Earth: The Basic Texts on Environment—Founex, Stockholm, Cocoyoc.* Nairobi: UNEP.

Chapter 7: UNEP, Petro-Canada and the Politics of Water

de Villiers, Marq. 1999. *Water.* Toronto: Stoddart.

Lotz, Jim. 1997. *Sharing a Lifetime of Experience: The CESO Story.* East Lawrencetown, N.S.: Pottersfield Press.

Steinberg, Eleanor, and Joseph A. Yager. 1978. *New Means of Financing International Needs.* Washington, D.C.: Brookings Institute.

Chapter 9: The Run-up to Rio

Brown, Lester, Christopher Flavin and Sandra Postel. 1991. *Saving the Planet: How to Shape an Environmentally Sustainable Global Economy.* New York: W. W. Norton.

IUCN (World Conservation Congress), UNEP, World Wildlife Fund. 1991. *Caring for the Earth: A Strategy for Sustainable Living.* Gland, Switzerland: IUCN.

Kirdar, Üner (ed.). 1992. *Change: Threat or Opportunity for Human Progress?* Volume 5: *Ecological Change: Environment, Development and Poverty Linkages.* New York: United Nations.

World Commission on Environment and Development. 1987. *Our Common Future: The Report of the World Commission on Environment and Development.* New York: Oxford University Press.

Chapter 10: The Earth Summit

Choucri, Nazli (ed.). 1993. *Global Accord: Environmental Challenges and International Responses.* Cambridge, Mass.: MIT Press.

Gardner, Richard N. 1992. *Negotiating Survival: Four Priorities after Rio.* New York: Council on Foreign Relations Press.

Grubb, Michael, et al. 1993. *The Earth Summit Agreements: A Guide and Assessment.* London: Royal Institute of International Affairs.

Johnson, Stanley P. 1993. *The Earth Summit: The United Nations Conference on Environment and Development.* London: Graham & Trotman.

Keating, Michael. 1993. *The Earth Summit's Agenda for Change: A Plain Language Version of Agenda 21 and the Other Rio Agreements.* Geneva: Centre for Our Common Future.

Middleton, Neil, Phil O'Keefe and Sam Moyo. 1993. *Tears of the Crocodile: From Rio to Reality in the Developing World.* Boulder: Pluto Press.

Mintzer, Irving M., and J. Amber Leonard. 1994. *Negotiating Climate Change: The Inside Story of the Rio Convention.* New York: Cambridge University Press.

Rogers, Adam. 1993. *The Earth Summit: A Planetary Reckoning.* Los Angeles: Global View Press.

Sachs, Wolfgang (ed.). 1993. *Global Ecology: A New Arena of Political Conflict.* London: Zed Books.

Schmidheiny, Stephan. 1992. *Changing Course: A Global Business Perspective on Development and the Environment.* Cambridge, Mass.: MIT Press.

Shabecoff, Philip. 1996. *A New Name for Peace: International Environmentalism, Sustainable Development, and Democracy.* Hanover: University Press of New England.

Sitarz, Daniel (ed.). 1993. *Agenda 21: The Earth Summit Strategy to Save Our Planet.* Boulder: Earthpress.

Thomas, Caroline (ed.). 1994. *Rio: Unravelling the Consequences.* Portland, Oregon: Frank Cass.

United Nations Conference on Environment and Development. 1992. *Agenda 21: Earth's Action Plan.*

Chapter 11: After Rio, the Earth Council and the Environmental Movement

Adams, W. M. 1996. *Future Nature: A Vision for Conservation.* London: Earthscan.

Brown, Harrison. 1954. *The Challenge of Man's Future: An Inquiry Concerning the Condition of Man during the Years That Lie Ahead.* New York: Viking Press.

Brown, Lester R. 1999. "Crossing the Threshold: Early Signs of an Environmental Awakening." *World Watch,* March/April 1999: 12–22.

Carson, Rachel. *Silent Spring.*

Easterbrook, Gregg. 1995. *A Moment on Earth: The Coming Age of Environmental Optimism.* New York: Viking.

Gore, Albert. 1992. *Earth in the Balance: Ecology and the Human Spirit.* Boston: Houghton Mifflin.

Holdgate, Martin. 1999. *The Green Web: A Union for World Conservation.* London: Earthscan.

Kendrick, Martyn, and Linda Moore. 1995. *Reinventing Our Common Future: An Exploration into Community Sustainability.* Hamilton, Ont.: Eco Gateway Group.

Lamb, Robert. 1996. *Promising the Earth.* New York: Routledge.

Marsh, George P. 1877. *The Earth as Modified by Human Action: A New Edition of Man and Nature.* New York: Scribner.

Salamon, Lester M. 1994. "The Rise of the Nonprofit Sector." *Foreign Affairs*, July/August 1994.

Schmidheiny, Stephan, Rodney Chase and Livio De Simone. 1997. *Signals of Change: Business Progress Towards Sustainable Development.* Geneva: World Business Council for Sustainable Development.

Shabecoff, Philip. 1993. *A Fierce Green Fire: The American Environmental Movement.* New York: Hill & Wang.

———. 1996. *A New Name for Peace.*

United Nations Development Program. *Human Development Report 1990–1999.* New York: Oxford University Press.

von Weizsacker, Ernst Ulrich. 1994. *Earth Politics.* London: Zed Books.

World Resources Institute (WRI), UNEP, United Nations Development Programme (UNDP) and World Bank. 1996. *World Resources: A Guide to the Global Environment, 1996–97.* New York: Oxford University Press.

World Resources Institute, United Nations Environment Programme, United Nations Development Programme, World Bank. 1998. *1998–99 World Resources: A Guide to the Global Environment—Environmental Change and Human Health.* Washington, D.C.: World Resources Institute.

Chapter 12: A Matter of Energy: Running a Power Utility

Freeman, Neil B. 1996. *The Politics of Power: Ontario Hydro and Its Government, 1906–1995.* Toronto: University of Toronto Press.

Task Force on Sustainable Energy Development. 1993. *A Strategy for Sustainable Energy Development and Use for Ontario Hydro: Report of the Task Force on Sustainable Energy Development.* Toronto: Ontario Hydro.

World Bank. 1995. *Mainstreaming the Environment: The World Bank Group and the Environment since the Rio Earth Summit.* Washington, D.C.: World Bank.

Chapter 13: Rio+5: Successes and Failures

de Moor, André, and Peter Calamai. 1997. *Subsidizing Unsustainable Development: Undermining the Earth with Public Funds.* San José, Costa Rica: Earth Council.

Earth Council. 1997. *Implementing Sustainable Development: Experiences and Recommendations from the National and Regional Consultations for the Rio+5 Forum.* San José, Costa Rica: Earth Council.

————. *Implementing Sustainable Development: Summaries of Special Focus Reports Prepared for the Rio+5 Forum.* San José, Costa Rica: Earth Council.

————. *Implementing Sustainable Development: Proceedings of the Rio+5 Forum.* San José, Costa Rica: Earth Council.

MacDonald, Mary. 1998. *Agendas for Sustainability: Environment and Development into the Twenty-first Century.* New York: Routledge.

Wackernagel, Mathias, and William Rees. 1996. *Our Ecological Footprint: Reducing Human Impact on the Earth.* British Columbia, Canada: New Society Publishers.

Chapter 14: Reforming the UN

Adede, Andronico O. 1993. *International Environmental Law Digest: Instruments for International Responses to Problems of Environment and Development 1972–1992.* Amsterdam: Elsevier Press.

Choucri. 1993. *Global Accord.*

Christopher, Warren. 1996. "American Diplomacy and the Global Environmental Challenges of the 21st Century." Speech at Stanford University, April 9, 1996.

Cleveland, Harlan, Hazel Henderson and Inge Kaul (eds.). 1996. *The United Nations: Policy and Financing Alternatives.* New York: Apex Press.

Commission on Global Governance. 1995. *Our Global Neighbourhood: The Report of the Commission on Global Governance.* Toronto: Oxford University Press.

ul Haq, Mahbub (ed.). 1995. *The UN and the Bretton Woods Institutions: New Challenges for the Twenty-First Century.* New York: St. Martin's Press.

Henderson, Hazel. 1996. *Building a Win-Win World: Life Beyond Global Economic Warfare.* San Francisco: Berrett-Koehlers Publishers.

Imber, Mark F. 1994. *Environment, Security, and UN Reform.* New York: St. Martin's Press.

Jasper, William F. 1992. *Global Tyranny . . . Step by Step: The United Nations and the New World Order.* Appleton, Wis.: Western Islands Press.

Korten, David. 1995. *When Corporations Rule the World.* West Hartford, Conn.: Kumarian Press.

Myers, Norman. 1993. *Ultimate Security: The Environmental Basis of Political Stability.* New York: W.W. Norton.

Sachs. 1993. *Global Ecology.*

Salamon. 1994. "The Rise of the Nonprofit Sector."

Serageldin, Ismail. 1995. *Nurturing Development: Aid and Cooperation in Today's Changing World.* Washington, D.C.: The World Bank.

Sjöstedt, Gunnar, Uno Svedin and Britt Hägerhäll Aniansson (eds.). 1993. *International Environmental Negotiations: Process, Issues and Contexts.* Stockholm: The Swedish Institute of International Affairs.

Spector, Bertram, Gunnar Sjöstedt and William Zartman (eds.). 1994. *Negotiating International Regimes: Lessons Learned from the United Nations Conference on Environment and Development.* London: Graham & Trotman.

Chapter 15: Can Technology See Us Through?

Criswell, David R. 1996. "Lunar-Solar Power System: Need, Concept, Pay-offs, Challenges." *IEEE Potentials,* April/May 1996: 4–7.

Strong, Maurice F. 1996. Speech: Crawford Memorial Lecture on the Consultative Group on International Agricultural Research.

Tapscott, Don. 1996. *The Digital Economy: Promise and Peril in the Age of Networked Intelligence.* New York: McGraw-Hill.

Utterback, James M. 1994. *Mastering the Dynamics of Innovation: How Companies Can Seize Opportunities in the Face of Technological Change.* Boston: Harvard Business School Press.

"When Virtue Pays a Premium." *The Economist,* April 18, 1998.

Chapter 16: Avoiding Doomsday: A Program for Action

de Moor and Calamai. 1997. *Subsidizing Unsustainable Development.*

Hawken, Paul 1993. *The Ecology of Commerce: A Declaration of Sustainability.* New York: Harperbusiness.

International Development Research and Policy Task Force. 1996. *Connecting with the World: Priorities for Canadian Internationalism in the 21st Century.* Ottawa: International Development Research Centre.

Myers, Norman. 1998. *Perverse Subsidies: Taxes Undercutting Our Economies and Environments Alike.* Winnipeg, Manitoba: International Institute for Sustainable Development.

Roodman, David M. 1996. Worldwatch Paper #133: "Paying the Piper: Subsidies, Politics and the Environment." Washington, D.C.: Worldwatch Institute.

Schmidheiny. 1992. *Changing Course.*

Schmidheiny, Chase and De Simone. 1997. *Signals of Change.*

Strong, Maurice F. 1997. "A lasting balance: toward a global sustainable energy policy," *Harvard International Review*, XIX, no. 3: 32–35.

UNDP. Human Development Report, 1999.

UNDP. Human Development Report, 1996.

World Energy Council. 1993. *Energy for Tomorrow's World: The Realities, the Real Options, and the Agenda for Achievement.* Report of the WEC Commission. New York: St. Martin's Press.

United Nations Development Program. 1996. *Human Development Report 1996.*

———. 1999. *Huamn Development Report 1999.* New York: Oxford University Press.

Chapter 17: And Now . . .

"The First King of the World." Southam Newspaper Group and *The Ottawa Citizen,* October 1997

Curriculum Vitae

The Honourable Maurice F. Strong, P.C., C.C., LLD.

Personal

Date of Birth: April 29, 1929, Oak Lake, Manitoba, Canada

Marital Status: Married to Hanne Marstrand

Children: (From former marriage to Pauline Williams) Frederick M., Maureen L., Mary Anne, Kenneth M., and Alice Szojka (foster daughter)

Education: Graduated from Oak Lake High School, Oak Lake, Manitoba, Canada

Honours: Honorary doctorates from 41 universities in Canada, the United States and Europe

Fellow, Royal Society (Great Britain), Royal Society of Canada, and Royal Architectural Society of Canada

Companion of Canada

Other Academic Activities

Montague Burton Professor of International Relations, University of Edinburgh, Scotland 1973

Visiting Professor, York University, Toronto, Canada 1969

Has lectured at a number of other universities

Other Awards

- Swedish Royal Order of the Polar Star, 1996
- IKEA Environmental Award, 1995
- Blue Planet Prize of the Asahi Glass Foundation, 1995
- Jawaharlal Nehru Award for International Understanding, 1994
- Lifetime Achievement Award, Environment Canada, 1994
- International Saint Frances Prize for Environment, 1993
- Cervia Ambiente Award, 1993
- Earth Day International Award, 1993
- Alexander Onassis Foundation DELPHI Prize, 1993
- New World Journal Award, 1993
- UN Writers' Award of Excellence, 1993
- Rotary Club McClure International Service Award, 1993
- National Parks Foundation Wirth Environmental Award, 1993
- National Wildlife Foundation Ding Darling Medal
- Pearson Peace Medal, 1989
- Member, United Nations Environment Programme Global 500, 1987
- René Dubos "Only One Earth" Award, 1983
- Gold Environmental Leadership Decade Award, United Nations Environment Programme, 1982
- Charles A. Lindbergh Award, 1981
- Tyler Ecology Award, 1979
- Commander of the Order of the Golden Ark (Netherlands), 1979
- Henri Pittier Order (Venezuela), 1977
- First United Nations International Environment Prize, 1976
- Order of Canada, 1976
- National Audubon Society Awards, 1975
- Mellon Award, 1975
- Freedom Festival Award, 1975

Current Appointments

Undersecretary-General and Senior Adviser to the Secretary-General of the United Nations

President of the Council and Rector, United Nations University for Peace

Chairman, Earth Council

Chairman, Stockholm Environment Institute

Senior Adviser to the President of the World Bank

Chairman, Strovest Holdings Inc.

Chairman, Technology Development, Inc.

Director, Environment Capital Corp.

Director, International Advisory Group CH2M Hill

Director, World Economic Forum

Director, Leadership for Environment and Development (LEAD)

Director, TOTAL Foundation Board of Directors

Member, Toyota International Advisory Board

Member, International Advisory Council, Federation of Korean Industries

Member, Lamonte-Doherty Observatory Advisory Board

International Advisory Council, Liu Centre for the Study of Global Issues at University of British Columbia

International Advisory Board, Center for International Development at Harvard University

Past Occupations and Associations

Member, High Level Advisory Committee to the Secretary-General of the United Nations

Chairman, World Resources Institute

Member of the World Business Council for Sustainable Development

Chairman, Trustees 21 Project of the World Economic Forum

Special Adviser to the Administrator of the United Nations Development Programme

Director, International Institute for Sustainable Development

Chairman, CORDEX Petroleums, Inc.

Chairman, Ontario Hydro, December 1992–November 1995

Secretary-General, 1992 United Nations Conference on Environment and Development (the Earth Summit), March 1990–September 1992

Chairman, Baca Resources Ltd., Calgary, Alberta, Canada

Chairman, American Water Development Inc.

Chairman, First Colorado Corporation and the Baca Corporation, Denver, Colorado, 1986–1989

Vice Chairman and Director, Société Générale pour l'Énergie and les Ressources, Geneva, Switzerland

Director, Better World Society, U.S.A.

Director, Consolidated Press Holdings, Inc., Hong Kong

Trustee, Fetzer Foundation, Kalamazoo, Michigan

Chairman, Strovest Holdings Inc., Vancouver, British Columbia, and Ottawa, Ontario

Co-Chairman, InterAction Policy Board, Vienna, Austria

Executive Co-ordinator, United Nations Office for Emergency Operations in Africa, January 1985–December 1986

Director and Vice Chairman, Tosco Corporation, Los Angeles, California, January 1983–March 1984

Chairman, Canada Development Investment Corporation, Vancouver, British Columbia, August 1982–October 1984

Director, Massey Ferguson, Canada, 1984

Director and Vice Chairman, Canada Development Corporation, Toronto, Ontario, August 1981–November 1984

*Chairman, International Energy Development Corporation, Geneva, Switzerland, January 1980–December 1983

President, National Council of YMCAs of Canada

Chairman, AZL Resources Inc., Phoenix, Arizona, September 1978–January 1983

*President, Chairman of the Board and Chairman of the Executive Committee, Petro-Canada (Canada's National Oil Company), January 1976–July 1978

Executive Director, United Nations Environment Programme, Nairobi, Kenya, January 1973–December 1975

Secretary-General, United Nations Conference on the Human Environment; and Undersecretary-General, United Nations, Geneva, Switzerland, November 1970–December 1972

Headed Canada's International Development Assistance Program, first as Director General, External Aid Office, and subsequently, when the role of the organization was enlarged and it became the Canadian International Development Agency (CIDA), as President and Chairman of the Canadian International Development Board, October 1966–October 1970

Alternate Governor for Canada, International Bank for Reconstruction and Development (IBRD), the Asian Development Bank (ADB) and the Caribbean Development Bank (CDB), October 1966–October 1970

Worked in industry, first as an Investment Analyst with James Richardson & Sons, specializing in oil and mining industries; as Executive Vice President and then President of Power Corporation of Canada, one of Canada's leading investment corporations (1962–1964); served as Director and/or Officer of a number of other Canadian and international corporations, September 1948–September 1966

Prior to this period, was employed by the Hudson's Bay Company at a trading post in the Canadian Arctic; as an accountant and analyst with Vincent Mining Corp., a group of mining companies in Toronto; and in 1947 as junior officer with the United Nations at Lake Success, New York

Vice-Chairman, Beijer Institute of the Royal Swedish Academy of Sciences, Stockholm, Sweden, June 1987–July 1989

Trustee of the Aspen Institute for Humanistic Studies, U.S.A., October 1973–April 1990

Member of the Executive Committee of the Club of Rome

Director, Lindisfarne Association, Colorado, U.S.A., August 1979–November 1987

Director, Renewable Energy Institute, Virginia, U.S.A., October 1983–

Director, U.S.A. for Africa, Los Angeles, California, April 1987–1989

Director, African-American Institute, New York, U.S.A., April 1987–December 1988

Vice President, Advisory Committee on Pollution of the Seas, London, United Kingdom, March 1987

Member, Board of Regents, Cathedral of St. John the Divine, New York, U.S.A., September 1985

Member of the Board, Bretton Woods Committee, Washington, D.C., April 1985

Member of the International Honorary Committee, Dag Hammarskjöld Foundation, Uppsala, Sweden, December 1972

Member of the President's Council (January 1984) and of the International Council (December 1980–December 1986) of the Asia Society, New York, U.S.A.

Member of the Advisory Board, Institute of Ecology, Padjadjaran University, Bandung, Indonesia

Member of the Advisory Board, Native Economic Development Programme, Ottawa, Ontario, October 1983–February 1985

*Director, Canadian Executive Service Organization, Montreal, Quebec, 1967–1987

Founding Member, Canadian Council for Native Business, Willowdale, Ontario, 1982–March 1987

Member of the Board, Institute for Resource Management, Salt Lake City, Utah, June 1984–January 1987

Special Representative, the Secretary-General for the United Nations Financing System for Science and Technology for Development, 1982

Chairman, Advisory Board, United Nations University, Tokyo, Japan, January 1981–December 1983

Chairman, Bureau of the International Union for Conservation of Nature and Natural Resources, Gland, Switzerland

Vice President (October 1978–December 1981) and Member of the Executive Council (October 1978–December 1986), World Wildlife International, Gland, Switzerland

*Chairman, the Board of Governors, International Development Research Centre, Ottawa, Ontario, October 1970–October 1972, December 1976–December 1980

President, National Council of YMCAs of Canada; and served in various capacities with World Alliance of YMCAs in Geneva, Switzerland; the International Committee of YMCAs of U.S.A. and Canada, 1956–1968

Trustee, Rockefeller Foundation, New York, U.S.A., July 1971–November 1977

Member of Council, Rockefeller University, New York, U.S.A., 1972–1978

Chairman, International Management Institute, Geneva, Switzerland, January 1972–September 1977

Member of Council and Executive Committee, Society for International Development, Geneva, Switzerland

Member, Society for Development, Justice and Peace, the Vatican, 1969–1973

Director, North-South Institute, Ottawa, Ontario, 1976–1978

Trustee, Eisenhower Exchange Fellowships, Los Angeles, California

Member of the Council, the Developing Countries Farm Radio Network, Guelph, Ontario

President, World Federation of United Nations Associations, Geneva, Switzerland, 1987–1991

Chairman, Council of the World Economic Forum, Geneva, Switzerland

Chairman, North-South Roundtable, Society for International Development, Rome, Italy, October 1984–October 1987

Member, World Commission on Environment and Development, Geneva, Switzerland, December 1983–December 1987

Member of the International Commission on Global Governance, Geneva

Member of the National Round Table on Environment and the Economy

*Organizations in which he was the Founder and/or First Head

December 1999

Name Index

S

Sahnoun, Mohammed, 382

Salamon, Lester, 339

Sandor, Richard, 239

Sandstrom, Sven, 277

Sarlos, Andy, 154, 256

Saul, John Ralston, 142–43

Säve-Söderbergh, Bengt, 198

Schmidheiny, Stephan, 235, 250, 348, 361

Schulthess, Beatriz, 198

Scott, Alan, 61–63

Scott, Sir Peter, 245

Seligman, Peter, 246

de Seyne, Philippe, 118

Shabecoff, Philip, 242

Shaib, Dr. Bukar, 190

Sharp, David, 147

Sharp, Mitchell, 105, 111–13, 147

Smallboy, Chief, 146

Smith, Arthur, 89

Speth, Gus, 234

Steinberg, Eleanor, 328

Stevens, Sinclair, 160

Stoby, Miles, 292, 305

Strong, Frank [brother of Maurice], 51, 385

Strong, Frederick M. [son of Maurice & Pauline], 90, 257

Strong, Frederick Milton [father of Maurice]. 51, 55, 60

Strong, Hanne [second wife of Maurice]. See Marstrand, Hanne

Strong, The Honourable Maurice F. See the Subject Index, 417

Strong, Joyce [sister of Maurice], 51, 385

Strong, Kenneth M. [son of Maurice and Pauline], 90

Strong, Lois [wife of brother Frank], 385

Strong, Mary [mother of Maurice], 51, 55

Strong, Mary Anne [daughter of Maurice & Pauline], 90

Strong, Maureen L. [daughter of Maurice & Pauline], 90

Strong, Pauline Williams [first wife of Maurice], 77, 90, 140, 153

Strong, Shirley [sister of Maurice], 51

Sununu, John, 206

Suzuki, David, 228

Szojka, Alice [foster daughter of Maurice and Pauline], 90

T

"Tadi," 20–22

Takeshita, Noboru, 196, 208–10

Tangiora, Pauline, 236

Taylor, Rod, 273

Thant, U, 118, 137

Thatcher, Margaret, 196

Thomson, Peter, 91–94

Thoreau, Henry David, 241

Tolba, Dr. Mostafa, 130, 138–39, 205

Töpfer, Klaus, 298

Torrance, Bob, 87

Towe, Peter, 102

Subject Index